D1269141

6/8/21

Black Saints in Early Modern Global Catholicism

From the sixteenth to the eighteenth centuries, Spanish and Portuguese monarchs launched global campaigns for territory and trade. This process spurred two efforts that reshaped the world: missions to spread Christianity to the four corners of the globe, and the horrors of the transatlantic slave trade. The intersection of these efforts gave rise to black saints. Erin Kathleen Rowe presents the untold story of how black saints – and the enslaved people who venerated them – transformed the early modern Church. By exploring race, the Atlantic slave trade, and Christianity, she provides new ways of thinking about blackness, holiness, and cultural authority. Rowe transforms our understanding of global devotional patterns and their effects on early modern societies by looking at previously unstudied sculptures and paintings of black saints, examining the impact of black lay communities, and analyzing controversies unfolding in the church about race, moral potential, enslavement, and salvation.

ERIN KATHLEEN ROWE is Associate Professor of History at Johns Hopkins University. She is the author of *Saint and Nation: Santiago, Teresa of Avila, and Plural Identities in Early Modern Spain* (2011) and co-author of the edited volume *The Early Modern Hispanic World: Transnational and Interdisciplinary Approaches* (2017).

BLACK SAINTS IN EARLY MODERN GLOBAL CATHOLICISM

ERIN KATHLEEN ROWE
Johns Hopkins University

CAMBRIDGE
UNIVERSITY PRESS

CAMBRIDGE
UNIVERSITY PRESS

University Printing House, Cambridge CB2 8BS, United Kingdom

One Liberty Plaza, 20th Floor, New York, NY 10006, USA

477 Williamstown Road, Port Melbourne, VIC 3207, Australia

314–321, 3rd Floor, Plot 3, Splendor Forum, Jasola District Centre, New Delhi – 110025, India

79 Anson Road, #06–04/06, Singapore 079906

Cambridge University Press is part of the University of Cambridge.

It furthers the University's mission by disseminating knowledge in the pursuit of education, learning, and research at the highest international levels of excellence.

www.cambridge.org
Information on this title: www.cambridge.org/9781108421218
DOI: 10.1017/9781108367578

First published 2019

Printed in the United Kingdom by TJ International Ltd, Padstow Cornwall

A catalogue record for this publication is available from the British Library.

Library of Congress Cataloging-in-Publication Data
NAMES: Rowe, Erin Kathleen, 1974– author.
TITLE: Black saints in early modern global catholicism / Erin Kathleen Rowe, the Johns Hopkins University.
DESCRIPTION: Cambridge, United Kingdom : Cambridge University Press, 2019. | Includes bibliographical references and index.
IDENTIFIERS: LCCN 2019040414 (print) | LCCN 2019040415 (ebook) | ISBN 9781108421218 (hardback) | ISBN 9781108367578 (ebook)
SUBJECTS: LCSH: Christian saints. | Catholic Church. | Blacks – Religion.
CLASSIFICATION: LCC BX4655.3 .R69 2019 (print) | LCC BX4655.3 (ebook) | DDC 282.089/96–dc23
LC record available at https://lccn.loc.gov/2019040414
LC ebook record available at https://lccn.loc.gov/2019040415

ISBN 978-1-108-42121-8 Hardback

For Richard R. Rowe

The best photographer and unpaid research
assistant a daughter could ask for

CONTENTS

The plate sections can be found between pages 106 and 107, and pages 202 and 203.

ILLUSTRATIONS

Plates

Figures

Maps

ACKNOWLEDGMENTS

It is a daunting task to acknowledge the many individuals and institutions that have advised, informed, and helped this project on its long path. It has challenged, delighted, frustrated, and surprised me at every step. The research took me to many unexpected places – geographic and intellectual – which rendered me particularly reliant on the generosity of people along the way. It is impossible to recognize all of them, in part because many who imparted crucial local assistance remain strangers.

On one of my many wild goose chases to find an image of Benedict of Palermo in a tiny village in Galicia, I drove in circles unable to rely on the GPS or to find the church in question. My father and I stopped to ask an elderly woman for directions. After a short conversation and a great deal of thought, she finally offered to have her son drive us to the church, as she worried that the instructions might be too convoluted for me to follow. I was embarrassed at the thought of imposing on her son, but she insisted, and we followed him to a tiny stone church, which indeed, I never would have found on my own. (The church was closed and impossible to access, but that is another story.)

Meandering through small towns and villages in the countryside or swallowed in unfamiliar cities, the generosity of locals proved critical to the many successes I achieved in viewing and photographing images of black saints. As at least half of my attempts ended in failure, every success felt like a major achievement. Some nuns turned on lights and supplied ladders; a custodian took us on an exhaustive search of an entire cathedral, including all the back areas and hidden nooks, in search of an image; a patient Portuguese priest waded through my halting French to direct me to the correct location of the sculpture; a kind elderly woman – the "keeper of the keys" – took us on a tour of the little church of which she was enormously proud, pointing out the most important works of art and providing brief histories of each; and an elderly gentleman in a suburb of Granada patiently detailed the complex schedule of processions and masses for Corpus Christi so we would know the right moment to enter the nearby churches. These are but a few anecdotes that help underscore the role that the kindness, magnanimity, and local pride of Spaniards and Portuguese played in this project.

Research and writing for this book would not have been possible without the generous support of the Edwin C. and Elizabeth A. Whitehead fellowship at the Institute for Advanced Study in Princeton, the American Council for Learned Societies, National Endowment for the Humanities, Council for American Overseas Research Centers, American Philosophical Society, University of Virginia, and Johns Hopkins University. The IAS played a particularly critical role in facilitating the completion this project by supplying much needed time dedicated solely to this effort, a period of intense productivity that I had never before experienced. I am indebted to the members of our early modern writing workshop who provided thoughtful advice on a difficult chapter: Alison Games, Guillaume Calafat, Marta Hanson, Jonathan Sachs, Timothy Brook, Silvia Sebastiani, Weijing Lu, and Ying Zhang. I am also grateful to Pamela Patton, Giulia Puma, Cynthia Hahn, and Patrick Geary.

Research for this project can be divided roughly among five geographic zones: Andalusia, Galicia, Portugal, Lima, and Rome. I am grateful to the many libraries and archives I consulted for providing access, advice, and permissions, with particular gratitude to the Archive of the Propaganda Fide, the Torre do Tombo, Biblioteca Comunale di Palermo, the Oliveira Lima Library (Catholic University of America), and the Archivo Histórico Nacional de España. My time in the Archivo Arzobispal de Lima proved invaluable, and owed its productivity to the advice of Carlos Gálvez-Peña and my two research assistants, Giovanna Pignano and Pablo Talavera. I am particularly grateful to Giovanna for sharing some of her master's thesis research on limeño convents.

Many churches and museums generously provided me access, information, and permission to examine images, including the Antiga Mercado de Escravos (Lagos, Portugal), Museu Municipal de Portalegre (Portugal), Museo Nacional de Escultura (Salamanca, Spain), the Museu de Arte Sacra de Arouca (Portugal), and the fantastic guía digital del Patrimonio Cultural de Andalucía created by the Junta de Andalucía. Conservators from the Museu Nacional do Azulejo (Lisbon, Portugal) kindly took the reliquary bust of Benedict of Palermo down from its current location and cleaned it so I could examine and photograph it better.

This project marks the first time I had engaged in research in – or indeed, visited – Portugal. I received invaluable information and advice from Liam Brockey, Mónica Leal da Silva, and Pedro Cardim, who helped me through archives, museums, cityscapes, and restaurants. Anyone who has had the pleasure to work with Liam or Pedro is well aware of their generosity, which was a great gift to me as I familiarized myself with Lisbon and its archives. My travels in central Portugal would not have borne fruit without the help of Arturo Jorge

Almeida of the Turismo Centro do Portugal (Aveiro) and Dr. José António Falcão, director of the Departamento do Património Histórico e Artístico da Diocese de Beja, both of whom took me on personal tours of several churches. Father Manuel Armando Rodrigues Marques kindly took a sculpture down from the altar of his church so it could be photographed. Rui Loureiro took me on a tour of the new Antiga Mercado do Escravos, which housed a painting of the Carmelite Virgin with Elesban and Efigenia that I particularly wished to see. He also generously supplied me with desperately needed photocopies of the relevant pages from Francisco Lameira's work on sacred art in Algarve. I am further grateful to Cristina Osswald, Fernanda Oliveira, and Mafalda Cunho – Malfalda in particular facilitated my access to the Convento das Chagas in Vila Viçosa.

In the United States, I would like to thank the Oliveira Lima Library at Catholic University (Washington, DC), where I spent a lovely day examining a beautiful compromiso and other manuscripts, and Yao-Fen You and Eve Straussman-Planzer at the Detroit Institute of Art for talking with me at length about their spectacular, newly purchased sculpture of Benedict of Palermo.

I received valuable questions, feedback, and stimulating conversation from many engaging interlocutors, including Simon Ditchfield, Harald Braun, Felipe Pereda, Richard L. Kagan, James Amelang, Mercedes García Arenal, Francisco Bethencourt, Juan Pimental, Fernando Bouza, Paul Kaplan, Giovanna Fiume, Kate Lowe, Pamela Patton, Andrew Beresford, José Miguel López, Vinicius Miranda, Anderson José Machado de Oliveira, Karen Graubart, Nancy van Deusen, Nick Jones, Ricardo Padrón, Teo Ruiz, Chloe Ireton, Jorge Fonseca, Daniel Hershenzon, Adam Jasienski, Charlene Villaseñor Black, Amy Remensnyder, Christina Lee, Rachel O'Toole, Tatiana Seijas, Pablo Sierra Silva, Elizabeth Wright, and Cory Conover. I received particularly important advice and recommendations from Mariana Dantas and Felipe Pereda on Chapters 3 and 4.

Chapters of this project were read and discussed at several seminars, including The Seminar on Slavery, Memory, and African Diaspora at Howard University; Early Modern Global History seminar at Georgetown University; UCLA's "Early Modern Cosmopolitanisms"; Jim Amelang's celebrated seminar at the Universidad Autónoma de Madrid; the Seminário Permanente de História Política e Institucional directed by David Martín Marcos at CHAM (New University of Lisbon); and an invited talk at Portland State University organized by Jesse Locker and Carmen Ripollés. Near the end of the project, I had the pleasure of attending a series of fantastic workshops: "Cross-Cultural Transformations in the Atlantic World," organized by Toby Green and Hugo Ribeiro da Silva at King's College in London; "Color of Faith" workshop at the

Detroit Institute for Art; and a symposium on Black Europe hosted by the German Historical Institute of Washington, DC.

I owe a significant debt to Allyson Poska, who provided careful and unsparing feedback on the entire manuscript at a critical juncture, and without whom this project would certainly be less than it is.

It is difficult to imagine a more ideal environment than the History department at JHU, with its blend of intellectual rigor and warm collegiality. I am grateful to all of my colleagues for supplying a stimulating atmosphere and, perhaps more importantly, friendship. I thank in particular Gabriel Paquette, Philip Morgan, John Marshall, Yumi Kim, Nathan Connolly, François Furstenberg, and Toby Ditz, as well as a number of graduate students from our Iberian and Latin America Workshop, including Yonatan Glazer-Eytan, María Lumbreras Corujo, Rebecca Teresi, Álvaro Caso-Bello, and Guillermo García Montufar. Álvaro provided important aid in preparing the manuscript for publication.

This project could not have been completed without the work of Liz Puhl, who designed the maps for the book, and Michelle Strunge, who provided additional copyediting. Lael Ensor-Bennett of JHU's Visual Resources Collection was pivotal for helping me prepare my images for publication. I would also like to thank Michael Watson, my editor at Cambridge University Press, for supporting this project, as well as the anonymous reviewers and the production staff.

I am deeply grateful for the web of love and friendship that supports me, particularly Matthew, Kate, and Marcella Figiel-Miller, Laura Howe, Aviva Cristy, Michelle Geck, Elliott Kennerson, Molly Warsh, Katie Stirling-Harris, Katrina Olds, Ricardo and Zoë Padrón, the Richilin-Paquettes, Kelly Barry, Michelle Strunge, Mike Ryan, Sasha Pack, and Geoff Jensen. I would also like to recognize Graham and Susan Ross, Sarah and Hartland Ross, my two delightful nephews, Bart Ross and Bianca Matheson, and Karen and Dick Brown – all of whom supplied love and refuge in British Columbia. I am further fortunate for my extended family on the Great Plains (and Florida) – my grandmother Bonnie, my aunts, uncles, and cousins – who have always offered support and, even better, lots of laughter. My parents, Richard and Cheryl, and my brother Matthew played integral roles in helping this project come to fruition, not only through emotional support but by providing the child-care that permitted many of my wide-ranging rambles.

Andrew, Daniel, and James – my own *flamantes luminarias* – for making sure I never get lost in the wilderness, and always bringing light and joy. Nothing is possible without you.

For this project, my father acted as my research assistant, photographer, and travel companion. Part way through our investigations, he experienced a devastating car accident. A difficult year ensued, but as soon as he could walk again, my father and I picked up where we left off. During a series of research trips between 2013 and 2017, we wandered throughout Iberia eating pumpkin compote, drinking Albariño, and bickering about highway tolls in Portugal. He charmed our way into a number of small churches and perched precariously on wobbly ladders to get the perfect shot of an altarpiece. It would, simply put, have been impossible for me to complete this work without him, and I am grateful every day for him.

NOTE ON TERMINOLOGY AND TRANSLATIONS

All translations are mine unless otherwise noted. I am grateful to Liam Brockey for his generous aid in translating a few Portuguese words and phrases, but any errors are solely my own.

I have also used the phrase "black confraternities" in cases that sometimes include both black and *mulato* brotherhoods, drawing on the American usage of the term "black" as defining all people of African origin or descent, largely because the majority of confraternities I study refer to themselves as "for black people." Early modern sources referred to Africans as "black," "Ethiopian," by various ethnic designations (Gege, Zape, Angolan), or status (enslaved, free, creole, *bozál*), not as Africans. The term *mulato* was usually used in Spanish sources to describe individuals with one black and one white parent, but in both Spanish and Portuguese sources, authors occasionally referred to such individuals as "*pardo.*" Yet in other cases (particularly New Spain), the term *pardo* could refer to those of mixed African and indigenous heritage. I have endeavored whenever possible to follow the terms used in the primary sources themselves; as a result, the reader will find both *mulato* and *pardo* used interchangeably but reflecting the language used in the example discussed.

INTRODUCTION

In the spring of 2015, I found myself standing outside the walls that led to a courtyard in front of a local church. The doors were supposed to be open according to the hours provided by the tourist office; after waiting a while, I went in search of help. Around the corner was a municipal library, where a librarian offered assistance. As he attempted to find more up-to-date information about the church (which was in the custody of a confraternity), he asked: "Why do you want to go inside the church?" I told him that I was writing a book about black saints and that I wanted to see the image of Benedict of Palermo inside. Before I finished talking, the man began shaking his head: "No, no, no, there is no black saint in that church. There are no black saints in Antequera." Despite this disappointing news, I decided to go back and wait longer. Eventually, the man responsible for unlocking the door, arrived and told me I could go in. And there it was in plain sight – a spectacular sculpture of Benedict of Palermo painted in a monochromatic black pigment. [**Plate 1**]

This incident would not be the only time someone in Spain or Portugal insisted that there was no black saint in a church that housed one. In cases where I knew the statue existed, I began to bring a Xerox of it to show the person who claimed there was no black saint in that church or museum. Upon viewing the photo, the person would sometimes exclaim: "Oh that image!" as though it had never occurred to him that the sculpture in question was a black saint, despite the dark pigment. Such encounters brought into relief the fraught relationship between memory and forgetfulness, visibility and invisibility, particularly in an Iberia that continues to struggle with its history of slavery.[1] Similarly, as I was writing this book, debates over Confederate flags and memorials intensified in the United States, leading to the removal of many prominent statues of

---

[1] Carrera, for example, argues: "'[S]eeing race' is not historically or culturally standard or universal. Rather, seeing is a historically and culturally-located practice that situates the reader/viewer so that s/he could see New Spain, its land and inhabitants": "'El Nuevo [Mundo]'," 70.

Confederate generals, including those in my home city of Baltimore. Such debates centered in part on what we can think of as misremembering – constructing a past in which the Confederacy could be separated from slavery. Misremembering and historical amnesia often plague contemporary views about the presence of enslaved people of African descent in medieval and early modern Europe.[2] The groundbreaking 2012–2013 exhibit at the Walters Art Museum, "Revealing the African Presence in Renaissance Europe," sought to render visible a hidden European past. Yet one of the most striking pieces in the exhibit was an empty frame on one wall. The information card described the frame as representing the sixteenth-century Afro-Iberian professor and poet, Juan Latino (d. 1596), whose only portrait had been destroyed in a fire. The absence provoked the viewer to consider what it means to have a past that cannot be made visible, and the multiple ways it is possible to resist erasure.

This book marks an attempt to uncover a past that is both shrouded and in plain sight. Images of black saints are both metaphor and evidence: their presence reveals the dynamic roles played by groups whose place as historical actors is often overlooked. While marginalized, unwilling members of a coercive institution, Afro-Iberians could also have a profound effect on Catholic belief and practice, for themselves and for the Church writ large. Recognizing how Afro-Iberians participated in the co-creation of devotional life allows us, in turn, to reconsider the evolution of early modern global Catholicism. The significance of the category of global Catholicism is less about specific geographic dispersion but rather its analytic potential: it provides a method for analyzing the processes of religious transformation occurring throughout the early modern Catholic Church as it began to spread across the globe.[3] It pushes us to displace the centrality of Europeans in the global "Christianization" that unfolded throughout early modern world.[4]

I assess the ways in which the early modern clergy understood the relationship between newly converted, non-European Christians and ecclesiastical and social hierarchies; more importantly, I examine how local devotions on the margins of Catholic society transformed spiritual practice back in Europe, specifically through the circulation of saints' cults. Much of the scholarship on missionaries has examined the dynamic between missionary and non/new Christians on

---

[2] For an American example of forgetting, see Melish, *Disowning Slavery*.

[3] Scholars working the Jesuits have provided much of the research on missionaries in a global framework: Clossey, *Salvation and Globalization*; Alden, *The Making of an Enterprise*; O'Malley et. al (eds.), *The Jesuits*; and Hsia (ed.), *A Companion to Early Modern Catholic Global Missions*.

[4] See Berg (ed.), *Writing the History of the Global*, esp. here Jean-Frédéric Schaub, "Notes on Some Discontents," 48–65; and Hopkins (ed.), *Global History*. See Gänger's critique of loose uses of the term "circulation": Gänger, "Circulation."

a local or regional level – that is, from the perspective of encounter and the dynamics such encounters produced in an environment where coercion and enslavement went hand in hand with conversion. The topics surrounding conversion have explored such questions as how baptisms took place, what level of coercion was involved, whether or not they were "successful," and local reactions to Christianity, including both rejection and syncretism.[5] All too often, religious practice of the ordinary laity is examined only in cases when individuals ran afoul of ecclesiastical authorities like the Inquisition, reducing lay devotions to resistance or punishment.

While the introduction of Christianity to non-Europeans through colonization and missions is one facet of early modern dynamics, it creates a picture of unidirectional influence and consistent maintenance of normative Catholicism. I argue, however, that the experience of transplanting Christianity altered normative practices in significant ways that brought non-European contributions into European churches, creating a circulation of ritual and ideas.[6] By expanding global Catholicism beyond a Eurocentric framework, my work exposes the ways in which Rome could be de-centered in early modern devotional practice, which, in turn, enables us to focus on actors who have traditionally been set to the side – the diverse lay populations of the Iberian empires, and Afro-Iberians in particular. Through the lens of global Catholicism, we see the participation of Afro-Iberians in the creation of new forms of Catholic ritual through active engagement with the divine. They organized acts of creativity that were not only accepted by the clergy, but that helped to shape devotional culture writ large. Through the organization of black confraternities and the veneration of black saints, Afro-Iberians took institutions and cults that were clerical in origin, and refashioned them into their own. This process, in turn, transformed the early modern Church in Europe as well as the Americas.

The process investigated in this book focuses on devotion to black saints and its dissemination by black confraternities, in which lay devotees ensured the expansion and significance of the cults of black saints first introduced by white clergy. The presence of black saints and their devotees legitimized the idea of black sanctity both among communities of color and white laity. Devotion to Benedict of Palermo (d. 1589) within black confraternities, for example, proved to be the primary factor that led to the saint's beatification in 1743, one of the first

---

[5] The historiography on this topic is vast, particularly in Latin America. See for example: Pardo, *The Origins of Mexican Catholicism*; Bailey, *Art on the Jesuit Missions*; Cymbalista, "The Presence of the Martyrs"; Tavárez, *Invisible War*; and Castelnau-L'Estoile, "The Uses of Shamanism."

[6] Scholars who discuss the impact of New World Christianity on Europe include Greer, *Mohawk Saint*; Vélez, "'A Sign that We Are Related to You'"; Kirk and Rivett, *Religious Transformations*; and Turley, *Franciscan Spirituality*.

early modern people of color so honored. In addition to Benedict, this book examines the cults of Elesban, Efigenia, and Antonio da Noto, with additional discussions of several living saints of color who did not attain official cults in the early modern period. While the number of saints is few, their influence was vast – cults to one saint can spread to hundreds, even thousands, of sites across the globe. There were altars dedicated to black saints in southern Italy, Portugal, Brazil, Spain, Angola, Mexico, Guatemala, Venezuela, Peru, and the Rio de la Plata, for just a few examples. In every place affected by the African slave trade, we find veneration to black saints, whose presence altered the spiritual landscape of global Catholicism.

The black saints themselves came to the forefront during the era of the transatlantic slave trade in response to the wide-scale baptism of newly enslaved people. Early modern authors explicitly used the term *negro* or *preto* to refer to these saints, echoing the most common monikers for individuals of sub-Saharan African origin or descent; therefore, ethnic origins, racial categorization, and skin color defined what it meant to be a black saint. Yet black saints were not the only non-European groups that white Catholics venerated or that religious orders attempted to have canonized during the early modern period. The globalization of Catholicism, in fact, spurred a competition to find new saints outside the bounds of Europe, the success of which would celebrate missionary endeavors. Black sanctity, then, developed alongside larger global patterns.

The indigenous peoples of America constituted one fertile area where non-European holy people could emerge. Perhaps the most famous examples of these are Juan Diego (the indigenous man who purportedly discovered the miraculous image of the Virgin of Guadalupe in Mexico) and Catherine Tekakwitha in New France.[7] Neither were canonized in the early modern period, however, and their influence remained relatively small. Nevertheless, Mónica Díaz points out that the French Jesuit Pierre Cholenec's hagiography of Catherine Tekakwitha was printed in Mexico City under the title *La gracia triunfante en la vida de Catharina Tegakovita, india iroquesa* [*Triumphant Grace in the Life of Catherine Tekakwitha, Iroquois Indian*], as part of a larger eighteenth-century effort to expand conventual access for noble indigenous women in New Spain.[8] This trans-imperial connection provides an example of the circulation of devotional patterns throughout the Atlantic – here Cholenec, a French Jesuit in New France,

---

[7] For a few examples of local veneration, see Ross, *The Baroque Narrative of Carlos de Sigüenza y Góngora*, who discusses two indigenous holy women: Petronila de la Concepeción and Francisca de San Miguel. Gunnarsdóttir has studied Francisca de los Ángeles, a mestiza from Querétero: *Mexican Karismata*; see also Rice, "La 'Teresa Indiana.'"

[8] Díaz, *Indigenous Writings*, 56.

printed his work in France for a French audience, and the work was quickly translated into Spanish in Mexico City for a different colonial audience.

Across the Pacific, accounts of local holy people circulated widely along oceanic networks that displaced the European node altogether.[9] A more successful (liturgically speaking) example of global saints resulted from the martyrdoms in Japan. Missionaries had begun to travel to Japan by the end of the century, in spite of the government's vigorous program of persecution of Christians from 1597 to 1640. In 1597, twenty-six Catholics, including six Franciscans and three Jesuits, were crucified; called the martyrs of Nagasaki, they were beatified in 1627, which marked the date of the official circulation of their cults. Liam Brockey notes the presence of portraits of the Franciscan martyrs, including the Japanese Diogo Kisai and João Soan de Gotó, in the Jesuit Church of São Roque in Lisbon, a rare example of individual portraits of the Japanese saints.[10]

The Nagaski martyr who achieved the highest profile in the early modern world was Gonçalo Garcia, whose cult proliferated in eighteenth-century Brazil and, to a lesser extent, Portugal. Garcia was himself a holy person of color – he had been born south of Bombay to a Portuguese soldier and a South Asian mother from the region of Vasai, not far from the early modern Portuguese stronghold of Goa. Janaina dos Santos Bezerra and Suely Creusa Cordeiro de Almeida have analyzed the promotion of Garcia's cult to and among the *pardo* population of eighteenth-century Recife via his patronage of confraternities for *pardos*.[11] In spite of his South Asian origins, black and mixed race people in the Americas and Portugal adopted Garcia as one of their own.[12] His devotional popularity, then, stemmed largely from his association with black confraternities. Like Catherine Tekakwitha, Garcia's cult demonstrates circuits of devotion that moved from the Lusophone Pacific to Brazil to Portugal.

Yet none of these individuals attained anything like the global impact of black saints. The question then becomes why, in the early modern Church's global search for non-European holy people, did the success of cults to black saints far outstrip the rest? It is a complex question, but one of the most fundamental

---

[9] See for example the important contributions of Ward, "Women Apostles," on Japanese women and their crucial roles in Christian Japanese networks, and the account of a Filipina *beata* in Manila, Fowler, "Illuminated Islands."

[10] Brockey, "Books of Martyrs," 211–12, 216–19.

[11] Bezerra and De Almeida, "'*Pompa e circunstância.*'" See also Viana, "Gonçalo Garcia."

[12] Another well studied and local famous South Asian holy woman, Catarina de San Juan (d. 1688), lived in Puebla, Mexico. For primary accounts of her life, see Ramos, *Primera parte de los prodigios*. The books' second part appeared in 1690, and included a print engraving of the saint in a tertiary's habit venerating a painting of the Madonna and child. For recent scholarship on Catarina: Seijas, *Asian Slaves*, ch. 1; Strasser, "A Case of Empire Envy?"; and Molina, "True Lies."

answers is precedence. Precedence was a core component of early modern Catholicism, because it established tradition, which followed closely after scripture as a form of authority. Anything that could be established as ancient could not be easily dismantled, and black saints maintained a lineage from the Old Testament all the way to Benedict of Palermo in the sixteenth century. When early modern authors searched for "Ethiopian" saints, they found abundant examples, which they painstakingly noted, offsetting some of the racial prejudices about Africans' moral potential.

The second major argument of the book assesses the ways in which sacred blackness was constructed, both by the clergy and by Afro-Iberians. White clergy produced copious meditations on the role of black Catholics in the Church, with a rhetoric that tended to be grounded in the intersection of sanctity with color difference – that is, blackness. The majority of their printed work was aimed at white audiences, and careful analysis of their rhetoric challenges scholarly views of race and blackness as inevitable or unchanging categories of otherness as constructed by white authors. Looking beyond textual evidence demonstrates how Afro-Iberians produced black sanctity through visible cultic devotion (in images and public processions) and by living holiness as members of religious orders. Like white clergy, Afro-Iberians grounded their relationship to black saints in terms of color, although of course for them, it was color sameness rather than color difference that explained devotion; they often referred to themselves as "those of the same color as the saint" as an explanation for their particular devotion. And the recurring presence of images of black saints carried by black Catholics reinforced powerfully the scriptural proclamation of the spiritual equality of all people, which acted as a visual resistance to the dehumanization of the slave system.

The representation of black saints – visual and textual – stands at the center of early modern debates over embodied difference and universal humanity, since these saints flourished at the same time that the transatlantic slave trade accelerated. Clergy imposing baptism and catechesis among enslaved people were often early promoters of black saints as evidence for the spiritual and moral capabilities of Africans. In arguing for the inclusion of Africans in the universal Church, clerical authors challenged the brutal treatment of the enslaved – although, notably, they did not speak out against the institution of slavery itself. Yet sacred blackness permitted Afro-Iberians to adopt the privileges of baptism to advocate for their civic participation, moral dignity, protection from brutal treatment, and freedom.

The complex ideas about sacred blackness were developed in part through the hagiographies of black saints, in which authors insisted on the spiritual equality of the souls of black and white Catholics. To do so, they played on tropes of blackness and whiteness, exterior and interior, which were deeply entrenched in scripture and theology. While the rhetoric of the white interior representing virtue could feed into early modern white supremacist thinking and the racial hierarchies of the Iberian world, hagiographers of black saints understood it differently. Sinfulness was a universal experience – anyone could be black on the outside, or white on the inside. Moreover, the exterior appearance of black saints acted as a form of martyrdom in hagiography, precisely because it was depreciated by society as whole. Such discourses added to and drew from ideas swirling around colonial Latin America that the sufferings of enslaved people on earth translated into a near guarantee of salvation. The idea of "spiritual slavery" took on a powerful force for white clergy writing about enslaved people as well as to white laity in relationship to their own piety. Furthermore, the claim by black confraternal brothers and sisters to public space and participation in the social life of towns and cities – most of which was organized by ecclesiastical rhythms of feast days and their attendant masses and processions – helped to create distinct spaces for black community members to gather and protect one another.[13] The performance of Christianity, whether from devotion or utility (not that these are mutually exclusive), forced shared public presence even as it could foster group consciousness among African diasporic communities.

The discourse of spiritual slavery, presence of black saints, and social capital of black confraternities did not lead to the end of slavery in the Iberian empires. They did not slow the slave trade, mitigate the great suffering of millions of enslaved people, or destabilize deep-rooted social and legal hierarchies. Yet they did provide vital opportunities for claimsmaking, arguments against the brutal treatment of enslaved people, and a push for universal humanity far into the eighteenth century, just as racism was becoming more firmly entrenched throughout the Atlantic world. Because members of the clergy were often complicit in maintaining the status quo and sustaining the system of slavery – as well as being major slave owners themselves – they have often been seen as uniformly participating in replicating structures of oppression. But close examination of textual and visual evidence of black saints demonstrates that some clergy constructed alternative discourses that were eventually replicated by anti-slavery advocates. Moreover, the idea of universal humanity (realized through baptism) and spiritual achievement fueled the potential of enslaved and free people of color to advocate on behalf of themselves and their communities in resisting colonial hegemony.

---

[13] We can see parallels between the processes I describe here in the context of confraternities and what scholars have argued regarding black militia soldiers: Vinson, *Bearing Arms*.

Methodology

The geographic reach of this study is vast: Sicily, Spain, Portugal, New Spain, Peru, Brazil, the Portuguese Atlantic islands, and West and Central Africa. It presents a synthetic analysis that connects a series of religious and social developments operating throughout the Iberian Atlantic and Catholic world. While synthetic studies run the danger of eliding local contexts, understanding the larger narrative creates the opportunity to recognize and analyze large-scale transformations. My focus on Spain and Portugal demonstrates their role as a nexus in the dynamic processes of global Catholicism that both fed spiritual developments across the Atlantic and was profoundly transformed by them. Yet it is also crucial to note that African diasporic people maintained a large variety of religious and social practices that could be more deeply tied to African than to Europe. Here, I focus on normative Catholicism, but I view this focus as a complement to important research on Candomblé, Santería, and Lucumí.[14] In the Americas, I chose Lima as my primary American case study because of its large black population and vibrant spiritual climate, which produced numerous American saints and holy people, including St. Martín de Porres. Furthermore, urban environments such as Lima were spaces where enslaved and free people of color could move with greater freedom and amass property and wealth, which, in turn, allowed black confraternities and their patronage of sacred art to thrive. As a result, colonial cities played a crucial role in the development of global Catholicism.

The printed textual sources I employ consist largely of ecclesiastical works including sacred histories, histories of orders, and, most of all, hagiographies, while the manuscripts consulted include confraternity statutes, beatification records, letters, and lawsuits. The latter proved particularly useful because they provided the richest opportunities to see sources written or dictated by enslaved and free people of color. At the same time, I found almost no manuscripts that provided information about the commission of images for confraternities, which leaves us with little sense whether or not the brothers and sisters requested specific elements in their images.

This project is by its nature interdisciplinary, with visual evidence taking center stage. The images act not as illustrations, but as objects providing critical information about the spread of cults of black saints and the meaning(s) of sacred blackness. They reveal histories that cannot otherwise be seen. My work,

---

[14] See for example, Parés, *The Formation of Candomblé*; Wirtz, *Performing Afro-Cuba*; Howard, *Changing History*; O'Toole, "To Be Free and Lucumí"; Sweet, *Recreating Africa*; and Sweet, *Domingo Alvares*.

therefore, engages with their materiality, though more precise dating and the techniques of sculpture and polychroming used in these images require further study by art historians and conservators.[15]

The process of finding and cataloguing images of black saints, even restricted to Iberia, was a challenging prospect. Despite an early hope that I could document all extant images in Iberia, the task proved impossible, as many were destroyed, lost, or hidden within monasteries and convents, even storage facilities. The first sculptures that I encountered were the fairly well-known ones of Benedict of Palermo and Efigenia in the Parroquia de Nuestra Señora del Rosario in Cadiz. In search of more images, I consulted a variety of sources: eighteenth-century hagiographies and beatification records; artistic guides of Andalusia; tourist offices; previous scholarly research, which occasionally included images; the digital archive for the Image of the Black in Western Art project available on Artstore; sacred art museums; and even simple internet searches. None of these sources proved comprehensive, although the Image of the Black digital archive includes a significant collection of images of Benedict in Portugal. The limitations of the extant source material stems in part from previous generations of art historians: Those who compiled artistic guides of Spain and Portugal sometimes did not include images of black saints in their descriptions of churches, since the authors restricted themselves to works they considered "of artistic merit," which rarely included black saints.

Images mentioned in early modern sources were the ones most likely to have vanished, largely through destruction from natural disaster or warfare. Others have been moved into storage, conservation, or are simply unseen by custodians. The images that I viewed were in various states of conservation – some had been conserved (which in Spain often included re-polychroming), others had not been but were in good condition, and still others were unconserved and in peril. I endeavored to view in person as many images as I could but have not included all of them in this work: in some cases, I was able to access the images but my photographs were not of sufficient resolution (churches are notoriously difficult to photograph in) and, in other cases, I was just not able to view the images. One good example comes from Oporto – I knew from a previous publication that there were beautiful sculptures of Elesban and Efigenia in the local Carmelite church, Santa Clara. Upon visiting, I discovered that the entire church was under conservation and the images were in storage. Discussions with local contacts yielded no useful aid. A year later, however, I stumbled across the Oporto image

---

[15] Metaphorical images of black saints also appear in literature, especially seventeenth-century Spanish theater. See important work black characters in Golden Age theater by Jones, *Habla de Negros*.

of Efigenia in the exhibit "Racisms" in Lisbon's Padrão dos Descobrimentos (2017), although I was unable to procure a publishable-quality photograph. On the opposite end of the spectrum, new images occasionally surface – the Detroit Institute of Art recently procured a magnificent baroque polychrome sculpture of Benedict of Palermo. Kind friends sometimes send me photos of images they encounter in Iberian churches, such as one of Benedict of Palermo I was recently sent by Cloe Cavero de Carondelet from a church near Valladolid.

During several visits to churches, officials who permitted me to photograph the images expressed great concern over their identification. They requested that the precise locations of the churches – many functioning parishes in smaller towns – be omitted from my work due to security concerns. The misplacement or theft of sacred art is no less common than the theft of manuscript and rare books from archives and libraries throughout Europe. Respecting their concerns and erring on the side of caution, I have chosen to omit the towns and churches associated with some of the images that appear in the book. Researchers who are interested in knowing those locations are welcome to contact me directly.

This book is divided into two parts. Part I, "Devotion," traces the processes through which devotion to black saints came into being, took root, and circulated. Key to this process was a medieval genealogy of sacred blackness in the Latin West. As the fifteenth century gave way to the sixteenth, the promotion of black saints became increasingly central to the clerical push to bring enslaved people into the fold of Christianity through evangelization, catechesis, and the formation of black confraternities. Quickly, however, black confraternities became social institutions that shaped part of a resistance to colonial hegemony, a fact that also made them subject to aggressive backlash by white Catholics.

Part II, "Illumination," shifts attention to representations of sacred blackness and whiteness developed by white clergy and artists. Such rhetoric helped to promote the cults of black saints and to produce discourses of universal humanity in ways that de-centered race as an exclusive lens through which to view Africans and their descendants. The approaches to sacred blackness taken by baroque artists developed differently from textual ones; this section, then, pays careful attention to images of black saints, their construction, and their meanings. The proliferation of images and texts discussing black saints created spiritual climates in which women and men of color could obtain reputations for holiness, even sanctity. As a result, clusters of holy people of color emerged in Iberia, New Spain, and Lima, including Martín de Porres (the only to eventually become a saint), Teresa Juliana de Santo Domingo, Úrsula de Jesús, Estefanía de San José, Juana Esperanza de San Alberto, and Magdalena de la Cruz. Close examination of Úrsula de Jesús's life, for example, provides a particularly important opportunity to unpack the experiences of a black holy person in her own words, since she produced a spiritual diary in seventeenth-century Lima.

The cathedral in Braga, Portugal, contains a side chapel with an altar and images that belonged to black confraternity, labeled "Nossa Senhora do Rosário dos pretos" (Our Lady of the Rosary of the Blacks). The Rosary Virgin stands in the center, the patronage image, and at her feet cluster four black saints. The name of the confraternity alone does not reveal the confraternity's devotion to black saints, yet the black brothers and sisters organized the altar and commissioned its images. It is, then, only by searching for surviving material evidence that we can uncover the full, rich history of black saints and their roles in global Catholic culture. Doing so helps to restore Afro-Iberians to the center of their own history and to the history of Christianity. The veneration of black saints was more than a spiritual preference – it was an act of creativity that resisted white hegemony, transformed the Church, and refuses to remain unseen.

PART I
DEVOTION

1 THE EMERGENCE OF BLACK SAINTS

In 1618, Philip III, king of Spain and Portugal, arrived in Lisbon as part of a royal visit throughout his kingdoms. During his stay, the city observed one of its most important feast days. Feast days were festivals celebrated throughout the Catholic world with the highest degree of sumptuousness, including processions that traversed the major thoroughfares of the city, elaborate decorations, games, poetry contests, and fireworks. Accounts of this particular feast were repeated throughout the Hispanic world and included one striking feature: a description of black members of a confraternity, free and enslaved, who participated in the procession, carrying with them several devotional images, including those of several black saints. Subsequent hagiographers described the black confraternal members as having "brilliant simplicity and sincere piety," carrying the standard of St. Benedict of Palermo, who was "their special patron and protector."[1] This festival marked an early period of devotion to black saints in Lisbon, which persisted for well over a century. In the middle of the eighteenth century, another visitor to the city, the British traveler William Beckford, witnessed a feast in honor of Portugal's patron saint, Anthony of Padua. Beckford, a Protestant, was inclined to be disgusted by the Catholic ritual, but had a particularly strong antipathy to images of "two blackamoor saints one never heard of" who "contribute[d] their share of ridicule to the procession."[2] The century and a half that spanned the celebrations of these two festivals provide a glimpse into the long and vibrant epoch of celebrating black saints in the early modern Iberian world.

Tracing the origins and early years of cults of black saints is vital for understanding how a black confraternity in Lisbon came to process through the streets carrying St. Benedict's image and standard. Close examination reveals the

---

[1] Mataplanes, *Vida de fray Benito de S. Fradelo*, 185. This procession was mentioned in several hagiographies in the seventeenth and eighteenth centuries.

[2] Beckford, *The Journal of William Beckford*, 81.

multiple strands of theology, political ideology, diplomacy, overseas expansion, and rapid economic change that came together to give rise to cults of black saints. Without all these elements cohering by the end of the sixteenth century, devotion to black saints could not have achieved the long geographic and chronological reach that it was able to attain. Yet the foundational elements grounding cults of black saints were a series of theological meditations on blackness, virtue, and holiness that evolved in the High Middle Ages. Such meditations were followed by a series of political-religious developments that culminated in the transformation of the figure of the Ethiopian to a symbol of universal Christianity and/or sovereignty. This symbolic read of blackness eventually became troubled by the rapid rise of the trans-Atlantic slave trade, which coded blackness quite differently. Yet the fusion of medieval ideas about sacred blackness and Ethiopia merged with the new colonial imperative to evangelize to thousands of newly baptized enslaved Africans to give rise to the spectacular emergence of black saints in the early modern world.

Blackness and Sanctity in the Middle Ages

The first representations of black sacredness in the Latin West appeared during the High Middle Ages, with the appearance of the Black Madonnas. Such images tend to be sculpture, most dating from the twelfth and thirteenth centuries, depicting the Virgin Mary sitting on a throne holding the Christ child in her arms (a position called the Virgin in Majesty), or standing, also holding Christ in her arms. Some of the most highly venerated images of the Virgin in medieval Europe were Black Madonnas, including Our Ladies of Montserrat, Guadalupe, Tindari, and Le Puy.[3] [Plate 2] The Virgins of Guadalupe (Extremadura, Spain) and Montserrat (Catalonia) maintain popular devotions to this day. Others, like the Puy Virgin, were destroyed and exist today only in copies, or not at all.

Black Madonnas have generated controversy among art historians, stemming from disagreements over when, how, and why such Madonnas came to acquire their black appearance – to put it simply, whether or not they had been intentionally made to appear black. As a result, scholars have sometimes argued that those originally painted white are not "real" Black Madonnas, leading to disagreement over how many existed in Europe, with figures ranging from dozens to hundreds. The darkness of many Madonnas can be attributed to environmental

---

[3] Moss and Cappannari suggest that the Black Virgin was associated with ancient pagan cults: "In Quest of the Black Virgin." Vilatte points out the divine origins of other Black Madonnas: "La 'dévote image noire de Nostre-Dame'," 754. The original Notre Dame du Puy was destroyed in 1794.

contamination and/or deterioration, rather than artistic intention.[4] The debate over materiality and intentionality complicate analysis of the possible meanings of their blackness. If, for example, the images of the Virgin holding the Christ child took on their darkened hue due to smoke or other kinds of environmental damage, then their blackness might have a different meaning to viewers than if the artist had deliberately painted them black.[5]

Jeanette Peterson and Monica Scheer argue that controversy regarding the origins of the black appearance is less salient than previous scholars have claimed; even if the images had been originally white, the faithful eventually began to recognize such images as black as they darkened. The images, therefore, accumulated new meanings for viewers over time. Once accepted as black, blackness itself developed specific associations with sacredness, especially because the audiences understood that the Virgin was *not* being depicted as ethnically or racially black.[6] Scheer contends that it was only in the early modern period that the blackness of these images was recognized, discussed, and explained, mirroring the increasingly fraught views Europeans developed about black skin during this period of the transatlantic slave trade, as well as the attendant rise in the visibility of black saints. As a result, early modern artists sometimes painted medieval black saints, spreading their cults even further. [**Plate 3**] The Virgin of Puy had been painted in the late seventeenth century, an important survival as the original image was destroyed during the French Revolution.

Significantly, however, most art historians agree that some of the Black Madonnas were originally created black, the result of a specific theology of sacred blackness.[7] The period of the introduction of Black Madonnas – the twelfth and thirteenth centuries – witnessed the explosion of devotion to the Virgin Mary in the Latin West.[8] Influential clergy such as St. Bernard of

---

[4] Ilene Forsyth rejects the idea that the French Madonnas were deliberately painted black: *The Throne of Wisdom*, 20–2. Moss and Cappannari argue that some of the images were darkened by pigment deterioration or environmental factors; others, in small numbers, were intentionally created as black, which were "Christian borrowings from earlier pagan art forms" that associated blackness with fertility (65): "In Quest of the Black Virgin." Miquel Ballbè i Boada refutes the syncretic argument: *Las Vírgenes negras y morenas*, 22.

[5] One image that darkened over time is Our Lady of Chartres, an object of much recent controversy when it was aggressively lightened to her "original" whiteness as part of a large-scale cleaning of the church.

[6] Peterson, *Visualizing Guadalupe*, 33; and Scheer, "From Majesty to Mystery," 1412–40. Victor Stoichita points out an engraving of Notre Dame du Puy from 1523 depicted her as white, while by 1627, another portrays her as black: *The Image of the Black*, 300–1.

[7] Ballbè i Boada, *Las Vírgenes negras y morenas*; Begg, *The Cult of the Black Virgin*; Moss and Cappannari, "In Quest of the Black Virgin."

[8] The rapid growth of devotion to the Virgin in the twelfth century is a well-recognized facet of medieval piety: Gold, *The Lady and the Virgin*, 43–75.

Clairvaux (d. 1153) promoted intense Marian piety. Many scholars have connected the surge of black images of Mary to commentaries and sermons on the Old Testament Song of Songs in twelfth-century France, particularly those of Bernard of Clairvaux.[9] Medieval commentators understood the "bride" in the Song as representing either the Church or the Virgin Mary, and the bride's self-described black appearance provides a possible explanation for the emergence of Black Madonnas. The pertinent line of the Song here is one of its most famous: "*nigra sum sed formosa.*" The entire passage in modern edition reads: "I am black and beautiful, Daughters of Jerusalem – like the tens of Qedar, like the curtains of Solomon. Do not stare at me because I am so black, because the sun has burned me."[10] While the modern edition translates "*sed*" as "and," most medieval and early modern authors translated it as "but," reinforcing the sense of contrast between beauty and blackness.[11] Bernard viewed the bride's blackness as displeasing, but simultaneously irrelevant to God, because He judges by the heart, not the face.[12] The monk further insisted that blackness was a gateway to greater grace precisely because it was less aesthetically pleasing, reminding his readers the apostle St. Paul's declaration that a true servant of Christ does not try to please others.[13] The inferior beauty of blackness, therefore, enabled the bride to avoid pleasing others:

> The outward blemishes that we may discern in any people are not to be condemned, because they play a part in the begetting of interior light, and so depose the soul for wisdom. For wisdom is described by the wise man as a reflection of eternal life, and brightness befits the soul in which it decides to dwell. If the soul of the righteous man is the seat of wisdom, I may certainly refer to such as a soul as bright. Righteousness itself can be called brightness.[14]

---

[9] Fazio, *La Madonna di Tindari*: "Questi comentari hanno probabilmente giocato un ruolo fondamentale nell nascita e nel diffondere delle 'Madonne nere'," 26.

[10] Canticles 1:4–5, Vulgate edition: "nigra sum sed formosa filiae Hierusalem ... nolite me considerare quod fusca sim quia decoloravit me sol." The English translations here and throughout the book come from the USCCB Bible.

[11] Kate Lowe discusses this phrase and its use in the later period: "The Global Consequences of Mistranslation."

[12] Bernard here cited 1 Samuel 16:7: "But the Lord said to Samuel: Do not judge from his appearance or from his lofty stature, because I have rejected him. ... The Lord looks into the heart."

[13] Galatians 1:10: "If I were still trying to please people, I would not be a slave of Christ."

[14] Bernard of Clairvaux, *Commentary*, 132. The original Latin can be found: Bernard of Clairvaux, *Sermons sur le Cantique*, v. 2, 266–9. The passage reads in Latin: "Non plane contemnenda in sanctis ista nigredo extera, quae candorem operatur internum, et sedem proinde praeparat sapientiae. *Candor est enim vitae aeternae* sapientia, ut Sapiens definit; et candidam oportet esse animam, in qua ipsa sedem elegerit" (268).

Being displeasing to others – here described in embodied terms as "outward blemishes" – acted as a gateway to Christian virtue and eternal life, since ignoring the values of this world cultivated virtue. While the English translator employed the phrase "outward blemishes," the Latin original emphasizes that the "blemish" in question is the Bride's blackness [*nigredo extera*].

Bernard reminds his readers that an outward blemish led to the cultivation of virtue and wisdom, which Bernard repeatedly described with the adjective "bright." Here the word translated into English as "brightness" is the Latin adjective *candor*. "Candor" connotes a bright light, associated with the divine in medieval Latin. Although "candor" is sometimes translated as "whiteness" in English, Bernard was not contrasting the colors white and black; rather, he spoke of darkness and light, using common Christian associations of darkness with the secular, the temporary, and the body (including its suffering), and light with the eternal, the permanent, the soul. For Bernard, and many other medieval Christians, the blackness of the Virgin represented the ultimate ability to conquer human weakness with the spiritual strength provided by divine grace.[15] This discourse of darkness and light produced two distinct but entangled results: on the one hand, Bernard is clear that blackness as a color was a "stigma" and "disagreeable"; at the same time, he insisted that the "form" or "shape of a thing" could be beautiful.[16] For Bernard, and other medieval theologians, the soul remained the locus of the true self. While blackness could represent sinfulness, its very sinfulness acted as the gateway to divine grace.

Sacred blackness could have meanings beyond those developed by Bernard of Clairvaux. Sylvie Vilatte has argued that the blackness of Notre Dame du Puy was a product of the second half of the fourteenth century, painted onto the Virgin's face and hands to symbolize her important role in the conversion of infidels.[17] Ballbè i Boada claims that the color of other Black Madonnas represented the triumph of the Church over the shadowy darkness of sin.[18] The Virgin was not the only saint in the Middle Ages who could be portrayed with black or dark pigments; Sicilian saints Calogero (d. 561) and Filippo di Agira (d.c. 453) could be depicted as white or black. Francesco Scorza Barcellona posits that the occasional representation of the two saints as black might have stemmed from their frequent struggles with demons, which were sometimes illustrated as black in medieval illuminations. The evil vapors of the Sicilian volcano, Mt. Etna, were

---

[15] Fazio, *La Madonna di Tindari*, 32; Scheer, "From Majesty to Mystery," 1430. I take up the language of "*candidez*" in Chapter 4.

[16] Bernard of Clairvaux, *Commentary*, 130–4.

[17] Vilatte, "La 'dévote image noire de Nostre-Dame,'" 751–3.

[18] Ballbè i Boada, *Las Vírgenes negras y morenas*, 40.

said to host demons, which Calogero and Filippo both battled.[19] The blackness of the saints' face and hands, therefore, represented iconographically the miracles with which they were associated, an equivalent to a saint holding a sword or a martyr's palm, as opposed to an attempt to highlight their bodily likeness. We can see, then, that blackness could have a number of meanings unrelated to skin color or ethnicity. It could be used to depict both a demon and a saint who triumphed over one, or it could represent suffering and penitence, key theological virtues. The theological meanings of blackness, therefore, were multifaceted throughout the Middle Ages – and richly intertwined with the sacred.

The First Black Saints

The appearance of the Black Madonnas throughout Europe marked the beginning of a slow process in which images of black saints began to appear more frequently. The next black saint to achieve popularity was the sub-Saharan African soldier, St. Maurice (d. 287). According to legend, Maurice was the leader of a Roman legion called the Thebians, all of whom were eventually executed by the emperor for refusing to persecute Christians. Their martyrdom purportedly took place in modern-day Switzerland, and his cult became associated with the Holy Roman Emperors. He was venerated in central Europe as early as the tenth century, and first depicted as a black African in the middle of the thirteenth. [Fig. 1.1] Jean Devisse argues that Emperor Frederick II (d. 1250) promoted Maurice as imperial patron to symbolize the empire's global dominion as the heirs to Rome. Such use of St. Maurice provides the first example of a European ruler employing an African as a symbol for imperial ambition. The connection between black Africans and universal sovereignty derived from the belief that a ruler whose territory reached the "Lands of the Blacks" – whose beginning and end could not be properly charted – could claim to be lord of the world. Because of its tie to the Hohenstaufen dynasty, this imagery of Maurice remained regional; in other kingdoms in the Latin West, Maurice was depicted as a white European.[20]

There is also evidence that medieval Europeans were aware of black saints who were venerated in the Greek Orthodox and Coptic churches from late antiquity. One of the most important of these black saints was an ascetic who lived in the

---

[19] Scorza Barcellona, "I santi neri di Sicilia," 270–1.
[20] On the cult of St. Maurice in central Europe, see Devisse's excellent section in "A Sanctified Black," 158–73. See also Kaplan, *Rise of the Black Magus*.

Figure 1.1 *Saint Maurice*, 1240, polychrome sculpture. Madgeburg Cathedral, Germany.

Egyptian desert named Moses the Ethiopian, although he could also be called Moses the Abyssinian, the Black, the Hermit, or the Robber. He was a fourth-century Ethiopian (Abyssinian) slave who spent many of his early years as a thief. He eventually experienced a spiritual conversion, which prompted him to live his life in the desert as a monk near Sketes, Egypt until old age. Around the year 405, however, a group of pagan Berbers raided the monastery; rather than flee or take up arms, Moses remained behind along with a small cohort of monks where they were all martyred. The main account of Moses's life can be found in Palladius of Galata's early fifth-century *The Lausiac History*. Palladius was a contemporary of Moses who wrote a collection of stories about Egyptian and Palestinian monks; he described the saint as a humble ascetic, a version largely followed in Athansius's *The Paradise of the Holy Fathers*, though Athansius included the account of Moses's martyrdom.[21] Moses's inclusion in these important works of the early Church, especially as it developed in the Greek Mediterranean, suggests widespread knowledge of his life. In the Latin Church, however, little has been uncovered about veneration of Moses until the fourteenth century, when authors in Europe

---

[21] Wortley, *Palladius of Aspuna*, 36–8; *The Book of the Elders: Sayings of the Desert Fathers*, 44–5; 200–1.

began to translate and rework the Greek *Sayings of the Fathers* into Latin and the vernacular.[22]

What little evidence we have for devotion to Moses in Western Europe comes from late medieval Castile, where authors provided commentary on passages in the *Sayings of the Father* that they considered of particular significance. Such authors focused particular attention on the sections of Moses's life that centered on his skin color. After Moses's ordination, the patriarch told him "[N]ow you are entirely white." Yet the patriarch wished to test Moses, so he told his audience to drive Moses from the sanctuary; when Moses entered, the other men forced him to leave, shouting, "Outside, black man!" Moses left without protest, speaking out loud to himself that he deserved their disdain, because his skin was "as black as ashes. You are not a man so why should you be allowed to meet men?"[23] While this anecdote was included in the *Sayings*, it took on a more central place in the commentary of the medieval Castilians, as they highlighted this passage while omitting others. The authors used the story to bolster a specific view of the aesthetics of blackness, and their decision to streamline Moses's life into a narrative of blackness, humility, and self-abnegation underscored the saint's lesser status – even lesser humanity. The themes echoed here – prejudice against black skin, the association of black sanctity and excessive humility, the interplay between interior and exterior – recurred in early modern hagiographies of black saints. It is therefore possible that translations of or commentaries on *Sayings* in the late medieval Mediterranean and early Renaissance helped lay the discursive groundwork for the black saints who emerged in later centuries.[24]

Another major innovation that had a dramatic effect on visual culture and black sanctity occurred just before these Castilian translations of Moses' life: the emergence of the black magus. The magi were the three kings who, according to the Gospels, visited the newborn Christ in the manger, offering lavish gifts and paying homage to him. They were later assigned the names Melchior, Gaspar (or Caspar), and Balthazar. This scene was frequently depicted in medieval and early modern churches as part of the Nativity cycle, where at a certain point they began

---

[22] On translations from Greek to Latin, see Beresford, "Sanctity and Prejudice," 19. For more on medieval ideas about blackness, see Heng, *The Invention of Race in the European Middle Ages*, ch. 4.

[23] This version comes from Ward, *The Sayings of the Desert Fathers*, 47. Wortley provides a slightly different translation, using the words "burnt-faced one" and "human" instead of "man": Wortley, *Sayings of the Desert Fathers*, 200–1. Beresford's study shows the similarities found in the Castilian translations: "Sanctity and Prejudice," 23–5. In Castilian, Moses referred to himself as "ashy" and "black as a kettle."

[24] For another example of the words of Abba Moses on the topic of obedience: Wortley, *Sayings of the Desert Fathers*, 184: "Let us acquire obedience, which begets humility." For more on early Christian discussions of Moses and Philip the Eunuch, see Byron, *Symbolic Blackness*, ch. 5.

to represent the three ages – one old, one middle aged, and one young – and eventually one became depicted as a black king. Paul Kaplan has traced the first depictions of black magi to between 1340 and 1375, though the spread of such iconography was slow. It was not until the fifteenth century that it began to spread rapidly, but once it did so, it became the standard iconography for the Adoration in Renaissance and Baroque works.[25] Koerner estimates that thousands of images of the Adoration were produced in northern Europe alone from 1480 to 1530 and that almost every household in Antwerp contained a print engraving of the Adoration with a black magus.[26]

Images of the Adoration took on specific iconographic features in addition to the black magus. The larger, more elaborate paintings often included other black figures, the magus's servants and companions. He was most frequently depicted as the youngest, Balthazar, often wearing more garish clothing than the other magi – lavish, bejeweled, colorful, and occasionally containing foreign elements such as feathers. He was also, as the youngest, the last of the magi to arrive, and was sometimes placed at a physical remove from the other magi, emphasizing his distance from the other figures in the scene.[27] [**Plate 4, Plate 5**] Yet his physical remove alongside the exoticization of his costume ultimately highlights the presence of a black African in the Adoration. The iconography, therefore, functioned on dual registers – simultaneously othering and inclusive.

Spanish baroque artists also took up the black magus by the early seventeenth century in works that included many of the standard elements developed in Northern European painting. Hundreds of Spanish churches contain Baroque bas relief, paintings, and frescoes of the Adoration including a black magus, many of which can be found in churches that also exhibit an image of a black saint. [**Plate 6**] Diego Velázquez painted an important Adoration while in Seville, a period of his early career where his work often included black slaves, presumably the result of living in a place with a large enslaved and free black population.[28] [**Plate 7**] In Velázquez's Adoration, the black magus is placed in the center of a triangle of figures; he stands, rather than kneels, revealing more of his figure than the other two magi, one of whom recedes into the left side of the frame. As a result, the viewer's eye lingers on him and his near-equal height to the

---

[25] Kaplan, *Rise of the Black Magus*, 85–100.

[26] Koerner, "The Epiphany of the Black Magus," 7–91.

[27] Trexler, *The Journey of the Magi*, 104–7. While the black magus is most frequently called Balthazar, he was not always referred to as such; occasionally he was called Gaspar, and, more rarely, by the third name, Melchior.

[28] Diego Velázquez owned at least one slave himself, Juan de Pareja, whom Velázquez later freed; Pareja became a well-known artist himself.

Virgin, the result of a spatial triangle created by the oldest magi kneeling between Balthazar and the Virgin. He is not dressed as garishly as other black magi, in spite of his rich red cloak and visible pearl earring; his white collar deliberately highlights the darkness of his skin (in a similar way to Bosch's), but he wears the somber black dress of a fashionable Spanish courtier.[29] Moreover, the magus's white collar picks up the whiteness of the Christ child's swaddling bands; the eye is drawn first to the baby, who occupies the central position, then moves to Balthazar's white collar followed by the creamier white of the Virgin's veil. From a distance, the repetition of whiteness creates a visual triangle – heightened by the triangular negative space between Balthazar and the Christ child – setting them apart from the others and emphasizing Balthazar's importance to the painting's meaning.

Sacred blackness, then, began with popular local cults of the Virgin Mary and evolved into presenting black Africans as historical saintly figures. During the transition from Black Madonna to black magus, we also see a shift in their symbolic significance – instead of spiritual blackness, black Africans became ambivalent symbols of both universality and foreignness. Yet such foreignness existed within the context of Christendom, and their antiquity created a genealogy of Ethiopian Christianity that was accepted throughout Europe.

Encountering Ethiopia

The shift in visual iconography of the Adoration did not occur in a vacuum. As Paul Kaplan aptly notes, "One of the preconditions for the remarkable expansion of the motif of the black King in the second half of the fifteenth century was unquestionably the progressively greater quantity of European contacts with black Africans which can be observed after about 1425."[30] European interest in Ethiopia was piqued by the rumors of a legendary Christian leader in a far distant kingdom called Prester John. European ideas about the location of Prester John's kingdom varied, but he became associated with Ethiopia more consistently by 1400.[31] Yet despite the strong emphasis in modern European historiography on the "discovery" of various places in Africa by European explorers, it was in fact the Ethiopians who established first – and persistent – contact with

---

[29] Serrera, "La Adoración de los Reyes Magos," 351–65; Brown and Garrido, *Velázquez*, 21–7.

[30] Kaplan, *Rise of the Black Magus*, 103.

[31] For an overview of the legend, see Kurt, "The Search for Prester John," 297–319. For a primary sources on the legend, see Barber et al., *Prester John*, which notes that the first reference to the Ethiopian negus as Prester John dates from 1400.

Europeans, which became robust in the fifteenth century.[32] One of the earliest recorded contacts between Ethiopians and Europeans was an embassy of around thirty legates sent to Europe by Wedem Ra'ad (d. 1314), most likely for the purpose of forging a military alliance with fellow Christians against an encroaching Islamic enemy.[33] Waylaid in Genoa, some of the Ethiopian party appear to have met with local cartographer Giovanni da Carignano (d. 1329).[34] Using the information gleaned from the Ethiopian party, Carignano compiled a map that correctly located Ethiopia with a corresponding commentary on the kingdom. From this moment on, Ethiopia evolved into a concrete, historical space for Europeans rather than a purely imaginary one. By the early sixteenth century, Europeans began visiting Ethiopia more regularly, forging stronger diplomatic, economic, and military ties.[35]

Ethiopian monks in particular initiated visits to Rome in greater numbers, beginning with two important fifteenth-century Catholic councils: The Council of Constance (1414–1418) and the Council of Florence (1431–1449).[36] Clergy at the Council of Florence discussed the possibility of reuniting the Eastern and Western branches of Christendom – e.g. Catholicism and the Orthodox Church. In celebration of that effort, Pope Eugene IV commissioned Filarete (d. c. 1469) to cast the bronze doors for the old St. Peter's basilica in Rome, which included a relief depicting Eugene handing the Bull of Union to Coptic and Ethiopian monks.[37] While the Ethiopian monks played a marginal role in the council, their presence was widely noted by contemporary Romans.

By the end of the fifteenth century, the number of Ethiopian monks in Rome was large enough that Pope Sixtus IV (d. 1484) dedicated a monastery with hospice, cloister, cells, and cemetery for Ethiopian pilgrims and monks. The complex was called San Stefano Maggiore (or San Stefano degli Abissini), and it became the center for contact between Ethiopian monks and Renaissance clergy and intellectuals, enabling Italian orientalists and antiquarians to access

---

[32] Salvadore, "The Ethiopian Age," 593. Salvadore refers to Ethiopian travelers to Europe as "agents of discovery and purveyors of geographical knowledge" (593–4).

[33] Salvadore, "The Ethiopian Age," 600–2.

[34] Beckingham, "European Sources for Ethiopian History," 169.

[35] Salvadore, "The Ethiopian Age," 604. Another European resident of Ethiopia was the artist Niccolò Brancaleon. On Brancaleon and Ethiopian sacred art, see Heldman, *The Marian Icons of the Painter Fre Seyon*, 149–50; and Heldman, "St. Luke as Painter," 125–48. In addition, Dawit I (d. 1411) sent two embassies to Venice and Rome in the early fifteenth century: Tedeschi, "Paolo Giovio," 94; and Salvadore, "The Ethiopian Age," 607–12. Another delegation was sent in 1449 to the Aragonese king Alfonso in Naples, headed by a Sicilian from Messina who had been living in Ethiopia.

[36] On the small Ethiopian delegation to the Council of Florence, see Lefèvre, "Presenze etiopiche in Italia," 21; and Tedeschi, "Etiopi e Copti al Concilio di Firenze," 380–97.

[37] Lowe, "Visual Representations of an Elite," 100.

direct information about Ethiopian history, culture, and languages.[38] The most well-known Ethiopian monk at San Stefano during this period was Tasfa Seyon (d.c. 1552).[39] It is difficult to summarize Seyon's wide influence briefly, but it is worth mentioning that one of his most famous friendships was with the founder of the Society of Jesus, Ignatius of Loyola. The friendship between the two men led Ignatius to consider evangelization efforts in Ethiopia and to pen his advice on conducting missionary work there.[40]

Medieval depictions of blackness and black Africans had changed considerably from the thirteenth to the fifteenth centuries. Accelerating diplomatic, religious, and cultural exchange that flowed between Ethiopia and Europe had a profound impact on the ways in which Europeans viewed Christian Africa. The association between Prester John and universal Christian sovereignty encouraged the popularity of the trope of saintly Ethiopian, particularly through the black magus. By the sixteenth century, authors of ecclesiastical sacred history increasingly integrated Ethiopian history into their studies of the universal church, including increasing numbers of Ethiopian saints in the Catholic liturgy.

Elesban and Efigenia

The black saints who became the center of cultic devotion in the early modern Ibero-Atlantic fall into two categories: the ancient Ethiopian saints (Moses, Elesban, Efigenia) and the early modern slaves (Benedict and Antonio). Even though the figures in both categories became popular around the same time, each followed a distinct trajectory that originated from a specific set of religious and political circumstances. The Ethiopian saints were ancient, but they did not maintain meaningful cults in the Latin West. It was not until the mid-to-late sixteenth century that ecclesiastical historians rediscovered Ethiopian saints and began to write them back into the liturgy. Promoters of ancient Ethiopian saints

[38] Esche-Ramschorn, "The Multi-Ethnic Pilgrim Centre," 183–4. Ethiopians were not permitted their own rite in their church, though they performed a Roman rite in their own language. For more on Renaissance interest in Ethiopian languages, see Kelly, "The Curious Case of Ethiopic Chaldean."

[39] Lefèvre, "Documenti e notizie su Tasfa Seyon," 74–133.

[40] Salvadore, "The Jesuit Mission to Ethiopia," 149–54; and Salvadore, "Gaining the Heart of Prester John." Seyon appears in several works of Renaissance art, including one of Pope Paul III receiving the rule of the Jesuits from Ignatius (1539, Il Gesù, Rome) and in one of the chapels in Santa Maria degli Angeli, which he was instrumental in founding: Catalani, *Historia dell'erettione della Chiesa di S. Maria degli Angeli in Roma*, Biblioteca Apostolica Vaticana (hereafter BAV), Ms. 8735, 36r-40v. Seyon was an inexhaustible resource for Europeans eager to know more Ethiopia, including Guillaume Postel and Paolo Giovio: Lefèvre, "Documente e notizie su Tasfa Seyon," 103.

were largely interested in the saints as participants in a sweeping historical drama about the origin and development of the papacy's claims to universal sovereignty. As we saw with St. Maurice and the Holy Roman Emperors, when the pope and cardinals in Rome sought justifications for their tradition and dominion, they turned to Ethiopia.

Yet Ethiopia itself, whether religiously or politically, was not a pressing concern of the Roman curia in the second half of the sixteenth century. Instead the Church found itself in the throes of a series of upheavals originating from the rise of the Protestant reform movement. Warfare, political instability, and theological uncertainty followed as the Church fought to regain control and limit damage wrought by Protestant leaders. While battles were fought on the fields, others took shape on the page as authors articulated bitter theological and historical disagreements. Protestant reformers accused the Church of having betrayed its early roots and to have fallen into corruption and superstitious heresy, which included most the institutional structure of the Church itself. As the Catholic Church regrouped following the Council of Trent and its reaffirmation of Catholic theology, a new generation of erudite clergy began to take up the challenge of Protestant attacks with vigorous defenses of Catholic tradition and history. The most devastating Protestant attack against Catholicism appeared in the *Magdeburg Centuries*, an ecclesiastical history covering the first thirteen centuries of Christianity; it appeared between 1559 and 1574, authored by a collaborative group of Protestant scholars.[41] It was imperative that Catholic authors respond with their own sacred history.

The leaders of the new intellectual and theological movement in the Church during the latter half of the sixteenth century originated largely from the Congregation of the Oratory, founded in 1575 by St. Philip Neri (d. 1595) as a community for priests to live and pray more simply.[42] An Oratorian service consisted of an informal sermon, another sermon on the life of a saint, a brief discussion of Church history, and another life of a saint.[43] This liturgy reflected the Oratorian view that ecclesiastical history, theology, and the lives of the saints were essential to piety and spiritual practice. To know history was to understand theology; to hear the lives of the saints was to understand both history and the

---

[41] Camilli, "Six Dialogues, 1566"; Lyon, "The Plan for the Magdeburg Centuries"; and Olson, *Flacius and the Survival of Luther's Reform*. The polemical uses of sacred history led both Catholic and Protestant historians to appeal back to the history practiced by Eusebius and his vision of the triumphant Universal Church: Momigliano, *The Classical Foundations*, 147–50.

[42] Touber, *Law, Medicine, and Engineering*, 85–97. Ditchfield notes "the importance of the Oratorian contribution to the rebirth of ecclesiastical historiography, hagiography, liturgical history and Christian archaeology": *Liturgy, Sanctity, and History*, 45.

[43] Connors, *Borromini and the Roman Oratory*, 6.

spiritual truths of the Church. The cult of the saints, therefore, rested at the center of intellectual efforts to reform and defend the Church.

One of the Oratory's most famous members was a rising star at the papal curia, Cesare Baronio (d. 1607). Born in the kingdom of Naples, Baronio became a member of the Oratory under Neri. Through his patronage networks, Baronio rose in power and prominence; he was eventually elevated the rank of cardinal (in 1596) when he became librarian of the Vatican, and he was widely considered a possible candidate to become pope. In his early career, Baronio enjoyed the support of the well-connected Cardinal Guglielmo Sirleto (d. 1585) with whom he shared scholarly pursuits, including a passion for history.[44] While Sirleto had a reputation as a Greek scholar, his career at the curia involved more practical efforts, such as overseeing many of the large-scale liturgical reforms that evolved out of the Council of Trent, which sought to strengthen Rome's control over its churches through strong assertions of authority. Such reforms began with the revisions to the Breviary (1568), which sought to standardize how services were performed throughout the Church.[45] Sirleto's next project was to gather a group of scholars, including his protégé Baronio, to work together on a major phase of liturgical reform: the revisions of the Martyrology, the authoritative catalogue of the holy people venerated in the Catholic Church.[46]

The Martyrology required a series of revisions following a rather dramatic reconfiguration of the Julian calendar by Pope Gregory XIII. In order to recalibrate the calendar to calculate Easter more accurately, in 1582 ten days were eliminated from the month of October.[47] But more than an adjustment of dates, revisions to the Martyrology included a reexamining of the individuals included with an eye to removing any saint judged historically dubious. As a result, the project of sacred history was at the heart of liturgical reform, and Baronio became deeply engaged with both. While Baronio and Sirleto were working on the Martyrology, Baronio was already at work on his magnum opus, a comprehensive history of the Church called the *Annales Ecclesiastici*.[48] The main goal of the *Annales* was to respond to the *Magdeburg Centuries* with a vision of an unchanging church from Christ's birth to the present day, with

---

[44] Guazzelli claims that Sirleto was Baronio's "principal contact inside the Curia": "Baronio and the Roman Catholic Vision," 54. For more on Sirleto, see Denzler, *Kardinal Guglielmo Sirleto*.

[45] Ditchfield, "Tridentine Worship and the Cult of Saints," 201–5.

[46] Baronio, *Martyrologium Romanum ad novam kalendarii rationem* (1586).

[47] That means that individuals went to bed on 4 October and woke up on 15 October. The first revised Martyrology was issued in 1583, but more major revisions occurred in the 1586 and 1589 editions.

[48] Keenan, "The Political Possibilities of Ecclesiastical History"; Tutino, "For the Sake of the Truth of History"; Tutino, *Shadows of Doubt*; Ditchfield, "Baronio storico nel suo tempo."

a particular emphasis on the first half-century of ecclesiastical history.[49] The revised Martyrology and the *Annales* were mutually reinforcing, as the Martyrology sought to keep veneration in line with new standards of sacred history while defending the Church from Protestant attacks on the cult of the saints. The authors of the Martyrology did indeed remove historically dubious saints, yet they also inserted a few, including a cluster of Ethiopian saints given a newly prominent place in Catholic liturgy – Moses the Ethiopian, Elesban, and Efigenia – who joined "Ethiopian" biblical figures such as Queen Candace and Philip, the eunuch who had been baptized by the apostle St. Philip.

The inclusion of the Ethiopian saints marked the first concerted effort to celebrate the place of Ethiopia in the Church's history in the Latin West. While each of these saints represented different centuries and backgrounds, they were all ancient saints, emphasizing the role that Ethiopia played in the development of the early Church. Rather than broad interest in Ethiopia per se, the Church included Ethiopia in their understanding of the Biblical Near East. The presence of Abyssinian or Ethiopian individuals in the Bible underscored the ancient tradition of Christianity in East Africa along with cultural similarities between Ethiopia and the Near East. For example, the two Ethiopian languages, Ge'ez and Amharic, were Semitic in origin and therefore related to Near Eastern language families like Hebrew and Arabic. Baronio highlighted Ethiopia as proof of the uninterrupted traditions of the Catholic Church.[50]

St. Elesban had been virtually unknown in the Latin West, although he was venerated in the Ethiopian and Coptic churches. His brief entry in the revised Martyrology followed the basic historical facts about the king and his reign, describing him as a king-saint famous for fighting the enemies of Christ.[51] His original name had been Kaleb (d.c. 520), and the moniker "Elesban" – by which he was known in the Latin West – derived from the name he assumed on the throne. Kaleb headed a period of expansion of the kingdom of Aksum across the Red Sea into Yemen and was an important leader in the early medieval world

---

[49] Guazzelli, "Baronio and the Roman Catholic Vision," 54–5. On the printing of the *Annales* and the Oratory, see Finocchiaro, *Cesare Baronio*. For more on this process, see Ditchfield, "Tridentine Worship and the Cult of the Saints"; Ditchfield, *Liturgy, Sanctity, and History*, 17–67; and Olds, *Forging the Past*.

[50] Others have noted Baronio's inclusion of the Ethiopian saints in the revised Martyrology: Lahon, "Le berger, le cuisinier, la princesse," 216–19; and Machado de Oliveira, *Devoção negra*, 138–9. For this section, I have consulted a Spanish translation of the revised Martyrology: Vázquez, trans., *Martyrologio Romano reformado* (1586).

[51] "En los reynos de la Ethiopia S. Elesbaan rey, que hauiendole Dios dado victoria, contra los enemigos de la religion Christiana, embio su corona real a Hierusalem, en tiempo del Emperador Iustino, y hizose ermitaño como lo hauia votado y en sancta vida acabo": *Martyrologio Romano reformado*, 27 October, f. 176r-v.

who exchanged diplomatic correspondence with the Emperor Justinian, but he rose to international fame when he fought the Jewish king Dunaan of Himyar in Yemen. The Jewish king had massacred a number of Christians at Najran, an event that sent shockwaves throughout the Mediterranean.[52] Kaleb's victory against the king of Himyar was interpreted as inspired by God, transforming him into a defender of Christianity. In later life, Kaleb retired to adopt ascetic practice and solitude, for which he became renowned in Ethiopian traditions.[53] In spite of this complex history – discussed at length in the *Annales* – Elesban warranted only one sentence in the revised Martyrology.[54] For the entries on both Elesban and Moses the Ethiopian, Baronio relied on Greek sources: the Greek Menology, Nicephorous, Theophanos, Symeon Metaphrastes, and Sozomen, highlighting their deep roots in Greek ecclesiastical history.[55]

Unlike Elesban and Moses, St. Efigenia's cult did not originate in the Ethiopian or Coptic churches; it was a product of the Latin church, most likely a ninth-century Carolingian fiction.[56] Efigenia had been a princess who, according to legend, converted to Christianity upon hearing the apostle St. Matthew.[57] Efigenia's life closely follows accounts of the typology of an ancient female martyr: the Ethiopian princess, renowned for her beauty, became the target of marital interest by the king (her uncle), who asked Matthew to help him persuade her to leave the convent in order to marry him. Matthew declared that Efigenia and her sisters had become brides to the king of kings, a greater honor than any earthly marriage. His response enraged the king, who had the apostle killed.[58]

---

[52] Munro-Hay, *Ethiopia, the Unknown Land*, 237. An account of the massacre appears in the Qur'an 85:4–8, among other sources. For one account, see Shahîd, *The Martyrs of Najrân*.

[53] In the eastern Mediterranean, a brief account of Elesban in the Byzantine abbot Theophanes Confessor's early ninth-century history of the world, which was translated into Latin: Theophanes, *The Chronicle of Theophanes Confessor*. Kaleb was also mentioned in Procopius of Caesarea's sixth-century history.

[54] For Moses's entry, see *Martyrologio Romano reformado*, 28 August, f. 140r.

[55] The Menology included lists of venerated saints and biographical details. Sozomen (d.c. 450) was a Palestinian Christian author of sacred history: Sozomen, *The Ecclesiastical History of Sozomen*. Nicephorous was a fourteenth-century Greek ecclesiastical historian. It is unlikely that Baronio read the texts in their original Greek: Machielsen, "Heretical Saints and Textual Discernment," 103–42.

[56] The only sustained study of the origins of Efigenia's cult is Carucci, *La Vergine Ifigenia*. Carucci posits the pseudo-Abdias as the most likely point of origin for her tale. For more on the Carolingian circulation of martyrologies, see Lifshitz, *The Name of the Saint*.

[57] Sixteenth-century Spanish ecclesiastical historian Juan de Pineda provides a brief explanation for the seeming double conversion of Ethiopia from the Matthew and Candace stories: Pineda, *Los treynta libros de la monarchia ecclesiastica* (1588), vol. 3, 92.

[58] Here I have used an early sixteenth century Spanish translation of Voragine's work: Jacobo de Vorágine *Leyenda de los santos* (1520–21 ed.), 462–5. Ribadeneira follows *The Golden Legend* in his *Flos sanctorum*, mentioning Efigenia, but only in the context of St. Matthew.

Jacques de Voragine's wildly popular thirteenth-century compilation of saints' lives, *The Golden Legend*, mentioned Efigenia, where, as in many medieval sources, she was folded into Matthew's entry. She played her part, but remained undeveloped, a prop to move the action forward.[59] The same proved true centuries later in the revised Marytrology, where Efigenia was mentioned merely as a holy virgin baptized by St. Matthew, yet by the sixteenth century, Efigenia was slowly accorded an entry separated from Matthew's.[60] A more dramatic rupture occurred in the seventeenth century when her cult separated from Matthew and instead became associated most closely with that of Elesban, a fellow Ethiopian nobleperson who rejected pagan enemies.[61]

In contrast to Elesban and Efignia, Moses the Ethopian's cult left far less of a trace on the early modern world. One noteworthy exception is Lope de Vega's early seventeenth-century play entitled *El prodigio de Etiopia* (*The Ethiopian Prodigy*), for which Lope apparently used an account of Moses's life from a *Flos Sanctorum* by either Alonso de Villegas or Pedro de Ribadeneira, as a source.[62] Moses also appeared in Alonso de Sandoval's 1627 section dedicated to black saints, for which he used the Martyrology as his primary source. I discovered no images of Moses in Iberia, but several polychrome sculptures of Moses survive from the early modern Iberian Atlantic, including one in Recife, Brazil, which depicts Moses dressed in black and gold robes, holding a whip in his right hand that represents ascetic practice.[63] This beautiful image provides a tantalizing hint of a current of devotion that carried the Ethiopian desert hermit from Egypt to Iberia and across the Atlantic.

To the ecclesiastical historians like Baronio, the significance of Ethiopian Christianity continued the medieval tradition of symbolizing universal Christendom and papal supremacy.[64] Bernard Vincent has argued that this move to highlight Efigenia's cult was part of the late medieval emphasis on the place of black people in the divine plan, as we saw in the example of the

---

[59] Paul Kaplan found an illuminated Czech manuscript of St. Matthew's life that included Efigenia, dating to 1402: Kaplan, *Rise of the Black Magus*, 83. In Holy Land, one of the Nazarene Capitals depicting Matthew included Efigenia: Folda, *The Nazareth Capitals*, 39–42.

[60] *Martyrologio Romano reformado*, 21 September, 156r.

[61] For the earliest example of a separate entry for Efigenia of which I am aware is in a martyrology along with a woodcut; see Petrus de Natalibus, *Catalogus sanctorum* (1534).

[62] Fra Molinero says that Lope also learned about Moses from Ribadeneira's *Flos sanctorum* for his play, *El prodigio de Etiopia*: Fra Molinero, *La imagen de los negros en el teatro*, 55–6. Lope also wrote a play dedicated to Benedict of Palermo, *Comedia famosa de el Santo Negro Rosambuco de la Ciudad de Palermo*.

[63] Whistler, *Opulence and Devotion*.

[64] Lahon argues that part of Baronio's motivation was an attempt to rouse the interest of Roman elite in the Jesuit missions to Ethiopia: "Le berger, le cuisinier, la princesse," 219. See also Mazurek, "Réforme tridentine et culte des saints en Espagne."

black magus.[65] The path that had begun with the darkening of the magus Balthazar and the recognition of Ethiopian Christianity transformed the figure of the Ethiopian into a representative of Catholicism's global dominion. This process, in turn, charged black saints with new meaning by the dawn of the seventeenth century. While Ethiopian saints helped to bolster the Church's post-Tridentine polemical vision, it was not until the turn of the seventeenth century that Ethiopian saints' cults began to attain greater visibility, which did not occur through Baronio, the *Annales*, or the Martyrology. Instead, their cults expanded rapidly after their adoption in the Spanish and Lusophone worlds, which occurred for another reason altogether: the accelerating slave trade.[66] Moreover, it was not Ethiopian saints whose cults initiated the dramatic spread of black saints in Catholic devotion – instead, a humble sixteenth-century Franciscan from the eastern reaches of the Spanish monarchy led the way.

The Mediterranean and Global Expansion

The first black saints who circulated widely in the Iberian Atlantic were Benedict of Palermo and Antonio da Noto, both sixteenth-century Sicilian Franciscans. Part of the far-flung Spanish monarchy, Sicily is one of the largest and most strategically placed Mediterranean islands.[67] From the ancient to the early modern period, it saw waves of invasions from different groups who sought to build fortresses and establish trade entrepôts there.[68] It had been ruled by Aragonese monarchs beginning in the late thirteenth century. Sicily joined the Spanish monarchy with the Aragonese crown, and oversight of Sicily moved to a centralized Council of Italy in Madrid in 1556. Once the Council of Italy was established, members of the council appointed administrative governors – i.e.,

[65] Vincent, "Saint Benoît de Palerme." Jean Devisse and Michel Mollat discuss an image of a black waiting woman in an early fifteenth century Book of Hours in the context of Ethiopians who "symbolize the universality of Christianity": Devisse and Mollat, "The Appeal to the Ethiopian," 136.

[66] Jeremy Lawrence has claimed that a hospital was dedicated to Efigenia in Seville as early as 1475, citing Alonso Franco Silva: Lawrence, "Black Africans in Renaissance Spanish Literature," 70. (He cites Franco Silva, *La esclavitud en Sevilla*, 222–3.) Tracing Franco's footnotes, however, I have not been able to corroborate it. There was a confraternity for black slaves (or including black slaves) in Seville by 1475, but its connection to Elesban and Efigenia is unclear: Ortiz y Zúñiga, *Anales de la ciudad de Sevilla* (1677), 374.

[67] Elliott, "A Europe of Composite Monarchies." References to the composite nature of the Spanish monarchy underscore the distinct laws, languages, and customs of each individual member.

[68] For more on medieval Aragon, its trade networks and merchants, see Muñoz and Corberta, *Crecimiento económico en Aragón*; and Constable, *Housing the Stranger*.

viceroys – in Naples and in Palermo-Messina.[69] Following the withdrawal of major naval forces after the Battle of Lepanto (1571), Sicily lost some of its strategic significance for the monarchy, and receded to the margins of Habsburg attention.[70]

Like Iberia, Sicily maintained sizable Jewish and Muslim populations throughout the Middle Ages. It also shared the Mediterranean tradition of the near-constant presence of slavery throughout the ancient, medieval, and early modern periods. It followed the slave demographics of peninsular Italy in the sixteenth century by seeing a gradual rise of slaves from sub-Saharan Africa, along with its well-established population of Muslim slaves.[71] During this period, however, the population of enslaved people on the island ranged between 1 and 3 percent, a lower figure than Mediterranean countries with major port cities, such as Spain, Portugal, and the Republic of Genoa.[72] Sicily, like many of its European Mediterranean counterparts, was the heir of a medieval legal system in which slaves were recognized as having, in the words of Nelson Minnich, "an attenuated personhood," rather than being understood as chattel. This status entailed limited protections of the bodies of enslaved people, which could not be killed or mutilated; they could travel, own property, and even sue their masters.[73]

While we know that legal prescriptions did not always translate into practice, Sicilians themselves had little direct involvement in the Atlantic-based slave trade of the early modern period. This distinction meant that in the sixteenth century, black slaves had a different relationship to the local population in Sicily than they did in Iberia, including greater freedom of movement, access to religious orders, and receptivity of black sanctity from the white laity. Yet, as we shall see, the hagiographies of both Antonio and Benedict contained a wealth of information about obstacles and color-based prejudice faced by the two holy men in a way that made their lives translate easily into the Iberian context.

In the sixteenth century, Sicily became home to at least five holy people of color, four of whom were Franciscan lay brothers. Two of these, Antonio and Benedict, rose to international devotional cults. Such a striking statistic

[69] On baroque Naples, its culture and politics, see Marino, *Becoming Neapolitan*.
[70] Smith, *A History of Sicily*, 136–9.
[71] On black African slaves and freed people in other regions of early modern Italy, see Tognetti, "The Trade in Black African Slaves," 213–24; McKee, "Domestic Slavery in Renaissance Italy," 311–12; Lowe, "Black Africans in Renaissance Venice."
[72] This statistic originates from Minnich, "The Pastoral Care of Black Africans," 283. He also puts the slave population of Genoa at 4–5 percent. See also Marrone, *Schiavitù nella società siciliana*.
[73] Minnich, "The Pastoral Care of Black Africans," 284. For a wider view of the history of "slaving," see Miller, *The Problem of Slavery as History*.

leads invariably to the question "Why Sicily? Why this moment?"[74] In addition to the long history of invasion, religious and ethnic plurality, and relatively low rates of slavery, the strong Franciscan presence on the island played a major role, as almost all the holy people of color during this period were Franciscan. Franciscan missionary work in the Mediterranean had deep roots – in fact, one of the most important celebrated events in Franciscan history was the thirteenth-century martyrdom of friars in Morocco.[75] It is likely, then, that Franciscans enthusiastically supported friars of color who died in the odor of sanctity as a way of promoting their own missionary successes.

In addition to Antonio and Benedict, Sicilian Franciscans counted at least three more living saints of color: there were two more Antonios and a holy woman of color, Benedetta. Benedetta was, in fact, one of Benedict of Palermo's nieces; she joined the Third Franciscan order and died with a reputation for holiness. Sicilian historian Pietro Tognoletto included a long vita dedicated to Benedetta's life and miracles in his work on the spiritual glories of Sicily.[76] Of these holy people of color, two gained official cults, although Antonio never achieved canonization. This is a remarkable statistic, considering the relatively small black population on Sicily.[77] Moreover, the holy people mentioned in Franciscan sacred histories did not necessarily represent the total number of Afro-Sicilians who might have died in the odor of sanctity. Looking back at the sixteenth century two hundred years later, Spanish Franciscan author Manuel Barbado de la Torre y Angulo declared: "Glorious was this century [the sixteenth] for black men!" after extoling the holiness of Antonio da Noto and Benedict of Palermo.[78] While enslaved black men would disagree vehemently with this characterization, sixteenth-century Sicily did provide fertile ground for Afro-Sicilians to join orders and earn recognition for their holiness.

---

[74] Giovanna Fiume talks about black sanctity in sixteenth-century Sicily as representing the victory of Catholicism over paganism and Islam, represented by Antonio and Benedict: Fiume, *Il santo moro*, 176.

[75] The Franciscan church in Assisi that houses St. Francis's sepulcher contains a cycle of frescoes dedicated to various Franciscan martyrdoms, including the Moroccan.

[76] Tognoletto, *Paradiso serafico*, 419–25; 468–82. She is currently interred in the cloister of Benedict's Franciscan convent in Palermo.

[77] Franciscans had always played a crucial role in Mediterranean life as martyrs and missionaries in North Africa. For additional background on religious orders, convents, and Sicily, see Manduca, "Uno spazio in movimento," 281–311.

[78] Barbado de la Torre y Angulo, *Compendio historico*: "Glorioso fuè este siglo para los Negros, pues ademàs de los referidos, florecieron en virtudes, y milagros en Sicilia San Benito de Palermo y … V. Antonio Africano" (409).

Antonio da Noto

The earliest known holy person of color was Antonio, sometimes given the epithet Etiope (the Ethiopian), da Noto, or some version of Caltagirone.[79] The issue of what Antonio was called is a bit of a tangle, because there were other holy men of color in sixteenth-century Sicily called "Antonio Etiope": one who died in 1550, another who died in 1561, and a third who died in 1580.[80] The earliest of these died in Noto and the last died in the convent of Santa Maria di Gesù in Caltagirone. Confusion arising from the multiple Antonios by later hagiographers and Franciscan historians mostly likely explains why the Antonio who achieved a formal cult, the earliest of the three, was sometimes referred to as being from Caltagirone, even though he lived in the coastal towns of Avola and Noto.[81] As a result, subsequent sacred historians outside of Sicily used the epithets "of Caltagirone" and "of Noto" interchangeably.

In contrast to Benedict of Palermo, Antonio has not been well-studied by scholars, most likely because Benedict's fame eventually eclipsed his and Antonio was never canonized, although a process was started soon after his death.[82] Antonio was born in Libya, a Muslim of sub-Saharan African origin; captured by Sicilian corsairs, he was brought to the island a slave. He converted to Catholicism and took Antonio as his baptismal name in honor of St. Anthony of Padua.[83] The most detailed information about Antonio comes from Antonio Daza, whose history of the Franciscan order and its saints was printed in 1611. Daza described the holy man as "black as people from Guinea, Xalose and Manicongo but also a Moor, born and raised in the law of Muhammad." This description is particularly interesting because it highlights the connections forged in Daza's mind between the Mediterranean and Atlantic contexts for early modern Spain. He brought together Antonio's background – North African, Muslim, captured by corsairs on the sea – with West and Central African

---

[79] "Caltagirone" appears in sources variably as Catagirona, Calatagirona, Catagerò, or Caltagirone. Antonio occasionally appears as Antonino, a diminutive form of the name ("little Anthony").

[80] Bono, "Due santi negri," 76–9. Bono cites the manuscript *Diario della citta di Palermo* for the year of the first Antonio's death.

[81] The three Antonios are discussed in Wadding, *Annales minorum* (1732 ed.), 19: 299; 21:138–9; 22:287–8; Fiume, *Il santo moro*, 175–6; and Barbado de la Torre y Angulo, *Compendio historico*, 408–9.

[82] The Biblioteca Comunale di Palermo (hereafter BCP) conserves a manuscript of an early canonization process: *Processo di beatificazione di Antonio da Noto redatto nel 1549*, BCP 3Qqc36, n. 15. The same volume contains a manuscript vita as well: Fra Vincenzo da Noto, "Vita del beato Antonio."

[83] Vincenzo da Noto, "Vita del beato Antonio," BCP 3Qqc36.

ethnicities and skin color in ways that were uniquely Spanish, absent from Sicilian sources.

After Antonio's recapture by Christian pirates, Daza claimed: "This blessed black man was not converted. It was only that he became Christian, content to have a common and ordinary life."[84] Here, Daza employs the term "conversion" in its Catholic context – a conversion involved the abandonment of secular life to focus wholly on a spiritual calling. Instead of entering a Franciscan convent after baptism, Antonio passed the majority of his life enslaved, working diligently for his master although he was eventually freed after performing a great miracle for his owners' benefit. During his time as a slave, Antonio achieved a reputation for holiness, particularly for distributing food and other alms to the poor as well as performing miracles in the towns of Avola and Noto on the east coast of Sicily, south of Syracuse. After his manumission, he joined the Third Order of Franciscans (the lay brothers), where he remained until his death in 1550.[85] Upon his death, great crowds surged into the hospital to kiss his hands and take some of his habit as relics. Daza remarked that if the Franciscan brothers had not stepped forward to guard the body, he would have been left nude, so great was the crush of people and their desire for pieces of his clothing.[86]

The early testimonies collected for Antonio's canonization process included individuals who knew Antonio as well as those who were strangers to him but claimed Antonio performed miracles for them after death. The vice-vicar of Noto, Giovanni de Donnis, began to collect witness statements about Antonio's life and miracles only a week following the holy man's death. While subsequent Franciscan chroniclers often referred to Antonio as "the Ethiopian," the canonization documents employed the epithet "Antonio the black" [*Antonij negri*]. Witnesses recounted Antonio's great piety, hatred of blasphemy, his solemn burial in the church of Santa Maria di Gesù (Noto), curing small children of illness (and other postmortem healing miracles), and preaching patience in adversity. One witness who knew Antonio in Avola, Nicolaus de Cazono, recounted the saint's ascetic practices, including flagellation, remarking that "he made penances and disciplined himself with ropes" in secret throughout

---

84 Daza, *Quarta parte de la chronica general*, 156. A brief reference to Antonio can also be found in Ferrari, *Catalogus generalis sanctorum*, 25–7.

85 Overviews of Anthony's life in scholarship can be found: Guastella, *Fratello negro*; Fiume, "Antonio Etiope e Benedetto il Moro"; Lahon, "Le berger, le cuisinier, la princesse"; Vincent, "Saint Benoît de Palerme," 222–3.

86 Daza, *Quarta parte de la chronica general*, 166: "Acuido toda la ciudad al hospital, por llegar a besarle las manos, y tomar algo de su habito, y con tan grande fuerça, que si no se guardara el cuerpo con otra mayor, en breue le dexaran desnudo." This type of scene was common upon the death of holy people who attracted the reputation for great holiness. For a lively description of the scene at a saint's sepulcher, see Eire, *From Madrid to Purgatory*, 440–2.

his life.[87] In the words of one contemporary Franciscan friar: "He was a man of good life, of the reputation [*fama*] for humility and charity, in which he lived a penitential life."[88] In these brief testimonies, Antonio emerged as a typical early modern holy person – secretly ascetic, devout, miraculous.

Antonio was set apart, however, by his deep sympathy with the impoverished and hungry, as well as his low social status, since most saints came from elite backgrounds. Antonio was poor and loved the poor among whom he lived, his compassion arising out of his own experience of enslavement and poverty. And it was precisely this element of his life that captured the interest of hagiographers and historians. Antonio's blackness is at once everywhere and nowhere in the beatification process, where he is repeatedly referred as "Antonio the Black." On the other hand, Antonio is never quoted referring to himself as "black" in the hagiography, although he called himself a "slave," particularly when deflecting praise and gratitude for the miracles he performed.[89]

In 1599, the Sicilian Inquisition granted permission for Antonio's image to be given a holy aura or halo, key visual signs of sanctity. That same year, his sepulcher was opened; his body was found to be incorrupt and giving off a strong, celestial odor.[90] The witness testimonies and an early hagiography by Vincenzo da Noto reached the attention of Franciscan Antonino da Randazzo, a local hagiographer of Sicilian saints who wrote prolifically in promotion of his compatriots. Randazzo played a key role in advancing the cult of Benedict of Palermo, as we will see, and he wrote a manuscript vita of Antonio da Noto sometime in the early seventeenth century. Randazzo was, by 1620, appointed to the role of procurator of canonization processes for the Franciscan Order, and thus a powerful figure in the world of Franciscan saint-making. His decision to distinguish Antonio with an entire vita speaks of Antonio's local importance and high profile among the Sicilian Franciscans.[91] Antonio also appeared in the *Catalogue of Saints Who Do Not Appear in the Roman Martyrology*, printed in 1625 Venice, with a brief entry.[92] Yet his cult lost its momentum, surviving to this day largely through sacred art, rather than

---

[87] *Processo di beatificazione di Antonio da Noto*, BCP 3Qqc36, n. 15, 237v-240v.

[88] Randazzo, "Vita del servo di Dio frate Antonino di Etiopia terziario, sepolto a Santa Maria di Gesù di Caltagirone de' Minori Osservanti," Biblioteca Regionale Siciliana (hereafter BRS), MS Misc. IIE13, 109r-110r. This vita follows the witness testimony in the processus closely: *Processo de beatificazione di Antonio da Noto*, 259v.

[89] *Processo di beatificazione di Antonio da Noto*, 253v (in the testimony of Orlando Rua).

[90] Fiume, *Il santo moro*, 171.   [91] Randazzo, "Vita del servo di Dio frate Antonino di Etiopia."

[92] *Catalogus generalis*, 25–6:13 Jan. Tuneti in Africa Antonius Naetinus a Mauris pro Christi fide combustus.

hagiography or sacred histories.[93] He became eclipsed by other, more successful saints, such as Benedict of Palermo.

Benedict of Palermo

Benedict, like Antonio, is known by a number of names; in early modern Sicilian sources, he was called Benedetto da San Fratello, sometimes translated into its Latin form, Benedictus de San Philadelphio.[94] It was the Spanish and Portuguese who christened him Benedict of Palermo, which was how his name appeared in most Spanish sources of the early modern period.[95] Unlike Antonio, Benedict was born in Sicily; his parents, Christoforo and Diana, were sub-Saharan African. His mother was free; his father enslaved, although they were both, hagiographers assured readers, good and virtuous Christians.[96] Diana had more children, including a girl named Fradella who married a black slave, Antonio Nastasi: Fradella's daughter, Benedetta, was the niece who died in the odor of sanctity.

Like most saints, Benedict grew up devout, free from the desires of the world; he eventually became a hermit in the hills outside San Fratello when he ran into a Franciscan brother who, inspired by the Holy Spirit, recognized Benedict's sanctity and invited him to live together in a hermitage. When reorganization of the Franciscan order compelled local hermits to integrate into a formal institutional structure, Benedict entered the convent on the outskirts of Palermo as a lay brother. During his time at the convent, he experienced great spiritual gifts, including visions, ecstasy, and shining with divine light while at prayer. He was further infused with divine wisdom, a spiritual gift that denoted a "supernatural intelligence" and deep understanding of scripture of divine origin occasionally

[93] One of the only extant stand-alone print hagiographies for Antonio is Bayão, *Historia das prodigiosas vidas dos gloriosos sanctos*. The full title translates: "History of the prodigious lives of the two glorious saints, Antonio and Benedict, greatest honor and light to black people."

[94] The life, canonization processes, and cult of Benedict of Palermo has received attention from scholars, most important the indefatigable research of Giovanna Fiume. Printed primary sources of the early phases of his *causa* can be found in Fiume and Modica, *San Benedetto il Moro: Santità*; and Giordano, *San Benedetto il Moro: Il Memoriale*.

[95] Eighteenth-century Italians professed confusion over the fact that Iberians called him "of Palermo" instead of "of San Fratello"; for one example, see: Archivio Segreto Vaticano (hereafter ASV) Congr. Riti, vol. 2179, 102r. I have found few references to Benedict as a "moor" in Iberian sources.

[96] Several hagiographers, at least, argued that his mother and he had been born free. Giovanna Fiume argues that the primary evidence demonstrates that Benedict had been born enslaved: Fiume, *Schiavitù mediterranee*, section 2.4.

granted to uneducated holy people.[97] His death produced the typical miracles associated with saintly passing – visions of saints, peaceful passing, celestial odors.[98]

Supporters moved quickly after Benedict's death. Led by a *palermitano* merchant, Gioan Domenico Rubbiano (d. 1613), information was gathered about Benedict's life and miracles and given to the archbishop in the hopes of beginning a formal process that would lead to his beatification and canonization.[99] The first stage of the report was complete by 1591, followed by a second solely on postmortem miracles. It was urgent, particularly in post-Tridentine canonization processes, to begin collecting eye witness testimonies as quickly as possible following the holy person's death in order to capture details that spoke to heroic virtue and penitential practices while memories were fresh. Rubbiano's treatises were sent on to Rome, where Cardinal Mattei began a correspondence with the guardian of the convent of Santa Maria di Gesù.[100] Acutely aware of the importance of the patronage of the Spanish crown, efforts were made in the early seventeenth century to reach out to Madrid as well as Rome.

Rubbiano's collected testimony included fifty-six witnesses. The miracles recounted were fairly typical accounts of cures, ranging from childbirth recovery to paralysis to restoration of speech.[101] Most cures occurred after Benedict's death, attributed to the power of relics, most of which were the less expensive ones known as contact relics – items or objects that contained transferred holiness after having touched the body. In one case, the contact relic was water in which a relic had been dipped. Petruccia, a thirty-six-year-old wife of a citizen of Palermo, owned a relic of Benedict – in this case, it was a tiny piece ("una minima particella") of the saint's tunic, the most common kind of relic specified by witnesses.[102] The local nobility also desired the relics of the holy man. The Baroness of San Fratello, for example, requested a relic of Benedict because she wished to found a convent of Reformed Franciscans in her territory to be

---

[97] Antonio da Noto was also described this way by Daza: "And as his zeal was so great and his charity so brilliant, not only did he not lose respect (even though he was black and a slave) but everyone treated him as though he was a great preacher and minister of the Lord." *Quarta parte de la chronica general*, 157.

[98] These events from Benedict's life are repeated in every version, though here I have followed Tognoletto, *Paradiso Serafico*, 283. A contemporary reference to Benedict's death can be found: Marzo, *Diario*, 116: "Forse fra Benedetto schiavo negro, dell'ordine Maria di Gesu; e fece molti miracoli, e poi fu diachiarta per beato."

[99] For more on the organization of the Sicilian church, see Fabrizio d'Avenia, *La Chiesa del re: monarchia e papato nella Sicilia spagnola (secc. XVI-XVII)* (Rome: Carocci, 2015).

[100] In the 1590s, Sicilian relics were systematically recorded, prompted through the viceroy, the Count of Olivares: Fiume and Modica, *San Benedetto il Moro: Santità*, 7–10.

[101] Ibid., 12.   [102] Giordano, *San Benedetto il Moro*, 74.

overseen by Randazzo.[103] The rapidly developing market of Benedict's relics demonstrates the quick spread of his reputation. While scholars often focus on the activities of ecclesiastical officials in the origins of cultic devotion, nearly all accounts of living saints tell us of the fierce popular devotion that engulfed towns and regions following a saint's death.

Rubbiano was instrumental in bringing Benedict to the attention of Philip III, king of Spain and Portugal (r. 1598–1621), sending the king a copy of his memorial on Benedict. In June 1608, Philip III offered alms of 1,500 escudos to move Benedict's body to a silver casket and received a relic of the holy man, provided by Rubbiano. Randazzo claimed that other relics were sent to the Franciscans in the Indies and other convents, and that images and relics of Benedict had performed miracles throughout the world.[104] Unfortunately, there is scanty evidence about the location(s) – past or present – of Benedictine relics outside of Palermo. An eighteenth-century reliquary bust located in the Lisbon convent church of Santa Madre de Deus is a unique survival in Iberia, although the whereabouts of the relic itself are currently unknown.

At the same time that Philip III wrote to the archbishop of Palermo to send the money for the sepulcher, he included reports of the great miracles the saint had already performed, facilitating the conversion of sub-Saharan Africans in the Indies.[105] Philip IV (r. 1621–1665) wrote a letter to his ambassador in Rome asking him to push Benedict's beatification case, citing his father's devotion to the holy man and the many miracles the saint had performed.[106] Beatification efforts continued throughout the first half of the seventeenth century, with processes in Palermo (1625–1626) and San Fratello (1626), which included testimony taken in the years 1620 to 1622.[107] Yet canonization efforts stalled after 1626, despite the warm support of the Spanish monarch and the persistence of the Franciscans. It is unclear why this occurred, although this period marked a relative dearth of canonizations and beatifications overall.[108] Benedict's cause was not picked up

---

[103] Daza, for example, noted that many learned people admired Benedict, including the viceroys of Sicily, the Condes of Alvade Liste, whom he described as "extremely devoted" to Benedict, *Quarta parte de la chronica general*, 68. Benedict's aristocratic support might help explain how Benedict's cult came to outstrip Antonio's, even though Antonio's was well-established by the time Benedict died in 1589.

[104] Fiume and Modica, *San Benedetto il Moro: Santità*, 175–81.

[105] Fiume and Modica include an excerpt of Philip's letter: *San Benedetto il Moro: Santità*, 175. The original can be found: Archivo General de Simancas (hereafter AGS), Stato, Regno Sicilia, box 1162, doc. 195.

[106] Fiume and Modica, *San Benedetto il Moro: Santità*, 190.

[107] Giordano, *San Benedetto il Moro*, provides the entire collection of testimonies for 1625–1626.

[108] Hsia, *The World of Catholic Renewal*. Hsia's table 8.1 shows that between 1630 and 1650 there were no canonizations, and only one between 1651 and 1660, which was not an unusual gap for the early modern period (p. 141).

again until the early eighteenth century with extensive witness testimony taken in Rome, a topic to which I will return later. Giovanna Fiume has suggested that the rise of the cult of St. Rosalia in the later 1620s eclipsed devotion for Benedict in Palermo; the discovery of Rosalia's relics outside of Palermo led to her quick promotion as patron saint of the city.[109] Although Benedict remained an important civic patron saint of Palermo, the excitement over his death and holiness in his own *patria* appears to have diminished as the seventeenth century wore on.

Growing Fame

Benedict's and Antonio's fame increased with the publication of Antonio Daza's work *Fourth Chronicle of the Order of Friars Minor*; Daza's inclusion of the Sicilian friars probably resulted from a 1606 Franciscan chapter meeting held in Toledo, where he undoubtedly gathered material.[110] Five years after the chapter meeting, his *Fourth Chronicle* appeared, providing the first account of the lives of Benedict and Antonio in Spanish, although his vita of Antonio da Noto was significantly longer than Benedict's. Rubbiano's memorial of Antonio and Randazzo's hagiography of Benedict (1623) remained in manuscript, and the first printed Italian hagiography would not be written for another several decades.[111] The next major mention of the two saints in Spanish came from Alonso de Sandoval, in 1627, eleven years following the publication of Daza's chronicle; Sandoval – to be discussed – cited Daza as his source for information on the two Sicilian Franciscans.[112] These works were seminal because they shaped the saints' cults for Spanish-speaking audiences.

While the exact date is unclear, around the time that Philip III sent his 1608 letter to Palermo, the Golden Age playwright Lope de Vega produced a work entitled *El Santo Negro Rosambuco, de la ciudad de Palermo*. Since plays about saints inhabited a gray zone between liturgy and entertainment, they tended to follow accounts of a saint's life enshrined in hagiography or the martyrology with some embellishment.[113] Yet there is little recognizable from the life of Benedict of Palermo in the play written by Lope; it does, on the other hand, sketch some of

---

[109] Fiume, *Il santo moro*, 154–7. The volume consists of an excellent and detailed overview of the entire canonization process.
[110] Fiume, "Antonio Etiope e Benedetto il Moro," 98.
[111] Randazzo, "Vita et miracoli del beato Benedetto di San Fradello," BCP, 3Qq E42, 125–93.
[112] Sandoval, *Naturaleza, policia, sagrada i profana*, 128v.
[113] Saints' plays were closely observed by the Church, and Lope himself, a tertiary member of the Franciscan order, would have known very well that ecclesiastical custom required the *comedia* to conform generally to Benedict's vita, lest it be censored by the Inquisition.

the key elements of Antonio's life. The eponymous saint begins the play as Muslim slave captured by Christians; after his captivity, he converts to Christianity, takes the name Benedict, and becomes a Franciscan. The next act follows Benedict's tribulations in his convent, where a jealous lay brother torments him and tries to kill him.[114] The Mediterranean landscape of Lope's play was most likely meant to entertain a Spanish audience so accustomed to stories of captivity, Muslim pirates, and conversion, though it had little to do with Benedict himself and reflected Antonio's life in only minor ways.[115]

Tracing the exact movement of Benedict's cult is challenging, but much can be gleaned from extant sources. The cult moved quickly from the early years of the seventeenth century as Rubbiano's activism on behalf of his saint began; Philip III received the relic in 1608; Daza's chronicle was printed in 1611; and Lope's play was performed in Madrid around the same time. Franciscan authors noted that in 1618, Philip III witnessed a procession in Lisbon that included some of the city's black confraternities, including one dedicated to Benedict of Palermo that had been established in 1609 at the Franciscan convent of Santa Ana.[116] As Bernard Vincent points out, the Spanish link was "essential" for the global circulation of Bernard's cult, as its broad diffusion required powerful support if it stood any chance at success. Vincent argues that Philip's support of Benedict's cult was part of his larger program of promoting holy people from different parts of his monarchy. Habsburg monarchs had begun an ambitious project of elevating holy people from all regions of its composite monarchy, including Rose of Lima, Isabel of Portugal, and John of God.[117] Philip had two levels of interest in Benedict's cult – first it highlighted the sanctity of Sicily, one of its dominions; and second, it offered help in the long effort of evangelizing to existing and new populations of enslaved Africans throughout his empire.

In spite of Lope's emphasis on the Mediterranean aspect of Antonio/Benedict's lives, from the very beginning of its introduction into the Spanish monarchy, the

---

[114] Lope de Vega, "El santo negro Rosambuco." For more on Lope, *comedias de santos*, and his sources, see Morrison, *Lope de Vega and the comedia de santos*, 166–74. Other plays about Benedict were written during this period, including Luis Vélez de Guevara, "El santo negro Rosambuco," Biblioteca Nacional de España (hereafter BNE), MS 17317.

[115] Another saints' play based on Antonio's life can be found: Rodrigo Pacheco, "El negro del serafín," in *Comedias famosas*, BNE, MS 14824. See also Beusterien, *An Eye on Race*; Panford, "La figura del negro." Eighteenth-century Castilian hagiographers of Benedict complained that Lope's *comedia* lacked historicity and confused the faithful about Benedict's life: Mataplanes, *Vida de fray Benito de S. Fradelo*, 5.

[116] For a discussion of the festival in Lisbon, see Tognoletto, *Paradiso serafico*, 322–3; Apolinário da Conceição, *Flor perigrina por preta* (1744), 253, 263; and Mataplanes, *Vida de fray Benito de S. Fradelo*, 185.

[117] Vincent, "Saint Benoît de Palermo et l'Espagne," 201–4; Conover, "Catholic Saints in Spain's Atlantic Empire"; and Rowe, *Saint and Nation*, 61–9.

cult of black saints was primarily grounded in a concern over the spiritual condition of enslaved sub-Saharan Africans, as we see in Philip III's foundational letter. The focus on conversion of black slaves marks a stark difference between devotion to Benedict in the Iberian world and in Sicily, where the earliest beatification testimony said almost nothing about devotion to the saint among slaves, and nearly all the accounts of miracles come from white devotees.[118] The path that Benedict's cult followed was not a linear one from Sicily to Spain and then the Americas. Instead, what we see is a simultaneous transmission of relics and images of Benedict to the peninsula and the Americas through the Franciscan network, as we saw when Randazzo sent a relic "to the Indies" at the same time he sent one to Madrid.[119] In both Iberia and the Americas, the promotion of Benedict's cult was tied to evangelization of black slaves, whose numbers were proliferating rapidly throughout the late sixteenth and early seventeenth centuries.[120]

The crucial connection between Ethiopian saints – both royal and enslaved – and the accelerating transatlantic slave trade in Iberia and Iberian America is exemplified in Alonso de Sandoval's *Naturaleza, policia sagrada i profana de todos los Etiopes*, which was published in Seville in 1627.[121] In Sandoval's text, we see the fundamental elements of devotion to black saints in the seventeenth and eighteenth centuries. Sandoval was born in Seville in 1576, but traveled as a child with his parents to Peru, where he spent the rest of his childhood. After he joined the Jesuits, he moved to Cartagena de Indias, the largest slave port in the Spanish Americas. There Sandoval dedicated his life to ministering to newly arrived enslaved people until his death in 1652. His book was part ethnographic study of African groups, including those from West, Central, and East Africa, and part polemic proclaiming the capabilities of sub-Saharan Africans to practice Christianity and to live moral lives.[122] The work consisted of four sections, each carefully arranged to emphasize its polemical purpose. The first subject tackled was the ethnography in order to establish the moral potential of Africans, whom

---

[118] Giordano provides a complete list of those who gave testimony in the earliest causa, 1594–1595: *San Benedetto il Moro: Il Memoriale*, 149–54.

[119] Tognoletto explained that Randazzo sent a reliquary containing a relic of the saint to the Franciscan commissioner of the Indies: *Paradiso serafico*, 320.

[120] The cults of Benedict and Antonio initially followed Franciscan networks in the Americas via Daza's work. See Fiume: "St. Benedict the Moor," 30–4.

[121] Sandoval, *Naturaleza, policia sagrada i profana*. It was republished under its more well-known title, *Tomo primero de instauranda Aethiopum salute: Historia de Aethiopia, naturaleza, policia sagrada y profana, costumbres, ritos y Cathecismo Evangelico, de todos los Aethiopes con que se restaura la salud de sus almas* in 1647.

[122] For an overview of Sandoval's ideas and beliefs, see Olsen, *Slavery and Salvation*; Morgan, "Jesuit Confessors, African Slaves"; Morgan, "Alonso de Sandoval's *De Instauranda Aethiopum Salute*"; and Stoichita, "The Image of the Black in Spanish Art," 195–8.

he put under a general umbrella of "Ethiopia," which he then divided into western and eastern parts. In spite of the fact that no enslaved people during this period originated from the kingdom of Ethiopia proper, Sandoval included ethnographic sections on Christian East Africa (gleaned from a Jesuit missionary returning from Ethiopia to Portugal via Cartagena), which helped to place West and Central Africa in a larger zone that included ancient Christian Africa. The subsequent sections of the book dealt with the proper treatment of slaves and their evangelization. Between these two major sections, Sandoval placed a section that acted as a bridge, one that described black saints.

Sandoval compiled an impressive number of black saints to include, among them Sephora (the Ethiopian second wife of the Old Testament Moses), the Queen of Sheba, Balthazar the magus, Candace, Efigenia, Elesban, Moses the Ethiopian, Serapion, and the two sixteenth-century Franciscans, Antonio and Benedict.[123] Drawing heavily on the Martyrology, Sandoval organized his list chronologically, beginning with the Old Testament and moving forward to the sixteenth century. In this way, he created a timeline of Ethiopian sanctity spanning the biblical centuries through the Middle Ages to the present day, which established the dignity and moral ability of "Ethiopians," from the Old Testament to the present century. Having proven that black Christians had the potential to become saints, Sandoval could then move on to attack those who argued that enslaved Africans lacked the reason required to partake in the Christian community. Sandoval's rhetoric demonstrates that the lives of black saints did not function as hagiographical oddities; rather, they served deeper political and spiritual purposes.

The arc of black sanctity stretched from Ethiopia representing universal sovereignty in the Middle Ages, to the Church's efforts to elevate the profile of ancient Ethiopia as part of its quest to bolster its own sacred history, and, finally, to the entanglement of black saints with the spiritual lives of enslaved and free Afro-Iberians. Within forty years of Benedict's death, then, their cults followed a rapid and multi-directional flow out of Sicily to Spain, Portugal, and the Americas, thanks to Sicilian patrons and the Franciscans, who worked in parallel efforts to raise the profile of their local holy men to global devotional phenomena. The interconnectedness of these geographic zones – Western Mediterranean, Iberian

---

[123] Sandoval, *Naturaleza, policia sagrada i profana*, 120v-30v. Not all the Ethiopian saints included by Sandoval and in the Martyrology generated devotional interest, including Abdemelech, Serapion the Ethiopian, and David the anchorite. Sephora, the Queen of Sheba, and Queen Candace and the eunuch, on the other hand, had more traction. Depictions of the eunuch's baptism by the apostle St. Philip proliferated in northern European art, especially Netherlandish. Massing connects such popularity to the Protestant emphasis on adult baptism: Massing, *The Image of the Black in Western Art*, v. 3: pt.2, 284–94.

Peninsula, the Americas – created a series of networks over which their cults could travel rapidly. Benedict's cult was the most important of the black saints, multiplying the most quickly and leaving behind the most visible reminders, but the waves of devotion to Benedict powered by missionary work with enslaved Africans swept the cults of Antonio, Efigenia, and Elesban along with him, across the seas to three continents.

2 SALVATION, BLACK CONFRATERNITIES, AND SAINTS IN GLOBAL CATHOLICISM

The spread of the cults of black saints followed imperial lines: From Sicily to Iberia and the Americas, Iberian clergy took the lead. In spite of local devotion to Benedict in Sicily, the cults of black saints arose from the needs of the empire. From the earliest Iberian expansion, friars followed merchants and conquistadores, entangling missionary work and empire-building. By the end of the sixteenth to the middle of the seventeenth century, the slave trade began to accelerate rapidly in the Spanish Atlantic, adding new pressure on the Iberian clergy to baptize and catechize enslaved Africans. While the clergy worked to baptize newly enslaved Africans as quickly as possible, providing substantial understanding of the Church's teachings to the newly baptized was a different problem altogether, starting with the basic issue of language barriers. For centuries, Iberian clergy debated a series of questions, including: Who should be in charge of the spiritual education of baptized slaves? Could non-Europeans be ordained as priests? By what methods should conversions be achieved? In theory, all baptized souls were equal, but in reality, people continued to be organized along entrenched social hierarchies, which were inflected with severe racial discrimination.[1]

Conversion itself proved haphazard and uneven, plagued by many problems, including the hostility of slave owners to catechesis, overworked clergy, and skepticism about the spiritual capabilities of new converts. The entanglement of Iberian clergy with colonization meant that Iberian clergy often benefited materially from oppressive structures like slavery. The papacy in Rome, on the other hand, played a limited role in monitoring overseas missionaries' efforts, and there were only a relatively small number of missionaries from non-Iberian regions in the Iberian Atlantic. In part to push back against the

---

[1] Such issues had been debated more broadly throughout the Spanish colonies when missionaries were confronted with indigenous groups and their various forms of resistance to Christianity: Tavárez, *The Invisible War*; Ramos, *Death and Conversion*; and Estenssoro, *Del paganismo a la santidad*.

near-monopoly Iberian clergy held on missionary zones, the papacy developed a centralized institution in 1622, the Congregation of the Propaganda Fide (the Propagation of the Faith), to organize overseas missionary work, though the Congregation exerted its greatest influence in the areas outside Iberian-held territories.[2]

The missionary and colonial imperatives merged in the need to create Christian subjects out of newly conquered and enslaved people. Baptism was the first stage, but Catholic subjecthood required continuous participation in a specific set of behaviors and events. In an attempt to integrate baptized Africans into orthodox conduct and practice, Iberian clergy encouraged Africans to join devotional societies called confraternities. Confraternities dedicated exclusively for the membership of people of color emerged as early as the fifteenth century when the first enslaved Africans were brought to Portugal. The tradition of black confraternities had been firmly in place for over a century before the entrance of Benedict's cult to the Iberian Atlantic, yet black saints and black confraternities quickly became intertwined. In fact, black confraternities became the primary vehicle through which devotion to black saints spread. Black saints, then, emerged out of the brutality of early modern slavery and the attendant collision of Africans and Christianity.

Slavery and Baptism in Early Modern Iberia

The slave trade that flourished in the medieval Mediterranean underwent a dramatic change in the mid-fifteenth century as Portuguese merchants moved down the western coast of Africa and began setting up trade citadels. The most important base of Portuguese Atlantic operations became the archipelago of Cabo Verde, where the Portuguese established settlements off the coast of West Africa in 1462. From here, Portuguese ships could move easily along the coast of West and Central Africa to trade with local leaders; trafficking in kidnapped Africans quickly became one of their most lucrative activities. From the late fifteenth century on, the Western Mediterranean saw rapidly expanding numbers of West and Central Africans in European slave markets via Lisbon.[3] Spain

---

[2] Santos Hernández, "Orígenes históricos," 543.

[3] Franco Silva, *La esclavitud en Sevilla*; Franco Silva, *La esclavitud en Andalucía*; Phillips, *Slavery*; and Stella, *Histoires d'esclaves*. Franco remarks that by the sixteenth century black slaves "fueron siempre los esclavos más numerosos, los más abundantes en el mercado, y los más demandados por los compradores" (150). For the development of the early Portuguese slave trade, see Green, "Building Slavery in the Atlantic World."

would emerge as one of the largest markets for enslaved people brought by the Portuguese even before the two crowns were joined in 1580.

By the mid-sixteenth century, as much as 10 percent of Lisbon's population was black African (mostly enslaved).[4] On the other side of the peninsula, Debra Blumenthal reports that by the end of the fifteenth century, in Valencia, as much as 40 percent of the slave population had been brought from West Africa.[5] The numbers grew steadily in Seville as well, as slaves disembarked both from the vessels sailing up Guadalquivir and overland through Extremadura. Southern Spain and the coastal cities of the Western Mediterranean saw the greatest concentration of West and Central African slaves overall.[6] Less scholarly attention has traditionally been paid to slavery in Spanish regions outside Andalusia, although Rocio Periáñez Gómez has called our attention to the need to study the presence of enslaved people in Extremadura, which saw a large influx of slaves via an overland trade route from Portugal.[7] The slave trade, then, was not merely maritime. In Portugal, relatively small with an extensive Atlantic coastline, slavery reached north along the coast to the border with Galicia as well as inland to the eastern regions.[8]

The exact numbers of enslaved people in early modern Iberia are subject to debate, but the overall patterns are clear: a steady rise in the number of slaves throughout the sixteenth century, peaking by the middle of the seventeenth century in Spain.[9] Following the separation of the crowns of Castile and Portugal in 1640, the importation of slaves throughout the Spanish empire slowed as their access to Portuguese trade was restricted. In Portugal, a temporary lull in the seventeenth century was followed by a dramatic acceleration of the

---

[4] For an exploration of black slaves and free people in early modern Portugal, see Lowe, "The Global Population"; and Sweet, "The Hidden Histories," 233–47.

[5] Blumenthal, *Enemies and Familiars*, 4–5; Cortés Alonso, *La esclavitud en Valencia*.

[6] Domínguez Ortiz, "La esclavitud en Castilla," 5–15. Allyson M. Poska discusses the transition from peasant to slaveowner that Gallegos underwent as they migrated from Galicia to the Río de la Plata: *Gendered Crossings*, 173–4.

[7] Periáñez Gómez, *Negros, mulatos, y blancos*; and Fonseca, *Os escravos em Évora*. For overviews on slavery and the black African presence in Portugal, see Henriques, *A herança Africana*; Saunders, *Social History*; and Fonseca, *Escravos no sul de Portugal*.

[8] Saunders, *Social History*, 49–61.

[9] Cortés López has calculated that in 1565, slaves accounted for 3 percent of the population in Seville, Cadiz, Huelva, Granada, Almería, and Malaga, with slightly lower percentages in other parts of Andalusia, like Cordoba and Jaén, and 2.5 percent for Valencia, with a dramatically lower number when factoring in the entire peninsula, at 0.2 percent: *La esclavitud negra peninsular*, 202–4. Keep in mind these numbers only count enslaved people, and not free people of color. For slavery in Malaga, see Gómez García and Martín Vergara, *La esclavitud en Málaga*; and González Arévalo, *La esclavitud en Málaga*.

slave trade in eighteenth and nineteenth centuries, driven largely by the economic demands of Brazil, but affecting Portugal as well.[10] We know considerably less, however, about peninsular slavery in the eighteenth century than in the sixteenth and seventeenth centuries, making it difficult to trace the long-term history of African-descended people in Iberia.[11]

During the first century of the sub-Saharan African slave trade, concern about the conversion and spiritual well-being of black slaves took a back seat to escalating persecution of Muslims and Jews. Following the 1492 expulsion of Jews from Spain, the Inquisition sought to squash any remaining practice of Judaism through a ferocious campaign, with the Portuguese Inquisition following suit not long after.[12] At the same time, the Spanish Inquisition sought to eradicate surviving Islamic practices following the forced conversion of all Muslims in the early sixteenth century. Baptized Christians of Islamic descent, called *moriscos*, were eventually expelled from the Spanish monarchy (1609–1614) for their purported inability to assimilate.

The issue of conversion and catechesis of newly arrived black slaves, then, was only part of a larger polemic about the (in)ability of certain groups to embrace Christianity. At the same time, the clergy treated black slaves as a category distinct in many ways from other New Christians. A series of questions emerged among the clergy when thinking about newly converted Africans: What part did early modern Iberians see African-descended people playing in Iberian society? Would conversion to Christianity combined with freedom mean that black members of society would be entitled to the same rights and privileges as whites? Were blacks subject to the same *limpieza de sangre* laws as descendants of Jews and Muslims?[13] These were complicated questions whose answers were in flux throughout the sixteenth and early seventeenth centuries.

In the earliest periods of West African slavery in Europe, there is some evidence that Iberians evinced an optimistic view of conversion and assimilation by enslaved people, particularly among the clergy. Contrasted with Muslim slaves who were viewed as intractable enemies, sub-Saharan Africans were sometimes

---

[10] Slavery in Portugal was not abolished until 1761. The excellent source www.slavevoyages.org illustrates the patterns of millions of enslaved Africans via the early modern Atlantic slave trade. See also Klein and Vidal Luna, *Slavery in Brazil*.

[11] Herzog, "How Did Early-Modern Slaves in Spain Disappear?" http://arcade.stanford.edu/rofl/how-did-early-modern-slaves-spain-disappear-antecedents.

[12] For the period of forced conversion of Jews and the early Portuguese Inquisition, see François Soyer, *The Persecution of the Jews and Muslims of Portugal*.

[13] The scholarship suggests that the answer to the question is murky, unfolding differently depending on time period and location. For the impact of *limpieza de sangre* laws on Spanish America in general and its black population in particular, see Martínez, "Black Blood"; and Martínez, *Genealogical Fictions*, ch. 6.

portrayed as eager to learn about Christianity and to speak European languages.[14] Such a view of enslaved Africans might have been partially influenced by the longstanding presence of Christianity in the Kingdom of Kongo, as well as Ethiopia.[15] The famous sixteenth-century Afro-Iberian poet, Juan Latino (1518–c.1594), emphasized the difference between those he called "Africans" (North African Muslims) and other Africans, whom he referred to as "Ethiopians." By employing distinct terms, Latino was able to distance Afro-Iberians from the Muslim enemies of the Spanish state. In addition to being "free" from Islam, Latino's "Ethiopia" invoked the kingdom in East Africa that had been Christian for many centuries.[16]

Latino's position, however, was defensive, and attitudes about the "civilizing" potential of black slaves remained in conflict with the realpolitik interests of owners who developed increasingly entrenched notions of racial superiority that underpinned the expanding slave trade.[17] More generally, an array of negative qualities were attached to black Africans that had deep roots in medieval Europe and were quickly mobilized against the newly enslaved population. Such stereotypes could be reinforced by the portrayals of black servants in Golden Age theatre, who became stock comic figures (often white actors in blackface), speaking broken or incorrect Castilian.[18] Moreover, the word "black" quickly became interchangeable with "slave" (i.e., to label a person as "negro" implied that he was a slave), in spite of the growing community of free people of color in Iberia.

During the early modern period, the biblical story of the Curse of Ham provided a scriptural justification for natural slavery, the idea that some groups were born with characteristics making them suited only for enslavement. The Curse of Ham – also called Cham – refers to the belief that God cursed Noah's son with perpetual slavery for laughing at his father when the patriarch was drunk and naked. Biblical exegetical traditions claimed that the sons of Noah had repopulated the earth following the Great Flood, each in his own region. As a result, Ham could be associated with Africa, and the punishment levied on Ham's descendants included both enslavement and blackness. In some interpretations of

---

[14] Saunders, "Legacy of Black Slavery," 18–19.

[15] For many years, members of the Kongolese nobility, including members of the royal family, sent its sons to Portugal for education.

[16] Wright, *Epic of Juan Latino*, especially pp. 101–12 on detailed analysis of Latino's positive polemic of blackness; and Fra Molinero, "Juan Latino," 337–42.

[17] Lahon, "Black African Slaves," 174. Lahon asserts: "contemporary accounts … show that the majority of owners had no interest in their slaves having a close relationship with the Church, and even objected to it."

[18] Beusterien, *Eye on Race*; and Fra Molinero, *La imagen de los negros*. For an important challenge to this view of black characters, see Jones, *Staging Habla de Negros* and Jones "Cosmetic Ontologies, Cosmetic Subversions."

the story of Ham, skin color and slavery could be linked with each other and with inherent sinfulness, providing a biblical justification for transatlantic slavery. The argument in favor of divine punishment drew its power from its ability to sidestep moral concerns about slavery by explaining that it had a divine origin.[19] Such ideas circulated in sixteenth-century Portugal, and spread throughout the Iberian Atlantic, particularly in the seventeenth and eighteenth centuries.[20] An early discussion of the Curse of Ham (here called "Can") appeared in the work of Father Diego Yepes (d. 1613), Bishop of Tarazona, who told the story of Noah's son Can as part of his history of the Mercedarian order; he described Can's children as "black, and ugly like the Egyptians and ... barbarian people ... black like coal."[21] Franciscan Juan de Torquemada echoed similar ideas in his early seventeenth-century work on New Spain, rejecting climate theories of color difference and describing the origin of black skin color as part of God's curse. He finished by deriding blackness as a deformity – so ugly it was clearly a punishment from God.[22] Sub-Saharan Africans were frequently disparaged throughout the Spanish monarchy as ugly, ignorant, ridiculous, disruptive, violent, and savage.

Such negative stereotypes of black Africans dominated in spite of older theological models in which true conversion to Christianity was considered the antidote for such "defects." The entanglement of civilization with faith meant that early modern Europeans associated right belief (Christianity) with cultural markers; a true Christian must be Christian, but must also dress, speak, and act like a European, an idea that intensified in the early modern period with its emphasis on policing community behavior.[23] In theory, a person who accepted Christianity and lived a "proper" life should be accepted as a full member of the community. Yet, such beliefs in the spiritual potential of all souls did not resolve structural inequalities and hierarchical understandings of purity and worthiness. In fact, the opposite began to occur in the sixteenth century as purity of blood laws began to proliferate across Spain and the Spanish empire, mobilizing

[19] Whitford, *Curse of Ham*; Kidd, *Forging of Races*; and Goldberg, *Black and Slave*.

[20] Russell-Wood, "Before Columbus."

[21] Yepes, *Discursos de varia historia*, 47v-48r. "[Nacieron] negros, y feos como los Egipcios, y los Getulos, gente barbara, que viuen en una region en lo interior de Lybia ... Son negros como carbon, y tienen la boca podrida."

[22] Torquemada, *I° parte de ... monarchia Indiana*, 611–12. José Gumilla, on the other hand, argued that it was the indigenous people of the Americas who were descendants of the cursed Ham: *El Orinoco ilustrado*, 56–8.

[23] Selwyn, "'Procur[ing] in the Common People,'" 5–34. The relationship between language and proper Christian devotion proved complicated in global missionary efforts. Zupanov argues that in some cases, European languages gave way to local ones: "Twisting a Pagan Tongue," 109–39.

medieval ideas about the inheritability of vice in a codified scheme of discrimination against *conversos, moriscos*, and their descendants.[24]

Like the indigenous peoples of the Americas, sub-Saharan Africans were categorized as pagans, free of the taint of infidelity that supposedly marred those of Jewish and Muslim descent.[25] It was therefore the moral and ethical responsibility of Christian political powers to bring the light of Christ to such groups; many considered this responsibility a justification for conquest and enslavement. Sub-Saharan Africans were imported for labor at a time when Spaniards were discouraged from enslaving indigenous people whose populations had declined precipitously from disease.[26] African-descended Americans were also bound to Castilian laws in ways that indigenous populations were largely exempt, as indigenous people maintained distinct legal rights as part of the so-called *república de indios*.[27] Black Africans, then, inhabited a legal and religious space distinct from other minorities, including *conversos* and indigenous people.

The increasing numbers of enslaved black Africans imported into the Iberian world in the later sixteenth century posed a growing problem for the Church. While technically masters were responsible for their slaves' religious education, they largely ignored this mandate. In fact, they had strong incentives to engage in passive resistance, because full membership into Catholicism gave slaves access to certain privileges, such as confraternities that could raise money to liberate members, avenues for complaint of violations of privileges, and a host of religiously mandated feast days on which no work could be done.[28] The general neglect of this duty both in Spain and the Spanish Americas was widespread.[29]

[24] Much has been written about *limpieza de sangre*, particularly in the context of the peninsula. For several recent works, see Hernández Franco, *Sangre limpia*; Cartaya Baños, *La pasión de don Fernando de Añasco*; and Soria Mesa, *La realidad tras el espejo*.

[25] On racial and ethnic hierarchies in New Spain, see Katzew, "Casta Painting," 8–29. On creole constructions of race, see Cañizares-Esguerra, "Demons, Stars, and the Imagination," 319–20.

[26] In spite of what scholars have often assumed, enslavement and forced labor of indigenous people persisted; see Goetz, "Indian Slavery"; Sherman, *Forced Native Labor*; and Seijas, *Asian Slaves*, chs. 6 and 7.

[27] The fact that "*indio*" itself was a legal as much as a racial category in the Spanish colonies promoted fluidity in colonial identities, including cases where individuals could claim the status of "white" or "Indian": Tavárez, "Legally Indian"; Twinam, *Purchasing Whiteness*; Restall, *The Black Middle*; and Owensby, *Empire of Law*.

[28] One document in the Archivo General de Indias (hereafter AGI) contains a royal edict for an ambassador to go to Rome to petition the pope to reduce the number of feast days celebrated by black slaves: AGI, Indiferente, 422, Leg. 16, 148v-149r. Martín Casares and Delaigue discuss a manual for penitents written by Martín de Azpilcueta Navarro in 1557, describing the "sins" of owners for refusal to catechize or to attend mass: "Evangelization," 217–18.

[29] The early Jesuits reported on efforts to evangelize to large groups of slaves in Seville as early as 1555, but with little success: *MHSI Literae quadrimestres*, vol. 3 (Madrid 1984–1932), 279, 551.

In April 1601, the bishops of Cuzco, Popayán, and Quito wrote to Philip III to complain about the magnitude of the problem of catechizing the enslaved populations. They pointed out that more than two thousand black people lived in Lima, knowing little of Catholic doctrine. The bishops requested that three or four priests take residence in specific neighborhoods to provide catechesis and the sacraments. The Jesuits attempted to organize religious festivals for the black population in Lima in order to provide opportunities for evangelization, as owners were compelled to allow their slaves to attend such celebrations. Yet few attended, and the Jesuits accused those who did of using the event as an excuse to rest, drink, and dance.[30]

By the beginning of the seventeenth century, the Jesuits began to concentrate more on the spiritual education of black slaves in Europe as an extension of their mandate to spread the Gospel throughout the world and to strengthen catechesis within Catholic Europe.[31] By far the most active center of Jesuit evangelization and ministry to slaves occurred in the largest Spanish American slave port, Cartagena de Indias, where Jesuits worked with newly arrived slaves, bringing them food, water, rudimentary health care, and catechesis. The most famous of such Jesuits were Alonso de Sandoval (d. 1652) and his follower, Peter Claver (d. 1654), who was canonized in 1888.[32] Claver, like Sandoval, was born in Spain, but arrived in New Granada as an adult, having volunteered for overseas missionary work. He joined Sandoval in his missionary work among the enslaved population of the city. The Jesuits in Cartagena, then, witnessed both the horrific conditions and the state of baptism and catechesis of the newly arrived enslaved.

[30] Archivum Romanum Societatis Iesu (hereafter ARSI), *MSHI Monumenta Peruana*, VII (1600–1602), 346. Jesuits in Peru launched a series of complaints against the behavior of enslaved people in the early seventeenth century, including lewd dancing on feast days: ARSI, *MSHI Monumenta Peruana*, VII, 109.

[31] Nelson Minnich and Jennifer Selwyn found Jesuits working with slave populations in Sicily and Naples, respectively, see Minnich, "The Catholic Church," 286–7; and Selwyn, *Paradise Inhabited by Devils*. Among *sevillano* Jesuits, Alonso de Avila (d. 1556) was described as preaching with a companion "in the parishes and teaching Christian doctrine to the blacks in la Espartería [a neighborhood in Seville]": O'Neill and Domínguez, *Diccionario histórico*, 1:304. Francisco Arias de Párraga (d. 1605), a native of Seville and professor of moral theology in Trigueros, was also greatly concerned about catechesis and marginalized communities, including the imprisoned, *moriscos*, and black slaves: ARSI, *Literae quadrimestres ex universis praeter Indiam et Brasiliam locis*, vol. 3 (Madrid: 1896), 379, 382–3, and 551. Arias, furthermore, strongly opposed the application of Spanish purity of blood laws to the Jesuits: O'Neill and Domínguez, *Diccionario histórico*, 1:231–2. See also El Alaoui, *Jésuites, morisques et indiens*.

[32] *Proceso de beatificación y canonización de San Pedro Claver*. This process contains many witness testimonies by enslaved men who acted as his interpreters, all of whom were owned by the Jesuits; see also Morgan, "Jesuit Confessors, African Slaves," 222–39. For a seventeenth-century hagiography of Claver, see Andrade, *Vida del venerable y apostolino padre Pedro Claver* (1657).

Baptized slaves were provided little to no information regarding the sacramental meaning of baptism, particularly if it had been administered at their ports of embarkment in Africa. It was often bestowed with no explanation at all, and was always compulsory. Even if the slaves were subject to a brief catechesis, it is unlikely that the significance of the ritual would have made sense in light of the linguistic and cultural incongruities. James Sweet's research reveals some of the responses provided by Central Africans when asked about the meaning of their baptisms, which included the idea that the ritual provided protection from illness, preparation for a sacrificial killing (at the hands of Europeans), or an enchantment against uprising on the slave ship. Central Africans, therefore, interpreted baptism within their own cultural framework and the horrors of captivity.[33]

One early ally of Jesuit efforts to improve evangelization to enslaved Africans began in Spain with the powerful archbishop of Seville, Pedro de Castro Quiñones.[34] After ascending to the archbishopric in 1610, Castro turned his attention to the spiritual education of black slaves, working with the Jesuits who lived in Seville's College of San Hermenegildo to evangelize the city's large enslaved population. In the process, Castro and the local Jesuits discovered that the sacrament of baptism had been applied improperly to the recent converts, whose ignorance of the sacrament's meaning violated canon law.[35] Castro consulted with theologians to examine how baptisms were being performed on slaves from Guinea and Angola. The Jesuits began to amass information from parish priests and captains of slave-bearing ships to get first-hand knowledge of baptisms occurring in West and Central Africa.[36] Jesuit networks spanned the Atlantic from Seville to Central Africa to the Americas, investigating the catechesis and baptism of enslaved Africans.[37]

---

[33] Sweet, *Recreating Africa*, 195–9. Not surprisingly, European clerical accounts of "successful" baptisms were self-congratulatory. In one anecdote a diplomatic envoy of "Arda" Africans who wound up in Cartagena and were baptized, see ARSI, *Litterae annuae societatis iesu anni 1601* (Antwerp: Heredes Martini Nutii & Ioannem Meursium, 1608), 7r-8r.

[34] Castro was in the middle of several high-profile seventeenth-century controversies: Harris, *From Muslim to Christian Granada*; Rowe, *Saint and Nation*, 56–60, 159–60; and Prosperi, "L'Immaculée Conception," 435–67.

[35] Martín Casares and Delaigue, "Evangelization"; Sweet, *Recreating Africa*, 198–201.

[36] Borja Medina, "La experiencia sevillana," 83–4.

[37] Borja Medina argues that the Jesuits created a network that reached from Cabo Verde and Angola to Lisbon and Seville and on to Brazil and Cartagena, and that the flow of ideas and news in this Atlantic circuit was crucial to Jesuit missions: "La experiencia sevillana," 76–7.

Among key Jesuit players in Castro's efforts was Diego Ruiz de Montoya (d. 1632), a professor of theology who was well-versed in catechizing children, *moriscos*, and slaves in Seville.[38] The two men developed new regulations governing the catechesis and baptism of enslaved people who had received the sacrament improperly – that is, without having any understanding of its meaning. The recommendations were subsequently printed in 1614 and were also included in Sandoval's 1627 work (which itself was printed in Seville).[39] These new recommendations argued that slaves who had received the sacrament without proper catechesis had not received the sacrament at all; rather, what had happened constituted a "sacrilege," and they should be rebaptized following adequate education.[40] Ruiz mandated that all priests keep records of individual black men and women, free and enslaved, in their parishes, as part of an effort to keep a closer watch on the spiritual lives of people of color.[41] Ruiz's approach to baptism soon became known as the "Jesuit method" and quickly spread throughout the Americas. The emphasis on baptism and catechesis at the beginning of the seventeenth century suggests that this period saw greater focus on the spiritual lives of enslaved people in an effort to bring them more firmly under the umbrella of the Church.

It was during this same time period – the first two decades of the seventeenth century – that devotion to black saints took off. Launched by the recent death and circulation of Benedict of Palermo's cult, it could not have been a more perfect moment from the perspective of the Spanish Church and monarchy. The clergy supported the advancement of devotion to black saints because they believed that the African origins of these holy people would facilitate conversion and

[38] Ruiz de Montoya was celebrated by the Jesuits for his work in baptism and catechesis of black slaves: ARSI, Baet. 19/I, Litt. Ann. 1632, 119.

[39] This document was printed, and can also be found in manuscript: "Para Remediar, y assegurar, quanto con la divina gracia fuere possible, que ninguno de los Negros, que vienen de Guinea, Angola, y otras Provincias de aquella costa de Africa, carezca del sagrado Baptismo," Biblioteca Arzobispal de Sevilla (hereafter BAS), Sig. 34–315, no. 8; see also Sandoval, *Naturaleza i policia*, 327–35. For a contemporary account of Ruiz de Montoya's life see Gálvez, *Carta sobre la muerte y virtudes del P. Diego Ruiz de Montoya*: "Muy sabida, y celebrada es la diligencia, que puso, en que los Negros, y Negras, que vienen de Guinea, y Angola, se baptizassen, haziendo instancia en ello con razones, que en un singular tratado deste articulo, represente al Ilustrissimo señor don Pedro de Castro y Quiñones Arçobispo deste Ciudad" (5v). This is a printed text, but rare; I accessed it at BNE, VE/1375/9.

[40] These ruminations – and particularly the use of the powerful word "sacrilege" – demonstrate both the connections to and stark differences in contemporary debates about forced baptisms of *conversos* and *moriscos*.

[41] *Para remediar, y assegurar, quanto con la divina gracia fuere posible* (1614, reprinted in 1627), ARSI, FG 720/III/4(b), 1r-2r. The Provincial in Peru met in the early seventeenth century to discuss the need to learn "la lengua Angola de los Negros" and to print a confessional in that language: ARSI, Linguae. Studium linguarum, FG 1488 int.1/II, 8ff.

participation in Catholic practice by black Iberians, who were arriving in much larger numbers by the early seventeenth century. One way to facilitate devotion to black saints was to introduce them to the lay confraternities that had been instituted for people of color for more than a century. Tying together the two – black saints and black confraternities – furthered the Iberian imperial agenda to transform enslaved Africans into Christian subjects. But, like the confraternities themselves, black Catholics quickly adopted black saints and made them their own.

Black Confraternities

Global evangelization was a process, rather than a singular instantiation. As a result, such efforts continued from first contact between missionaries and non-Europeans through the eighteenth century. Yet the practice of Christianity by people of color cannot be viewed solely through the clerical lens. The Atlantic Jesuit network we have discussed provides a top-down model for understanding the process of global Catholicism – that is, one in which the spread of Christianity was initiated by the clergy, who in turn imposed it on the newly baptized. Closer examination reveals that communities of color quickly took charge of their own devotional lives, primarily through the organization of lay confraternities. Their status as baptized members of the Church enabled people of color – even those enslaved – to form lay devotional groups, which provided opportunities for independent group organization, mutual support, and the celebration of religious festivals. Perhaps more significantly, confraternities created spaces where people of color could escape the white gaze, even if only for short periods of time. And it was through such confraternities that devotion to black saints spread throughout the Iberian Atlantic.[42]

Each confraternity was embedded in a local context that includes how it was formed, its history over time, and how it developed in relationship to its host church and town, which varied widely depending on location. While study of individual confraternities within specific towns or regions is vital, the intention in this section is to provide a broad overview of the geographic spread of black confraternities. Mapping the presence of black and *mulato* brotherhoods throughout the Iberian Atlantic demonstrates that such organizations were a transnational phenomenon, quickly taking root from the arrival of the earliest

---

[42] The history of confraternities whose memberships included indigenous and *mestizo* populations falls outside the scope of this project, but such brotherhoods did exist, called *cofradías de indios*, or *de mestizos*.

enslaved people and accelerating along with the slave trade. Moreover, hagiographers and sacred historians discussed devotion to black saints in Spain, Portugal, and the Americas indiscriminately, clearly seeing them as interconnected systems of Iberian devotion, even across imperial lines, which is also visible in the overarching patterns. Because communities of color formed their own confraternities, they also chose their patron saints and the sacred images that stood on the altars they rented from host churches. Analyzing the broad sweep of brotherhoods and their sacred art, then, provides a glimpse into the formation of global Catholicism originating from communities of color.

It would be difficult to overstate the cultural and social significance of confraternities in the late medieval and early modern Catholic world.[43] Confraternities emerged out of the High Middle Ages as the laity began to desire increased participation in spiritual experiences that could be folded into the rhythms of their lives. Like guilds, confraternities were urban institutions, organized by profession or neighborhood, generally housed in local churches (both parish and religious) where the members could rent an altar or side chapel. The chapels provided spaces for confraternal celebrations of private religious services and the rights to appeal for alms on certain days. Organized around one saint or cult, members went on procession on feast days, carrying the image of their patron saint. This patron saint is referred to as their "avocation," in keeping with the tradition of adopting a personal patron to act as one's "advocate" in heaven; the confraternity would then be named for its patron (e.g., the Confraternity of Our Lady of the Snows, the Confraternity of St. Nicolas). In addition to their spiritual functions, confraternities served as outlets for community creation and mutual support, playing key roles in the structure of the spiritual, social, and political lives of urban residents.

Some of the most important social functions of confraternities involved raising funds to support members and members' families for events such as burial and dowries.[44] Being hosted by a specific church provided confraternities with rights to burial inside the church and on its grounds. Burial was an important facet of medieval and early modern Catholic culture, because it was necessary to be buried in consecrated ground. Moreover, the faithful needed to memorialize the dead and pray for their souls. Such prayer had traditionally been the preserve of monks and nuns, who prayed ceaselessly for the souls in Purgatory.

[43] For some recent work on early modern confraternities, Dompnier and Vismara, *Confréries et devotions*.

[44] Banker, *Death in the Community*; Eisenbichler, "Italian Scholarship on Pre-Modern Confraternities"; Terpstra, *Politics of Ritual Kinship*; and Black and Gravestock, *Early Modern Confraternities*.

Figure 2.1 The sign outside Hermandad de Nuestra Señora de los Ángeles, Seville, Spain.

Confraternities permitted lay people to bury and remember their dead as a community.

Individual brotherhoods maintained constitutions or statutes, called *compromisos*, formulaic documents that detailed the number of members, required qualifications for membership as well as office-holding, administrative structure, feast days celebrated, alms-collecting policies, and description of burial practices and rights. Despite the formulaic genre, they also provide important information about the confraternities' elections, officials, and purpose, which can be crucial for analyzing their social networks. Yet the *compromiso* did not necessarily mark the beginning date of a brotherhood's organization, only when it was written and ratified by ecclesiastical authorities. The first meeting of the brothers and sisters often occurred years before the official ratification of the confraternal constitution. For example, one of Seville's oldest and most famous confraternities, Nuestra Señora de los Ángeles (Our Lady of the Angels), nicknamed *Los negritos*, has an uncertain origin date with estimates ranging between the late fourteenth to the mid-sixteenth centuries.[45] [Fig. 2.1] Such ratification dates can,

---

[45] Isidoro Moreno dates the beginning of the confraternity to the fourteenth century: *La antigua hermandad de los negros de Sevilla*, 26–41, largely based on evidence that Archbishop Gonzalo de Mena (d. 1401) established a hospital and house. Moreno claims that the hospital was for "*morenos*" (his word, without citation), which he takes to mean black slaves (p. 39). Yet it is unlikely that a hospital would be established solely for black slaves at a time when the majority of slaves were Moorish. There is, however, evidence of a significant population of black slaves by the end of the fifteenth century, including the appointment of a black "mayor" in 1474: Ortiz y Zúñiga, *Anales eclesiásticos*, 374.

however, provide a general timeframe for the establishment of new brotherhoods in the early modern period.

The most important functions of lay confraternities were their participation in public festivals, which occurred on significant liturgical feasts, such as Corpus Christi and Holy Week, as well as their patron's feast day. These feasts were public and civic; they took place on the streets of the town and often in conjunction with the processions of other confraternities, praying for the well-being of the community and safeguarding it against disasters like flood and drought. For example, Nuestra Señora de los Reyes, the black confraternity in Jaén, celebrated its principal feast on Epiphany (6 January) the last feast of the Christmas season; Epiphany commemorates the arrival of the three kings(los reyes), or magi, to bring gifts and homage to baby Jesus in Bethlehem. The confraternity processed again on Corpus Christi, although not during Holy Week.[46] Presumably, the reformation of the brotherhood by Cristóbal de Porras in the 1620s (to be discussed), led to the addition of the feast of St. Benedict to its calendar of processions. Nuestra Señora de los Ángeles in Seville participated in three public festivals by the mid-sixteenth century: the Incarnation, Holy Cross, and the Nativity of the Virgin. They also celebrated two additional Marian feasts: the Immaculate Conception and the Virgin of the Angels, their patron.[47] A group of brothers would carry the confraternity's image or images on platforms large enough to look like floats, called pasos.[48] Even though they are hollow within, polychrome sculptures can be quite heavy, requiring, in some cases, dozens of men to bear the weight of a single structure and move it at a glacially slow pace through the streets, although such pieces were sometimes carried on wheeled carriages.

Brotherhoods for enslaved people of color emerged as quickly as newly arrived enslaved people were baptized.[49] For people of color, confraternities supplied the same benefits as for white Christians, but in a context where such benefits were more desperately needed and could develop uses exclusively significant to them.[50] Roquinaldo Ferreira remarks: "In many ways, the social and cultural lives of free and enslaved residents of the city centered

---

[46] Ortega, "La cofradía de los negros," 6.   [47] Moreno, La antigua hermandad, 65, 116.

[48] Monti, Week of Salvation, 63. A "paso" refers specifically to a platform mounted with a sculpture; in Spain, many of the sculptures with polychrome wood were "vestido" – that is, dressed in sumptuous clothing and jewels. See also Webster, Art and Ritual.

[49] "Brotherhoods" emerged as a distinct form of confraternities, and had a strong focus on penance and penitential rites, yet the two terms were often used interchangeably during the early modern period, and this is how I use them throughout.

[50] This aspect of black confraternities will be assessed in greater depth in Chapter 3.

on religious services and activities organized by Christian lay brotherhoods, churches, and convents."[51] While Ferreira's comment described Luanda, Angola, the same could be said about almost every region of the Iberian Atlantic. The first black confraternities were founded around 1500 and continued to thrive in some places in the Iberian world to the end of the eighteenth century and beyond.[52] The majority of black confraternities in the Spanish Atlantic were founded between 1575 and 1700, the same period that witnessed the sharp rise in the slave trade in Iberia and the Spanish Americas. Because the foundation of brotherhoods followed the patterns of the slave trade, new brotherhoods continued to proliferate in eighteenth- and nineteenth-century Brazil. [Fig. 2.2]

While occasionally the result of outreach from specific religious orders, most black confraternities formed in the same way as white confraternities – a group came together, decided to organize, adopted an avocation, and found a sympathetic host church. Eventually, they drafted a *compromiso* detailing the brotherhood's organizational structure and requesting official ecclesiastical approval. [Fig. 2.3] Two examples of individuals responsible for organizing black confraternities in Spain were Juan Cobo and Cristóbal de Porras. Cobo founded Nuestra Señora de los Reyes in Jaén, although it struggled financially and collapsed. In 1627, however, Cristóbal de Porras arrived in Jaén as part of a trek across Andalusia for the express purpose of founding black confraternities in Franciscan convents dedicated to Benedict of Palermo. A document recording Porras's desire to establish a Cofradía de San Benito de Palermo in Jaén noted that he had established one previously in Baeza and "others in other places." In Jaén, Porras discovered the defunct Cofradía de los Reyes and sought to bring it together with an avocation to Benedict of Palermo. Cobo resisted the effort and the two ended up engaged in a lawsuit, which Porras eventually won, bringing the new, joined confraternity into existence.[53] The lawsuit in Jaén demonstrates the process through which black confraternities could be founded by black leaders or communities. Moreover, Porras's focus on creating black confraternities under the patronage of Benedict of Palermo speaks to the confraternal devotion to him throughout the Iberian Atlantic.

---

[51] Ferreira, *Cross-Cultural Exchange*, 91.
[52] For more on early confraternities in Valencia and Portugal (Lisbon, confirmed 1505), see Blumenthal, "Casa del Negres," 225–46; and Lahon, "Black African Slaves," 261–79. The earliest confraternity in Africa was established in Cabo Verde, Nossa Senhora do Rosário, in 1495: Green, "Building Slavery," 233. Confraternities that welcomed black slaves and free people were also established in Italy: Minnich, "The Catholic Church," 296.
[53] Ortega, "Cofradía de los Negros," 6–7, 127, 131.

Figure 2.2 Igreja de Nossa Senhora do Rosário dos Pretos in Pelourinho, Salvador (Bahia), Brazil.

Some of the earliest black confraternities took root in the Portuguese territories. The constitution of Lisbon's Nossa Senhora do Rosário dos Homens Pretos (Our Lady of the Rosary of Black People) declared in its prologue that "we, black men, came from the regions of Ethiopia and its territories," and that they had venerated the titular Virgin in their chapel in

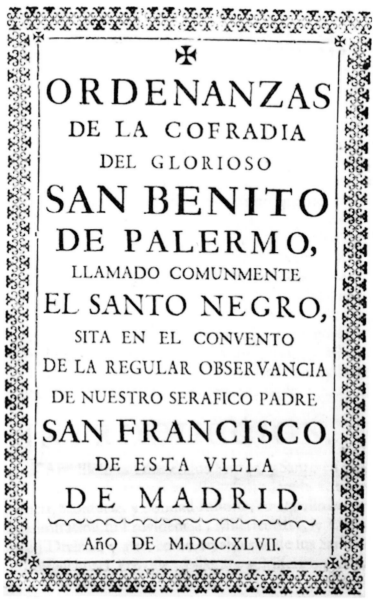

ORDENANZAS
DE LA COFRADIA
DEL GLORIOSO
SAN BENITO
DE PALERMO,
LLAMADO COMUNMENTE
EL SANTO NEGRO,
SITA EN EL CONVENTO
DE LA REGULAR OBSERVANCIA
DE NUESTRO SERAFICO PADRE
SAN FRANCISCO
DE ESTA VILLA
DE MADRID.
AñO DE M.DCC.XLVII.

Figure 2.3 Cover page of *Ordenanzas de la Cofradia del Glorioso San Benito de Palermo, llamado comunmente El Santo Negro*, 1747. Archivo Histórico Nacional, lib. 5224, Madrid, Spain.

Lisbon "since the year 1470."[54] While the *compromiso* was dated 1565, the members maintained a communal memory of their confraternity's antiquity

---

[54] "Compromisso da Irmandade de N.S. do Rosario dos Homens Pretos, [Dec. 1565]" MS F. 975, Biblioteca Nacional de Portugal (hereafter BNP), f. 1v. Surviving *compromisos* from the

and date of origin.[55] Lisbon had several black confraternities by the end of the sixteenth century, including the aforementioned Rosary brotherhood, which was housed in the Dominican convent and was the oldest of all known black confraternities in the city. By the dawn of the eighteenth century, then, Lisbon housed nine confraternities for its black community, the most of any city in Iberia.[56] One late Rosary confraternity in Lisbon was founded at the royal Monastery of Santa Joana. Santa Joana (d. 1490) had been the daughter of the Portuguese king Afonso V; she became a nun renowned for her piety and achieved beatification in 1693. Six years after her beatification, a convent was established under her patronage in Lisbon, amply funded and supported by the royal family.[57] While the dates of the Rosary confirmation at Santa Joana are uncertain, it was probably established around the turn of the eighteenth century, and it remained active until at least the mid-eighteenth century.[58]

Brotherhoods fanned out to other regions in Portugal, north as far as Braga and to the eastern section of the central region of the Alentejo. [Map 2.1] The port city of Oporto housed four: three separate brotherhoods dedicated to Nossa Senhora do Rosário, including one that added St. Benedict to its name, and one dedicated to San Gonçalo García.[59] Brotherhoods in the eastern Alentejo – Evora, Vila Viçosa, and Elvas – created a line from west to east from central Portugal across the border

sixteenth century are rare, but abound for eighteenth-century Brazil in the Arquivo Nacional Torre do Tombo (hereafter ANTT), Lisbon.

[55] There are additional primary source documents related to this confraternity from throughout the sixteenth century, discussed in Lahon, "Black African Slaves," 261–79.

[56] Reginaldo, "'África em Portugal'"; *Os negros em Portugal*; Lahon, "Exclusion, integration et métissages"; Lahon, "Les confréries de noirs"; Saunders, *Social History*. Lisbon confraternities: Nossa Senhora do Rosário dos Homens Pretos (Dominican, 1470); Nossa Senhora de Guadalupe e São Benedito (Franciscan, 1500s); Jesus María José (Carmelite, 1500s); Nossa Senhora do Rosário (Trinitarian, 1600s); Nossa Senhora do Rosário (Augustinian, 1600s); Jesus María José (Franciscan, 1600s); Nossa Senhora dos Reyes Magos (1700s); and Nossa Senhora do Rosário (Santa Joana, 1700s).

[57] "Mosteiro de Santa Joana de Lisboa (1318–1889)," ANTT, PT/TT/MSJL. It is uncertain when the confraternity at the Mosteiro de Santa Joana was founded but it must have been between 1699 and 1740. The monastery has been converted into a hotel, and the sepulcher of the saint moved to the Convento de Jesus da Ordem Dominicana, today the Museu de Aveiro.

[58] See "Livro da esmolas que da a casa real para a irmandade dos homens pretos de Santa Joana," ANTT, PT/TT/MSJL/MF.LA; and "Ação cível de embargos a primeira em que são autores o juiz e irmãos da irmandade Nossa Senhora do Rosario dos homens pretos," ANTT, MS. PT/TT/CCPP/0036/0009.

[59] Reginaldo, "'África em Portugal'," 296–8. There is Igreja de Nossa Senhora da Purificação de São Gonçalo. On confraternities to São Gonçalo, see Arquivo Histórico Ultramarino (hereafter AHU)_ACL_CU_004, Cx. 3, D. 175; AHU_ACL_CU_015, Cx. 63, D. 5379 (1746); and AHU_ACL_CU_015, Cx. 222, D. 15068 (1800). Garcia's cult was also extant in Portugal; an inventory for the black confraternity housed in Lisbon listed St. Gonçalo among its images, as well as a later note about celebrating his feast day: ANTT, 27v.

Map 2.1 Locations of black confraternities in early modern Portugal

to Badajoz and Zafra, Spain, which had its own black confraternities, following the overland slave trading route from Portugal to Andalusia. Although such land-locked regions are not generally associated with slavery in the same way as major port cities like Lisbon and Seville, the overland slave trade created diverse paths for the movement of slaves and the creation of enslaved and freed black communities. Tracing such alternate paths of slave trafficking can help us understand the spread of slavery in regions distant from the sea.[60]

In the Kingdom of Castile, black confraternities were established in urban areas with the largest populations of enslaved people of color: Andalusia and Extremadura. Little is known about the histories of many of these brotherhoods, especially those outside Andalusia and Extremadura. For example, there were brotherhoods established on the Canary Islands (Telde), Mallorca (Las Palmas), and various locations in the Kingdom of Aragon (Barcelona and Valencia).[61] [Map 2.2] Tantalizing fragments of evidence demonstrate that their dissemination might have encompassed a broader geographic range than has yet been studied.[62] Two black confraternities were founded in Madrid – Nuestra Señora de las Estrellas from the middle of the seventeenth century and the Cofradía de San Benito de Palermo in the middle of the eighteenth century – although they have been little studied. A small museum in the Castilian town of Arenas de San Pedro, located in the province of Avila near the border with Extremadura, houses a statue of Benedict of Palermo labeled as having been part of the black confraternity's chapel.[63] The presence of a black confraternity here suggests that numbers of enslaved people sufficient to sustain a confraternity might have existed in other parts of Castile-León.[64] José Luis Cortés López discusses several cities in Castile outside of Andalusia that maintained enslaved and free black populations, including Madrid, Toledo, Ciudad Real, and Valladolid.[65]

In addition to challenging previously assumed geographic borders of black confraternities in Iberia, it is also important to expand their histories

---

[60] Periáñez Gómez, *Negros, mulatos y blancos*.

[61] Armenteros Martínez, "De hermandades y procesiones"; and Vincent, "Pour une histoire des confréries de noirs," 247–50.

[62] Estaban Mira Caballos includes a table of black brotherhoods founded in early modern Castile, almost all of which were in Extremadura or Andalusia: Badajoz, Seville, El Puerto de Santa María, Jerez de los Caballeros, Cádiz, Málaga, Granada, Jerez de la Frontera, Usagre, Segura de León, Bujalance, Jaén, Úbeda, Baeza, Madrid, Toledo, and Almendral: "Cofradías étnicas," 61–3. There were also two in Medina Sidonia: Martínez Delgado, *Historia de la ciudad de Medina Sidonia*, 232. For more information on the sculpture of Benedict now housed in the Museo del Carmen y franciscano in Pastrana, see: Muñoz, *Museo de arte sacra*, 220–1.

[63] Dell'Aire, *Da San Fratello a Bahia*, 37.

[64] Bernard Vincent has traced evidence of devotion to Benedict throughout Castile and Aragon through the late eighteenth century – Valladolid, Toledo, Barcelona, Aranjuez, and Guadix: "San Benito de Palermo," 23–38.

[65] Cortés López, *La esclavitud negra*, 21–4.

Map 2.2 Locations of black confraternities in early modern Spain

chronologically. While many black brotherhoods in Spain disappeared in the eighteenth century – whether by force or through dwindling membership and poverty – confraternities in Spain and Portugal persisted throughout the eighteenth century, even to the beginning of the nineteenth.[66] Three confraternities were founded in Castile in the mid-eighteenth century – in Madrid, Almendral, and Toledo.[67] Little is known about them; the Cofradía de San Benito de Palermo in Madrid, for example, appears to have shut its doors a mere twenty years after its foundation.[68] Yet that still extends the presence of the black confraternity in the royal capital to the 1770s, suggesting a long-enduring population of enslaved and free people of color.[69] Moreover, additional archival evidence might be uncovered that that pushes the dates of persistence of black confraternities into the early nineteenth century in places beyond Lisbon.[70]

Black confraternities quickly spread beyond the Iberian Peninsula to its imperial territories.[71] Not surprisingly, their numbers in the Americas far outstripped those in Iberia, reflecting the significantly larger African-descended populations as well as a larger geographic area. The confraternities in Lima, New Spain, and Brazil have been the best studied, though the extant scholarship on the Spanish Americas represents the tip of the iceberg.[72] The largest-scale analysis of black

---

[66] Survivals of black confraternities in Brazil are unsurprising, given the rapidly escalating slave trade of the eighteenth century, the late abolition of slavery (1888), and the large Afro-Brazilian population. Much of the collection dealing with confraternities held by the AHU has been digitized, and can be found: http://brasilhis.usal.es/pt-br. For a few examples, see AHU_ACL_CU, Cod. 1677 (1) and Cod. 1931 (1) for two compromisos from 1803. For Lisbon, see ANTT, PT/TT/JIM/JA/0041/00005 (a lawsuit involving the Rosary brothers of the Igreja da Graça, 1811); ANTT, PT/TT/JIM/B/0033 /00004 (a lawsuit involving the brotherhood of Nossa Senhora de Guadalupe e São Benedito, 1814).

[67] On Almendral, see Pérez Guedejo, *Cofradías y hermandades*, 112–14.

[68] Documentation for the confraternity can be found at the Archivo Histórico Nacional (hereafter AHN). The "*ordenanzas*" can be found both in print and manuscript: AHN, "Ordenanzas de la Cofradia de San Benito de Palermo," Libro 5224 and Consejos lib. 5496, ff. 1–27. Additional documents, including the order for the confraternity's suppression, can be found: AHN, Legajo 4006, exp. 86; and Libro 1355, ff. 848–56.

[69] For more on slavery in eighteenth-century Madrid, including a discussion of this confraternity, see López García, Castroviejo Salas, and Pozo Rincón, "Entre la marginación y integración."

[70] See, for example, a few lawsuits (*acção civil*) from mid-eighteenth-century Portugal: ANTT, PT/TT/CSFP/CNSR/004/0001, Registro de esmolas, 1739–1767, liv. 9, 6r-26v, 38r-40r; ANTT, PT/TT/JIM/JA/0041/0005, Execuçao de sentença cívil (Igreja de Graça, Lisbon, 1811); and ANTT, PT/TT/MSJL/MF.L121A, "Libro da esmolas que da a casa real para a irmandade dos homens pretos de Santa Joana," liv. 121-A. 16r-23v.

[71] While our focus here remains on black confraternities, a variety existed in Colonial America: brotherhoods for "whites" only; "mixed" – which did not have ethnic restrictions; indigenous, *pardo*, and black. For more on indigenous confraternities, see Schroeder, "Jesuits, Nahuas, and the Good Death"; Bechtloff, *Las cofradías en Michoacán*; and Charney, "A Sense of Belonging."

[72] Roselló Soberón, "La Cofradía de San Benito de Palermo"; Childs, "Re-Creating African Ethnic Identities," 86–9; and Childs, "Gendering the African Diaspora." For a brief description of two

brotherhoods in New Spain has been developed by Nicole von Germeten, who studied fifty-six black brotherhoods founded in the late sixteenth to eighteenth centuries. She compiled an appendix of these brotherhoods, including their town, church, name, and date of foundation (if known). Many towns in New Spain hosted more than one black confraternity, including Valladolid and Quéretero, while Mexico City boasted the most with eight.[73] It is difficult to know the exact date of the first confraternal foundation in New Spain, but the viceroy of Mexico, Martín Enríquez, mentioned several black and *mulato* confraternities in a letter to the king dated 1572.[74] In several of these avocations, we can see the presence of black saints. For example, one *mulato* confraternity founded in Mexico City took the name La Coronación de Christo Nuestro Señor, y S. Benito (The Coronation of Our Lord Christ and St. Benedict), by 1599.[75] Another black confraternity in Mexico City was dedicated to Efigenia, though its altar included an image of Benedict as well.[76] Brotherhoods continued to be founded through the first half of the seventeenth century. Castañeda noted four black confraternities founded between 1599 and 1646: Puebla, Veracruz, Mexico, and Querétaro.[77]

One of the best-known black confraternities in New Spain was located in Puebla de los Ángeles, which maintained perhaps the earliest devotion to Benedict in the Americas, housed in the Franciscan church.[78] The confraternity's presence was significant enough to be mentioned in a number of sources, particularly in the early eighteenth-century beatification process for Benedict of Palermo, which included the *compromiso* for the *poblano* confraternity – the

black brotherhoods in sixteenth-century Havana, see Fuente, Garcia del Pino, and Iglesias Delgado, *Havana and the Atlantic*, 168–70.

[73] Von Germeten, *Black Blood Brothers*. See also Von Germeten, "Black Brotherhoods in Mexico City." Von Germeten's list is wide-ranging, if not complete – Puebla de los Ángeles, for example, does not appear. For a critique of von Germeten's analysis of one *cofradía*, see Moriel-Payne, "La cofradía de la Limpia Concepción."

[74] Archivo General de Indias (hereafter AGI), Mexico, 19, n. 82, n.f. Enríquez mentioned processions by "*indios*," "*mestizos* and *mulatos*," and "blacks," as separate devotional groups.

[75] Vetancurt notes one *cofradía de morenos* in the convent of Santa Maria Redonda (Mexico City), called La Coronación de Christo Nuestro Señor, y S. Benito. He claimed the confraternity was confirmed by Pope Clement VIII in 1599, though it is likely that Benedict was named patron later (it was common for the second patron to be added later): *Chronica*, vol. 2, 36. He also mentioned a Cofradía de San Benito in Veracruz, p. 76. The *veracruzano* confraternity (and its statues) has been examined by Roselló Soberón, "La Cofradía de San Benito de Palermo."

[76] ASV, Processus, MS 2179, 385v. This testimony was provided by Francisco del Rosario, a Bethlehemic brother.

[77] Castañeda, "La devoción a Santa Ifigenia," 155. Von Germeten listed two others founded in 1646 and 1679: *Black Blood Brothers*, appendix.

[78] For the local history of Puebla including its enslaved population and confraternities, see Sierra Silva, *Urban Slavery*; and Ramos, *Identity, Ritual, and Power*.

only such document incorporated into the volume. The *compromiso* contains little information about the reason for its foundation; like most other *compromisos*, it used boilerplate language about the brotherhood's structure and purpose.[79] Its presence alone speaks to the importance both of devotion to Benedict in Puebla and the interest evinced by *poblanos* in the saint's beatification. Moreover, witnesses in the beatification testimony and hagiographers who discussed the confraternity mentioned the confraternity's image of St. Benedict, making it a particularly renowned object.[80]

Lima, the viceregal capital of Peru was home to a large African-descended population – nearly 50 percent of the entire population by some calculations – and its black confraternities were numerous. The exact number is difficult to pin down, but at least seventeen have been identified, with at least six additional brotherhoods permitting members of color. The numerous brotherhoods for black and *mulato limeños* were founded between the sixteenth and seventeenth centuries, headed by the wealthy and powerful Nuestra Señora de la Antigua (Our Lady of Antiquity) and Nuestra Señora de los Reyes (Our Lady of the Kings).[81] Most of the "mixed" confraternities were housed in parish churches, suggesting that neighborhood parishes might have organized around specific communities, as opposed to those in convent churches, which might have been chosen specifically by members as exclusive spaces. Presumably because they were more accessible, parish churches such as San Marcelo and Santa Ana were more likely than convent churches to house multiple confraternities that admitted members of color. It is important to add, when thinking about the overall numbers of *limeño* confraternities, that they were not all active at the same time – some closed, split, or changed avocations over time, which accounts for variation in numbers gathered by scholars.

While Lima might have maintained the greatest concentration of black confraternities in Spanish America, Brazil hosted the greatest overall number in the Iberian Atlantic, the result of its immense enslaved population by the late eighteenth century. The first Rosary confraternities were established by the Jesuits in 1552, and subsequently could be found throughout the coastal cities, in addition to the region of Minas Gerais, north and inland from Rio de Janeiro.[82] Patricia Mulvey and Barry Crouch argue that the church in Brazil was weaker than the church in Spanish America, which meant that lay brotherhoods could step into

---

[79] For the entire *compromiso*, see ASV, Procesos, MS 2179, 200v-241v.   [80] Cited at, n. 1.

[81] Graubart, "'So Color de una Cofradía,'" 48–9; Tardieu, *L'eglise et les noirs au Pérou*, 1:554–61; Jouve Martín, "Public Ceremonies and Mulatto Identity"; and Egoavil, *Las cofradías en Lima*. A table can be found in Bowser, *The African Slave in Colonial Peru*, 249.

[82] Dantas, "Humble Slaves," 130–1; and Russell-Wood, "Black and Mulatto Brotherhoods," 567–602.

the power gap and become "tremendously powerful."[83] The high proportion of enslaved Africans brought to Brazil in the eighteenth century built upon older Afrocreole populations; during this period, the black population outnumbered the white in many regions, and black brotherhoods not only proliferated, but played crucial roles in the social, cultural, and even political structures of Brazilian communities.[84] The large numbers of black confraternities have yet to be studied comprehensively, although their historiography in specific cities or regions is rich.[85]

Significantly less is known about the black brotherhoods founded in the areas of West and Central Africa that had been evangelized by Portuguese and Spanish friars. The first such confraternities appeared in Portuguese settlements on the previously uninhabited African islands, including Cabo Verde and São Tomé, as well as Portugal's northern Atlantic islands, the Azores and Madeira.[86] The Irmandade de Nossa Senhora do Rosário for enslaved people was founded in Cabo Verde as early as 1495, following the same timeline as the earliest foundations in Lisbon.[87] Despite the fact that Christianity had been introduced to the Kingdom of Kongo by the Portuguese at the end of the fifteenth century, there is no evidence for the formation of confraternities during the period before Portuguese incursions into the region. Confraternities are a European institution, after all, and the Manikongo worked hard to separate the Church in his dominions from Portuguese institutional oversight, although this was a losing battle – the governance of the diocese remained firmly in the hands of the Portuguese clergy.[88] Nevertheless, Kongolese Christianity in the sixteenth century maintained a great deal of

---

[83] Mulvey and Crouch, "Black Solidarity," 53. See also Cardozo, "The Lay Brotherhoods"; Santana, "Nossa Senhora do Rosário"; and Scarano, *Devoção e escravidão*.

[84] ANTT and AHU in Lisbon house many documents related to eighteenth-century Brazilian confraternities. For a few examples of *compromisos*, see: ANTT, PT/TT/MR/NE/06/47; AHU Códice 1789; AHU Códices 1664, 1950, and 919; Mulvey, "Slave Confraternities in Brazil"; and Kiddy, *Blacks of the Rosary*.

[85] In addition to the above, see Reginaldo, "Irmandades e devoções," 25–36; and Santana, "Nossa Senhora do Rosário."

[86] Jorge Fonseca provides an excellent overview of Portugal's black confraternities, including three black confraternities in the Azores and two in Madeira: *Religião e Liberdade*, 68–9. For more on the Rosary confraternity in Faro, see Fonseca and Sabóia, "Os Negros de Faro," 113–31, which includes its statutes.

[87] Green, "Building Slavery," 233. See also Green, "Building Creole Identity."

[88] For a few examples, see Biblioteca Apostolico Vaticano (hereafter BAV) Vat. Lat. 12516, 5r-18r, 43v-45v100r; ASV, Ep. Ad Princ., 86, Letters from the Pope to the rulers of Kongo and Matambo, 82v-85v. See also Heywood, "Angolan-Afro-Brazilian Cultural Connections"; Thornton, "Development of an African Catholic Church"; Kenny, "The Catholic Church in Tropical Africa"; and Felsi, "Enrico, figlio del re di Congo."

independence, and the first lay confraternities were founded in Angola when the Dominicans established a Rosary brotherhood in 1610.[89]

The greatest concentrations of black confraternities in Central Africa were located in Angola, where the Portuguese gained a foothold after founding the coastal city of São Paulo da Assunção de Loanda (today Luanda) in 1575, and began aggressive missionary – and military – incursions further inland. António de Oliveira's history of the Angolan wars (1680) contains abundant references to black confraternities in its descriptions of cities and towns. In a description of Luanda, he lavished praise on the Jesuit College, mentioning that it housed a Rosary confraternity for blacks, including slaves. He continued that they celebrated processions alongside white confraternities.[90] Luanda was not the only town that Oliveira claimed had a black confraternity; for example, he described the town of Victoria de Mansangano as having four churches, including a parish church for the "pretos [blacks] Quimbares."[91] In another Angolan town, the black residents had their own church dedicated to Nossa Senhora do Rosário with a corresponding confraternity.[92]

Mapping the locations and dates of confirmation of black confraternities allows us to understand their reach and rapid development. Local and regional approaches to their study has militated against viewing black confraternities as a global institutional network, both initiated by European clergy and organized on the ground by people of color. The earliest foundations of black confraternities throughout the Iberian Atlantic were considered part of missionary work, rather than the ordinary rhythm of parish life like most other lay brotherhoods. Ecclesiastic leaders such as the archbishop of Mexico, Francisco Aguiar y Seixas clearly expressed his belief that confraternities would aid the "civilizing"

---

[89] Kiddy, *Blacks of the Rosary*, 32. For more on Angolan confraternities, see Reginaldo, "Rosário dos Pretos," which discusses Angola in the second half of the article.

[90] Cadornega, *História Geral das Guerras Angolanas*, 15. For more on Luanda, see Ferreira, "Slavery and the Social."

[91] Cadornega, *História Geral das Guerras Angolanas*, 119–21. The term *"quimbares"* referred to free black groups who engaged in itinerant trade: Ferreira, *Cross-Cultural Exchange*, 59. Robert Harms mentions the black Rosary confraternity, saying that King João III had "given the brotherhood the right to demand freedman for any black man or woman who was a member of the order": *The Diligent*, 284. For more on slavery in São Tomé and Principe, see Izequiel, *São Tomé et Príncipe*.

[92] Cadornega, *História Geral das Guerras Angolanas*, 27. He claims that Benedict of Palermo was celebrated by "gente preta, e particularment a Sra do Rozario." The potential institutional relationships between Central African and American confraternities merits further scholarly attention. Two recent studies focus on cultural ties between Central Africa and Brazil including black confraternities: Kananoja, "Central African Identities," 175–96; and Reginaldo, "Rosários dos pretos."

process to African populations, and thus promote colonial authority.[93] Yet evidence also demonstrates that many black confraternities – particularly those established in the late sixteenth and mid-eighteenth centuries – were founded by the members themselves, run by their brothers and sisters. And those brothers and sisters quickly adopted black saints as their own, rapidly expanding these new cults throughout the Iberian Atlantic.

Black Confraternities and Benedictine Devotion

The richest evidence we have for the wide-ranging influence of black devotion to Benedict comes from the beatification process that took place in the Roman church of Santa Maria sopra Minerva in 1716, which was administered by the Congregation of Sacred Rites. This process acted as a follow-up to the late sixteenth- and early seventeenth-century testimonies collected in Sicily. A century later, the Congregation decided to take up the question of Benedict's beatification again, and gathered witnesses to give testimony about devotion to the holy man. The records of this process fill two volumes, divided into two parts, the second of which focused on testimony from Sicily. The first volume, however, consists almost exclusively of testimony about the Iberian world. Eight witnesses – almost all friars – reported on the spread of Benedict's cult in New Spain, Lima, Brazil, Portugal, and Spain.

In questioning the witnesses, representatives of the Congregation of Sacred Rites expressed curiosity and confusion over the reach of devotion to Benedict. Following the reforms of beatification and canonization from the late sixteenth to the mid-seventeenth centuries, no widespread public cult was permitted until the holy person's beatification. In fact, in the Spanish monarchy, the Inquisition – the gatekeeper on early cultic devotion – decreed that new saints could not be beatified unless they were proved not to have a public cult. As a result, those venerating a local holy person had to be careful not to represent the individual with the visual markers of sanctity, which included halos and rays around the head and images on altars with candles.[94] Yet Benedict's cult in the Iberian world contained all such markers and more. When asked about what they called Benedict and why they were venerating

---

[93] Von Germeten, *Black Blood Brothers*, 15. See also Meznar, "Our Lady of the Rosary."

[94] For more on early modern rules about beatification and canonization, see Gotor, *I beati del papa*, 285–319; Ditchfield, "Tridentine Worship," 205–24; and Renoux, "Canonizzazione e santità femmenile," 735–6. One example of the search for "ancient" images as part of a seventeenth-century canonization effort is that of the king-saint Fernando III: Wunder, *Baroque Seville*, ch. 3; and Quiles, "En los cimientos de la iglesia sevillana."

him, the witnesses replied in much the same way – they called him a saint, insisting that his cult was public and permitted by local ecclesiastical authorities; several thought he had already been canonized.[95] The breadth of the veneration of Benedict demonstrates the unevenness with which papal requirements were applied, as well as the Congregation's ignorance about the devotional landscape of the Americas.[96]

Most of the witnesses emphasized the universality of devotion to Benedict, repeatedly insisting that people of all ranks and ethnicities venerated him. Parish priest Giuseppe Lacienego asserted that devotion to Benedict was particularly intense in the Spanish Indies, while another Franciscan friar, Nicola di Lione, claimed that altars and veneration could be found in Iberia as well as the Americas.[97] The witnesses all mentioned specific towns and cities, as well as more general regions such as Spain, Portugal, New Spain, or "the Indies." Specific cities that recurred in multiple testimonies include Mexico City, Lisbon, Rio de Janeiro, Bahia, and Lima. Other friars based in New Spain mentioned Tolucca and Puebla de los Ángeles as well as Mexico City. [Map 2.3] It is not surprising that cities listed frequently by itinerant friars were home to large enslaved and free black populations. Some witnesses, however, mentioned smaller towns – Baltasar de San Diego, for example, was a Franciscan friar from Cañete de Torres, located outside

---

[95] These testimonies are found in ASV Processus, MS 2179, ff. 256r; 366v-367r; and 614v-625r, respectively. Massimo Navares, providing testimony on New Spain, argued that in Puebla and Tolucca, devotion to Benedict was "most ancient," as well as public and constant. Navares's formulation closely followed ecclesiastical requirements for the path to official cultic recognition. One can find defenses of the proper conduct of Iberian devotees in hagiography. Antonio Vicente de Madrid, for example, argued: "Tambien pudieron fundarse en la Bula de Gregorio Decimotercio, dada en el dia treinta de Diciembre del año de mil quinientos y setenta y tres. ... En esta Bula concede su Santidad à las Iglesias de España, que de sus Santos naturales, ò Patronos de alguna Diocesi, ò Iglesia, ò que en ellas se veneran sus Cuerpos, ò notables Reliquias, aunque no estuviessen escritos en el Breviario Romano, pudiessen rezar de ellos con Oficio proprio," *El Negro más prodigioso*, 167.

[96] While some argued in the eighteenth century that Benedict's cult qualified as having existed for "time immemorial" (i.e., for more than a century), he did *not* meet the requirement that the cult could only exist privately, rather than publicly (*non cultu*). Ditchfield stresses that the rules were applied unevenly, particularly in the early seventeenth century, "Tridentine Worship," 210. Giovanna Fiume discusses Benedict's case in more detail: "Il processo 'de cultu'," 231–52.

[97] The records were preserved in Italian; as a result, the names of witnesses were rendered in Italian, rather than their Spanish originals. ASV, Processus, MS 2179, f. 252r; 113v. Antonio Attayde used similar language to Fernández Zagudo when described the universal devotion to Benedict in Lisbon: "origine da persone nobili, letterate, discrete prudenti e d'ogni grado tanto in Sicilia, quanto in Lisbona" (502r.) See also ASV, Processus, MS 2179, Baltasar de San Diego, 322r-332r: "e uenerato publicamente da quei popoli di qui luoghi ... . Non solo da christiani etiopi neri, mà anche da christiani bianchi" (322r).

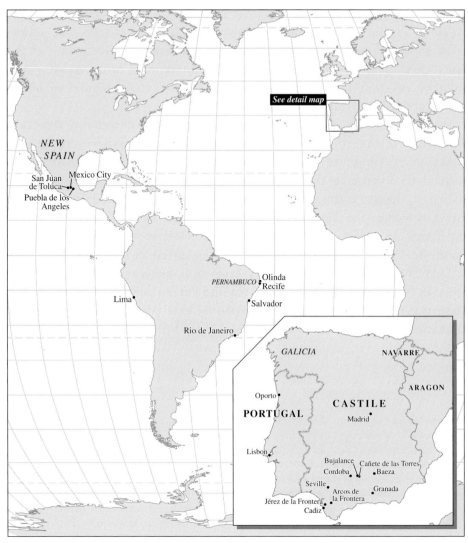

Map 2.3 Cities mentioned in beatification testimony for Benedict of Palermo

Cordoba; he testified to devotion to Benedict in his hometown, which suggests that he witnessed veneration to Benedict in his youth.[98]

In spite of assertions of universal acclaim, witnesses invariably reported at length the "particular" love shown the saint by black and *mulato* Catholics. Jesuit Antonio Maria Bonuccio reported several altars in Recife dedicated to Benedict that were housed in churches for free blacks, and said that he witnessed a procession by the brothers of the Confraternity of San Benedict, whom he

[98] ASV, Processus, MS 2179, f. 359r.

described as "black Christians."[99] Fernández Zagudo noted that the confraternity carrying Benedict's image during processions was "black and *mulato*."[100] Baltasar de San Diego and Lanciego noted devotion to the holy man in Spanish cities – specifically, Cadiz and Jerez de la Frontera, "especially in which places there are blacks."[101] Di Lione mentioned a black confraternity in Lima, where they celebrated a mass in the Franciscan church at the altar of Blessed Benedict, which also included an image of the saint. He noted that there were in fact two images of Benedict in the Franciscan church there – the sculpture on the confraternity's altar, and a painting on another altar also dedicated to the holy man.[102] Almost all of the witnesses, in fact, made explicit connections between black confraternities and devotion to Benedict. The persistent singling out of black devotion to Benedict underscored the saint's special significance to a group of Christians considered by those witnesses to be vulnerable, or in particular need of devotional support.

Because Benedict was being venerated as a saint, the members of the Congregation discussed the suppression of his cult and asked witnesses about this possibility. Members of the Congregation persisted in asking a series of questions aimed at uncovering the breadth of Benedict's public cult – how he was represented, if his images stood on altars, whether or not there were candles burning or masses said on the altars. At stake appeared to be the Congregation's agitation over the potential widespread misuse of Benedict's cult in the Iberian world and their uncertainty about whether it should be suppressed. Benedict had been venerated not just as a *beato*, but as a saint; he was called such, had masses celebrated with lit candles at his altars, processed through the streets, and had images in churches throughout the Iberian world. Responses given by Alessio Solitudine, Fernández Zagudo, and Francisco de Santa Elena describing the importance of Benedict's cult to the spiritual well-being of black Christians sometimes read as panicked fear of its suppression.

Alessio Solitudine's and Fernández Zagudo's testimonies in particular reflected considerable concern for the effects that suppression of Benedict's cult might have on Afro-Iberian communities.[103] Fernández Zagudo, a Franciscan posted in

---

[99] ASV, Processus, MS 2179, 402v-417r. He also mentioned a small church erected by the "slaves of the Jesuit fathers," f. 403v.

[100] ASV, Processus, MS 2179, Fernández Zagudo, 216v.

[101] "Specialmente in quei lochi doue sono li mori." Some of the witnesses use the term "mori/Moor" to describe African-descended people, although Lanciego specified, after mentioning the "*mori*," that they were called "black" in Spanish, suggesting that the use of the term *mori* might have resulted from the translated into Italian. ASV, Processus, MS 2179, 357r, 633r.

[102] ASV, Processus, MS 2179, Nicola di Lione, 120v-122r.

[103] Giovanna Fiume also discusses this aspect of Benedict's beatification process in *Saints and Their Cults*, 16–21.

Puebla, declared that seeing the sculpture of Benedict wearing the Franciscan habit gave hope to black Christians that they too one day might make a formal religious profession and don a habit on their deathbeds. Solitudine noted a similar effect on Afro-Iberians when they saw that someone like them could become a saint.[104] He reminded his listeners that Afro-Iberians, whom he referred to as Ethiopians, were heirs to ancient Christianity and as such they deserved particular consideration. Early in his testimony, he defined Benedict as Ethiopian, arguing that one of the three magi had been Ethiopian, "and Saint Benedict of Palermo was a religious Ethiopian, and also a black saint."[105] He continued throughout to refer to Afro-Iberians as "Ethiopians," each iteration an audible cue to his listeners that Benedict was an Ethiopian saint for Ethiopians in America, co-heirs to salvation from Christ's first days on earth, and equally worthy of sanctity and veneration of a saint of their own.

Solitudine, Fernández Zagudo, and Francisco de Santa Elena informed the Congregation of the scandal and disorder that would result from any effort to suppress Benedict's cult. Solitudine pointed out that Afro-Iberians would never believe it possible that they too could become saints if the cult were suppressed, implying that taking away this belief would seriously undermine their spiritual practices and efforts. He warned that it would further weaken not only Christian piety, but faith in God altogether, presumably unraveling the Church's centuries of missionary efforts among Africans and African-descended people.[106] Francisco de Santa Elena agreed that cultic prohibition would result in "a most grave scandal."[107] Another Franciscan witness replied at great length to the question regarding the prohibition of Benedict's cult. He cleverly pointed out that the removal of a public cult to a saint would fuel the fire of "calumny" against the Church by those in Holland and England who denied the cult of the saints and the infallibility of the pope.[108] The question of the Dutch and English was particularly pressing, as both nations maintained significant presences in the Circum-Caribbean and Brazil. Their heresy, therefore, had the potential in infect Afro-Iberians.[109]

---

[104] ASV, Processus, MS 2179, 262r, and 300r and 311r, respectively. Solitudine added that many blacks named their children after Benedict. The use of the term "Ethiopian" by Solitudine and Fernández Zagudo here is striking – they are the only two to use it consistently (although it appears a handful of times in other testimony). The word "Ethiopian" conferred dignity to black communities, connecting them to a nation, a specific group identity, rather than lumping them together indiscriminately by skin color.

[105] ASV, Processus, MS. 2179, f. 193r.   [106] ASV, Processus, MS. 2179, f. 311v-312r.

[107] ASV, Processus, MS. 2179, f. 332v. This phrase – "most grave scandal" – was repeated by another witness in the Articuli of the volume, f. 270r.

[108] ASV, Processus, MS. 2179, f. 272v.

[109] Protecting enslaved Africans from heresy is discussed in Meznar, "Our Lady of the Rosary."

The same witness added that should the cult of "one of their nation" be removed, the doubt created "would create such confusion that their belief could collapse, and they could fall into indifference over the Divine goodness, and ... if the cult were removed it would ruin inducement and erode so many exercises of Christian piety, on which this cult is founded."[110] He proclaimed that the example of Benedict's holiness had a profound impact on black Christian devotion because it inspired them to their own spiritual practices and desire for living a holy life. The hope of the possibility of achieving sanctity was considered crucial to the spiritual good of Afro-Catholics. The friar furthermore cited two holy people of color whose processes were currently underway in Rome – one *mulato* and one indigenous: Martín de Porres and Nicolás de Dios Ayllón (d. 1677) – declaring that their aspirations to religious life had been inspired by Benedict.[111]

Most importantly, at the end of his response to the question, Fernández Zagudo declared that Benedict's cult inspired slave owners to treat their slaves with greater kindness and "humanity" (*humanità*) and enslaved people to live with greater patience in their suffering and terrible situation, following Benedict's example, and reassured by it that they too could attain Paradise.[112] Here Fernández Zagudo specifically addressed the colonial context of Benedict's cult, connecting it not only to the need to inspire devotion in the relatively new members of the Catholic Church (Ethiopians) but the saint's role in maintaining colonial order. Masters would become kinder, slaves more willing to endure suffering. Echoing the rhetoric of Alonso de Sandoval from a century before, Fernández Zagudo's words open a window to the advantages that many clergy saw for black saints to maintain the status quo vis-à-vis slavery – the celebration of the holiness of black saints, and its attendant public participation in black confraternities, would help to sustain colonial order through modeling humility and patience.

The story of baptism and catechesis, black confraternities and black saints, cannot be told simply in terms of black empowerment or ecclesiastic oppression – both are crucial aspects of this multi-faceted narrative. Clergy such as Fernández Zagudo could easily see Benedict's cult as a way of maintaining social tranquility, which he viewed as the desired result of providing spiritual hope to enslaved and free people of color. Yet they also explained that devotion by black communities were essential to Benedict's cult, and predicted dire consequences should the cult be shut down. And, surprisingly considering the early eighteenth-century Church's position on the celebration of unofficial holy people, the Congregation of the

---

[110] ASV, Processus, MS. 2179, f. 271v.

[111] ASV, Processus, MS. 2179, f. 272v, 279r. Nicolás de Dios Ayllón (d. 1677) was a *limeño* son of a Chiclayo cacique. On Ayllón, see Espinoza Rúa, "Un indio camino," 135–80.

[112] ASV, Processus, MS. 2179, f. 279v.

Sacred Rites ultimately decided that their only choice, given how widespread and deeply entrenched Benedict's cult was, would be to provide him the official status. A few decades later, the process was complete, and Benedict was beatified. The Church had been forced into a corner by the prolific spread of the Franciscan holy man's cult, which had been propelled energetically by black and *mulato* confraternities throughout the Iberian world. While the accounts themselves are one-sided, as they articulate only white, clerical perspectives (with the exception of Paulino de Velasco), they do illuminate the breadth of his cult and the role of black confraternities in its dissemination. The presence of images of black saints in confraternity chapels tells a similar story.

Confraternal Images

Avocations shaped confraternities beyond lending them a name. An image of the patron saint stood on the brotherhoods' altar, usually a statue or, more rarely, a painting. The main devotional image would not only be placed in the center of an altar, it would shape the brotherhood's participation in public ritual; special masses and processions would be performed on the associated feast day, and the image would often be taken out for major festivals. [Fig. 2.4] While most confraternities were organized around cults to the Virgin Mary or Christ, some brotherhoods adopted other patrons, including those of black saints. In a few cases, brotherhoods employed a black saint as sole patron, but more commonly they added the patronage of a black saint to the original avocation. For example, one of the black confraternities in Cádiz was Nuestra Señora de la Salud y San Benito y Santa Efigenia (Our Lady of Good Health and St. Benedict and St. Efigenia), and Jaén housed the Cofradía de Nuestra Señora de los Reyes y San Benito de Palermo (Brotherhood of Our Lady of the Kings and St. Benedict of Palermo). In these two cases, the confraternities established in the sixteenth or early seventeenth centuries added an avocation of a black saint once the cults of black saints began to spread later in the seventeenth century. While black confraternities predated devotion to black saints, then, they adopted the new cults quickly.

Due to the types of surviving documentation, we do not know what members of the black confraternities thought or felt about the images on their altars. Their choices reflected preferences that largely mirrored dominant devotional trends in early modern Catholicism. The clergy believed that exposing baptized Africans to black saints would help draw them into the Christian fold. Such reasoning, however, reflected early modern European ideas about blackness, whiteness, and holiness. Few documents suggest what black Christians thought or saw when they looked at an image of a black saint. In a few instances, however, individuals referred to shared skin color as a reason for devotion. For example,

Figure 2.4 Main altar, Iglesia de San Juan, eighteenth century, Écija, Spain.

Paulino de Velasco, a witness in the early eighteenth-century beatification processes for Benedict, proclaimed his veneration of an image of Benedict in the Franciscan church in Lima, explaining that he felt drawn to it because "he was black like me." Other references come from confraternity records, where the brothers mentioned that they had chosen Benedict as a patron or object of devotion because they were "of the same color."[113] Moreover, black saints in confraternal devotions remained solely the provenance of black Catholics. The presence of images of black saints is a lasting legacy of their importance for the devotions of black confraternities and, in turn, for the brotherhoods' role in circulating the cults of black saints.

In spite of the significance of images for the devotional practice of confraternities, art historians have paid little attention to the art of confraternal altars.[114] But such focus is particularly significant for the history of black saints as close evaluation of surviving confraternity chapels in Iberia reveals the ways black saints could penetrate into confraternal devotions beyond named avocations.[115] In Brazil, for example, the 1733 festival of the Triumph of the Eucharist featured the black Rosary members carrying images not only of their titular Rosary Virgin, but also Antonio da Catagerona (a.k.a. Antonio da Noto) and St. Benedict.[116] Many cases follow a similar pattern: A confraternity had one main patron saint, reflected in its name, but it also maintained devotion to black saints on altars and in processions. If we used only avocation patterns as evidence for devotion to black saints among black confraternities, then, we would have diminished understanding of the reach of black saints. Rather, the deep ties between black brotherhoods and black saints are demonstrated in archival records (however spare) and the enduring presence of sacred art in confraternity altars.

There are dozens, if not hundreds, of images of black saints in the Iberian world dating from the seventeenth and eighteenth centuries that had once stood on confraternity altars or chapels, such as the altar of Nuestra Señora de Salud in the Iglesia de Nuestra Señora del Rosario in Cadiz. [**Plate 8**] This altar is structured in a typical fashion for a confraternal altar: the patronal image, usually of the Virgin Mary, standing in the center, bordered by ancillary saints. The titular Marian image is flanked by two polychrome sculptures of Benedict (left) and Efigenia (right). Although the sculptures of Efigenia and Benedict date to the mid-eighteenth century, the confraternity records show evidence of earlier

---

[113] ASV, Processus, MS. 2179, 71r.; *Ordenanzas de la Cofradía de San Benito de Palermo*, AHN, lib. 5224: the brothers claim "que sean Christianos, *del color del Santo*" [emphasis mine]. I thank Jesús Tellez Rubio of the CSIC for providing me with the latter reference. John Thornton points out Beatriz Kimpa Vita's complaint that the Church did not have any black saints: *The Kongolese Saint Anthony*, 113.

[114] Wisch, "Incorporating Images," 243–63.

[115] Nicole von Germeten's table of black confraternities in New Spain reveals that most were dedicated to the Virgin and to Christ, followed overwhelmingly by Nicolas de Tolentino (d. 1305), an Italian Augustinian friar: *Black Blood Brothers*, appendix.

[116] Kiddy discusses the lateral altars of the Rosary confraternity church that held images of Benedict and Efigenia: *Blacks of the Rosary*, 85–8. The black Rosary confraternities, as Kiddy mentions here, were unlikely to add another avocation, although they venerated images of Benedict of Palermo quite frequently.

images of the saints.[117] These are large, impressive works, decorated with lavish gold work, both on the front and back, and larger in size than the patronal image in the center, unusual proportions for such an altar, where the flanking saints are almost always smaller than the central image. The images have been recently restored and re-polychromed, enhancing the contrast between the intricate floral designs in gold leaf and the deep matte black of the *encarnaciones* (the flesh tone pigment). The altarpiece itself is nineteenth-century marble, so it is difficult to know what the eighteenth-century structure might have looked like, and how exactly the original images might have been placed in relationship to one another.[118]

The most well-known black confraternal art can be found in Brazil, where the cities and landscapes are dotted with breathtaking baroque churches constructed by black confraternities and dedicated to black saints. [Fig. 2.5] All surviving chapels are crucial for studying African diasporic lives and practices; they permit scholars access to the spaces inhabited (and in some cases, designed) by Africans themselves. Even in the absence of the original confraternal altar, we are often left textual descriptions as in hagiographies and sacred histories. Apolinário da Conceição, for example, described the confraternal chapel at the Igreja de Santa Ana in Lisbon, where the confraternity housed their main image of Benedict (presumably a sculpture). Benedict appeared there with a great silver diadem, robes decorated with flowers, holding a cross in his right hand and a cleaning rag (*esfragão*) in his left. Apolinário added that Mexico City's Hospital de Jesús Nazareno contained a black confraternity altar with statues of Efigenia and Benedict.[119] Pietro Tognoletto later reported the same information, adding that, in 1632, two Spanish Calced Carmelites made their way to Palermo to venerate Benedict's relics, where they told the Sicilian brothers about the veneration of Benedict in Puebla, where an image of the saint provoked "intense devotion." This fleeting encounter between *palermitano* Franciscans and Spanish Carmelites indicates the transnational networks of communication that could spread knowledge of cultic devotion across geographies and religious orders.[120]

---

[117] It is unclear when the image of Benedict was commissioned. In 1702, while engaged in a lawsuit against one of the church's priests, the leaders of the confraternity refer to their patrons and images as those of the Salud Virgin and St. Benedict, with no reference to Efigenia. By 1734, however, they began to refer to themselves as "Nuestra Señora de la Salud, y Santa Efigenia y San Benedicto": Archivo Diocesano de Cadiz (hereafter ADC), Leg. 520–1.

[118] Sancho de Sopranis included a black-and-white photograph of the Cadiz altarpiece from 1931 that shows the Salud Virgin flanked by two oval-shaped oil paintings of what appear to be Efiginia and Elesban; it is not clear what happened to these images, and the reproduction is so poor it is impossible to see the details clearly: *Las cofradías de morenos a Cádiz: Ensayo histórico* (Cadiz, 1940), n.p.

[119] Apolinário, *Flor perigrina*, 263–4. The Church of Santa Ana was destroyed in the eighteenth century; as a result, this description is all that survives of the image.

[120] Tognoletto, *Paradiso serafico*, 321.

Figure 2.5 Interior of the Igreja de Nossa Senhora do Rosário dos Pretos, Tiradentes (Minas Gerais), Brazil. Sculptures of Sts. Antonio and Benedict can be found in the left and right niches, respectively.

While most surviving confraternal chapels in Iberia displayed one or two black saints, two rare examples from Portugal contain all four: the Capela da Antiga Confraria de Nossa Senhora do Rosário dos Pretos (Chapel of the Ancient Confraternity of Our Lady of the Rosary of the Blacks) in Lisbon's Igreja da Graça; and a chapel for a confraternity with the same name in Braga's cathedral. In the Igreja da Graça, the Rosary Virgin is flanked by all four black saints at her feet, two on each side, with parallel pairs corresponding to the shared orders – that is, the Carmelite saints Elesban and Efigenia are on the top row, with the Franciscan saints Antonio da Noto and Benedict of Palermo on the bottom.

[Plate 9] Each order is recognizable by its signature habits – Elesban and Efigenia in the brown with cream cloak and wimple of the Carmelites, and Benedict and Antonio in the simple brown habit of a Franciscan with its knotted belt. Unlike Cadiz, where the black saints are larger than the titular Virgin, here we see the black saints clustered at the Virgin's feet in a smaller size, though crafted with great detail and decoration.[121]

The chapel off the central courtyard in the Cathedral of Braga bears some similarities to the Graça altarpiece. [Plate 10] In this example, the Rosary Virgin is again flanked by all four black saints at her feet, neatly labeled, and organized by religious order – with the Carmelite saints on the inside, one on each side of the Virgin, and the Franciscans on the outside. But here the four saints are not stacked but instead form a straight line, and the figures themselves are rather crude – the facial features sculpted without the detail and nuance one finds in the striking Graça images. Organizing multiple saints on the same level as each other while flanking a central image of the Virgin is an unusual presentation for a baroque altar; as we have seen, altarpieces with multiple saints around a central sculpture display the saints arranged vertically, one on each side of the image in their own niche, with the other two (or four) arranged above. It is possible that it was less expensive to line up the saints at the Virgin's feet more informally because such a structure did not require a large and elaborate altarpiece. Yet the presentation also creates an unusual method for portraying the intercessory power of the Virgin and the black saints as her supplicants, mirroring the roles that the brothers and sisters played in relationship to the titular image, and collapsing the space between devotee and saint.

Other images once in the custody of black confraternities have been removed in the intervening years. The modification of altarpieces and dispersal of their images makes contextualizing sculptures of black saints in the history of black confraternities more challenging. In the Franciscan church in Oporto, one can find a late seventeenth-century image of Benedict of Palermo on a base attached to the pillar to the left of the main altar, freestanding rather than integrated into an altarpiece. [Plate 11] In eastern Alentejo, an image of Benedict of Palermo stands on the collateral altarpiece of St. Anthony of Padua in the local Franciscan church. [Plate 12] In both places, scholars have established the presence of black confraternities in the churches in question, and one can hypothesize that the images might have been part of the original confraternal altars, as images were often moved around churches in subsequent centuries.[122]

---

[121] Os negros em Portugal, 136. The original Igreja da Graça likewise did not survive the devastation of 1755; the present buildings and altars were rebuilt.

[122] Reginaldo mentions that the Confraternity of Our Lady of the Rosary and St. Benedict had been housed in Oporto's Franciscan church, where an image of St. Benedict remains: "'África em Portugal,'" 296–8.

Figure 2.6 Symbol of the Rosary confraternities (black Rosary confraternity in the center, with white Rosary symbols on left and right), Igreja de São Domingo, Elvas, Portugal.

Another town in eastern Alentejo that housed a black Rosary confraternity demonstrates how the black confraternal images could be moved and decontexualized. In one Dominican church, a sculpture of St. Benedict stands in the church's small museum [**Plate 13**]. The sculpture's original location had been in an altarpiece in the small chapel immediately to the right of the main altar, which had once belonged to the Rosary confraternity. The black confraternity in this town must have been large and important, as it maintained its own meeting room attached to the main nave, marked by the sign of the confraternity.[123] [Fig. 2.6, Fig. 2.7] The church also hosted another Rosary confraternity, this one dedicated solely to white members, whose sign is located next to the black confraternity's. It is difficult to know, then, if both shared the altar, or if the black confraternity had been awarded sole use of this prominently placed chapel. In any event, in the original wood altarpiece, St. Benedict had stood on the right lateral next to a central image of the Rosary Virgin. As part of renovations of the church in the early twentieth century, the wood altarpiece was dismantled and replaced with a marble one, which stands today. While the original Rosary Virgin can still be

---

[123] In addition, I viewed the table used for the black confraternity's meeting, their processional images, the jewelry, and silver objects for devotional use (chalice, thurible, etc.).

Figure 2.7 *Our Lady of the Rosary*, polychrome sculpture with silver, property of the Nossa Senhora do Rosário confraternity, Igreja de São Domingo, Elvas, Portugal.

found at the center of the new altarpiece, St. Benedict was removed and eventually placed in the museum.[124]

The wealthiest confraternities built free-standing chapels separate from the dependence of a host church, though few black confraternities in the Iberian Peninsula had such financial resources at their disposal. One of the few exceptions was Nuestra Señora de los Ángeles in Seville. The confraternity still exists today, one of the city's oldest and most important, the brothers still maintaining its original chapel. While the confraternity today is all white, it retains its historical nickname "los negritos" and houses images that reflect its history, including nineteenth-century frescos of black angels, as well as a baroque sculpture of Benedict of Palermo. The silver float for carrying the titular Virgin in the festival is further decorated with small images of Benedict, Martín, Efigenia, and

[124] On my visit to the church, I was able to see a deteriorated black and white photo from the early twentieth-century of the original altarpiece, showing the Rosary Virgin with Benedict to her left.

Elesban. Isidoro Moreno's history of the confraternity's inventories establishes that it had commissioned the sculpture of Benedict of Palermo by the mid-seventeenth century and, by the eighteenth century, it procured two oil paintings of Sts. Elesban and Efigenia, which unfortunately disappeared in the twentieth century.[125]

Examples of surviving confraternal altars offer important insights: while some surviving altars are still known by their original ownership (as in Cadiz), others stand in churches estranged from their original connection to black confraternities, even in cases where we know black confraternities had once worshipped. Still other images have been separated not only from the altar in question, but from the church itself, as in the case of San Pedro de Arenas in Spain. Such displacements can challenge our ability to connect black saints and confraternal devotions. In some cases, however, it is possible to infer the provenance of the image based on the correlations between known confraternities and extant sculptures of black saints. The complexity of recreating black confraternal altars merits further research. At the same time, the surviving evidence substantiates the vital role that black confraternities played in the dissemination of black saints.

The expansion of black confraternities across the Iberian Atlantic occurred rapidly in tandem with the slave trade. Initially organized and encouraged by the clergy, baptized Africans soon organized brotherhoods, chose patron saints, purchased images for their altars, and went on procession. The geographic sweep of black confraternities illustrates their popularity and influence on small- and large-scale Catholic culture. We have less information about the relationship among confraternities, but the example of Cristóbal de Porras traveling throughout Andalusia with permission to establish black confraternities dedicated to St. Benedict provides a window into how such foundations could occur. By founding black confraternities and promoting the cults of black saints, Afro-Iberians centered themselves in Iberian civic life and, in the process, of global Catholicism.

[125] Moreno, *La antigua hermandad*, 120–1.

3 "BLACK LIKE ME": COMMUNITY FORMATION AND WHITE BACKLASH

Black confraternities were organized the same ways as white ones in terms of institutional structure, patron saints, and participation in ritual life. Yet, their very existence had radical potential in the context of colonial norms and oppressive power structures. The simple act of participating publicly in feast days, which involved processing in the streets, carrying sacred images, music, and dance, reflected more than acquiescence to the strictures of the Catholic Church. It was an assertion of inclusion in a society whose civic and political life was structured around the liturgical calendar. Firmly grounded in Catholic practice, black confraternities could become wealthy through alms collecting and dues, property owners, participants in civil lawsuits, and emancipators of fellow members. People of color organized their own brotherhoods in ways that were the most meaningful to them, in avocation, composition of membership, and specific membership require-ments. Moreover, in addition to public acts of civic engagement, black confraternities provided private spaces for African and African-descended people to engage in rituals in ways that were the most meaningful to them.

When challenged legally, people of color invariably appealed to their status as baptized Christians as justification for their full participation in Catholic imperial life, and the collective organization provided by confraternities added institu-tional heft behind individual claims. The power of confraternities more generally permitted some Catholics of color to act as representatives for entire groups of black and *mulatos*, a leadership role not often accorded to people of color, especially in the Americas. In some ways, we can measure the successes of black confraternities by the amount of hostility they generated on the part of white Catholics, who were often determined to silence or sideline black brother-hoods. Fights could break out between blacks and whites over procession pre-cedent, membership in brotherhoods, or the rights to certain images in ways that reveal the vibrant participation of black Catholics in Iberian civic life. It also demonstrates how threatened white Catholics felt by the civic and theological claims of black confraternities.

Afro-Catholicism

In order to discuss the rhetoric of shared baptism by Afro-Iberians, it is important to unpack the complex ways African diasporic people engaged with and transformed Christianity. The entanglement of the slave trade with coerced baptism has led to much scholarship on the extent to which Africans and their descendants were stripped of their cultural and religious traditions and forced into conformity with Catholicism. Such scholarship has approached the topic from many different perspectives; some scholars have contended that, while compulsory baptism was imposed on African slaves, the clergy itself was largely negligent and indifferent to their religious education. As a result, little effort was put into the process of catechesis (as we have seen) and in turn Christianity was accepted "superficially" by African and indigenous people.[1] Others have argued that Catholicism itself acted as a tie back to Africa for slaves brought to the Americas, particularly during the eighteenth century, as many Central Africans would have been exposed to Catholic ritual and practice from at least the seventeenth century, and might even have been born Christians themselves.[2] When considering individuals who were forcibly converted, some scholars have emphasized the survivals of African culture in the Americas that persisted hidden inside Christianity frameworks in the Americas.[3]

The question of conversion itself – what does it mean to be "converted"? What is the difference between genuine and superficial adoption of a new religion? – lies at the center of these different avenues for thinking through African participation in Christianity, particularly in Europe and the Americas. Natalie Rothman describes conversion as "a set of interlinked social practices employed in the project of subject making and the perpetuation of imperial power relations."[4] In other words, imperial authority was constituted through forced conformity to a number of European cultural norms, including language, dress, and

---

[1] *La devoção negra*, 28–9.

[2] Heywood, "The Angolan-Afro-Brazilian Cultural Connections"; Bastide, *African Religions of Brazil*, 109–42; Thornton, "Afro-Christian Syncretism"; and Thornton, "The Development of an African Catholic Church." Kongolese Christianity developed independently of colonialism, and preserved greater autonomy from European oversight.

[3] Thornton, "The Development of an African Catholic Church"; Frey, "The Visible Church"; Lovejoy, "African Diaspora"; and Sweet; *Recreating Africa*. Thornton and Sweet engaged in a debate over "syncretic" vs. "parallel" systems of belief among Afrocreoles.

[4] Rothman, "Becoming Venetian," 40.

comportment. Because of the role that Catholicism played in Iberian empires, all such norms were filtered through religion. Religious conversion and subject making became entangled in the imperial framework, which needs to be understood as a category distinct from mission fields in spaces outside coercion, such as Tokugawa Japan. Those who were the victims of forced conversion could face intense scrutiny and oversight by imperial-ecclesiastical forces intent on maintaining social order.

As a result of the entanglement of conversion with empire, many scholarly debates about African Christianity revolve around the central question of belief, practice, sincerity, and authenticity.[5] Yet such approaches have the potential to replicate problematic conceptualizations of how faith operated in the premodern Christian world. The terms "religious" and "conversion" had multiple meanings in the early modern period, some of which do not align with modern definitions. For example, "religious" was most often a noun, not an adjective, referring to a person who followed a rule, like a monk or a friar. "Conversion," for its part, was most often employed in the context of a Christian person who turned his or her back on secular life to embrace a religious one. We must therefore employ some caution when applying terms whose modern meanings do not invariably correlate to the premodern. The concept of religious itself and what it means to proclaim membership in a particular religious sect is one crucial example of modern notions not aligning with earlier eras. The Catholic laity existed in a nebulous world below the religious and clerical; they attended mass infrequently in a language they could not understand, took communion once a year at Easter, and possibly knew one or two rote prayers. As the early modern period progressed, more emphasis was placed on lay religious education by Catholic clergy, but such oversight did little to create homogeneous thought and practice.

One of the most well-known critics of the scholarly overemphasis on the framework of belief is Talal Asad, who maintains that the premodern concept was distinct from the present day. He argues that premodern religious practices were "embedded in distinctive social and political relationships and articulated distinctive sensibilities. They were first of all lived and only occasionally theorized."[6] Opening up a space between the theoretical and lived aspects of Christian practice allows us to see the frequency with which the two did not align in the premodern era. It is important to question to what extent an individual had to understand or agree with official precepts in order for religious practice to hold spiritual and cultural meaning. Sociologists often point out the frequency with

[5] Federico Palomo has recently counseled against employing a binary of "acceptance vs resistance" when examining the early modern Spanish world: "Un catolicismo en plural."

[6] Asad, "Thinking about Religion," 47. The question of what a Catholic ought to "believe" in order to achieve salvation remains a subject of debate: Lombardi, *Salvation of the Unbeliever.*

which lived religion fails to maintain doctrinal or intellectual coherence.[7] What does it mean to interrogate someone's "beliefs" in an era when time itself was calculated by the Church, both by the calendar and the daily bells that told the canonical hours throughout towns and villages? Early modern Christians lived their religion, even when they did not understand its theology.

Any discussion of African diasporic practices ought to be placed within a larger framework that acknowledges the diverse and lived nature of early modern global Catholicism. We should resist the temptation to posit the existence of two mutually exclusive experiences of religion: on the one hand, stable, normative Christianity practiced by Europeans, and on the other, superficial or hybrid Christianity practiced by non-Europeans. The Catholic Reformation marked a period when the Church endeavored to inculcate the laity with correct doctrine, and the Inquisition took root in many Catholic spaces to oversee orthodoxy and punish heterodox behaviors ranging from apostasy to blasphemy. Using inquisitorial records as source material provides an important perspective on early modern religious culture, but they sometimes give the impression of rapid and ruthless response to deviation from orthodoxy, when they can also be employed as a window into the diversity of beliefs circulating.[8] While the Inquisition did try to stamp out practices it considered superstitious or heretical, it hardly had the power to eradicate them all – indeed, it had limited knowledge of everyday practices, and sometimes simply did not care.[9]

In fact, early modern people – white and non-white – on both sides of the Atlantic frequently engaged in practices condemned by the Inquisition. The most popular of such practices was witchcraft, particularly healing and love magic. In Iberian America, the marketplace of magic often acted as a zone that brought together people of all castes, as appealing to whites as to people of color.[10] The difference between appealing to a witch or a saint was much less than we sometimes assume – in both cases, the supplicant's goal was to achieve supernatural aid for their worldly problem. The same individual might chose to try both witch

---

[7] Sociologist Meredith McGuire comments, "when we consider all these aspects of individual religiosity and spirituality, we discover that they rarely resemble the tidy, consistent, and theologically correct packages official religions promote"; she further remarks on the "diverse and complex, eclectic, and malleable" religious forms of the early modern period: *Lived Religion*, 17.

[8] For one example of the latter approach, see Stuart Schwartz, *All Can Be Saved*.

[9] One example of a "folkloric" survival is the Toro Jubilo festival in the Castilian town of Medinaceli, in which a bull's horns are set on fire until he dies; the bull is then butchered and meat consumed by the community. Of pre-Christian origin, the festival was eventually Christianized as a celebration of the arrival of the relics of five martyrs: https://guiadesoria.es/agenda-cultural/fiestas-y-tradiciones/fiestas-de-interes-turistico/1624-el-toro-jubilo-de-medinaceli.html. The event is celebrated to the present time.

[10] Lewis, *Hall of Mirrors*; Von Germeten, *Violent Delights*, ch. 2; Sweet, *Domingo Alvares*; and Restall, *The Black Middle*, ch. 7.

and saint, perceiving few distinctions or contradictions in such movement between marketplaces.

A significant part of the power of the Catholic Church throughout its history derived from its plasticity, both in its willingness to incorporate non-Christian ideas or concepts and, even more importantly, its acceptance of an array of local traditions (once incorporated into a nominally Christian framework).[11] Christianity was embryonic when it first began to absorb Greek and then Latin linguistic and cultural influences.[12] The process of transformation continued throughout the history of the Church both in terms of doctrine and ritual. While core beliefs have remained relatively stable in the Latin Church following the Council of Nicaea, practice and theology were never static, which adds to problematic efforts to generalize about an "authentic" Catholic belief or practice.[13] From Bill Christian's work on Spanish peasants to Alexandra Walsham's study of sacred springs to David Luebke's work on plural faith communities in Germany, the defining feature of Christianity in the early modern period was its many permutations.[14] The focus on "how genuine" or "authentic" the beliefs of non-European Christians were misses how seldom the European laity reflected the orthodox theology of the hierarchical Church.

Moreover, normative Christianity – that is, what the Church considered licit – could encompass practices outside strict orthodoxy. The cult of the saints existed throughout the premodern world as the zone where illicit beliefs (often termed "superstitious" by the Church) most often collided with normative Christianity. The widespread practices that surrounded the saints' veneration proliferated with abuses that brought down the derision of Protestant Reformers and critics such as Erasmus.[15] While the Church viewed many such practices as superstitious, those participating in them did not. Catholic saints acted as bridges between the living and the dead, receiving prayers and gifts in return for favors. Many individuals or communities abandoned saints who stopped performing beneficial miracles in favor of a new one who might be more amenable to their

---

[11] Rubiés, "The Concept of Cultural Dialogue"; and Pardo, *The Origins of Mexican Catholicism*.

[12] Peter Brown's seminal work demonstrated that the veneration of saints resulted from Roman burial practices: *The Cult of the Saints*.

[13] On the problem of the idea of cultural authenticity in the context of the African diaspora, see Scott, *Refashioning Futures*, 106–27. He argues, "authenticity still lingers in the idea of a cultural tradition understood as an identifiable and representable ensemble of essential – if now heterogeneous – elements" (122). The same could be said for premodern Christianity.

[14] Christian, *Local Religion*; Walsham, *The Reformation of the Landscape*; and Luebke, *Hometown Religion*.

[15] Erasmus, *The Praise of Folly*; Waldron, *Reformations of the Body*, ch. 1. For a few examples of local religion, see Schmitt, *The Holy Greyhound*; Christian, *Local Religion*; and Ginzburg, *The Night Battles*.

requests. Furthermore, the saints were not always benign or helpful; they could be angered and exact retribution from the living. While many beliefs about "bargaining" with saints – or even praying directly to them for favors – were not orthodox in Catholic theology, they dominated the devotional culture.[16] The line between European veneration of a saint and what was deemed idol worship by the Church was much more porous than the Church admitted.

The cult of the saints took on new significance in the context of baptized slaves, as the promotion of saints could be influential in drawing Afro-Iberians into Catholic practice. Veneration of saints created what Cécile Fromont has referred to as a "space of correlation" between Catholic practice and West and Central African beliefs.[17] Many Central Africans understood the world as consisting of two parts – one for the living and one for the dead – that were simultaneously parallel and fluid. Sweet describes them as "a single community with social and moral obligations flowing in both directions."[18] In some cases, the whiteness of the saints might have appealed to Central Africans, who associated the color white with the world of the dead.[19] Roger Bastide has argued that Bantu slaves were mostly likely attracted to the cult of the saints because of the saints' function as intermediaries, as ancestors played similar roles in Bantu religion.[20]

Scholars have noted that African Christians evinced specific devotional interest in saints renowned for their ability to aid souls in Purgatory, such as the Virgin Mary (often described as the most important advocate for those suffering in Purgatory) and Nicholas of Tolentino.[21] Such saints were the ultimate intermediaries between the living and the dead because their appeals could pull a suffering soul out of Purgatory and into final peace in Heaven. The souls of

---

[16] Catholic doctrine specifies that the saints only pray to God on behalf of the suppliant; any subsequent miracles originated from God alone. But early modern people appealed directly to the saints, clearly believing that miracles came directly from the saint.

[17] "Spaces of correlation are cultural creations such as narratives, artworks, or performances that offer a yet unspecified domain in which their creators can bring together ideas and forms belonging to radically different realms, confront them, and eventually turn them into interrelated parts of a new system of thought and expression": Fromont, *Art of Conversion*, 1.

[18] Sweet, *Recreating Africa*, 104; and Tardieu, *L'église et les noirs*, I:624.

[19] Kiddy, *Blacks of the Rosary*, 56.

[20] Bastide, *African Religions*, 60. In some cases, there was a one-to-one correlation of Catholic saint with Yoruban orishas (emissaries of the gods), though such melding was not always deliberate. Nancy van Deusen argues that devotion to the cult of the saints was enhanced through the use of grave dirt and human relics for ritual purposes: *Souls of Purgatory*, 45. On the circulation of relics in Central Africa, see Silva Santos, "Uma política de ossos."

[21] Nancy van Deusen points out that sorceresses could also be renowned for their ability to communicate with deceased family members who wanted help in getting out of Purgatory: "Circuits of Knowledge," 140. On religious belief and practice in the Americas, see Seeman, *Death in the New World*; Roach, *Cities of the Dead*; and Vollendorf and Kostroun, *Women, Religion and the Atlantic World*.

living saints – particularly female saints – could also act as intermediaries to aid souls in Purgatory. Others, most famously Martín de Porres, could slip out of their bodies while sleeping and travel freely, a gift that correlated with Central African beliefs.[22]

The lines between West and Central African and Catholic religious traditions could be blurred in complicated ways. My intention here is not to elide or ignore crucial aspects of diverse African cultural practices in the Iberian Atlantic, which require recognition. The lived religions of Afro-Iberians were rich, complex, and multifaceted. Joan Bristol tells a story about a group of people caught by the Inquisition in Mexico City for dressing like priests and nuns (the women called themselves "Iphigenias," after the Ethiopian saint). While those involved were condemned by the Inquisition, the existence of this ritual reflected the engagement of marginalized people with ecclesiastical hierarchy – a subversion that returned power to the black participants – though these activities took place behind closed doors, hidden from the white clerical gaze.[23] Even African Catholics who considered themselves devout Christians could employ their faith as a form of resistance precisely because faith was lived. For the forcibly converted, acceptance of the social reality of baptism opened pathways to the participation in specific social and judicial avenues that would have been closed to them as nonbelievers. While the acceptance of a Christian mantle and its opportunities – however limited – required a performance of subjecthood, it also provided significant potential for various kinds of claimsmaking and subversions.[24]

Confraternities have a particularly complex history: they operated as orthodox Christian institutions embedded in European practice, while at the same time the private spaces inhabited by the brothers and sisters provided some protection from imperial and ecclesiastical authorities.[25] In addition, claims by confraternal brothers and sisters to public participation in the social life of towns and cities went hand in hand with a push for formal recognition of Afro-Iberian status. In confraternal devotions, then, the saints acted as intermediaries not only between heaven and earth, but between Afro-Iberians and colonial society. The presence of the saints assured authorities and fellow citizens of the Afro-Iberian

[22] Sweet, *Re-Creating Africa*, 104. See also Manrique, "Marabilla de la cardidad perfecta," 194–6. Manrique writes: "el Sieruo de Dios fue muchas veces trasportado e su Conuento de Lima a los Reynos de la China, y Iapon con el don de agilidad."

[23] Bristol, *Christians, Blasphemers, and Witches*, 191–3.

[24] Jason Young argues that "religion operated as a central form of resistance not only against the system of slavery but also against the very ideological underpinnings that supported slavery in the first place": *Rituals of Resistance*, 11.

[25] Local authorities sometimes prohibited black confraternities from processing, although when they appealed to Rome, the papacy almost always sided with the confraternities.

willingness to conform to colonial norms.[26] The performance of Christianity, whether from devotion or utility or both, offered opportunities for social inclusion and its attendant privileges even as it fostered group consciousness among African diasporic communities.

Creating Diasporic Communities

From their earliest forced removal to Cabo Verde and Lisbon, black Catholics participated in confraternities and public ritual life in the same ways as white laity. From Spain and Portugal to Central Africa and the Americas, they gathered in brotherhoods to process, play music, dance, speak their own languages, pray, support, and protect each other. Contemporaries frequently remarked on the music and dance performed by members of black confraternities during festivals – sometimes disapprovingly and sometimes with admiration.[27] Afro-Catholics took great care with the musical portions of their processions; Rafael Ortega points out that Nuestra Señora de los Reyes paid to hire the best singers in the area, as well as two guitar players. At the end of the procession, the members of the confraternity dressed in colorful uniforms performed a dance in front of the images to the sound of rattles, little bells, drums, and a hornpipe.[28] Elsewhere, additional rituals made black confraternities distinctive: Rosary brotherhoods in Brazil and Lisbon elected a king and queen to preside. The royal pair sometimes took the names of historically important Central African rulers, such as King Henrique and Queen Njinga, maintaining the living memory of Central Africa in the Iberian Atlantic.[29]

The preservation of culture could be enhanced in black confraternities that were divided not only by *casta* (imperially defined social and racial categories), but by ethnicity (general language and cultural groups originating from

---

[26] The cultural-preservation aspects of confraternal life also parallel some of Vinson's assertions regarding the creation of black identity: Vinson, *Bearing Arms*.

[27] See in particular Voigt, *Spectacular Wealth*, ch. 4.

[28] Ortega, "La cofradía de los negros," 5. For more on "ethnic" music (and dance) in black confraternal celebrations, see Fiume, "St. Benedict the Moor," 26–7; and Martín Casares and Barranco, "The Musical Legacy of Black Africans." Musicologist Kydalla Etheyo Young discusses the specific instruments used by limeño brotherhoods: "Colonial Music, Confraternities, and Power," 188–201.

[29] For more on the "kings and queens of Kongo" in Brazilian confraternities, see Kiddy, *Blacks of the Rosary*, 77–9; Fromont, "Dancing for the King of Congo"; Souza, "Kongo King Festivals"; and Heywood, "Angolan-Afro-Brazilian Cultural Connections," 20. Sweet discusses the Angolan and Mina "kings" of eighteenth-century Lisbon: "The Hidden Histories of African Lisbon," 243–6. Dewulf traces the spread of the ritual to Protestant zones of the Caribbean and North America: "Black Brotherhoods in North America."

geographic zones in Africa), a trend that proliferated in places with large populations of Africans and Afrocreoles.[30] Enslaved people were brought to Europe and
the Americas from regional zones that varied over time; while such zones
reflected a large diversity of ethnicities, enslaved people often maintained as
close ties as possible to each other – privileging first specific ethnic groups, and
members of shared regions.[31] Such tendencies can be seen reflected in patterns of
marriage and larger social ties such as godparentage, in addition the organization
of brotherhoods.[32] Elizabeth Kiddy remarks that brotherhoods created and
maintained a sense of community among black residents, "an identity formed
by the annual reaffirmation of a shared, remembered history as descendants of
Africans and devotees of Our Lady of Rosary."[33] The maintenance of
a corporate identity, even as it evolved over time, was a crucial component to
black confraternities.

There were a number of ways that black confraternities could define their
membership. In places with large enslaved and free populations of color, like
Lima and Minas Gerais, confraternities often included or excluded specific
groups by criteria such as legal status (free or enslaved), *casta* (black, *mulato*,
indigenous), or level of creolization (Afrocreole versus those born in Africa).[34] In
Lima, for example, there were separate brotherhoods for Terranovos, Lúcumes,
Cambundas, Carabalíes, Cangoes, Mandingas – all West African groups – as well
as Chalas, Huarocharíes (indigenous), Congos, and Misangas.[35] The confraternity of Nuestra Señora de la Candelaria in Santo Domingo, for example, was
specifically for the use of "negros biofras."[36] The deliberate creation of confraternities with such criteria came from the ground up, and reflected the desire by
members to gather together in groups from similar regions and language families.

---

[30] Matthew Restall cautions against over-interpreting the presence of "ethnic" confraternities given
the numbers of "mixed" brotherhoods: *The Black Middle*, 237.

[31] Sweet, *Recreating Africa*, 15–18. Sweet divides the regions that slaves came from three general
zones: Upper Guinea, Lower Guinea, and Central Africa.

[32] Graubart, "'So color de una cofradía'"; Martín Casares and Delaigue, "Evangelization"; Sweet,
Recreating Africa, 45. In eighteenth-century Brazil, 94 percent of Africans who married did so
with others from similar or the same cultural zone.

[33] Kiddy, *Blacks of the Rosary*, 5.

[34] Graubart, "'So color de una cofradía,'" 47; Kiddy, *Blacks of the Rosary*; and Childs, "Retaining
and Recreating African Ethnic Identities." See also the important article, Sidbury and Cañizares-
Esguerra, "Mapping Ethnogenesis."

[35] Such ethnic designations reflect the problematic categories ascribed to Africans in Latin America:
Lipski, *A History of Afro-Hispanic Language*, 96; Hall, *Slavery and African Ethnicities*; and
Law, "Ethnicity and the Slave Trade." But they also provided opportunities for community
formation: O'Toole, "From the Rivers of Guinea"; and Mangan, "A Market of Identities."

[36] AGI, Santo Domingo, 869, L. 6, 154v-155r.

In Brazil, which saw the highest concentrations of black confraternities of anywhere in the Iberian world, Nossa Senhora dos Remedios in Rio specified that it was "for the nation of Mina."[37] Another from a town near Salvador de Bahia claimed that it had been founded for people "from the *Gege* nation." Later in the document, it acknowledged "creoles" as a distinct group who could be members once they paid an entrance fee and understood the condition that they would never be allowed certain offices that were reserved for the Gege.[38] A black Rosary confraternity (officially titled *Nossa Senhora do Rozario dos homens pretos*) in the parish of San Miguel de Ipojuca specified in its first constitution that it admitted as members any man or woman, black as well as creole – using the association of "black/preto" with "enslaved" and "Creole/crioules" as "free" – from Angola, Mina, São Tomé, or Mozambique. The ethnicities represented here covered a wide geographic swath, from East Central Africa to West Central Africa to the "Gold Coast" of West Africa.[39] Another brotherhood, located in Recife, designated almost identical ethnicities: those from Angola, Cabo Verde, Santo Thomas, and Mina, free or enslaved, although in this case the *compromiso* stated that the elected king and queen had to be Angolan.[40] Even in brotherhoods where multiple ethnic groups were admitted, then, further divisions could occur along more specific ethnic lines.

Specifications on the backgrounds of members could be even more fine-grained. For example, the founders of the Cofradía de Fray Juan de la Buenaventura in the Church of San Francisco in Lima described themselves as "morenos of the Bioho caste, native to Guinea." Here they specified themselves not only ethnically, but by place of birth. They launched a lawsuit requesting the immediate expulsion of some of the members, whom they called "creoles from Panama, of the Bioho caste." Rather than drawing lines between ethnicity or race, Antón Calafate, Manuel de Aramburú, and Alonso de Niza, the authors of the lawsuit and founders of the confraternity, distinguished between places of birth (Guinea vs. Panama). Here the Guinean brothers condemned the Panamanian Biohos for being "restless, with bad

---

[37] AHU, Códice 1300(1), "Compromisso da confraria de Nossa Senhora dos Remedios dos pretos da Cidade do Rio de Janeiro de Nascoa Minas' colocada na Capela de Santa Efigenia, 1788."

[38] AHU, Códice 1666 (1), n. 127, "Compromisso da irmandade do senjor Bom Jesus com a soberano titulo de Senhor dos Martirios erecta pelos Homens pretos de nasção Gege.. este anno de 1765"; s.f. Kraay ponts out that the "Gege" (Aja-speaking people of southwestern Benin and southeastern Togo) were the largest group of enslaved people in eighteenth-century Bahia: *Afro-Brazilian Culture*, 80.

[39] AHU, Códice 1667 (1) "Compromiso da muita Veneravel Irmandade da Virgem Nossa Senhora do Rozario dos homens pretos desta freguesia de S. Miguel de Ipojuca 1724 Outubro 15," 2r. The confraternity also accepted white and *pardo* members.

[40] AHU, Códice 1179 (2), "Compromisos que nouamente faz a Irmandade de N. Snr.a do Rozario dos homens pretos da Villa do Reciffe neste prezente anno de 1782," s.f. On ethnic identity in black confraternities in Rio, see Soares, *People of Faith*, 183–221.

impulses and reputation, raised in vice and liberties," accusing them of various thefts and drunkenness.[41] The rhetoric here is particularly striking, as it echoes accusations leveled against black brothers by whites, suggesting that the *limeño* Biohos worried about their reputation as good and pious Christians.[42] In another example from Lima, Nuestra Señora de la Antigua – which described itself simply as "*moreno*" – launched a lawsuit alleging that due to its antiquity, it had the exclusive right to ask for alms at the cathedral door. While the initial complaint was general, the authors of the lawsuit elaborated in a subsequent suit that a confraternity of the "casta Caboverdian" had violated their monopoly by collecting alms on their designated day.[43] Competition and quarrels erupted between confraternities for people of color just as they did between black and white brotherhoods.

One striking element of the Brazilian *compromisos* of the eighteenth century is that, in spite of their titular designation as a confraternity of blacks, they frequently admitted not only *mulato* members, but white (*branco*) as well. Nossa Senhora do Rosário dos Pretos from Rio stated that it did not matter if the office holders were black or white as long as they were qualified.[44] One from Recife (another Rosary "dos homens pretos") declared that members included men of "black faces" (*cor preta*), men and women, enslaved or free, creoles or those from Angola, Cabo Verde, San Tomé, or "of the casta of Mina." While these specifications were laid out in the statute, the authors added later in the text but that black members owed an entrance fee of 1,320 reis, while white and *pardo* had to pay a heftier sum – 2,000 reis. As a result, the "mixed" nature of the confraternity's membership was buried in the document.[45] The Ipojuca Rosary brotherhood made sure to underscore that white brothers also had to pay alms every year, "like our black brothers."[46] Another black Rosary confraternity – this

---

[41] "De Panamá eran virtuosos y capaces de nuestra hermandad, los cuales con el tiempo han dado muestras de gente inquieta, de mala inclinación y malos respectos, criados en vicios y libertades": Archivo Arzobispal de Lima (hereafter AAL), Cofradias, Leg. 51, exp: 1 (1607), 1v. The Panamanian Biohos responded by requesting a separate confraternity and chapel devoted to San Juan de Buenaventura, whom they referred to as a "fraile moreno": ibid, 5v. The most common ethnonyms used by individual people in the AAL were Bran, Fula, and Zape.

[42] There are numerous sources that report such insults, some of which will be discussed below. See also AGI, Lima 94 (1602), in which the author lamented the lack of law and order in the city as it was "dominated by *mestizos, mulatos*, and blacks" who exhibited "liberty and vices" (s.f.).

[43] AAL, Cofradias, 64:9.

[44] "Compromiso da Irmandade de Nossa Senhora do Rosario dos pretos da vila de Ribeira do Rio de Janeiro: ANTT, PT/TT/MR/NE/06/47, Ministerio do Reino, lib. 528-D, 6r.

[45] AHU, Códice 1179 (2), "Compromisos que nouamente faz a Irmandade de N. Snr.a do Rozario dos homens pretos," s.f. Another example can be found AHU, Códice 1939 (1), "Compromisso da Irmandade de N. Sr. do Terço, erecta na Igreja de N. Sr. do Rosário dos homens pretos da Vila de Santo António do Recife de Pernambuco, 1758," s.f. (Brazilian brotherhoods tended to employ the term "*pardo*" to refer to people of mixed white–African ancestry.)

[46] "com os nossos Irmaos pretos": AHU, Códice 1667 (1), 10r. This *compromiso* is dated 1803.

time in Arrayal, near Rio de Janeiro – specified that white members ("of good name and intelligence") could serve in the offices of treasurer or notary, but only in the case that there were no qualified black men available to take the role.[47] On the other hand, the body approving the *compromiso* for the confraternity of St. Anthony insisted that the treasurers of the brotherhood be white, since they (whites) were more "trustworthy," indicating that official oversight could circumscribe the designs of black founders.[48]

In-depth examination of confraternity *compromisos*, then, reveals a story more complex than the brotherhood's name or description implied, even in cases where it declared itself for a certain *casta* or ethnic group and specified the founders' membership requirements. The admission of *pardo* or white individuals in black confraternities could have occurred for multiple reasons: The black confraternity in question could have been particularly desirable because of wealth or connection to a miraculous image; whites and *pardos* might have been a minority in certain regions (like Minas Gerais) and therefore unable to form their own brotherhoods; or the white members might have been poor or otherwise unable to join other confraternities. Whatever the specific reason, organizers of black confraternities underscored that their founders were black, whether enslaved or free. Moreover, in cases when the founders of confraternities that specified their membership as black – seen in the amended titles as Nossa Senhora do Rosário "for black people" or "for *pardos*" – the decisions about membership, office-holding, and entrances fees were made by Afro-Iberians, even if the brotherhood included white members. Black confraternities, particularly in the Americas, remained under the control of black members.

In addition to public processions, one of the most significant functions that confraternities served was to guarantee rights to burial spaces. Such access was emphasized not only in *compromisos*, but in some of the lawsuits in which confraternities engaged. The brothers of the confraternity of San Bendito in Bahia, Brazil, for example, requested permission from the king in 1734 for the right of burial in their chapel.[49] Another Bahian brotherhood – this time a Rosary

---

[47] "sirvão dous homens brancos de bom nome, inteligencia para o governo.. em quanto nao houverem homens pretos com sufficiencia para os referridos cargos": AHU Códice 1814 (1), "Compromisso da Irmandade de Nossa Senhora do Rozario dos Pretos do Arrayal ... anno de 1777," s.f.

[48] "Compromisso da irmandade de S. Antonio de Catagero na cita na Matris des Pedro desta Cidade da Bahya: que seus devotos hao de guarder feito no año de 1699," Oliveira Lima Library, Catholic University.

[49] AHU, Bahia, Caixa 37, doc. 58, a concession they were granted the following year: AHU, Bahia, Caixa 51, doc. 28 (1735). Alonso de Sandoval commented on the frequent refusal of owners to provide burials for their slaves: "sino es que pidan para su entierro limosna sus parientes, contribuan todos los de su casta ... echese derrama, dando aviso a su cofradia, donde no, ay está el cimenterio, aunque sea muy ladino, y muy antiguo en casa": *Naturaleza, policia, i religiosa*, 136.

confraternity – requested a judgment requiring the custodian of the Igreja de Nossa Senhora de Conceição, Rodrigues Landim, to fulfill the permission granted to the Rosary members to accompany the bodies of the deceased brothers to their sepulcher.[50] Securing the rights of burial granted to them by the official approval of their *compromisos* was therefore a primary concern for the brothers. All brotherhoods – black and white, European and American – fiercely guarded burial rights at their host churches, so this aspect of confraternity life is not specific to black brotherhoods. Yet black brotherhoods engaged in distinct rituals connected to their burials, and they occasionally had to push for the fulfillment of such rights by the host churches, with whom they were often at odds.[51]

Black confraternities played crucial roles in mutual protection as well as preservation of culture.[52] They frequently raised money to manumit fellow members, an activity that was occasionally enshrined in their *compromisos*, in the same way that white confraternities raised money to provide poor girls with dowries or widows of brothers with financial support.[53] In Mexico City, black brotherhoods rose up in outrage to fight in the slave revolt of 1611–1612 when a female member of the confraternity died at the hands of her master.[54] Members of brotherhoods could also protect enslaved members from white predation on a less dramatic scale. The Rosary confraternity (*dos homens pretos e pardos*) in Lisbon represented Maria Joaquina, a "*mulher preta*" (black woman) and most likely a sister of the confraternity, who had been arrested. It appears to have paid of a fine in her name of eight gold coins.[55] The confraternity of the Rosary in

[50] AHU, Bahia, Caixa 96, doc. 33 (1747). In a report on Jesuits' activities in Brazil, the authors mention that in "all the cities of Brazil" black confraternities buried their brothers and sisters "decently": Misc. Papers III (n. 45), 1693, Oliveira Lima Library, Catholic University Library.

[51] On African cultural practices in burial rites, see Neves, Almeida, and Ferreira, "Separados na vida e na morte."

[52] Mariana Dantas discusses the number of ways membership in eighteenth-century Brazilian confraternities could "empower" communities of color, including property ownership: "Humble Servants and Loyal Vassals."

[53] For a few examples of freeing members from the eighteenth-century Lusophone world, see AHU_ACL_CU, Cod. 1300 (1); ANTT, PT/TT/ JIM/ JA/ 0011/00017. The enforcement of letters of manumission could also be important; see ANTT, PT/TT/JIM/B/0033/00004. Mariana Dantas notes that some ecclesiastical authorities restricted provisos in eighteenth-century *compromisos* about the confraternity's intention to manumit fellow members: Personal communication on March 14, 2018.

[54] Proctor, "Slave Rebellion," 27–31. Proctor warns that the events of the so-called revolt have been debated, but the execution of black confraternity members for rebellion is established. See also Martínez, "The Black Blood of New Spain." It is significant to note, however, that the role of confraternities in manumitting fellow members could be contested by colonial authorities, especially in Brazil.

[55] ANTT, PT/TT/JIM/JA/0041/ 00005, "Ação cível em que é autor António José Texeira e Ré a irmandade de Nossa Senhora do Rosário dos homens pretos e pardos," n.f.

Mosteiro de Santa Joanna in Lisbon launched a lawsuit (*ação cível*) by José Ferreira da Fonseca against his owner José Ferreira Baptista. In this extensive lawsuit, the confraternity attempted to block Baptista's efforts to sell his slave abroad against his will, which was contrary to the privileges granted the brotherhood stating that their members could not be so sold.[56] This Rosary brotherhood appears to have been particularly powerful relative to other black confraternities; the convent's relationship to the royal family provided black brothers and sisters with a special relationship with the royal family, who frequently gave alms to them.[57]

Communities of color, then, could organize themselves along multiple lines in the early modern Atlantic – they might do so by ethnicity in combination with place of birth; they may have no distinctions besides African origin or descent; and they might focus exclusively on *casta* (as in the case of confraternities exclusively for *pardos*). Black confraternities allowed brothers and sisters opportunities for positions of leadership and responsibility, in the same way that female monasteries could for early modern women. One of the most significant aspects of black confraternal life throughout the Iberian Atlantic – although such ceremonies are particularly visible in the Lusophone world – was their election of kings and queens, which created continual ties to Central African origins. The histories of black confraternities in the Americas and Iberia were formed in similar ways but followed distinct trajectories. While black confraternities in Iberia often separated themselves from white brotherhoods, and *pardo* confraternities from black ones, they almost never divided themselves by ethnicity, except possibly in Lisbon. Not surprisingly, ethnic or more fine-grained divisions were possible only in places with large black populations. Yet the fundamental features of black confraternities that distinguished them from white ones were replicated throughout the Iberian Atlantic.

Equality of All Souls

These examples of black confraternity members' ability to organize themselves, preserve aspects of African culture (even if such aspects were reshaped through creolization), and advocate on behalf of fellow members demonstrate how

---

[56] ANTT, PT/TT/CCPP/0036/00009, "Ação cível de embargos à primeira em que são autores o juiz e irmãos da irmandade Nossa Senhora do Rosario dos homens pretos e reú José Ferreira da Foncesa," 3r-20v.

[57] ANTT, PT/TT/MSJL/MF.L1212-A, Livro da esmolas que da a casa real para a irmandade dos homens pretos de Santa Joana, 16r-19r. James Sweet mentions that King João V and his queen attended a festival honoring St. Benedict in 1744: "The Hidden Histories of African Lisbon," 245.

participation in black confraternities permitted Afro-Iberians to mediate between black communities and white authorities. Such opportunities had the potential to extend beyond local instances of manumission, paying a debt, or suing on behalf of a member. Afro-Iberians frequently deployed their status as baptized Christians to argue for their right to access courts, certain professions, property ownership, and public space.[58] Public participation in religious festivals in particular acted as a way of staking a claim to inclusion on the streets and in a larger civic, as well as religious, community. The act of insisting on ecclesiastically sanctioned privileges as fellow Christians allowed black members of the community to advocate for each other and defend their innate human dignity.

The power of brotherhoods in the Catholic world meant that its leaders could stake claims to authority in civic spheres; such powers could extend to black leaders of brotherhoods as well as white. Perhaps one of the best examples of this possibility comes from the travels of Lorenzo de Silva Mendoza (d. 1698).[59] Not much is currently known about Mendoza's background – surviving documentation about him in Rome provides thin details about his origin. Mendoza referred to himself simply as a descendant of the king of Kongo and Angola, and the prior of a Rosary confraternity for blacks and *mulatos*.[60] Portuguese papal nuncio Gaspar da Costa Meschita described Mendoza as "a man of olive color" who was "the leader of all the men of his color in all of this kingdom [Portugal]." After this description, Mischita broadened Mendoza's authority to encompass Spain and Brazil as well as Portugal ("come nella Spagna et Brasile"). The letter also refers to Mendoza as a "natural" of the kingdom of Portugal, suggesting his long-term residence there, although he had at an earlier point lived in Brazil. Now, Mendoza was traveling to Rome to procure a brief from the Pope about "a certain business."[61]

On his way to Rome, Mendoza stopped at the royal court of Charles II in Madrid. Another document preserved in Rome provides a few additional details about Mendoza's time in Spain. The purpose of the document was also connected

---

[58] Herman Bennett discusses the processes through which the Church viewed Afro-Mexicans as Christians and Afro-Mexican responses to the processes of Christianization: *Africans in Colonial Mexico*. On the rhetoric of Christianity in advocating for privileges, see Ireton, "'They Are Blacks of the Caste of Black Christians.'"

[59] Richard Gray's elegant essay provides an overview of the case: "The Papacy and the Atlantic Slave Trade." All the documents in Rome refer to him as Lorenzo de Silva Mendoza, although his Portuguese name was most likely Lourenço da Silva Mendonça or Mendouça. For current research being conducting on this important figure that promises to elucidate more about Mendoza's early life and career, see Dr. José Lingna Nafafé's article: https://mmppf.wordpress.com/2019/03/12/lourenco-da-silva-mendonca-the-first-anti-slavery-activist/.

[60] Archivio Storico de Propaganda Fide (hereafter APF), SOCG 490, 140v.

[61] APF, Serio Africa, Angola, etc., I, Gaspar da Costa de Mischita to the Propaganda Fide, February 25, 1681, 488r.

to black confraternities – that is, to extend to Mendoza the right to establish the confraternity of Madonna della Stella de'negri (Nuestra Señora de las Estrellas de los Negros) wheresoever Mendoza might choose in the realms of Charles II for the express purpose of catechizing "infidels" and providing instruction on Catholic dogma.[62] This right was conferred on Mendoza by Lorenzo de Re, described as Knight of the Order of Christ, master of music, native of Lima, and leader in the said confraternity.[63] The bulk of the letter is largely formulaic, laying out the terms of Mendoza's privileges as a potential founder of Nuestra Señora de las Estrellas. Mendoza's arrival in Madrid under the aegis of the leader of black confraternities in Portugal led to a doubling of the privileges accorded him. He clearly captured the attention of important people at the royal court, and was welcomed there by the king and the archbishop, presumably because they did not know his true intentions in traveling to Rome.

After leaving Madrid and Lisbon, Mendoza went to Rome and took up his main purpose: to complain to the Propaganda Fide about the horrific mistreatment of enslaved people in Brazil. Highly educated, he distilled his critique to two main points – inhuman treatment and perpetual slavery. He wrote baldly about the dire situation, calling the perpetual enslavement of blacks a form of "tyrannical cruelty" that was contrary to both divine and natural law. He insisted on the equality of all souls, that God has infused every baptized person with a soul, no matter their skin color. Here, Mendoza explained that people were separate only "by a small accident of blackness or whiteness," a similar formulation to what appears in hagiographies of black saints. He emphatically declared that God would "unsheathe the rigorous sword of his justice to punish such impiety resulting from the tyrannical sale of human and Christian blood." Here, the slave trade was a form of impiety, an affront to God. Tellingly, Mendoza qualified the bodies of the enslaved as both human and Christian. The inclusion of "human" here is significant, because, while it underscores the shared origins of all God's children, it provides a new emphasis on humanity itself as a shared characteristic.[64] Moreover,

[62] APF, SC Africa, Angola, etc. I, Giacinto Rogio Monzon to the Propaganda Fide, September 23, 1682, 487r-v.

[63] Lorenzo de Re emerges as a somewhat shadowy figure here, in spite of the titles attributed to him by Monzon. The Order of the Knights of Christ, for example, was a Portuguese order, not Spanish, yet the letter clearly designates him as *limeño*. Re's membership in the confraternity further suggests that he himself was black, though Monzon did not describe him as such, which could imply that Re was in fact white, but maintained a position of oversight to the brotherhood. I have so far been unable to learn more about Re.

[64] APF, SOCG 49, 140v. The phrases that I have translated above are in the original: "tirannica crudelità, che con i ridotti alla uera religione di Christo usano contra ogni legge diuina ... ancorche.. della legge natural"; "un minimo accidente di negro, ò bianco"; and "chi il diuino Giudice sfoderi la rigorosa spade della sua giustitia e castigar tanti empietà, che da tal tirannnica uendita d'humano e Christiano sangue deriuano."

his use of the word "tyranny" invoked a legal category that denoted rule without constraint by the law, one area that some political theorists of the time argued justified revolt.[65]

In his second main point, Mendoza condemned the death of "innumerable souls" of black Christians due to their maltreatment and punishments. But switching quickly from murder, Mendoza turned to the condemnation of Africans to "perpetual slavery," which encompassed people who remained enslaved after baptism, as well as those who were born slaves as the children of enslaved people ("even if their children are white"). These points were critical because part of the Church's support for enslavement stated its desire to bring Christianity to pagans. But what happened once pagan slaves became Christian? The legal status and moral ambiguities would resonate with the clergy of the Propaganda Fide in ways that they did not in the Iberian imperial context. Mendoza's decision to emphasize the problem of perpetual slavery was particularly well chosen because it side-stepped the thornier questions of the legitimacy of the slave trade itself, something that the Church had already deemed licit. Mendoza's impassioned letter spoke both to his high level of education, powerful rhetorical abilities, and knowledge of theology. As someone surrounded by the horrors of slavery, Mendoza discussed the miseries inflicted on enslaved people through their masters' behavior, yet he kept his main focus on arguments most likely to gain the sympathy of the pope and the clergy of the Propaganda Fide – i.e., the immoral and illegal imprisonment of Christian souls.

Mendoza's powerful words survive in the volumes at the Propaganda Fide along with documents by members of the Congregation who composed various responses. The reports were overwhelmingly sympathetic to Mendoza. The congregation's first step was to unearth independent corroboration of his assertions. Archbishop Edoardo Cibo, the secretary of the Congregation, demanded to know whether or not any Spanish or Portuguese priests in the Kongo abused their role and participated in the slave trade. He wanted information specifically about the theft of children from their mother "with violence," and the forcible removal of said children to Spain on ships where they were treated "like animals," a phrase that recurred in the document several times. The accusation that people were treated like animals contrasted with Mendoza's emphasis on the humanity of Africans throughout his argument. If enslaved people were animals, then they had no souls to save, an idea that the Church soundly rejected.

---

[65] The subject of tyranny, just rule, and revolt took center stage in the late sixteenth and seventeenth centuries, largely inspired by religious wars, as well as increasingly consolidating monarchical power. For an overview, see Lagerlund and Hill, *The Routledge Companion*.

Cibo directed his ire at the Christian merchants who controlled the slave trade, condemning roundly their role in such abuses. He was particularly concerned with Mendoza's accusation that slavery had become "perpetual," including children born Christian. He announced his intention to write the kings of Spain and Portugal prohibiting such actions, and suggested that enslavement be restricted to a period of no more than ten years, and that all children born of enslaved people be free from birth. He later declared that the apostolic nuncios to Spain and Portugal would declare to their monarchs that they were prohibited from such actions under grave penalty.[66] Moreover, the nuncio in Portugal would "punish severely" everyone who stole Africans, and to promulgate excommunication against such thieves ("*ladroni*").[67]

The Propaganda Fide's seeming ignorance of the dire situation of enslaved people in the Americas is striking, and a bit bewildering, considering that the Congregation was responsible for overseas missionaries who worked with both West and Central Africans and enslaved people in the Americas.[68] The most likely explanation is the near-monopoly in missionary work exercised by Iberian clergy in Iberian-held territory (both in the Americas and Africa), and the Iberian monarchs' efforts to limit the interferences of the papacy in Iberian churches. The establishment of the Propaganda Fide, however, led to an increased presence of non-Iberian missionaries, particularly in West and Central Africa. Italian Capuchins in Central Africa seem to have been a major conduit of information back to Rome, breaking the imperial silences of Spanish and Portuguese clergy. In fact, in 1687, Capuchin missionary Giuseppe Maia da Busseto wrote an angry letter from Luanda denouncing the abuses of buying and selling slaves in that city; at the end of the letter he pointed his finger particularly at the Jesuits whom he claimed were supplying slaves to Brazil.[69] The Capuchin's accusations against the Jesuits for serving their king and personal economic interests rather than upholding their vows to the Church is particularly telling as it speaks to the

---

[66] APF, SOCG 490 (1684), 136r-138v. In March 1684, from Monsignor Cibo to Cardinal Millini, Cibo denounced the "fraud and violence" of the slave trade and perpetual slavery violated "Catholic liberty": APF, Lettere 73 (1684), "Monsignor Cibo to Cardinal Millini, March 6, 1684, 9v-10r. Additional discussions of Da Silva can be found: APF, Lettere 75 (1686), 21v, 39r-40v, 56v, and 191r-v, and SOCG 490, 139r-v, 145r-147v.

[67] APF, Lettere 75 (1686), 141r-v. He further repeated the stricture that enslavement last a maximum of ten years.

[68] For additional information about discussions about slavery in the 1680s spearheaded by two important Capuchins (Francisco José de Jaca and Epifanio de Moirans), see López García, *Dos defensores de los esclavos*.

[69] APF, SC, Africa-Angola, II (1686–1692), Giuseppe Maia da Busseto to the Congregation of the Propaganda Fide, March 8, 1687, 92r. On Capuchin missions, see Carrocera, "Misión capuchina."

powerful grip that imperial policies and clerical collaboration had on the continuance of the slave trade.

The power of Iberian empires shut down the Propaganda Fide's threats as soon as they were uttered, and Silva's labors ultimately came to nothing. Yet it is important to note that Silva's efforts, his elegance and effectiveness at gaining the ear of the powerful Congregation, and his deft use of Christian rhetoric found a sympathetic reception in Rome. His self-declared position as leader of his people and as the head of a black Rosary confraternity paved the way for his journey to Europe, his welcome in Madrid, and his ability to be heard in Rome. His emphasis on enslaved people as baptized Christians acted as the foundation on which his claims of black humanity and spiritual equality were built. Critiques of the treatment of the enslaved in the seventeenth-century Catholic world, like those articulated by Mendoza, Sandoval, and Brazilian Jesuit António Vieira, were grounded in the fact that baptized Africans were Christians, endowed with the grace, reason, and dignity of God. As a result, the embrace of Christianity – and the attendant public practice of it through black confraternities – proved central to the efforts by black Christians to advocate for themselves and to improve their status in European-colonial society. Widespread visibility of black saints enhanced this process, because they proved that black Africans could achieve the same levels of spiritual perfection as white Christians.

White Hostility

Efforts by Afro-Iberians to claims of status and public space, however, could produce a vicious backlash from Iberian and colonial observers, lay and clerical, who wished to maintain the status quo and reinforce extant hierarchies. Owners in particular did not wish their slaves to have access to the limited freedoms provided by Catholic inclusion, and such animosity extended to white laity in cities and towns. Contestation over racial hierarchies, public space, the production of power, and, in the Americas, the maintenance of imperial authority could manifest itself through conflict over the role that black confraternities played in civic life. Participation in festivals by black confraternities could lead not only to derision, but to violence as white parishioners sought to erase the black presence from public Catholic ritual.

The complaints of white laity against black Catholics tended to be grounded in arguments that black people were "senseless" and "barbaric." Such claims expanded outward from there: black slaves and free people drank and stole; they were aggressive and disrespectful, disruptive, noisy, and generally behaved inappropriately, particularly at religious festivals.[70] Although such complaints reveal little about the actual behavior of black Catholics during religious festivals, they do illustrate common racist tropes. It was common for ecclesiastic authorities to complain about the music and dance performed by black confraternity members as part of public processions, deriding it as "an offense to Our Lord."[71] Music and dance were one important area of distinction between black and white confraternities, marking out black brotherhoods as "different" in a way that white observers found offensive. It is difficult to gauge what exactly whites found distasteful about the music and dance – for example, whether if the issue was unfamiliarity in music types that were not considered appropriate for religious solemnities or if the complaining whites were reacting to the public presence of black Christians on the streets in general.

Ecclesiastical authorities were often receptive to white complaints, occasionally refusing to permit black confraternities to participate in important festivals.[72] In 1604 Seville, the archbishop responded to complaints leveled by white confraternity members against the black confraternity Nuestra Señora de los Ángeles, declaring that Los Ángeles could not participate in Corpus Christi celebrations.[73] Another incident occurred in seventeenth-century Mexico City, when the viceroy prohibited the "cofradía de los negros" (no name given) from processing as a result of the "inconveniences" that thus resulted.[74] In eighteenth-century Bahia, the leaders of the Casa da Santa Misericórdia sent a letter complaining to the king that the Irmandades da Santa Cruz and dos Martiros – "composed of *mulatos* and blacks, respectively" – persisted in processing during Lent, despite having been forbidden from doing so by the viceroy.[75] Thus, black confraternities throughout the Iberian Atlantic suffered from periodic prohibitions and backlash in the seventeenth and eighteenth centuries.

[70] Lahon, "Black African Slaves and Freedmen," 268.

[71] ARSI, *MHSI Monumenta Peruana*, VII (Rome, 1981), 109, 373–4. See also Moreno, *La antigua hermandad*, 85; and Sweet mentions white observers of black confraternities as sneezing as they walked by, presumably to disrupt: "Hidden Histories," 245.

[72] Sancho de Sopranis likewise cites complaints made by white ecclesiastical authorities about black processions as noisy and indecent: *Las cofradías de los morenos*, 14. Sancho's work is occasionally marred by a tendency to accept primary source criticisms of the black confraternities at face value. Young provides another example from seventeenth-century Lima, when locals were scandalized by the "licentious dancing" of black participants in *autos sacramentales*: Young, "Colonial Music, Confraternities, and Power," 86–7.

[73] Moreno, *La antigua hermandad*, 83–4.   [74] AGI, Mexico 1090, L.8, 42v-43r.

[75] "Referente à insistência das Irmandades de Santa Cruz e dos Martíros, composta de mulatos e pretos, respectivamente, em saírem em procissão por ocasião da quaresma levando suas varas, mesmo tendo há muito sido proibidas pelo vice-rei do Brasil": AHU, Bahia, Caixa 151, doc. 49, s. f. The complaints resumed in AHU, Bahia, Caixa 152, doc. 10.

Plate 1 *St. Benedict of Palermo*, Altar of San Diego de Alcalá, eighteenth century. Andalusian school, gilded wood sculpture, 80 × 25 × 25 cm. Andalusia, Spain.

Plate 2 *Our Lady of Guadalupe*, Guadalupe, Spain.

Plate 3 *The Black Virgin in the Chadaraita*, seventeenth century, oil on canvas. Musée Crozatier, Le Puy-en-Velay, France.

Plate 4 Detail of Hieronymous Bosch, *The Adoration of the Magi*, 1492, oil on panel, 147.4 × 168.6 cm. Museo Nacional del Prado, Madrid.

Plate 5 Detail of Balthazar in Francesco Polazzo, *Magi Adoration*, 1735–1738, oil on canvas. Chiesa di Sant'Agata del Carmine, Bergamo, Italy.

Plate 6 Antonio del Villar, *The Adoration of the Magi*, bas-relief, Altar of la Expectación, 1722. Cathedral of Tui, Spain.

Plate 7 Diego Velázquez, *The Adoration of the Kings*, 1619, oil on canvas, 203 × 125 cm. Museo Nacional del Prado, Madrid.

Plate 8 Altar of the Black Confraternity of Nuestra Señora de Salud, Iglesia de Nuestra Señora del Rosario, Cadiz, Spain. The altarpiece is nineteenth century, but the sculptures of Sts. Benedict and Efigenia date from 1650 to 1699.

Plate 9 Chapel of the Ancient Confraternity of Our Lady of the Rosary of the Blacks, eighteenth century. Convento e Igreja da Graça, Lisbon, Portugal.

Plate 10 Altar of Black Confraternity, Cathedral of Braga, Portugal.

Plate 11 *St. Benedict of Palermo*, eighteenth century, polychrome wood sculpture. Igreja de São Francisco, Oporto, Portugal.

Plate 12 *St. Benedict of Palermo*, eighteenth century, polychrome wood sculpture in collateral altar. Eastern Alentejo, Portugal.

Plate 13 *St. Benedict of Palermo*, date unknown, polychrome wood sculpture. Igreja do Santo Domingo, Elvas Portugal.

Plate 14 Ex-voto for *St. Benedict of Palermo*, 1724, oil on wood. Eastern Alentejo, Portugal.

Plate 15 Detail of *estofado* work, *St. Benedict of Palermo*, eighteenth century, reliquary bust, polychrome and gilded wood sculpture. Convento da Madre de Deus, Lisbon, Portugal.

Plate 16 *St. Efigenia*, eighteenth century, polychrome wood sculpture. Algarve, Portugal.

Plate 17 *St. Benedict of Palermo*, eighteenth century. Polychrome sculpture, wood and cloth, 110 cm. Central Portugal.

Plate 18 Pedro de Mena, *San Pedro de Alcántara*. Spanish, c. 1663–1670, polychrome wood sculpture with ivory and glass. Cleveland Museum of Art, Ohio.

Plate 19 Here you can see extensive termite damage and some chipping (which is more extensive on the feet [not shown]). Unknown artist, *St. Benedict of Palermo*, polychrome wood sculpture. Central Portugal.

Plate 20 Deteriorated polychrome work in unknown artist, *St. Efigenia*, eighteenth century, polychrome wood sculpture. Museu Municipal, Portalegre, Portugal.

Plate 21 Detail with brown and pink pigments, *St. Efigenia*, eighteenth century, polychrome wood sculpture. Igreja e Convento de Santo Domingo, Betanzos, Spain.

Plate 22 José Montes de Oca, *St. Benedict of Palermo*, Spanish, c. 1734, polychrome and gilt sculpture. Minneapolis Institute of Arts, Minneapolis, Minnesota, the John R. Van Derlip Fund.

Plate 23 Detail, unknown artist, *St. Efigenia*, seventeenth century, polychrome wood sculpture, 60 × 36 cm. Algarve, Portugal.

Plate 24 Detail of *St. Benedict of Palermo*, seventeenth century, polychrome wood sculpture, 86 cm. Northern Portugal.

Plate 25 Detail of feet, *St. Benedict of Palermo*, eighteenth century, polychrome wood. Igreja do Santo Domingo, Elvas, Portugal.

Plate 26 Detail of *St. Benedict of Palermo*, reliquary bust, eighteenth century, polychrome wood sculpture, 48 cm. Convento da Madre de Deus, Lisbon, Portugal.

Plate 27 Detail of *St. Efigenia*, polychrome wood sculpture. Iglesia del Carmen, Cadiz, Spain.

Plate 28 Detail of *St. Benedict of Palermo*, late seventeenth century, polychrome wood sculpture, 168 cm (height). Museo Nacional de Escultura, Valladolid, Spain.

Plate 29 Detail, unknown artist, *St. Benedict of Palermo*, eighteenth century, polychrome wood. Southeastern Portugal.

Plate 30 Detail, unknown artist, *St. Benedict of Palermo*, eighteenth century, polychrome wood sculpture. Convento de San Francisco, Pontevedra, Spain.

Plate 31 Detail of *St. Elesban*, eighteenth century, polychrome wood sculpture, Altar of Our Lady of the Rosary of the Blacks. Convento e Igreja da Graça, Lisbon, Portugal.

Plate 32 *St. Benedict of Palermo*, eighteenth century, polychrome wood sculpture. Northern Portugal.

Plate 33 Detail of bloody rag, *St. Benedict of Palermo*, eighteenth century, oil on wood. Southeastern Portugal.

Plate 34 Detail of the bloody rag, *St. Benedict of Palermo*, polychrome wood and cloth. Southeastern Portugal.

Plate 35 Detail of *St. Benedict of Palermo*, polychrome wood sculpture. Central Portugal.

Plate 36 Francisco de Zurbarán, *Queen Saint Elizabeth of Portugal*, c. 1635, oil on canvas, 184 × 98 cm. Museo Nacional del Prado, Madrid, Spain.

Plate 37 Detail, *St. Benedict of Palermo*, eighteenth century, polychrome wood sculpture. Igreja Matriz, Santiago do Cacém, Portugal.

Plate 38 Detail of *St. Benedict of Palermo*, late seventeenth century, polychrome wood sculpture, 168 cm. Photo courtesy of the Museo Nacional de Escultura, Valladolid, Spain.

Plate 39 *St. Antonio da Noto*, eighteenth century, polychrome sculpture. Altar of Nossa Senhora do Rosário dos Pretos. Cathedral of Braga, Lisbon, Portugal.

Plate 40 *St. Antonio de Catagerona*, eighteenth century, watercolor. "Compromiso da Irmandade de S. Antonio de Catagerona," Brazil. Oliveira Lima Library, Catholic University of America, Washington, DC.

Before delving more deeply into specific case studies of violence and hostility between black and white confraternities, it is important to remember that it was common for early modern confraternities to wrangle with each other, particularly in the seventeenth and eighteenth centuries as the processions of Holy Week and Corpus Christi took on heightened religious and social significance.[76] Like nearly every aspect of early modern Iberian life, processions were deeply hierarchical and often involved conflicts over the most pressing of all issues: precedence. The problem of precedence often appeared during large, complex festivals with many participating groups; the question of who would walk in front of or behind another person or group was a matter of great importance in a society that emphasized the continuous, public performance of rank and status.[77] Both white and black confraternities launched lawsuits against each other over such issues. In late seventeenth-century Lima, for example, the "moreno" brotherhood Nuestra Señora de los Reyes (in the church of San Francisco) insisted that Nuestra Señora de la Antigua (of the "blacks") recognize Los Reyes' place of primacy.[78]

Bitter conflict between confraternities over precedence and resources could be inflected with particular malice when it occurred between white and black confraternities. Two examples of black confraternities under siege in Iberia occurred in the seventeenth-century Andalusian cities of Seville and Cadiz.[79] Both cities had large enslaved and free black populations (though Cadiz's grew large slightly later than Seville's), and multiple black and mulatto confraternities. Several long-term conflicts developed in these two cities throughout the seventeenth and eighteenth centuries between black and white confraternities. Such conflicts highlight both the tenacious efforts by black Catholics to participate in public festivals and the enduring challenges they faced in maintaining their role in civic life. Seville was home to three confraternities for its enslaved and free population of color. Two were dedicated to black brothers – Los Ángeles, and a Rosary confraternity housed across the Guadalquivir in the poor neighborhood of Triana – and a third for the *mulato* population, which eventually moved to the Church of St. Ildefonso.[80] All three brotherhoods faced criticism, white takeover, and/ or eventual disappearance resulting from demographic shifts (i.e., a dwindling population of color).

---

[76] Monti, *Week of Salvation*, 61.

[77] For arguments over precedence in early modern processions, see Webster, "Sacred Altars"; Melvin, *Building Colonial Cities*, 23–4, 114, 169–70; and Poska, "From Parties to Pieties."

[78] ALL, Cofradias, 64:2.

[79] Didier Lahon tells a similar story about one of Lisbon's Rosary confraternities: Lahon, "Black African Slaves and Freedmen."

[80] Moreno, *La antigua hermandad*, 75–6.

The oldest and best studied of these three brotherhoods is Nuestra Señora de los Ángeles. Renowned for its lavish Corpus Christi processions, Los Ángeles became sufficiently wealthy and well-established to build a freestanding chapel and hospital in the neighborhood of San Agustín, just outside the center of town.[81] In 1604, however, the confraternity became embroiled in a nasty confrontation with another confraternity during Holy Week that resulted in a string of lawsuits. While all of Holy Week had spiritual significance, the processions that occurred on Maundy Thursday and Good Friday were the most prestigious, since they acted as the climax of the liturgical celebration of Christ's arrest and torture. To settle the issue of precedence – that is, how to determine which confraternities were given which slots in the procession – cities turned to tradition. The prime spots on the processional calendar were given to the oldest, considered the most prestigious.

The manuscript of the ensuing lawsuit, housed in the archive of the Palace of the Archbishop of Seville, contains the recorded testimony of dozens of participants and witnesses. While accounts differ about what exactly transpired, witnesses generally agreed on the main events: Los Ángeles and a prominent all-white confraternity, Nuestra Señora de la Antigua, were both processing on Holy Thursday. La Antigua was leaving the Church of San Salvador (its home church) and, entering onto the Plaza de San Salvador, it ran into Los Ángeles, which was also converging on the plaza from another street. Here the issue of precedence took center stage – giving way in the street was abandoning the right of precedence, which both parties were loath to do. Members of the two confraternities began yelling at each other to yield; both refused to do so, and an altercation ensued in which stones were thrown, swords brandished, and blood shed. The scene grew chaotic and several people were injured. La Antigua accused the members of Los Ángeles of instigating the violence, claiming that the black brothers tried to physically force La Antigua aside with their weapons drawn, throwing stones and even striking the female members of La Antigua.[82]

All the witnesses outside the membership of the confraternities were white men and women who happened to be in the neighborhood. Witness Jorge Fernández claimed to have seen a white brother from Antigua rush into the hospital, Nuestra Señora de la Paz (directly across the plaza from the church), with blood flowing from a head wound.[83] One of the hospital's friars, Pasqual Baca, also noted to the presence of bloodied and wounded men in the hospital that

---

[81] Moreno, *La antigua hermandad*.

[82] Archivo General del Arzobispado de Sevilla (hereafter AGAS), Justicia, Hermandades, Leg. 94, n. (09885), "Pleito de la cofradía de Nuestra Señora de los Angeles con la de la Antigua," 1r.

[83] AGAS, Justicia, Hermandades, Leg. 94, n. 5 (09885), "Pleito de la cofradía de Nuestra Señora de los Angeles," 5r.

night (presumably all white).[84] One member of the white confraternity, Juan Pérez, claimed that the members of Los Ángeles initiated the violence "without cause or reason."[85] Witnesses uniformly supported the account of the Antigua brothers – a story of aggressive and violent black men who drew swords, threw rocks, hurled insults, and generally caused chaos and scandal on one of the most holy nights of the year.

Not surprisingly, the Los Ángeles brothers told a different story. They refused to accept the status ascribed to them by the white witnesses. In the upheaval of that Holy Thursday, Bartolomé de Celada argued that despite the accounts by white onlookers, the brothers from Los Ángeles had not initiated the violence; rather, it was the Antigua brothers who left the church with swords drawn, and the free black members of Los Ángeles rushed to arm themselves with swords to defend their right to precedence on the street and to defend each other from bodily harm.[86] Those who were not armed threw stones at powerful white *sevillanos*. Regardless of who started the violence, they considered their confraternity as having the right to precedence as the older of the two confraternities; it insisted on its rank as *"antiquissima"* ("most ancient"). Celada advanced his confraternity's position vigorously: Los Ángeles was more ancient than La Antigua, and it was unjust for a "modern" confraternity to try to exclude a more ancient one. Second, he defended himself and fellow brothers against the claim that they were behaving in a scandalous fashion – rather, he insisted, "the confraternity always makes its procession with much devotion and decency."

On the question of violence, Celada insisted that his brothers had not come armed with the aim of causing trouble; rather they acted in self-defense, which they were permitted by "natural law." Celada would not cede the right of white *sevillanos* to inflict harm on black *sevillanos* (free and enslaved) out of spite. Celada described the members of his confraternity as "black," suggesting that members of La Antigua attacked and insulted them for this reason. He clearly considered being black an illegitimate foundation for violence, and they had every right to protect themselves. Later in the legal wrangling, Juan de Santiago, a (white) priest who was processing with Los Ángeles gave testimony that supported Celada's: the white brothers accosted the black brothers, hissing

---

[84] AGAS, Justicia, Hermandades, Leg. 94, n. 5 (09885), "Pleito de la cofradía de Nuestra Señora de los Angeles," 8r. The hospital during this period was run by the Orden Hospitalaria de San Juan de Dios, a Spanish religious order dedicated to hospital work.

[85] AGAS, Justicia, Hermandades, Leg. 94, n. 5 (09885), "Pleito de la cofradía de Nuestra Señora de los Angeles," 6v.

[86] AGAS, Justicia, Hermandades, Leg. 94, n. 5 (09885), "Pleito de la cofradía de Nuestra Señora de los Angeles," 14r.

unprovoked insults at them (including "*borrachos*" [drunks]). Juan de Santiago characterized such behavior as a great dishonor both to the brothers and to the image of the Passion of Christ they carried, reminding his listeners that the members of Los Ángeles were pious Christians.[87]

Celada's deposition is immediately followed by Francisco de Acosta's rebuttal. Acosta was enraged by Celada's defense of himself and the other black brothers. In his next statement, it becomes clear that there was more at stake in this fracas than precedence – it had become a referendum on the place of black Catholics in church and society. For the members of La Antigua, it was incomprehensible that they would be forced to give way to group that consisted of "ignorant blacks and slaves" who behaved with "much indecency and without any devotion, which provoked laughter from those who watched them."[88] While the accusations of indecent behavior by black brothers is prominent in the complaints of the members of La Antigua, it derived from the simple idea that it was unacceptable for white people – slave owners among them, more than likely – to give way to black slaves in the street.

Acosta aggressively countered Celada's claims to the equality of all souls by proclaiming:

> Our holy mother Church does not deny that there are orders and grades here on earth just as there are in Heaven – and it is against good order and natural reason that the brothers of that confraternity, being slaves who do not descend from Old Christians, should try to compete with this confraternity of white men.[89]

Acosta's proclamation of white supremacy in the face of the historic right of precedence could not have been clearer – what did it matter if Los Ángeles was older than La Antigua if the members of Los Ángeles were New Christians and those of La Antigua were Old Christians? Here Acosta coded blackness with New Christianity and whiteness with Old Christianity. The status of "New Christian" was also a legal category that forbade such individuals access to certain offices and roles in the Church; it was most commonly applied to those of Jewish and Muslim descent, and carried connotations of heresy and danger to the faith. With this argument, Acosta sought to replace the older model of order

---

[87] AGAS, Justicia, Hermandades, Leg. 94, n. 5 (09885), "Pleito de la cofradía de Nuestra Señora de los Angeles," s.f. This later group of testimonies focuses on the use of injurious language rather than violence or bloodshed so heavily emphasized in the first round.

[88] AGAS, Justicia, Hermandades, Leg. 94, n. 5 (09885), "Pleito de la cofradía de Nuestra Señora de los Angeles," 27v.

[89] AGAS, Justicia, Hermandades, Leg. 94, n. 5 (09885), "Pleito de la cofradía de Nuestra Señora de los Angeles," 18r-19r.

(antiquity of organization regardless of ethnicity) with a new model rooted in *limpieza de sangre* laws.

Acosta's appeal to a natural order that originated in Heaven and ought to be replicated on earth was key to the argument against Los Ángeles. What would happen to the general order of a slave society if slaves were permitted to force free white men to stand down? Here we see a strikingly illustrated example of the potential promise of spiritual equality offered to black Catholics colliding with the social realities of a white slaveholding society. White residents would, under no circumstances, accept the premises of baptismal equality, insisting instead that inequality structured Heaven itself. Furthermore, nearly all the (white) witnesses of the melee supported the account of La Antigua, claiming that the black confraternity members had hurled insults at whites (including "dogs" and "Jews"), justifying violence against them. They further described the black brothers as "rustic," "barbarous," and "ridiculous."[90] As in other cases where white authors or witnesses described black participants in religious festivals with this kind of language, they provided no examples to illustrate their claims. It is possible that the very presence of black bodies on the street, carrying *pasos* with their patronal images to the sound of their own music, struck many seventeenth-century white *sevillanos* as inherently ridiculous and barbarous.

For his part, Celada proclaimed that the Church itself did not consider black Catholics "less than." He declared that "there are many black priests (*sacerdotes*) and prebends throughout Spain," which itself proved that blacks were not excluded from the Church because of their skin color.[91] Celada and his fellow brothers, therefore, mounted a legal defense that rejected every one of La Antigua's racist premises, particularly about black decorum and place in the Church. Los Ángeles drew its strength from its members' status as baptized and practicing Christians, which meant they could not be barred from admission within the Church, even among the ecclesiastical hierarchy. Another member of the confraternity, Luis de Mendoza, complained bitterly about the expense of the lawsuit, which naturally worked to benefit La Antigua, which, he noted, was full of "very powerful men," whereas his poor confraternity was being driven to bankruptcy by the lawsuit's cost.[92]

---

[90] AGAS, Justicia, Hermandades, Leg. 94, n. 5 (09885), "Pleito de la cofradía de Nuestra Señora de los Angeles," 1r-v ("gente barbara"), and additional references in AGAS, "Continuación del pleito entre las cofradías de los Angeles y la Antigua," Leg. 92, no. 2 (09883), s.f. to gente (people) "barbara," "rustica," and "ridicula." Note here the insult of calling someone "Jewish" was also echoed in Acosta's description of Afro-Iberians as "New Christians."

[91] AGAS, Justicia, Hermandades, Leg. 94, n. 5 (09885), "Pleito de la cofradía de Nuestra Señora de los Angeles," 14r-v. I have found no evidence to support this claim by Celada, at least in Spain.

[92] AGAS, Justicia, Hermandades, Leg. 94, n. 5 (09885), "Pleito de la cofradía de Nuestra Señora de los Angeles," 56r-v.

Not surprisingly, however, the archbishop of Seville, Ambrosio Roche, sided with La Antigua and, in 1606, forbade Los Ángeles from going on procession because of the scandal they caused.[93] He further tried to effectively quash the confraternity by excommunicating its members. Isidoro Moreno points out that the subsequent archbishop, Pedro de Castro, lifted the ban, but that it was reinstated by Philip III, who, in 1614, accused members of Los Ángeles of lacking due dignity and stealing from their masters to buy candles.[94] In spite of this royal decision, the members of the confraternity apparently continued fighting, this time moving the conflict to Rome. Luis de Mendoza, alcalde of the confraternity, together with other leaders, presented their case to the papal nuncio, who transmitted the information back to Rome.[95] Their effort was successful, and Pope Urban VIII reconfirmed the confraternity's rule in 1625, safeguarding it from further such attacks.

There are many facets of early modern Spanish religious and social life revealed by this fracas. It represents clearly that black *sevillanos* faced constant hostility and derision. Yet the outburst of violence occurred precisely because of the elevated position of the black confraternity, rather than its marginalization – the claims of antiquity and spiritual equality that derived from the prominent participation of Los Ángeles in the Holy Week processions, and from the refusal of the members of the confraternity to recognize the claims of the powerful white members of La Antigua. It is entirely possible that, tired of the verbal abuse and ridicule to which they were regularly subjected, the black brothers did instigate violence against white brothers – and no matter who threw the first rock, it seems clear that members of Los Ángeles defended themselves physically. Surrounded by prejudice and hostility, black *sevillanos* staked out the public space accorded to them as baptized Christians. In Celada's and Mendoza's testimonies, we see the potential fruit of participation in black confraternities. We see clearly how adeptly Afro-sevillanos adopted and adapted Spanish laws and traditions in ways that bolstered their status and situations, in similar ways as other marginalized groups throughout the Spanish empire.[96]

Most conflict between black confraternities and white authorities did not draw blood; instead, long-term wars of attrition were waged. Cadiz, a port city on Spain's Atlantic coast, hosted three confraternities for its population of color: Nuestra Señora del Rosario, the oldest of the three, founded before

---

[93] AGAS, Justicia, Hermandades, Leg. 94, n. 5 (09885), "Pleito de la cofradía de Nuestra Señora de los Angeles," N. 9885 (1).

[94] Moreno, *La antigua hermandad*, 89–90. [95] AGAS, III.1.6, N. 9885, f. 56v.

[96] Villa-Flores, *Dangerous Speech*; McKnight, "Blasphemy as Resistance"; and Twinam, *Purchasing Whiteness*. The topic has been well-studied for indigenous populations, especially in New Spain: Yannakakis, *The Art of Being In-Between*; Owensby, *Empire of Law*.

1590; Nuestra Señora de la Salud, founded in the early seventeenth century; and the short-lived *mulato* confraternity, Santísimo Ecce Homo, which disappeared by 1675.[97] The Rosary confraternity was originally housed in the Hospital de la Santa Misericordia, located on the Plaza de Corredera along a vibrant route in the town center.[98] At the end of the sixteenth century, the confraternity's popularity and wealth had accumulated to the point where it could move to its own space, the hermitage of San Antonio, afterwards called El Rosario. In the same period, the city's Dominican order worked to expand its influence and power base in the city. The hermitage offered one such opportunity; the Rosary Virgin was a Dominican cult, and the friars offered to act as the confraternity's chaplain and overseer. The confraternity resisted but lost its battle in a lawsuit, which resulted in the confraternity's removal with its titular images and goods to another chapel on Esteban de Sopranis street in 1635.

The Dominicans might have cast their eyes to exert control over the hermitage because of the elevated profile of devotion to the Rosary Virgin in Cadiz at this time. She became the patroness of the Spanish fleet at a time when the economic success of the city depended on transatlantic trade; she remains the patroness of the city to the present day.[99] Tension between the confraternity and the Dominicans continued as the brothers attempted to establish firm rights to their own goods, alms, and prerogatives.[100] Such increasing prominence of the Rosary cult led to increased interest in the black Rosary confraternity by members of the white community as well. As in Seville, white laity were perfectly happy to join historically black confraternities once the brotherhoods became sufficiently visible, historic, and/or wealthy. Sancho de Sopranis notes that on the membership rolls of the brotherhood we can find the names of the oldest local nobility as well as powerful Genovese patricians.[101] In 1734, the confraternity lodged a complaint against the Dominicans over their church, staking a longstanding claim to the image of the Rosary Virgin following their loss of San Antonio in the early seventeenth century. As part of this complaint, they explained that they did not have the earliest documentation proving this ownership, because it had been destroyed when the English sacked the city in 1596.[102] Presumably this absence of documentation opened the door for the Dominicans to deny their rights.

---

[97] Sancho de Sopranis, *Las cofradias de morenos en Cádiz*, 12–13.

[98] Lomas Salmonte, *Historia de Cádiz*, 216–17.

[99] Every year during the feast of Corpus Christi, an image of the Rosary Virgin is carried from the cathedral in a large procession during which the path is strewn with rosemary.

[100] Sopranis, *Las cofradías de morenos*, 19–21.   [101] Sopranis, *Las cofradías negras*, 22.

[102] Archivo Diocesano de Cádiz (hereafter ADC), Caja 520, 6r.

As in the case of Los Ángeles in Seville, once the wealthy and noble white members of *gatidano* society began to participate in the confraternity, they worked to wrest control of the offices from enslaved and free black members. When the black Rosary confraternity moved to the Dominican church in 1635, their brotherhood had been "combined" with a white Rosary brotherhood to share the altar and image. The black leaders of the confraternity declared that after this merger, the black members had kept their right to hold the highest positions of office and thus to lead the brotherhood.[103] They organized a judicial complaint to protest efforts by the white members to systematically block the election of black members to higher office, arguing: "Naturally the Spanish members [*hermanos Españoles*] favor those of their kind [*clase*]," but insisting that the Spaniards still violated the privileges assured to Ethiopian members. Here, the author employed significant terms to describe the two groups of members: Spaniard and Ethiopian. The language distinguished the two groups, by conferring a national status, rather than referring to them by skin color.[104] Black leadership of the confraternity remained solidly in place, then, for a century following the union of the two brotherhoods: In contrast to eighteenth-century Brazil, in Cadiz, white members began a campaign against the monopoly on leadership by black members, and ultimate succeeded in this endeavor.

Not all the black members remained in the confraternity after the initial conflict. Some broke off and formed a new brotherhood exclusively for members of color. They could not take their patronal image – the Rosary Virgin – with them, and therefore had to find a new patron. They settled on Nuestra Señora de la Salud, eventually adding two co-patrons: Benedict of Palermo and Efigenia. During the first years following the split, Salud appeared to have shared the hermitage San Antonio with the Rosary confraternity, but by the turn of the eighteenth century, they had settled in a collateral altar and vault of the Dominican parish church called the Iglesia del Rosario, where the confraternity's images stand today.

Yet the relationship between the Salud confraternity and their Dominican hosts soured quickly and they engaged in increasingly bitter conflict throughout the first half of the eighteenth century. The first record of conflict comes from a simple lawsuit from Father Tomás de Cantalejos, the sacristan at the Iglesia del Rosario against the Salud confraternity for failing to pay him his annual fee of thirty-six ducados. The subsequent documents by the leaders of the confraternity – including Francisco Antonio, Julian Antonio, and Antonio Faustin de Soto, among others – issued a petition defending their right to their collateral altars and

---

[103] ADC, Caja 521, 5r.
[104] ADC, Caja 520, 23v-24r. The brothers do earlier use the terms "black" and "white."

images which they had erected "with all devotion, reverence, and worship that was, and is, well known." The church, it seems, had undergone a major renovation, after which the confraternity's altar had been moved, and the members of the confraternity denied access pending payment.[105] The fiscal general of Cadiz's ecclesiastic court responded by asserting that the issue of the collateral altar had nothing to do with the petition at hand, which was about the salary owed Cantalejos. Julian Antonio and the others persisted, which apparently irritated the fiscal general sufficiently that he issued a declaration of perpetual silence on the issue and then denied their right of access.[106] The Salud confraternity did not give up, once again petitioning the court for the return of their altar, insisting that their brotherhood had been in existence "for at least a century," and was of good standing; therefore, they deserved their proper place in the church. They further noted that for the previous year, their image (of the Virgin) had been kept in a "private house," presumably because they no longer had access to the church.[107] Their petition must have been unsuccessful, because their fights with the church over the altars continued into the mid-eighteenth century.

By 1734, conflict between the two groups became particularly embittered, when the Salud brothers accused the Dominicans of having "repossessed" and "violently despoiled" the confraternity's altar, turning them out of the church once again.[108] The Dominicans continued to accuse the brothers of "altercations and grave scandals."[109] The bishop of Cadiz, Manuel de Ypenza wrote from Madrid ordering the church to return the altar to the possession of the confraternity.[110] The two sides clashed again in 1759 over the theft of a silver lamp and a bronze bell, which occurred during Dominican efforts to have the Salud confraternity extinguished. The Salud confraternity lost the initial battle with the Dominicans, and appealed three times (tercera instancia) to one of the priors of the archdiocese of Seville in charge of hermitages after the receipt of a papal bull in their favor. Ownership of the lamp and bell were tied, then, to the

---

[105] ADC, Caja 520, "Cadiz año de 1702: Autos que sigue de Thomas Cantalejos sacristan mayor de la yglesia del Rosario. contra el Fran.co Antonio negro el mayo de la cofradia de nra snr de la salud," 5r. The series of lawsuits and wrangling between the Salud brothers and the Dominican priests fills Caja 520, half of 521, and 522, spanning the first six decades of the eighteenth century.

[106] ADC, Caja 520, 7r–14r.　　[107] Ibid., 16r.

[108] ADC, Caja 521, f. 107r-v. Salud confraternity member Francisco Muñoz Temprada accuses the Dominicans of "despojado violentamente a esta cofradia de la posesion, que tenia de altar, capilla, y demas en dha Ig.a" (107v).

[109] Sopranis, Las cofradías de los morenos, 34–6.

[110] ADC, Autos 1734, 378v. Ypenza wrote: "mandò se reintegre a la expresada cofradia en la possession y uso, del altar, bobeda, y demas altaxas; y los referidos curas sitienen algo que pedir contra dicha hermandad y cofradia en razon de la indecencia de retablo used de su derecho como les convenga."

extinguishment and reformation of the brotherhood, which was still a point of contention in spite of the papal bull.[111] The matter was decided in 1760 by Cristóbal de Morales, notary and secretary for the Archbishop of Seville, who had ultimate jurisdiction over Cadiz as its suffragan.[112]

The black confraternities of Los Ángeles, Salud, and Rosario lost control of their offices and possessions to white members or white clergy bent on stripping black members of as much ceremonial honor as they could. The example of Los Ángeles demonstrates that the process of attempting to silence and suppress black public participation in Spanish social and religious life stretched from the early seventeenth century to the eighteenth. Facing dwindling numbers and increasing economic hardship, black confraternities became more vulnerable to white predation and Los Ángeles eventually went the way of Cadiz's Rosary confraternity. Its antiquity and place of honor in Seville's public rituals led to its infiltration by white members, who eventually took control of it and drove out black members in the late seventeenth century. The long eighteenth century, then, saw the end of almost all the black confraternities in Spain, many through force.

We need not see the history of black confraternities only through the lens of white supremacy and ruin. The brothers of the Rosary, Los Ángeles, and Salud resisted attempts by white clergy and brothers to wrest control of their offices and sacred spaces. They engaged in lawsuits, correspondence, and recourse to historical documentation to bolster their claims. The conflict in the streets of Seville took place at the dawn of the seventeenth century, one hundred and fifty years before Nuestra Señora de la Salud was successfully repressed by its enemies. Their history, then, was long and left an indelible impression on the landscape of Iberia. Salud and Los Ángeles maintained prominent cults to black saints, including images on their altars that survive to this day, a lasting visual legacy of both the saints and the groups of black men and women who venerated them.

White Spiritual Slavery, Black Saints, and Ambivalence

Eager for new avenues to access the divine, white lay people in Iberia increasingly appropriated more than important sacred images and the confraternities that held them – they also associated themselves with the rhetoric of spiritual slavery. While the ideas discussed here all drew from ancient and medieval tropes, they began to take on new intensity during the seventeenth and eighteenth centuries

---

[111] ADC, Caja 522; and *Defensa juridica por la cofradia de N. Sra de la Salud* (Seville: Imprenta de la Universidad), 1759.

[112] Information regarding this quarrel can be found in Biblioteca Universitaria de Sevilla (BUS), "D. Christobal de Morales Pastor ... certifico, que autos se han seguido en tercera instancia."

While suffering had been intertwined with slavery in Christian spirituality from the earliest period, the elaborate public performance of penance and the transatlantic slave trade elevated practices that brought together enslavement and suffering in new ways. One of the main vehicles for these new spiritual developments was a new type of confraternity that flourished in the Iberian world, dedicated to penitential acts. Penitential confraternities focused on Holy Week with its commemoration of Christ's suffering and death, mirroring His suffering with their own as expiation of their sins in an effort to render themselves worthy of salvation.[113]

Confraternal devotions could be associated with the concept of spiritual slavery in several different ways: the veneration of a formerly enslaved image; Christ as slave-on-earth; and Catholic laity as slaves of the divine. During the early modern period, raids by Islamic corsairs along the coasts of Spain and Portugal often led to the despoiling of local churches. Images could be taken and held in North Africa. Rulers of Islamic states recognized that the objects had value to Spanish clergy and often offered to ransom them back the same way they would return prisoners for a price. One of the most important "rescued" images was the Cristo de Medinaceli, which was an Ecce Homo – a sculpture of Christ with hands bound in front, crown of thorns pressing into his head. [Fig. 3.1] The image's suffering was doubled – it represented Christ's earthly suffering, and it had been subject to violence while in Morocco.[114] The confraternity that developed around the Cristo de Medinaceli was called "Real y Ilustre Esclavitud de Nuestro Padre Jesús Medinceli," and it took root in multiple sites, including Madrid, Zaragoza, and Alicante. Brotherhoods devoted to this sculpture celebrated the joyous reunion of a precious image taken in violence and commemorated the threat of enslavement that hung over white Europeans in the Mediterranean.

Other discussions of the "slavery" of Christ referred to His time on earth as a human being. Christ's humanity was described as a form of slavery because it chained Him to His earthly body and its attendant suffering. While Christ's slavery was more impressive because He was also God, all humans could claim a kind of earthly exile or enslavement of their flesh that would end with death and the return of their true selves to God's presence. Through Christ's decision to endure brutal physical punishment and death in order to bestow salvation on all people, the everyday human experience of suffering became connected to salvation, imbuing it with spiritual meaning. The greater the suffering, the greater its salvific potential. Slavery, then, with its utter debasement, operated metaphorically as a form of

[113] Penitential confraternities were (and are) particularly visible in Seville. See Webster, *Art and Ritual*; and Schneider, "Mortification on Parade."

[114] A miracle involving the newly returned image appears in Paniagua's hagiography of Teresa Juliana de Santo Domingo, along with a brief account of its travails: *Compendio*, 40–1.

Figure 3.1 *Jesús de Medinaceli*, seventeenth century, polychrome sculpture, Sevillian school, Madrid.

imitatio Christi, and the expansion of this metaphor paralleled the sharp rise in the popularity of penitential confraternities and the slave trade. Rather than remind white Christians of the appalling suffering they directed at enslaved people, such rhetoric expanded the category of slave to one that any person could claim.

Declaring one's slavery to Christ or Mary had scriptural roots – in the New Testament, Paul refers to himself as a "slave of God" (Titus 1:1).[115] We see such

---

[115] This word is sometimes translated as "servant." The Vulgate Bible term is "servus," which could mean either servant or slave.

ideas reflected in the titles of confraternities: for example, La Cofradía de Esclavos del Santísimo Sacramento, or the Cofradia y esclavitud de Nuestra Señora de la Merced. In the latter case, the members of the organization referred to themselves as "*esclavos*" rather than the typical "*hermanos.*" The Church's promotion of slavery as a state of particular grace resonated with white Christians.[116] Such ideas are echoed in the proclamation by seventeenth-century Jesuit Pedro Claver that he was the "slave of slaves," as he ministered to newly arrived enslaved Africans in Cartagena de Indias. In the same way that the holiness of poverty tended to be reserved for those who practiced voluntary poverty rather than to the poor themselves, seventeenth- and eighteenth-century white Catholics desired a self-imposed mantle of slavery.[117] They performed a spiritual slavery that would gain them special access to salvation, without any attendant interest in or sympathy for those enslaved by Europeans.

Just as the white laity were happy to take over a black confraternity and associate themselves voluntarily with slavery, they also venerated black saints, particularly in Iberia. In early modern America, devotion to black saints continued to be largely the preserve of communities of color. While several of the witnesses to Benedict's beatification noted the presence of white devotees to the holy man in Brazil, in most cases, veneration of black saints remained largely driven by people of African descent.[118] In Iberia, by contrast, we see devotion to black saints taking root in predominantly or exclusively white spaces, following aggressive efforts by Franciscans and Carmelites to promote their saints in their convents and churches. The embrace of black saints by white devotees enhanced the saints' status and public presence, while simultaneously diminishing the more radical possibilities offered by black holy authority.

Alonso de Torres mentioned devotions to Benedict in Ubeda, Cordoba, and Bujalance in his 1683 chronicle of Andalusia. Bujalance was the only city of the three where Torres cited the black community as the principal driver of devotion to the black saint. He recounted how devotion to Benedict began in Ubeda: during a terrible drought, the community's white saints were taken on procession to beg their aid in rescuing the community. When they all failed, one nameless devotee of Benedict suggested processing with the Franciscan's image. The townspeople agreed, and rain poured down on the parched town. "With this,"

---

[116] The trope of being a slave to the divine reinforced elaborate strains of penitential devotion emerging from the early seventeenth century. Carlos Varona notes that the "congregaciones de esclavos" proliferated throughout this century: "Una propuesta devocional femenina," 85.

[117] On ideas about poverty and work in the early Church, see Brown, *Treasure in Heaven.*

[118] Devotion to black saints as sites of racially mixed devotional spaces in the Iberian Americas would be a fruitful avenue for future research, since the general focus until now has been on black confraternities.

Torres concluded, "devotion to the saint was greatly increased."[119] Torres's miracle accounts began with white people, even when tied to black confraternities. For example, Fray Sebastian Herrera was on the verge of death; "Inspired by God," Torres claimed, Herrera appealed to St. Benedict for the return of his health. He offered, in return for a successful cure, to commission an image of the saint. Herrera was healed and followed through on his vow, and the image was later given to members of a black confraternity for use in their chapel.[120]

Torres described another miraculous image of Benedict, this time in San Pedro el Real in Cordoba. The sculpture of Benedict was, he declared, "so miraculous," that for more than a year he was without his roped belt, crucifix, and heart from his hands because the devoted had taken them to help heal the ill. Presumably, Torres meant that the objects were removed to bring them to those too ill to visit the church. The objects held in Benedict's hands acted like contact relics – that is, because they were a part of the sculpture, they could act as a conduit for the saint's miraculous power. Torres followed with an account of a miraculous cure of a three-year-old white child. The child's father, Juan Casa de Eza, had brought his child a number of images of the saints to help to cure him. But the child said, "Bring me the little black saint from San Francisco." They brought it to him and placed it in the bed with him. The child put his arms around the saint and afterwards said that the saint had held his hand. And he was cured. Afterwards, Juan Casa also appealed to Benedict to help his son-in-law in his efforts during a bullfight; in gratitude, Juan took the saint as his "particular patron."[121] By the middle of the seventeenth century, then, around one hundred years before his beatification, Benedict had gained a reputation for performing miracles for white devotees in Andalusia. While in both Ubeda and Cordoba, appeals were made to Benedict as a last result, a successful miracle led to long-lasting devotion.

While it is unclear if the images from Ubeda, Cordoba, or Bujalance have survived, visual evidence for miracles by St. Benedict for white devotees can be found throughout Iberia in spaces that were devoted to white clergy or in contexts that make it clear that black saints were performing miracles for white devotees. In central Portugal, two eighteenth-century ex-voto paintings have survived depicting Benedict performing miraculous cures. An ex-voto painting was a commemoration of a miracle by a saint, containing a depiction of the miracle and an inscription at the bottom telling the story of what occurred. Ex-

---

[119] Torres, *Chronica de la Santa Provincia de Granada*, 41.

[120] Torres, *Chronica de la Santa Provincia de Granada*, 127.

[121] Torres's account of the child's cure is a little unclear. While he previously mentioned that there were pieces of the sculpture removed, here it appears that an entire statue had been taken to the child: Torres, *Chronica de la Santa Provincia de Granada*, 49.

votos' artists tended to be amateurs, producing low-cost works on wood that were often displayed in churches near images of the saint in question. One of the two ex-votos from central Portugal was painted in 1724, showing a family clustered around a white man lying prone in bed who was saved from a near-death illness by Benedict, who stands in the back-right corner. Because Benedict's face and hands were painted a very dark pigment with a brown habit, he is difficult to see.[122] [Plate 14]

While the search for the miraculous was a significant factor in the spread of new cults, interorder competition also played an important role in the introduction of saints to lay audiences. Saints of specific orders were aggressively promoted by their orders. Orders worked tirelessly on the canonization of their own, because each new saint represented increased prestige for the order. The religious orders existed in a permanent tangle of competition with each other, fighting over worldly matters like patronage and precedence, and spiritual matters like specific cults of the Virgin and their own saints. Certain types of saints brought heightened prestige to their orders, especially those considered rare, such as martyrs and women. Throughout the early modern period, we also see the religious orders in competition for non-European saints as another type of saint bringing particular fame to an order.[123]

Teresa of Avila, for example, was famous for her mysticism, but her role as the founder of the Discalced Carmelites was perhaps her most significant achievement by early modern standards. Her accomplishments were heightened by her femininity because early modern clergy believed that women were morally and intellectually weaker than men, making their sanctity a greater gift. Like women, non-European holy people – African, indigenous, Chinese, South Asian, etc. – brought glory to their order as a symbols of successful overseas missionary efforts. Such holy people represented the power of God's grace, and reflected glory on the entire order, although such interest in holy women or people of color remained small in comparison to the time, expense, and successes of canonizations of white, European clergy.

Yet several orders worked assiduously to promote holy people of color, including the Franciscans, Dominicans, and Carmelites. The Calced Carmelites began to promote their two saints – Elesban and Efigenia – aggressively throughout the seventeenth and into the eighteenth century. There is less textual evidence for Elesban and Efigenia than for Benedict: the main source we have for the dispersal of their images and cults comes from the Portuguese Carmelite historian

---

[122] The second ex-voto, not provided here, also depicts a miracle on behalf of a white man.

[123] One of the few exceptions to this rule were the early modern cults to the patron saint of Madrid, Isidore the Laborer, and his wife, María de la Cabeza. Venerated in the Middle Ages, Isidore's cult received a significant boost with his official beatification in 1619.

José Pereira Santana, who had little interest in discussing devotion to the saints among black Catholics or black confraternities. Like Torres, Santana centered discussions about the presence of cults to Elesban and Efigenia on white friars. He explained that devotion to the saints had originally arrived in Portugal from Spain. It was, Santana explained, friar Francisco de Santa Helena, who "was the first and principal method of introduction of St. Elesban in Portugal and its Dominions." Francisco had learned about Elesban on a journey to Rome; stopping over in Seville, Francisco visited the Calced Carmelite convent, the so-called Casa Grande (now defunct), a "sumptuous" church, "first among architecture." Here stood an image of Elesban on the altar of Nuestra Señora de la Antigua, "of medium height" and "superior perfection," surrounded by many ex-votos offered in thanksgiving from devotees who received aid from the saint. Francisco met another Carmelite friar, João Affonso (José Alfonso) de Aguiar, prior in the town of Trigueros near Huelva, northwest of Cadiz. Aguiar promised to send Francisco copies of the image of Elesban from Trigueros to the Carmelite house in Lisbon: "[Francisco] received these paintings ... and so one began to see the two Ethiopian saints in Portugal."[124] Santana attributed veneration to Elesban in Portugal, then, to Carmelite networks spanning southern Europe, rather than black confraternities.[125]

Spanish Carmelite friar Joseph de Navia preached a sermon in Avila in the middle of the eighteenth century as part of a celebration of the arrival of images of Elesban and Efigenia in 1752, brought by the confraternity of Nuestra Señora de las Angustias. Navia provided no additional information to explain why the confraternity wished to commission these images for their chapel in the Carmelite church. He did mention the miracles that the saints performed in Seville and Lisbon, suggesting that knowledge of the Ethiopian saints was slim in the region around Avila.[126] Works such as Santana's panegyric and Navia's sermon in Avila worked to promote the two saints among the white laity in Portugal and Spain, clearly part of a larger Carmelite effort to elevate Elesban's and Efigenia's profiles in the order's pantheon of saints.

Black saints and their cults held significance to white laity and clergy. Franciscans and Carmelites had the most at stake in the promotion of their saints, but fame was only possible if the cults were embraced by white laity as well as black. White embrace of black saints rested largely on their interest in access to miracles, but it is less clear what meaning they ascribed to the blackness of the saints they venerated; presumably their devotion rested on the ability to

---

[124] Santana, *Os dous atlantes*, 1:317–21.

[125] Santana provided a string of examples of miracles performed by Elesban: *Os dous atlantes*, I:324–9. He described miracles performed by Efigenia in Cadiz: *Os dous atlantes*, II:113–17.

[126] Navia, *Sermon pangyrico-historico*.

sever the tie between black saints and the promise of spiritual equality that they embodied, in the same way that their performances of slavery had nothing to do with the actual enslaved bodies who lived among them.

The existence of black saints proved that black Catholics could reach the highest levels of sanctity. Their quick adoption by members of black confraternities was the logical extension of their insistence on their rightful participation in public festivals and civic life. We can speculate that members of black confraternities adapted such saints to reinforce established rhetoric. The visible presence of black saints on the streets and in churches acted as the ultimate reminder to white viewers of spiritual equality mandated by God and to black Catholics that justice through awaited them in the next life if it never occurred on earth. Cults of black saints, then, formed a circuit between black devotees, religious orders, and the white laity, creating powerful and ambivalent nodes of discussion about spiritual equality, racism, color prejudice, and sanctity. We must not, however, forget Paulino de Velasco, the enslaved man standing in the Franciscan church in Lima. Surveying the saints in the church's magnificent altars, his eyes rested on Benedict of Palermo. Deeply moved that the saint was black like him, Paulino returned again and again to venerate at Benedict's altar.

PART II
ILLUMINATION

4 BEAUTIFUL BLACKNESS: REPRESENTING BLACK SAINTS IN BAROQUE SCULPTURE

When the Congregation of Sacred Rites gathered people to testify in the early eighteenth-century beatification process for Benedict of Palermo, witnesses were asked a series of prepared questions, including a request to name any place where they had seen images of the holy man. All the witnesses reporting about the Iberian Atlantic testified to having viewed more than one statue or painting. We have seen how their reports and similar accounts from hagiographies make it possible to map the breadth of devotion to Benedict as well as the other black saints. Such reports also provide crucial insight into the ways in which early modern people reacted to and remembered the images in their midst. Sacred art acted as visual reminders, foci for meditation, and spiritual inspiration; perhaps most importantly for the laity, statues and paintings of the saints could often work miracles in ways similar to relics. Images – and their miracles – attracted devotees, fame, and even wealth from the alms of visitors. Like other saints, images of black saints saturated the devotional landscape of the Iberian Atlantic, projecting spiritual truths and shaping perceptions of how to see and understand sacred blackness.

Sacred art was created through dynamic interactions between artists and patrons on a variety of spiritual, theological, and aesthetic matters. As a result, holy objects engaged with multiple meanings and purposes simultaneously, which also varied based on the interaction between the object and a specific viewer. In addition to these devotional purposes, sacred images also provided powerful evidence for the existence of a saint's cult. Early modern clergy could, therefore, use the presence of images to defend the legitimacy of a particular cult, to protect it from criticism, or to elevate its significance, as we saw with the beatification testimony for Benedict. Images could prove particularly useful to the religious orders as they launched intense campaigns to spread devotion to their own saints, including black saints. Elesban and Efigenia, for example, operated as evidence for the Carmelites as they sought to defend a specific version of their order's history dating from the Prophet Elijah.[1] The Franciscans, on the other hand, viewed Benedict's cult as a way for them to promote their success as global missionaries, a reputation under threat by the Jesuits. Beyond clerical concerns, images of black saints communicated spiritual truths to viewers about blackness, color difference, and the spiritual potential of Africans. All these aspects of sacred art – spiritual, polemical, aesthetic – must be examined together in order to understand the richness and complexity of images of black saints.

Before analysis of the sacred art of black saints, a brief word must be said about chronology, since the study here encompasses two centuries in which we know significantly less about the earlier century than the later, and sources about both can be thin. In many cases, there are no surviving sources to describe exactly when or why a given image was commissioned. There are many surviving references to images commissioned during the seventeenth century in printed sources, but many of the images mentioned do not appear to have survived to the present day. For example, the image in Puebla appears to have vanished, as have the three mentioned by Alonso de Torres – Cordoba, Ubeda, and Bujalance – as well as the *sevillano* paintings of Elesban and Efigenia. Witnesses in the beatification testimony for Benedict describe images that existed in the Iberian Atlantic at least by the end of the seventeenth century, since they viewed the artwork in person before 1713.[2] Like the beatification testimony, hagiographies and sacred histories also mention images at length, although they do not provide concrete information about dating. Most of these printed works were printed between 1702 and 1770, although some specifically refer to early seventeenth-century images.[3] What we are left with, however, are two distinct threads of evidence: textual references to seventeenth-century images that have vanished; and the surviving sacred art, which largely dates to the eighteenth century. Surviving print engravings of black saints also overwhelming date to the middle of the eighteenth century.[4]

While most images of black saints have unknown artists, several of Benedict have been attributed to well-known artists: Bernardo González and Mateos Bermuda (Iglesia de San Antonio da Padua, Seville, 1702); José de Mora

---

[1] For an overview on early Carmelite history, see Jotischky, *The Carmelites and Antiquity*.

[2] Ironically, the images that were the most often mentioned in the beatification testimony were the ones I was least likely to find and view in person – Lima, Puebla, Cañete, and Cordoba.

[3] The hagiography printed in 1779 is a chronological outlier, as 1702–1752 marks the period of most concentrated writing on the saint: Benegasi y Luján, *Vida del portentoso negro San Benito de Palermo*.

[4] Celia Cussen's important study of Martín de Porres includes several seventeenth-century paintings and engravings of the holy man: *Black Saint of the Americas*.

(d. 1724); José Montes de Oca (d. 1754); and José Salvador de Carmona (largely worked in the 1770s). Most works, however, are simply labelled by century without further information about their commission or artists involved. Yet the patterns suggest that the period 1720–1770 was a crucial one for the cults of black saints, precisely the period leading up to and following Benedict's beatification in 1743. The increasing prominence of Benedict's cult affected devotion to all black saints, as it sparked competition with other orders, particularly the Carmelites, who ramped up the visibility of their own saints at the same time. The increasing promotion of black saints by Franciscans and Carmelites throughout the late seventeenth to mid-eighteenth centuries led to an attendant proliferation of their images, which began to dot the sacred landscape of the Iberian Atlantic.

Mapping Images

From the end of the sixteenth to the beginning of the seventeenth centuries, a series of reforms by the papacy in the liturgy and process for canonization led to increased bureaucratic hurdles for legitimating saints' cults. Local communities and religious orders responded with a flurry of effort to establish the antiquity – a catch-all term for a cult with a long history – of certain cults too old to have undergone papal canonization. Whether a preliminary effort for a saint's canonization or an attempt to validate a centuries-old cult, the presence of sacred art played a key role in determining the existence, spread, and significance of a cult.[5] Because early modern clergy viewed the presence of sacred art as essential to demonstrating devotion to particular saint in a specific location, they always included lists of places where such images could be found in their hagiographies. Close examination of such references allow us to map cultic devotion.

Witnesses in Benedict's beatification cause noted the presence of his image throughout Spain, Portugal, New Spain, Peru, and Brazil. [Map 4.1] Authors of hagiographic texts likewise provided a wide geographic landscape for Benedictine devotion. Although there is much overlap between places mentioned in beatification testimony and those mentioned in hagiographies, they do not fully replicate each other. The Iberian clergy gave testimony predominantly about the Spanish Atlantic, whereas hagiographers mentioned more diverse locations, largely in Portugal. It was perhaps easier for hagiographers to collect

---

[5] One example of the search for "ancient" images as part of a seventeenth-century canonization effort is that of the king-saint Fernando III: Wunder, *Baroque Seville*, ch. 3; Quiles, "En los cimientos de la iglesia sevillana." For studies that address responses by local authorities to the problem of authenticity, see Olds, *Forging the Past*; and Ditchfield, *Liturgy, Sanctity, and History*.

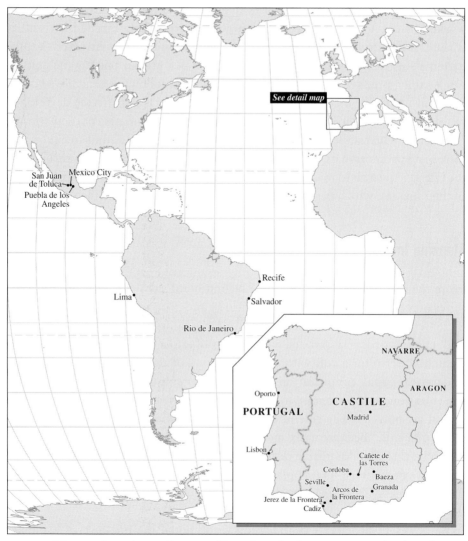

Map 4.1 Locations of images of Benedict of Palermo mentioned in beatification testimony

accounts of images than for the witnesses who could only testify to what they had seen with their own eyes. [Map 4.2] Taken together, the maps reveal the geographic reach of Benedict's cult throughout the Iberian Atlantic by the turn of the eighteenth century.

Those promoting the cults of black saints centered their arguments on the claims of antiquity and universal devotion, particularly those advocating Benedict's beatification. Sometimes authors and witnesses provided general dates for images, confraternities, or devotions to Benedict, some reaching as far

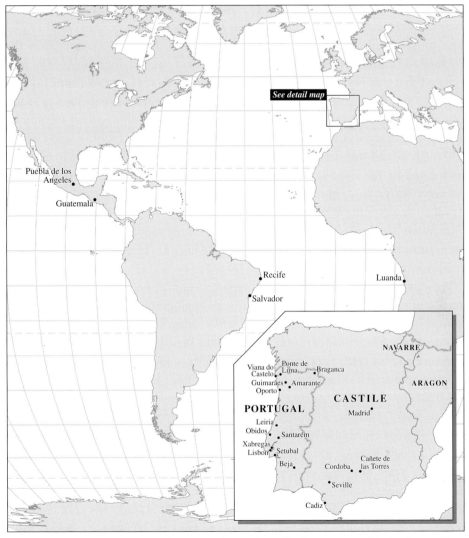

Map 4.2 Locations of images of Benedict of Palermo named in hagiographies

back as the early seventeenth century. They often commented that a work was "most ancient," which referred to a period of one hundred years or more, as antiquity was one of the requirements for an official cult. Witnesses and hagiographers further emphasized the large numbers of extant images in diverse places in order to indicate how widespread the cult was.[6] Occasionally, they provided

---

[6] For example, Francisco Antonio Castellano mentions "the many and singular marvels bestowed to his devotees accomplished through his prints and images": *Compendio de la heroyca, y maravillosa vida*, 119.

precise information: for example, one manuscript hagiography mentioned an image of Benedict that had been placed in Madrid's Franciscan convent in 1733.[7] The most detailed information about images of Benedict comes from the Portuguese author Apolinário de Conceição's 1744 hagiography.[8] He proclaimed that not only had Sicily "benefited from the rays of this beautiful son, but its warm light spread over all of Catholic Europe, and its benign warmth extends all the way to the Indies and Brazil." He followed this general account by mentioning specific cities: Rio de Janeiro, Leiria (Portugal), Oporto, and Lisbon. Although he did not describe the images, he included accounts of the miracles performed by the saint in each location, therefore reinforcing the relationship between image and miracle in the making of a devotional cult.[9] Because Apolinário was a prominent Franciscan author, his works spread quickly along Franciscan networks; the same year *Flor peregrina* was printed, Spanish Franciscan Antonio Vicente de Madrid wrote his own hagiography in which he cited Apolinário's work as a source.[10]

Perhaps the "most ancient" of all Iberian images of Benedict dates to the first decade of the seventeenth century. Nearly all hagiographers mentioned the 1618 festival in Lisbon attended by Philip III, which occurred ten years after the establishment of a black brotherhood dedicated to Benedict in the city. The earliest reference to this festival occurred in Tognoletto's 1667 work; a more detailed account appeared in Mataplanes's 1702 hagiography, where the author described the black brotherhood moving through the streets with "simple *candidez* and sincere piety," carrying a "costly" standard with a painted image of Benedict.[11] Hagiographers clearly viewed the Lisbon procession as a foundational moment for Benedict's cult, because it was performed in a major city with a royal audience, less than fifty years after the saint's death. Tognoletto described the movement of Benedict's relics to the "Indies," and the "many altars and solemn festivals" that were celebrated throughout the "east" and "west," particularly among black communities, providing geographical reach to go with its antiquity. Some of his evidence for the Atlantic reaches of Benedict's cult came from a visit by a group of Spanish Franciscan brothers to Palermo in 1632, where the Spaniards told the *palermitano* brothers about the profound devotion to Benedict in New Spain,

[7] Francisco de Hoyo, "Doctrina mysticas, morales, fundadas, y elucidas de la vida del santo Negro san Benedito de San Fratelo," BNE 3418 (1744), 101–2.

[8] Apolinário de Conceição, *Flor peregrina*. For more on Apolinário and his influential Franciscan writing, see Palomo, "Conexiones atlánticas."

[9] Apolinário de Conceição, *Flor peregrina*, 237–45.

[10] Antonio Vicente de Madrid, *El negro mas prodigioso*, 164.

[11] Mataplanes, *Vida del fray Benito de S. Fradelo*, 185. Mataplanes, who lived in Palermo, lifted much information and detail from Tognoletto's earlier text.

particularly in Puebla de los Ángeles.[12] This small moment in Tognoletto's text tells us much about knowledge of the saints traveling across the Iberian Atlantic, and it is particularly significant that the Iberian Franciscans', report about New Spain – that is, information circulated from the Americas all the way to Sicily.

Although Carmelite promoters of Elesban and Efigenia did not need to persuade the papacy to approve beatification or worry about the proper representation of their saints, they also called attention to the wide dispersion of images of their saints. Their efforts to map this devotion in printed texts acted as advertising that they hoped would help spread cults to new locations. The most vigorous promoter of the cults of Efigenia and Elesban was Santana, whose work encompassed a large geographic swath including Lisbon, Oporto, Seville, and Trigueros. For example, Santana reported that, in Oporto, the Benedictine brothers in the royal monastery desired an image of Efigenia in order to obtain "her most effective protection," adding that the brothers celebrated a solemn procession the day they received their images of the two Ethiopian saints. The Benedictine nuns at Santa Clara likewise requested images, magnificent sculptures that are housed there to this day.[13] Accounts like these communicated to readers that certain saints were efficacious in performing miracles, and therefore desirable additions to local devotions. [Map 4.3]

Images, then, acted as the central way early modern people learned about saints, especially new ones, even when our evidence comes from texts rather than surviving images. The Iberian clergy who gave testimony to the Congregation in 1713 almost universally reported that they had never read a hagiography of the saint, in sharp contrast to the witnesses in Palermo, almost all of whom had read Tognoletto's hagiography. The gap most likely resulted from the fact that most hagiographies of Benedict in Castilian had not been printed yet – except for brief accounts in sources like Daza or Sandoval, Mataplanes's 1702 hagiography was the first. In Palermo, then, clergy had a textual knowledge base for the saint's life, while Iberian clergy and laity relied predominantly on visual evidence.[14]

Blackness in Baroque Polychrome Sculpture

Nearly all the surviving images of black saints are polychrome sculpture, in large part because of the enormous popularity of this medium in the seventeenth- and

---

[12] Tognoletti, *Paradiso serafico*, 320–1.
[13] Santana, *Os dous atlantes*, 2:211. For more on the Santa Clara images, see Lopes, "Imagem-objeto."
[14] ASV, Processus, MS 2179 and 2180. The second volume (MS 2180) consists almost exclusively of testimony about devotion to Benedict in Sicily.

eighteenth-century Iberian world. The uses the images were variable. Some polychrome sculptures were taken out in procession – they were formed from wood, and hollowed out to make them lighter for carrying. Others remained permanently in their altars. While witnesses at Benedict's canonization mentioned many examples of images taken out, the sculpture and banners cited tend to be the ones that have not survived or cannot be clearly attributed. We can sometimes learn about an image's use by looking at the back. Many of the images were decorated with gold leaf or by using a technique called *estofado*. In *estofado* work, gold leaf is painted over the part of the sculpture, and then covered with the intended colors for the clothes – in these cases usually brown and cream. Next, the artist carefully created designs by punching through the paint to reveal the gold in sophisticated and complicated patterns. [**Plate 15**] Because gold leaf and certain pigments were expensive, many images that were not meant to go out on procession had plain, undecorated backs, thus reducing the amount of material required. [**Plate 16**] Such images were most likely placed in the church where their backs would not be seen by the viewer, like in an altar niche.

Another common type of sacred sculpture in early modern Iberia is called an "*imagen de vestir*." This means that the image was meant to be dressed with real cloth. The most lavish of these – usually sculptures of the Virgin Mary – might have several expensive outfits into which they would be lovingly dressed, particularly for special occasions like processions. *Imágenes de vestir* were constructed differently from other polychrome sculpture. Although they too were fashioned from wood, their arms and legs were jointed for easier dressing and undressing.[15] Few surviving sculptures of black saints in Iberia are dressed, although two in central Portugal appear today clothed in brown Franciscan robes, one tied with a knotted rope. The habits in both sculptures swamp the saint, and it is difficult to tell whether the images had originally been designed to be clothed or if the robes were added more recently.[16] [**Plate 17**]

Polychrome sculpture emerged as a powerful force in baroque piety because of its dramatic ability to invoke the living presence (*praesentia*) of the holy to the viewer. It had, and was meant to have, a profound spiritual and emotional impact on devotees, capable of collapsing visible and invisible, temporary and eternal, the illusions of the profane in contrast to the omnipresence of the holy. The temporary and eternal did not exist in separate spheres; rather, the sacred operated in the liminal zone between the physical and the spiritual; the image

---

[15] Webster, *Art and Ritual.*
[16] Looking underneath the clothes would have answered this question; unfortunately, I was not able to do so.

Map 4.3 Images of Black Saints in Iberia, which I have seen or for which I have concrete information that they exist or existed at one time.

was the bridge.[17] The key to achieving *praesentia* was to create a sculpture so convincing that it could startle the viewer into imagining that it had come to life. The technical work of the sculptor naturally played a crucial role in developing the perfect proportions, the sense of movement, the detail of bone and facial features/expression and hair (which very often required the technical skill to create swirls of waves in order to give movement and personality to the work). The second phase involved the decoration – a second artist, the painter, was responsible for the intricate *estofado* work of the garments, which provided not only detail, but also a play of pattern, light, and movement to complement the

[17] For important discussions of the role of polychrome sculpture in Spanish spiritual life, see Kasl et al., *Sacred Spain*; and Bray et al., in *The Sacred Made Real*.

sculptor's work.[18] More importantly, the painter completed crucial work on the body of the figure. A sculptor would create the veins in a hand or face, for example, while the painter's job was to make such details vivid, often applying a blue pigment on the veins, which were then painted over with cream-beige fleshtones to provide the appearance of veins under skin, as well as the appearance of stubble on the face and head.[19] [Plate 18] The synergy of sculptor and painter generated works of magnificent detail and impact.

Most early modern artists – such as the influential theorist and painter, Francisco de Pacheco – agreed that the most important aspect of polychrome sculpture was the process referred to as *encarnaciones*. The *encarnaciones*, translated as "flesh tones," involved the application of the pigmentation and shading of the figure's skin.[20] As scholars have described it: "the application of translucent oil layers over a white round, as in the *encarnaciones* technique, yields a result that – even on close inspection – mimics the luminous translucency of human flesh, thus enhancing the realism of the figures."[21] The word "*encarnación*" (incarnation) itself is significant, because it is the theological term for Christ taking human form. The term, therefore, referred both to an artistic technique wherein the artist applied flesh tones to the sculpture of a human, and to the spiritual process of transforming something without flesh into flesh. This is not the realism of a wax work, which might resemble its human counterpart but maintains a stiff blankness; rather it is an effort to startle, to move, to bring the sacred to life.[22]

Yet the concept of "incarnation" in the context of sacred sculpture suggests a deeper theological significance than bringing flesh to life. Felipe Pereda argues that "realism" in sacred sculpture mattered less than the artists' ability to convey theological and spiritual truths. Through this process, the viewer is transformed into witness and believer.[23] Similitude, therefore, operated on one level in the creation of sacred sculpture, but the *meaning* of the work – the proof it provided to divine truth, to use Pereda's framework – went much deeper than technique.

---

[18] A fascinating look at the mechanics of creating a polychrome sculpture was found at www.getty.edu/art/collection/video/399883/making-a-spanish-polychrome-sculpture/.

[19] See also this study of the polychrome sculpture by sculptor Luisa de Roldán and painter Tomás de los Arcos: Bassett and Alvarez, "Process and Collaboration."

[20] Pacheco, *El Arte de la Pintura*, 252–3.

[21] Bassett and Alvarez, "Process and Collaboration," 21.

[22] For more on this theme in Spanish baroque polychrome sculpture, see: Bray, Rodríguez G. de Ceballos, *The Sacred Made Real*; and Kasl and Alonso Rodríguez G. de Ceballos, *Sacred Spain*. Baroque painters and sculptors engaged in a lively debate in seventeenth-century Seville over which medium was superior, the so-called parangón: González García, "Spanish Religious Imagery," 175–252; and Ostrow, "Zurbarán's Cartellini."

[23] Pereda, *Crimen e ilusión*.

This point about evidence and realism is particularly important when beginning to assess images of black saints and to understand the spiritual meaning that artists meant to communicate through their works. It is clear through close examination of sculptures of black saints that the key to the spiritual truths they expressed was their blackness. The black pigments employed were both aesthetic and theological, working together to convey meaning to the viewer about blackness, sanctity, and salvation.

Baroque polychromers highlighted their subjects' blackness in a way that achieved a visual effect not only of great beauty, but that also played with the relationship between pigment and light. Aesthetic theories of color and light could transgress the standard binary of light and dark through an awareness of the visual impact of light on color. Because black, like all colors, exhibits shading and depth, it can react to different light in distinct ways, some of which are capable of achieving a special brightness, while some emphasized rich darkness.[24] Masterpieces of baroque polychrome sculpture like those by Luisa Roldán and Tomás de los Arcos depict white Europeans. In doing so, artists chose fleshtones from a range of hues – that is, shades of beige, from a pale that is almost white to olive-brown. Because almost all fleshtones reflected shades of whiteness, analysis of the *encarnaciones* of black saints is a new area of study, both in terms of technique and symbolism. Sculptors and artists approached images of black saints in fundamentally different ways from white saints, supplying them with a spiritual truth distinct from that of white saints.

The vast majority of sculptures of black saints were painted with uniform black pigment. There are a few examples where the fleshtones appear with medium-brown pigment used on the skin, although in most cases the pigment tends to be so dark that it looks black from a distance. When looking at baroque sculpture of black saints today, it is important to keep in mind that conservation of sacred art in Iberia often includes re-painting, making it more difficult to assess the original pigments used. The recently conserved images have uniform pigment, very dark and without blemish or crack. Other examples, however, are poorly conserved with chipped paint, visible cracks, or substantial termite damage. Such damaged images suggest the original composition of the pieces, revealing that flesh tones in conserved images used similar pigments to originals.[25] [**Plate 19, Plate 20**]

---

[24] For early modern theories on vision, color, and light, see Barasch, *Light and Color*; Hendrix and Carmon, *Renaissance Theories of Vision*; Hall, *Color and Meaning*; and Pastoureau, *Black*.

[25] I am currently waiting for the pigment testing results for the image of St. Benedict housed in the Detroit Institute of Arts.

The intense blackness of the pigments used in sculpture and painting of black saints was much remarked on by contemporary viewers. The Franciscan friar Massimo Navares, a native of Malacatepec in the diocese of Mexico, noted an image of Benedict in the Franciscan church in Mexico City. While he could not recall if it had been a statue or painting, he did remember that it had a "black face" (*faccia nera*), a description he used for images he also saw in Spain. It is telling that he could not remember the media of the images – despite the significant difference between painting and sculpture, in their dimensionality, placement in a church, and a viewer's aesthetic response – yet he vividly remembered their black facial pigment.[26] Francisco del Rosario described an image of Efigenia which stood along with Benedict in Mexico City's Hospital of Jesus Nazarano as "also black" (*parimente nera*).[27] Nicola di Lione described one image as a statue of Benedict in the habit of a Franciscan with a black face (*il uolto nero*), while Giuseppe Saportui described an image "with a totally black face."[28] Such descriptions echo Santana's stricture that Elesban and Efigenia should be depicted as "black."

In addition to the pigments chosen for the flesh tones of black saints, there are other striking departures in the artistic techniques of *encarnaciones* from what we see in white saints. For example, painters did not employ the same depth and detail of shading in black saints that helped to create the intense life-likeness of white saints. Such details created highlighting and shading, pinkening of cheeks and lips, blue veins, and contrast between hair and skin (since most white saints had dark hair). Two outliers survive of black saints polychromed with medium-brown flesh tones with some basic *encarnaciones* (pink tones in the cheeks), although it is unclear if these images were lightened to a medium brown following conservation, which is entirely possible. [Plate 21] In the vast majority of sculpture, however, the beauty and intensity of the black skin remains their most striking feature, even as it has the effect of highlighting the detailed and beautiful *estofado* work of many. The black and gold combination renders them particularly eye catching and a contrast to the white saints around them. [Plate 22]

It would be a mistake, however, to imagine that artists of sculptures of black saints merely applied uniform dark pigment in a careless or indifferent way. The dark pigments of skin and hair did not, in fact, preclude shading. One image of Efigenia in the Algarve shows remarkable details in her face – the faint pink of the lips, her lips parted to reveal small white teeth, pink pigment inside her nostrils and faintly rimming the inside of her eyelids, which appears to be the same shade. While her face and hands echo the black pigmentation of almost all other images,

---

[26] ASV, Processus, MS 2179. 614r.   [27] ASV, Processus, MS 2179, 385v.
[28] ASV, Processus, MS 2179, 111v., and 646r.

the details of her face reveal the painter's efforts to create realism of facial details while simultaneously maintaining the uniform blackness of her skin. [Plate 23] We can see another example of the rimming of the eyelids with the same pigment as the lips in the sculpture from northern Portugal, where the lower lids are dramatically big, rendering the pink highly visible. [Plate 24]

Close attention to the hands and feet of black saints reveals further details, subtler than the lips, that testify to the care of the painters involved in the production of sculpture of black saints. Sometimes fingernails and toenails were the same monochromatic black as the skin and hair; in many cases, however, nails could be rimmed either with pinkish or grayish tones. In one image from southern Spain, the Benedict's foot is encased in his signature sandal, his toenails painted pinkish-red. [Plate 25] In the reliquary of St. Benedict in Lisbon, the fingers are painted with greater detail, with grayish-white nails ringed with thin lines of reddish-pink, giving the nails depth and presence. [Plate 26] Pinks and grays in eyes, nose, fingers, and toes throw the sculptural details of face and hands into relief, creating additional levels of visual interest. We can see in these examples the ways in which artists employed many of the traditional techniques of the medium for black saints, modified for their specific characteristics. The subtlety of the details contrasts with the general uniformity of pigment in skin and hair, underscoring the precision of the artists' vision.

Another striking feature of black saints in sculpture is the careful attention artists paid to their heads – specifically, facial features and hair. As with other sculptures of saints, their facial features varied greatly from image to image, yet almost all were crafted with distinct appearances, such as sharp and expressive features, which are enhanced by the uniformity of black fleshtones and the simplicity of the *encarnaciones*. Without elaborate *encarnaciones* as seen in sculptures of white saints, the faces and hair of black saints take on greater power. Santana was the only author who described the appearance of a black saint beyond skin color, declaring that Elesban had "curly hair, like that which decorates the heads of men of his color; with features similar to those of Europeans, with a straight nose in a pleasing shape."[29] Here we see some ambivalence about the relationship between skin color and other markers of difference – Elesban should have the hair of fellow Africans but facial features similar to Europeans, which for Santana included a thin nose. Many sculptures of black saints followed Santana's recommendations, particularly those of Efigenia, but others reflected great diversity in facial features including various sizes and

---

[29] Santana, *Os dous atlantes*, 1:332: "cabello revolto, a semelhança daquelle; com que se ornão as cabeças dos homens da sua cor: as feiçoens parecidas as dos Européos, nariz afilado, forma gentil."

shapes of noses and mouths. The marriage of European facial features with "African" hair and black pigmentation indicates the aesthetic parameters of black sanctity and which characteristics were considered to constitute ideal beauty. [Plate 27]

Almost all sculptures of the male saints followed Santana's recommendation that their hair be "boisterous" or "curly" like other black men. Sculptors, in fact, took great care crafting the hair for black saints. Hair was an important component of polychrome sculpture more generally because it could emphasize the saint's tonsure or express movement, particularly through length and waves. Yet the hair in sculptures of black (male) saints has unique qualities not replicated in the hair of sculptures of white saints. For black male saints, the sculptors engaged in work of exquisite detail that resulted in images with heightened beauty and visual interest. The sculptures of Benedict in Valladolid and in southeastern Portugal, for example, portray the curls of the hair as coiled spirals connected tightly to the scalp. [Plate 28, Plate 29] Others have hair that is a riot of waves with heightened volume. [Plate 30, Plate 31] A few are quite playful, infusing the image with a hint of respectful humor and boyish charm. [Plate 32] The style of hair is as unique as the facial expression of each image; it is incredibly detailed, a crucial element of the saint's personality. Artists therefore crafted sculpture of black saints of great beauty and emotional resonance through ways that were unique to them.

Most of the images I have viewed were *in situ* (some in their original locations, others not), but we cannot recreate the experience of being in a church without electric lights. How would the blackness have been experienced? How did the original finishes affect the viewer's experience of the image – many originally matte, even when conserved with a glossy overcoat? It is difficult to know how viewers might have reacted to images of black saints, either aesthetically or spiritually, other than knowing that many generated great devotion. Additional research might yield more information about the response of black viewers in particular. It does bear keeping in mind that the color black had a myriad of meanings in premodern Europe. As we have seen in the case of the Black Madonnas, blackness could be tied to penance, penitential practice, and spiritual gifts, as well as darkness, sin, and the diabolic. In early modern Spanish culture, black was the color of fashion and the court, representing wealth and luxury.[30] As a result, the blackness of the saints did not align with general attitudes that tied black skin color with inferiority, ugliness, and sin.

Larissa Brewer-García's study of the beatification processes for Pedro Claver in seventeenth-century Cartagena, for example, includes a description by Claver's

---

[30] Colomer, "Black and the Royal Image."

black interpreters of a painting of a black man being baptized. One of these witnesses, Ignacio Angola, described the baptized man as "very beautiful because of the baptism."[31] The transformation of baptism from ugliness to beauty could, therefore, be recognized as part of the spiritual truth being conveyed by the painting. Here, the external features of the baptized man were not whitened or lightened, yet the interior spiritual transformation rendered the man beautiful. Beautiful blackness itself represents a key spiritual truth to be conveyed to the viewer, particularly for black viewers. As a result, people of color in Europe and the Americas could see themselves as holy and beautiful.

The predominance of polychrome sculpture in the sacred art of black saints resulted in specific ways of viewing black sanctity. In spite of the efforts of sculptors and artists to create vivid and lifelike images of human beings, their choices in the process of *encarnaciones* were not as naturalistic. Yet realism was not always the sole goal of works of white saints either: In Luisa Roldán and Tomás de los Arcos's work, San Ginés (c. 1692), Los Arcos chose a pigment that was close to a translucent white, blending almost perfectly with his hair. The choice of flesh tones at the extreme of human variation mirrors what we see in images of black saints.[32] The choice of uniform black pigment rather than a more "realistic" fleshtone without differentiation between flesh and hair (in most cases) transform blackness from simple visual identifier to a key component of the holiness of the saints. Such blackness could encompass a variety of meanings – a reminder that even the most humble could be transformed by divine grace, encouragement to populations of color to abandon their "idolatry," or the meaning accorded humility and suffering through acceptance. Moreover, such sculptures underscore the embodied nature of Catholic spirituality. Rather than an intrinsic enemy of the spirit, the body could be harnessed as a powerful force to fight evil and achieve the heights of holiness. More than a just a visual identifier (i.e., saying to the viewer "this is a black saint"), blackness acted as a key component of the saints' holiness and of holiness more broadly.

Attributes of Black Sanctity

In addition to pigments applied by artists and sculptural details, saintly attributes were integral to each work's story of sanctity. Attributes included a variety of features in addition to flesh and hair, including garments and any added elements such as objects in the saints' hands. Authors did not usually provide details about

[31] As quoted by Brewer-García, "Imagined Transformations," 131.
[32] Bassett and Alvarez, "Process and Collaboration."

the appearance of images of black saints alongside their remarks on the saint's blackness and religious habit. The habit itself – denoting the saint's religious order – remained stable over time and place. Other features, however, could differ greatly based on time period or geographic location of the image. Benedict's images show significant variety, divided fairly neatly between the Spanish and the Lusophone Atlantics.[33] Benedict's attributes in the Lusophone world included flowers, bread, and/or a bloody cloth, while in the Spanish, the saint was depicted mostly commonly with a burning heart and/or symbols of penitential practice (particularly whips), although penitential attributes appeared almost exclusively in print engravings. Lusophone images occasionally included the burning heart, but the surviving Spanish ones never included the bloody rag, bread, or roses, with one important exception.

Sometimes the attributes associated with a given saint are relatively straight forward – St. Teresa holding a pen, for example, or St. Peter with his keys – but part of what makes these meanings obvious is the iconographic knowledge layered onto the saint, reinforced by labels, liturgy, and hagiography. Drawn from accounts of a saint's life, textual accounts of images sometimes explain the spiritual meaning of specific attributes. Of all of Benedict's attributes, the rag he occasionally holds requires particular unpacking because it is not always obvious what the object even is by looking at it. Apolinário da Conceição described a sculpture of Benedict standing on the altar of a black confraternity in Lisbon's Igreja de Santa Ana, the church attached to the convent for the tertiary Franciscans and home to the earliest cults to black saints. He explained that Benedict stood with a great silver diadem, robes decorated with flowers, holding a cross in his right hand and a cleaning rag (*esfragão*) in his left.[34] In his beatification testimony, Solitudine likewise mentioned the bloody rag appearing in an image, adding specifically that it was "a pink, or rather bloody, rag signifying a prodigy."[35] In this panel, the blood dripping from the cloth is vividly apparent. [Plate 33]

The object in some sculptures is not obviously a rag, but rather curled up (with swirls indicating folds). The blood can be difficult to discern, because the paint has chipped off or faded or, as in this example from the eastern Alentejo, the red-pink color swirls inside the cloth rather than dripping down as we see in the wood panel. [Plate 34]

---

[33] Though Italy falls outside the scope of this project, most baroque images of Benedict there represent the saint holding a baby, which was much less common in the Iberian world.

[34] Apolinário da Conceição, *Flor perigrina*, 263–4. Santa Ana was damaged in the 1755 earth-quake. It was subsequently rebuilt, but the image of Benedict was most likely destroyed.

[35] ASV, Processus, MS 2179, f. 294r-v. The Italian phrase is "scopetta rosa anzi insaguinata significabiuo di qualque prodigio."

Another beatification witness, Bonucci, explained the story behind the prodigy mentioned by Solitudine in a passage describing a different image of Benedict, this one in Recife. The sculpture, he said, was wood, four or five palms high, holding a bloody piece of cloth (*tutto insaguinato*). He then recounted the miracle associated with this specific iconography: while cleaning the kitchen Benedict saw an ill-treated cat (presumably bloody), and the saint, struck with pity, dipped his cloth in hot water and cleaned it.[36] For Bonucci, the rag symbolized Benedict's charity and love for all living creatures, no matter how humble.

While Bonucci's anecdote about the cat appears in Tognoletto's hagiography, other moments of Benedict's life provide an alternative origin story for the attribute. Francisco Antonio Castellano recounted a meeting between Benedict and some young friars in the kitchen. Benedict began collecting small pieces of the food that had been left on the plates of the friars after the meal because their thoughtless waste pierced the saint's soul. He considered such profligacy as an insult to the spirit of humility in which the brothers were supposed to dwell. The young friars laughed at Benedict for engaging in this "impertinent and frivolous" activity. (It is unclear in the story what Benedict intended to do with the bread and meat he gathered, though presumably he meant to give it away to the hungry.) Benedict responded forcefully by telling the brothers that he was actually collecting "the blood of the poor," whereupon Benedict squeezed the rag in his hands, which began to drip fresh blood.[37]

In spite of Bonucci's description, Castellano's aligns more strongly with the saint's iconography in Portugal, where images of Benedict often portray him with the bloody rag in one hand and roses or bread in the fold of his other arm. [**Plate 35**] Other images include the flowers with the second hand curled but empty, making it less clear if the original object had been a rag, cross, or another item, although presumably some had been rags.[38] Nearly all Portuguese images of Benedict included flowers. [**Plate 26, Plate 32**] Unlike the bloody rag, however, the flowers do not correspond to a story from Benedict's hagiographies. Instead,

---

[36] ASV, Processus, MS 2179, 403v. An anecdote involving a cat and meat appears in Tognoletto's seventeenth-century hagiography of the saint – and is repeated in later, Spanish ones: Tognoletto, *Paradiso serafico*, 238. The cat steals a piece of meat that was for the brothers and refuses to give it back until Benedict speaks patiently to it, whereupon the cat drops the meat at the saint's feet. Vicente concluded this account: "Por este caso suelen en algunas Pinturas poner un Gato à sus pies con la carne en la boca": *El negro mas prodigioso*, 93.

[37] Castellano, *Compendio de la heroyca y maravillosa vida*, 45–6: "Tomò el bendito Negro en sus manos un estropago, y comprimiendole entre los dedos, destilò bastante porcion de sangre viva en la presencia de todos. Quedaronse los pobres jovenes, no solo confundidos, sino tambien afrentados, al ver que aquellos pedacitos de pan, y carne, que a ellos les parecia cosa de tan poca entidad, le havia costado a la probreza de Benito un milagro con tan sangrienta execucion."

[38] It is possible to hypothesize about the previous contents of the hand based on its position, as it would clutch a crucifix differently than a rag.

they replicate a miracle and attribute of another Portuguese saint – the queen-saint Isabel of Portugal, sometimes called Isabel of Aragon (d. 1336).

Isabel was the sister to two Aragonese kings, eventually marrying the king of Portugal and becoming queen. She bore two children, one of whom eventually ascended the throne. Renowned in her life for her piety and charity, she retired to a Franciscan convent in Coimbra after her husband's death and died in the odor of sanctity. She was canonized by Pope Urban VIII in 1625, and her image proliferated quickly, especially within the Spanish-Portuguese monarchy. For two decades following Isabel's beatification, the kingdom of Portugal remained part of the Spanish monarchy; this union intensified the spread of her cult throughout the peninsula.

Isabel's iconography mirrored that of an earlier medieval queen-saint, Elizabeth of Hungary (d. 1231), who had been both Isabel's great-aunt and the relative for whom Isabel was named. Elizabeth's life paralleled her namesake's closely, including retirement to a Franciscan convent. Legends of Elizabeth of Hungary and Isabel of Portugal include nearly identical miracles, in which their husbands grew impatient with their constant almsgiving. One day, she was distributing bread to the local poor, and when her husband appeared, the bread miraculously turned into flowers so he would not know what she had been doing. While the queens were sometimes depicted wearing their Franciscan habits, they were more often dressed sumptuously and adorned with jewels and royal crowns. [**Plate 36**] Zurbarán's decision to paint Isabel of Portugal in profile rather than facing forward provides a different angle from which to view the flowers, but he is careful to render them clearly visible. Zurbarán's portrait closely mirrors his depiction of another Spanish princess-saint, Santa Casilda, which solidifies the association between flowers and royal women. The miracle associated with the bread and flowers was central to the queens' sanctity: While experiencing a deep desire to live a fully spiritual life, they were secular leaders, loyal to their husbands and dutiful in fulfilling queenly obligations. But in private they prayed constantly and performed acts of charity, leveraging their wealth and privilege to help those who were desperately poor, feeding and clothing the hungry just as Christ had demanded.

The association of the flowers with Benedict acts as a significant departure for this iconography. While Benedict's cult was circulating at the same time as Isabel of Portugal's, the two represent opposite ends of the socio economic spectrum. Their greatest common experience was that they were both Franciscan tertiaries, which suggests that the Franciscans deliberately developed their parallel iconographies.[39] The saints did share key virtues, however – submission to authority

---

[39] Alessandro dell'Aira mentions the parallel rise of the two saints in Portugal, and two mid-seventeenth-century images in Lisbon that were a matched set: "Le navire de la reine."

and great concern for the welfare of the poor. The flowers represent both, although in a highly gendered way. Only queen saints performed the balancing act of the requirements of wifely submission in tension with her higher calling to do God's work. While the subversion of authority was a common theme in hagiography, it appeared more frequently in that of female saints, since, as women, they faced additional layers of patriarchal authority. The parallel iconography suggests that Portuguese Franciscans viewed Benedict and Isabel as similar because they both bore the double burden of submission.[40] Other than the presence of flowers, however, there is little else that gendered Benedict feminine; his images portray the saint with strong, even stern, masculine features.

Occasionally, Benedict holds bread instead of flowers, either in the folds of his habit or holding it in his hands. [Plate 12, Plate 37] Because of the role that bread played in the miracles of the roses, they can be read as having the same iconographical meaning. In Benedict's case, the presence of either bread or roses was amplified by the presence of the bloody rag. In one example in Spain, the saint holds an object in his hand that, on first glance, could be a flaming heart – but closer observation reveals that the object is in fact a piece of bread, an oval with an indention in the middle like the split in a roll of bread. At the bottom of the roll we see three separate large drops of blood frozen mid-drip, the most literal representation of the story where Benedict wrung the blood from the bread itself. [Plate 38] Humility and heroic charity were central to Benedict's iconography, then, even in cases when it involved challenging authority. The saint's spiritual imperative released him from secular strictures and allowed him to resist social hierarchies.

Benedict's fellow Sicilian, Antonio da Noto, has left fewer images than the other black saints. Both surviving Iberian images that I know of are in Portugal – in Braga and Lisbon – though they also dot the spiritual landscape of Brazil. [Plate 39] While Antonio occasionally held a cross or crucifix, his most distinctive attribute was the Christ child he occasionally cradled in his arms, in a way nearly identical to Anthony of Padua, the patron saint of Portugal. The print engraving of Antonio holding the Christ child was included in the *compromisos* of a black brotherhood in Brazil dedicated to the saint in Bahia (here called Antonio de Catagerona) [Plate 40]. In this beautiful watercolor, most likely painted by one of the brothers, the saint stands simply in his Franciscan robes, cross in left hand, a naked Christ child perched in his right arm. In such images, the contrast between the white child and the black man is striking, each emphasizing the color of the

---

[40] Saints from peasant backgrounds were rare; one notable exception is the peasant Isidro Labrador, patron saint of Madrid, who was canonized in 1622, but Isidro never entered a religious order and was thus represented as a farmer.

other to great visual effect. The Church officials reviewing the brotherhood's *compromiso* complained about the saint's iconography, specifying that the saint should appear neither with a hooded cowl nor with the Christ child. In the first case, they insisted that because Antonio had been a tertiary, rather than a friar, the cowl was inappropriate, as the habit of a tertiary did not include one. On the question of the child, they claimed that it reflected no miracle in Antonio's life.[41]

In fact, the image of the Christ child was associated with Benedict from the early days of his cult in Sicily; therefore there was some iconographic confusion between the two Franciscan black saints in the Iberian Atlantic. While images of saints holding the Christ child were fairly common in baroque art, Jesus's presence in conjunction with Antonio created a visual connection between the black saint and St. Anthony of Padua, the patron saint of Portugal. Associations between the cults of black saints and two high profile saints (Antonio and Isabel) established the black saints' position in a larger Franciscan-Portuguese genealogy.

Elesban and Efigenia inhabit a different spiritual-symbolic zone than the Franciscan black saints. While we do not have as many examples of authors describing their images as we do for Benedict, there are important details provided in the works of José Pereira de Santana and Joseph de Navia. Santana described how the two should be represented in sacred art generally: Efigenia had black face and hands, was "of middle age," and very beautiful (*sumamente fermosa*). She wore a Carmelite habit of a brownish-black tunic and scapular with a white cloak on her shoulders and a black veil on her head. One hand held a cross and the other the burning convent.[42] Santana described images of Elesban in a similar way: black of face and hands and any visible part of the body, as a "grown man" (*idade varão*), dressed in a Carmelite habit, which he described in the same colors and general style as Efigenia's. He further specified that King Dunaan – whom the saint defeated in battle – should be placed in a position of submission at the saint's feet.[43] The appearance of the two saints in their Carmelite habits distinguished them from other ancient saints, because saints who lived in the earliest centuries following Christ's death were not usually associated with the religious orders, which developed later. The Carmelites, however, claimed an ancient lineage predating all the other orders; as a result, it was crucial to portray the Ethiopian saints clearly as members of their order.

In addition to the habits, Elesban and Efigenia often shared one of the most important attributes common to images of holy kings and queens: their crowns.

[41] "Compromisso da irmandade de S. Antonio de Catagerona," Oliveira Lima Library, Catholic University of America, n.f. It is likely that the complaints about the image referred to an image on the brotherhood's altar, rather than the small watercolor in the private *compromiso* document.

[42] Santana, *Os dous atlantes*, 2:107.   [43] Santana, *Os dous atlantes*, 1:332.

It was common for royal saints to be depicted with their crowns – as we saw with Elizabeth – which sometimes appeared on their head and sometimes at their feet. The crown at the feet signals the saint's abandonment of secular rulership in favor of spiritual life; because royalty involved the heights of secular power, the conscious rejection of it represented heroic self-denial. In sculpture, we are more likely to see the crown on the saint's head, although in their case, it remained a particularly powerful symbol in conjunction with the habit, since the two worked together to tell the story of a royal person's transformation into a religious. [Plate 41, Plate 42] Many viewers might not know that the saints were ancient or Ethiopian, but they would recognize them as royal. Images of black saints as royalty acted as a challenge to a world where most people encountered black Africans as enslaved or low-status free people. Unlike the black magus, Elesban and Efigenia stood on their own, wrapped in the clothes of a respected religious order, fully integrated into the fold of Catholicism.[44]

As recommended by Santana, Efigenia was depicted in typical ways for early modern holy women, with a facial expression of great serenity, kindness, or a kind of placid prettiness, although usually as a young woman rather than middle aged. In addition to being a princess, Efigenia was the patroness of protection from fire and was almost always depicted holding a burning convent – the convent that her pagan uncle had set on fire to punish her. Her role as patroness of fire was the most important element to her cult in the seventeenth and eighteenth centuries, which might explain some of the growth of her cult beyond black confraternities.[45] Santana described one Portuguese countess who claimed to have received aid from Efigenia after an enormous fire that broke out at her convent was miraculously extinguished through the saint's intercession.[46] Almost all the convents were small sculptures swirling with flames, which added both drama and dimensionality to the attribute. In this sculpture from southern Portugal, the exceptional detail work, including red-gold flames, demonstrate the care and attention the sculptors and artists paid the building. [Plate 43]

Elesban, for his part, could be depicted holding the convent he retired to late in life, or, more dramatically, as a heretic-slayer.[47] While some sculptures of Elesban were relatively static, others demonstrated great theatricality: the depiction of the

---

[44] Residents of Iberian courts might have encountered one of the many embassies from West or Central African kingdoms (particularly, though not exclusively, the Kongo).

[45] I was told anecdotally that there used to be frescos of Efigenia over the doors of houses in Lisbon to protect them from fire.

[46] Santana, *Os dous atlantes*, 2:128–9.

[47] In Plate 21, the convent is clearly a modern replacement for a lost or damaged original. The attributes in the hands of baroque sculptures are the most likely to have been lost and replaced with modern objects.

saint in his triumph over his enemy, Dunaan, the evil king of Himyar. Such iconography associated Elesban with other saints renowned for their battles against enemies of the faith, including Santiago (St. James), St. George, and Michael the Archangel. Because Santiago and George are most often depicted on horseback, Elesban's iconography aligns him most closely with Michael, whose cult was exceptionally popular in the early modern Iberian world. [Plate 44] Elesban, like Michael, usually stands on the neck or back of his enemy, his spear-like crozier on the enemy's neck; the enemy king lies on his stomach or back, hands often bound, face upraised and contorted in pain. [Plate 45] Elesban's depiction as a heretic-slayer is all the more striking because there are so few saints who are represented in this way. While heretic-slayers were usually ancient kings, the problem of heresy and unbelief were reactivated in the early modern period, as the global reach of the Church meant continuous contact with non-Christians and "relapsed" heretics. The Carmelites shaped Elesban's iconography in a way that allowed them to stake a claim to militant defense of the faith (with which they were not generally identified) as well as to the ancient church.

The appearance of the king at Elesban's feet varies – sometimes King Dunaan is depicted with white skin and sometimes with black skin. When King Dunaan is depicted black, the pigments used for the evil king often match those of the saint. The kings with white skin add drama and visual interest to the scene. This oil painting from central Portugal [Plate 46] presents Elesban with his convent and as a heretic-slayer. Here the evil king crumpled at the saint's feet, pointed spear in the back of his neck, is white. In an example from Andalusia, the saint's spear is missing, though the curling of his right hand indicates that it had been there. The king (represented only from the shoulders up) rests under Elesban's foot, which is pushing down at the center of the king's head. The king gazes upward, his hands bound with gold chains. In a sculpture from Antequera, the inclusion of the enemy king and crozier adds both movement and emotional impact to the image. Elesban's cloak swirls around him as though the viewer catches him in the precise moment of victory, and the careful details on the body and expressions of the defeated king enhance the saint's triumph over evil. [Plate 47] Despite the power of these particular images, the variations in the vanquished king's skin color hint at an underlying anxiety about portraying a black saint – even a king – standing with his foot on the neck of a white ruler.

In addition to heretic-slayer, king, and monk, Elesban's iconography includes patronage over sailors. Though rare in visual culture, one surviving sculpture – significantly, from seafaring Galicia – depicts him holding a ship, as does an eighteenth-century engraving. [Plate 48] [Fig. 4.1] A panegyric to the saint in eighteenth-century Portugal proclaimed him "the advocate against storms and

Figure 4.1 José Patiño, *San Elesban*, c. 1753–1781, print engraving, 110 x 86 mm. Biblioteca Nacional de España, Madrid.

the dangers of the sea."[48] There is no clear explication for the evolution of his attribute, though it was likely inspired by his journey from Aksum across the Red Sea to Yemen to expand his territory and attack the evil king. Yet his sea travel inspired no commentary in his hagiography – there were no descriptions of

---

[48] "O Glorioso Saõ Elesbão da Ethiopia Altar, preto na cor," Biblioteca Nacional de Portugal (hereafter BNP), RES. 1353/20.

miracles involving storms at sea, for example. The choice to promote Elesban as a patron over sailors, like Efigenia with fire, provided an avenue for the Carmelite-driven expansion of his cult beyond black confraternities to more general audiences. Not surprisingly, Elesban was popular in seafaring regions – Galicia, Spain and the Algarve, Portugal – but whether this iconography was developed to suit the needs of seafaring populations, or if sailors adopted Elesban because of this patronage, we do not know.

Images of Elesban and Efigenia were most often placed together on an altarpiece, though Efigenia sometimes appeared on her own. They are usually presented as a matched set – that is, their sizes and decorative colors and patterns echo each other in ways that make it clear that the images were designed together. [Plate 49] One exception is in Faro, Portugal; Elesban and Efigenia are displayed together now, but are dissimilar enough to suggest they were not originally together. Today they stand in the left and right niches, but they are sized and positioned differently. Efigenia faces forward, looking ahead and slightly upward, eyes averted from what most likely had been a cross in her right hand, the burning convent in her left, with a sweet, serene expression on her face. [Plate 50] Elesban, by contrast, is turned slightly to the side, gazing downward toward the viewer. [Plate 51] Elesban's arms are raised dramatically, the right higher than the left, which creates ripples in his cape and the illusion of movement. The Ethiopian king holds his convent, but the building is modern and wooden, presumably a replacement for the lost original. The item in his right hand is a long pole, likely a replacement for a broken version of the saint's staff.[49] Both display rich *estofado* work, dominated by gold and pale black designs on their habits, the gold contrasting vividly with the black pigment of their face and hands. Elesban's cape – and parts of his habit and scapular – show faded paint in pinks and greens (or blues) that appears to have covered some of the goldwork in the lavish floral patterns.[50] The decorations on the scapular, robe, and habit contrast with the whimsical gold polka-dots on his black shoes – a detail found on an image of Efigenia in a different church. [Plate 52] The patterns on Efigenia's habit are bigger and bolder, with distinct but echoing shapes of fanning petals or leaves on both scapular and robe, more static and less dramatic than Elesban's image. [Plate 53]

The extravagant richness of the previous images is thrown into relief by others that are much simpler and more plainly constructed. In another sculpture of Efigenia, we see that, although the sculpture is quite small and not nearly as lavish

---

[49] It does appear likely that Elesban has been re-polychromed, based on the richness of the black pigment.

[50] The blues and pinks of Elesban's cape proved difficult to photograph clearly, but in person they are easy to see.

or dramatic as others, the details are quite precise and beautiful. The cream cape swirls over her habit, tucked under the burning convent she holds in her left hand. The robe is decorated with small star-shaped flowers (painted in a faint rose color) which then increases in gold until reaching the broad gold band around the front of the robe, which swirls and drapes around her in a similar movement to the previous one of Elesban. Her habit is dark brown with large flowers contrasting the smaller ones of the cape. The scapular swirls up on one side, revealing the playful polka dot pattern underneath. The flames are large, undulating red and gold, rich and lively in color. The convent is beautifully decorated with a subtle striped pattern in its cream walls that echoes the faint gold stripes of her wimple. [**Plate 54**] The attention to detail suggests the importance of the image to devotees, in spite of its small size and their relative poverty (indicated by the small size and the plain back). Although composed with differences in skill, detail, and expense, the sculptures of Elesban and Efigenia were imbued with the drama, movement, and charisma necessary to provoke a spiritual and devotional reaction from the viewer.

Contemplation

One common feature of baroque sculptures of saints was their active state of contemplation. Two of the most famous saints portrayed this way were Mary Magdalene and Jerome, who were also accompanied by symbols of ascetic discipline, such as stages of undress or blood from bodily mortifications. While dramatic and important, images of ascetic saints in the acts of penance were not the most common representations of contemplation. [**Plate 55, Plate 18**] Most were presented in a quieter way: eyes fixed on a crucifix, mouth open, sometimes in a grimace, brow creased. We see images of Benedict, Elesban, and Efigenia in such poses; the relative lack of ascetic or visionary elements to their hagiographies suggest that they were depicted this way because most saints were. Efigenia's expression of contemplation followed the gendered pattern, in which her countenance remained more placid and gentle rather than depicting virile agony. [**Plate 56**] The preponderance of contemplative saints in baroque sculpture signifies the importance of prayer, meditation, and the attendant cultivation of virtue in the post-Tridentine Church, communicated to the laity through the expressions on their saints' faces. [**Plate 57**]

Yet contemplation is a key aspect of Benedict's life and, therefore, of his iconography, where it could manifest in several different ways, ranging from the more placid contemplation in most saints to dramatic rendering of an ecstatic experience. Castellano described this moment:

According to natural philosophy, a flame is burning smoke, and our Black Saint was the flame. The proof of this truth is a repeated miracle in which his heart left its place and elevated to his face; his heart exhaled burning flames, appearing on his heart and blazing in the fire of Divine love, illuminated by these beautiful rays. This is the reason why our black saint is painted or drawn with a Heart in his hand, enflamed, with his face showing the fire of divine Love scorching his interior, like an ardent Seraphim.[51]

This account begins with the rich metaphorical language frequently employed in the hagiographies of black saints – his black body is the smoke, alight with divine love, which transformed him into a flame, bright and dark together, the entire passage replete with the language of light. Flames had long been associated with the divine, particularly the communication of divine wisdom or love, as in the New Testament account of Pentecost during which flames descended on the apostles and the Virgin after Christ's Ascension into Heaven. Castellano added another, specific vision at the end of the saint's life. After receiving Extreme Unction, Benedict asked to be left alone in order to experience full devotion "in his heart" to the Crucified Christ, whereupon his "flaming heart" (*encendido corazón*) flew outside his body into union with the divine, because the saint "yearned so much for God."[52] Castellano's vida included a print engraving of the saint in this moment, crucifix in left hand, right hand reaching up to his chest to support or reveal a heart. A similar engraving appeared in Antonio Vicente de Madrid's hagiography of Benedict, complete with symbols of penitence at the saint's feet. [Fig. 4.2] The rhetoric of being enflamed by divine love was relatively common in early modern hagiography, but here the placement of the heart keeps the focus on the saint rather than a dynamic interaction with Christ playing an equal role. Benedict's heart reaches out of his body to unite with the divine, rather than God reaching down to him.

But the specific meanings the artists wished to impart on the ecstasy of the heart iconography in Benedict's images require further unpacking. A visionary experience that included one's heart was not unprecedented – perhaps one of the most vivid and influential examples can be found in images of Catherine of Siena (d. 1380), who was one of the most famous saints of the premodern

---

[51] Castellano, *Compendio de la vida*, n.f.

[52] See Castellano, *Compendio de la vida*, 78: "Llegada en fin la ultima hora, pidiò à la Comunidad le administrasse el Santo Sacramento de la Extrema Uncion, y haviendole recibido, pidiò lo dexassen solo, porque queria en la libertad de la soledad desahogar los afectos de su corazon con Christo crucificado. En este lance fueron frequentissimos los vuelos de su encendido corazon à la dichosa esfera de la divinidad, anhelando tanto mas à la union con el Sumo Bien, quanto mas de cerca miraba su possession feliz." Other authors mention Benedict's fixation on the crucifix on his deathbed, without mentioning the details of this specific miracle.

Figure 4.2 Julián Rodríguez, *San Benito de Palermo*, 1744, print engraving for Antonio Vicente de Madrid, *El negro mas prodigioso*, Biblioteca Nacional de España, Madrid spain.

Church [Plate 58]. Here we see Catherine presented in much the same way as the engraving of Benedict – she stands holding a crucifix (and lily) in her right hand. Her eyes are fixed on the corpus of Christ, while in her left hand she holds a brilliant red heart that contains the initials of Christ (IHS) in gold lettering. The connection between Catherine and Christ's heart was further reinforced by

Figure 4.3 *St. Jean Eudes (1601–1680)*, seventeenth century.

a vision recounted in her vida in which Christ lifted her heart out of her body after she begged him to remove her sinfulness; later, Christ gave His heart in exchange for hers. In this account, the focus remains on exchange – while the gift is Christ's, the process is dynamic where both participated.

The heart in Christian iconography took on new prominence in the seventeenth century, when the cult of Christ's Sacred Heart began to proliferate. In this cult, Christ was most commonly depicted with His heart outside His body, usually surrounded by flames and crowned with thorns, either on its own or with a saint (rather than with Christ Himself. This new devotional focus was widely popularized by the French mystic Mary Magdalene Alacoque (d. 1690) as well as her contemporaries, Francis of Sales (d. 1622), Jeanne de Chantal (d. 1641), Vincent de Paul (d. 1660), and Jean Eudes (d. 1680). [Fig. 4.3] Unlike the stigmata, the early modern cult of the Sacred Heart did not represent experiencing the pain of Christ's earthly suffering – rather it was Christ's love manifest.

Seventeenth-century people who promoted the cult of the Sacred Heart tended to be deeply engaged with the world, rather than separate from it in solitary prayer. Vincent de Paul was a priest and zealous reformer of clerical abuses, while Eudes founded Our Lady of Charity to help former prostitutes find redemption and solace. Francis of Sales and Jeanne de Chantal formed the Order of the Visitation in 1610 – a female monastic order where the sisters focused on ministering to the sick and poor. Such movements implicitly criticized the traditional monastic calling in which monks and nuns were permanently cloistered, sealed off from the world; instead early modern holy people throughout Catholic

Europe created new hybrids like the Society of Jesus or the Ursulines.[53] The Visitidines and the Sisters of Charity fashioned such active piety specifically for women, who were largely excluded from public action.

Although many seventeenth-century French holy people were associated with the Sacred Heart, Alacoque had the most profound influence on the early modern period and was widely credited with the rapid expansion of the Sacred Heart, which quickly took deep root in Spain and Spanish America.[54] Alacoque (canonized 1920) was a renowned visionary who took vows in the relatively new Order of the Visitation. The French archbishop Jean-Joseph Languet wrote a hagiography of Alacoque to promote her cult, and the cult of the Sacred Heart more broadly, which was printed in 1729. A decade later, it was translated into Spanish, along with other works on the Sacred Heart.[55] In the seventeenth and eighteenth centuries, meditation on Divine Love – embodied in the heart – took center stage, ushering in a newly intense spiritual emphasis on changes wrought through love alongside other models of *imitatio Christi* through bodily penance.

As the iconography of Benedict emerged during these same centuries, it became intertwined with that of the Sacred Heart, sometimes blurring the line between the visions of Benedict's heart rising from his body and the Sacred Heart. The heart that Benedict holds could be encircled with thorns and flames, while being pierced with three nails, which was the traditional iconography for the Sacred Heart, rather than the saint's own.[56] [**Plate 59**] Another from Portugal depicts Benedict's heart in the middle of his chest, likewise surrounded by thorns, creating an ambivalence between the saint's heart and Christ's, perhaps suggesting a heart-switching miracle as seen in Catherine of Siena [**Plate 60**]. In other examples, however, the portrayal suggests that the flaming heart is Benedict's own (as in Castellano's anecdotes) or it is unclear.

Benedict appears with the flaming heart in three main positions: in his hand held away from his body, in the center of his chest and emerging from the chest. Usually, when the saint holds the heart out away from his body, it is in his right hand with the left hand grasping a crucifix. In one sculpture from Galicia,

---

[53] Allegorical paintings of Charity often include her holding a flaming heart. See for example, Francisco de Zurbarán, *The Allegory of Charity*, c. 1655, oil on canvas, Museo Nacional del Prado.

[54] For brief overviews of the cult of the Sacred Heart, see Meyer, "The Sacred Heart of Jesus"; Kilroy-Ewbank, "Holy Organ"; and Morgan, "The Visual Piety of the Sacred Heart," 232–6. See also Alacoque, *Letters*.

[55] Juan de Loyola wrote a hagiography of Francis of Sales, followed quickly by a work on the Sacred Heart: *Vida de el dulcissimo director*; Loyola, *Thesoro Escondido*; Languet de Gergy, *Historia de la Devoción*; and Croiset, *La devocion al Sagrado Corazon*.

[56] The debate over whether or not the Christ Crucified should be portrayed with three or four nails was a lively one in seventeenth-century Spain.

Benedict's arm is outstretched, hand open to reveal the whole heart, which here appears a dark grayish-black, although some deterioration of the polychroming suggests that the dark pigment might cover a faint pink. [Plate 61] In an image from Cambados, the arm holding the heart curls around to the front of his torso, close to his right side, but not near his chest; the heart itself is displayed clearly, with its flames crowning the top. [Plate 62] Benedict stands in a similar pose in an image from Andalusia, where the reddish-pink heart rests on his chest, his hand around it, fingers splayed against his chest. [Plate 63] In many sculptures, as in these two, the heart and the flames are painted pink, red, or reddish-orange, sometimes quite subtly, sometimes vibrantly; such pigments usually mirrored the lips, creating a visual connection between the two, although in many cases the vibrancy of the pigments suggest recent repolychroming that results from a kind of garishness.

Several images reveal the heart emerging from the chest more explicitly, sometimes subtly and sometimes dramatically. This painting from Andalusia depicts Benedict, eyes fixed on the crucifix in his right hand, his left hand curled up to his chest where the heart lies. While painting does not offer the same dimensionality that sculpture does, here the artist adds a striking detail – a slit along his right side, gaping open, painted the same red as the heart that was positioned slightly to the left of the cut. The side wound indicates that the heart has just been removed from Benedict's chest. [Plate 64] In a sculpture from central Portugal, the effect of emergence is subtler; here, the saint stands in the typical position of his right hand cradling the heart at his chest. His left hand is curled into a holding position, though the crucifix is currently absent. Rather than a red side wound, the sculptor created a split in the front of the saint's habit, almost a deep fold. It is shaped like a V, with the point at the saint's belted waist, and opening up through his chest, heart at the top of the V-shape. The V-shape provides a visual effect of depth, out of which the heart emerges. [Plate 65]

Three particularly dramatic examples survive in the region around Granada where the artists capture the movement of the heart's emergence as well as the emotional drama of the physical rupture. Two of the three share such vivid artistic similarities that they may have been produced by the same workshop. One of the most striking features they share is the level of intensity in Benedict's ecstatic contemplation. While previous examples often represent the saint with lips parted (teeth showing) and a crease in the brow to express the emotion of a mystical experience, in all of the *granadino* images (particularly the first two), the saint's facial expression is more passionate, holding the familiar ecstatic line between pleasure and pain. In all three, the saint holds his cross (most likely a crucifix in the original) in his left hand, with his right up to his chest and heart. One of the three sculptures bears the least similarity to the others – Benedict's expression is more placid and his habit designed more simply. In this simpler image, the heart emerges from his habit, surrounded by cloth, particularly where the bottom of the heart emerges, seemingly last. There is little detail in the boundary between heart and habit, just a line where the heart begins. [Plate 66] In the other two examples, however, the sculptors created a more detailed effect, with greater movement, depth, and emotion. In both these cases, the saint's face is contorted with ecstatic pain, with his habit folding and swirling around the heart. In one, Benedict's hand in clenches dramatically with magnificent detail in the clutching fingers, actually pulling the heart out in a moment that is clearly agonizing. [Plate 67] In the other, the saint's hand more gently pulls back the fold of the habit to reveal the emerging heart, with the flames fully exposed and three-dimensional. [Plate 68] In contrast to the previous sculptures, the iconography in these three capture the moment of the miracle itself, telling the story of ecstatic contemplation of the corpus on the cross and the flaming heart appearing from the saint's chest.

Such images of Benedict reflect the specific miracles of his life, while simultaneously connecting to deeper artistic, theological, and spiritual shifts in late seventeenth- and early eighteenth-century Catholicism. The ubiquitous images of the Sacred Heart of Jesus can be found in significant numbers in churches throughout Iberia, but have been less well studied than other Christological images like the *Cristos yacentes*.[57] A shift of emphasis away from bodily mortification to the heart reveals not only an artistic or iconographic innovation, but also a spiritual one. The Sacred Heart in the lives of the saints remained grounded in visionary experiences yet it moved from being acted upon by an outward force – as in the stigmata – to one that originates from within the individual and bursts forth from his own body. Benedict's love for Christ was so powerful that it literally ripped his heart out of his chest. The movement of the internal to the external furthermore supplies a powerful message about the proper spiritual relationship between the inner and the outer – through love of Christ, our interior (soul) breaks free from the prison of flesh to be reunited with Christ. The message about the irrelevance of the body and the flesh as prison is highlighted in Benedict's case by his blackness, as black saints above all other types require liberation from the flesh, whether because of the chains of slavery or the assumption directed at them about their unworthiness. Inside, the sculptures emphasize, we are all one body in Christ.

Devotion to the Sacred Heart emphasized the experience of love. Juan de Loyola proclaimed that when we meditate on the Sacred Heart "it is not something inanimate, devoid of life and feeling ... but above all like a heart, something that lives, that feels, that loves, adorned with the perfection that one finds in the

---

[57] For one example, see Cólon Mendoza, *The Cristos yacentes*.

most sacred humanity of Christ."[58] While Juan de Loyola maintained the equal sanctity of Christ's body, he emphasized Christ's Heart as the locus of His *emotions* – it feels and loves; as such, he implied, it is the true center of Christ's humanity. This idea represents a fundamental shift from earlier models that had fixed Christ's humanity in His body more generally, as the site through which He experienced the ordinary sufferings of being human (hunger, thirst, exhaustion) as well as the excruciating punishments of the Passion. If the heart is the center of Christ's humanity, then the main conduit through which humans could experience Christ was through their own hearts. Exposed hearts – Christ's, Mary's, and Benedict's – reminded early eighteenth-century viewers that the divine fire of God's love was waiting only for them to open their hearts to it.

Printed Images

Another common way for early modern people to encounter devotional images was through black and white print engravings. Some engravings were included in books – particularly hagiographies – while others were printed in single sheets that were cheap and easy to disseminate. Because they were portable, engravings played a crucial role in early modern lay devotion. They further provided opportunities for artists to produce their own ways of imagining the saints for a wider audience than what could be achieved by a sculpture or painting, even in cases when an engraving was a copy of a known image. Yet because they were printed in single sheets, print engravings were easily destroyed; as a result, our knowledge of the scope of their dissemination is often fragmentary.[59]

Like paintings, print engravings sometimes included a background or scene from the saints' lives to help create a narrative; others were standing figures, positioned much like those found in sculpture surrounded by additional iconography. [Fig. 4.4] Engravings of Benedict tend to remove the saint from a terrestrial landscape and place him within a celestial one. In this eighteenth-century image, the saint sits on a cloud, head surrounded by rays, in a Franciscan robe with knotted belt and rosary, his gaze raised to heaven. His skin is inked darkly, shaded to produce the illusion of light and shadow in order to give the figure dimension. The saint is surrounded by angels, two of whom hold attributes – the one on the left holds his lily, while the one at his feet holds instruments of penitential practice, including ropes ending with barbed spikes,

---

[58] Loyola, *El Corazon Sagrado de Jesus*, 48.
[59] For an important analysis of prints and lay devotion in colonial New Spain, see Taylor, *Theater of a Thousand Wonders*.

Figure 4.4 *San Benito de Palermo segun esta en la Capilla de San Diego de Alcalá*, engraving in *Ordenanzas de la Cofradia del Glorioso San Benito de Palermo, llamado comunmente El Santo Negro*, 1747. Courtesy of Archivo Histórico Nacional, Madrid, Spain.

which signal his humility and self-imposed suffering. Underneath the image, the engraving includes an inscription that identified the saint, first by name and then by his nickname – "*santo negro*" – and lists in phrases his markers of sanctity, including his gift of prophecy and miracles, beginning with "candido por la grazia" ("bright through grace"). [Fig. 4.5] Togneletto's *Paradiso serafico*, in contrast, includes an engraving of Benedict where the saint experiences a vision, holding the Christ child in his arms in front of an altar, as an angel reaches down in the act of having delivered the child to the saint. Benedict holds the baby tenderly as they gaze at each other in absorption.[60] [Fig. 4.6] Like the watercolor of Antonio da Noto, black confraternities could produce smaller, less expensive devotional images than a painting or sculpture that might stand in a church.

Tognoletto's *Paradiso serafico* included another engraving where Benedict appears in a garden surrounded by his fellow Franciscans, all wearing patched habits, tending the orchard together. [Fig. 4.7] Three main trees, heavy with fruit, reach upward and connect to three figures, from left to right: the Virgin Mary, Christ, and St. Francis (with his stigmata). All three water the orchard with their divine fluid – Mary squeezes milk from her breast, Christ's side wound flows down as does Francis's side stigmata, though his trickles rather than pours, signifying Francis's lesser miracle. Four friars stand in the center of the engraving, the middle one embracing the middle tree, with Benedict on the right. These friars are all labeled with their names: Simon, Matteus, Benedict, and Paulus a Palatiola. Tognoletto described four men in his work as individuals who maintained reputations for sanctity in Sicily. The scene emphasizes the hard work of the figures – one picks fruit, although most are engaged in planting a new tree. The tree's main branch is held by Benedict, and Paulus holds a pitcher out of which water pours, partially covered by the label "I watered" ("*ego rigavi*"). The engraving represents the enduring cultivation of holiness of the Franciscan order, particularly in Sicily, both by brothers and by Christ, his mother, and the order's founder. Benedict was clearly central to the Franciscan order in Sicily, but one of many brothers, an idea mirrored in the examples from Iberia.

---

[60] In the middle of the eighteenth-century, Francisco Ajofrín travelled to New Spain to tour the region on behalf of the Propaganda Fide to record the religious houses and major devotions, which included a series of eighteenth-century engravings from Mexico. One of these was the Virgin flanked by four black saints: Efigenia and Benedict (right and left, respectively) with Melchior and Moses on the bottom (right and left). The four faces ring the central image of the Virgin, who stands holding the Christ child, mantle held back by Benedict and Efigenia, while Melchior and Moses cluster at her feet. Efigenia holds a lily, and Benedict a flaming heart, while the two saints on the bottom do not have attributes. Written underneath is the description: "Our Lady of Mercy: who is venerated in the Chapel of the Blacks and Pardos in this court of Mexico." Ajofrín, *Diario del viaje*, 142–3. This image is reproduced and discussed in Alcalá, "Blanqueando la Loreto mexicana." On the next page is included an engraving of Efigenia, inscribed: "Sta Ephigenia. Venerado en Mexico en su Capilla del Convento Grande de la Merced."

Figure 4.5 *Retrato de San Benito de Palermo llamado comunmente por todos SANTO NEGRO*, eighteenth century, engraving. Schomburg Center for Research in Black Culture, The New York Public Library Digital Collections.

Figure 4.6 *P.F. Benedictus a S. Fratello*, seventeenth century in Pietro Tognolleto, *Paradiso Serafico del Regno de Sicilia*, 1667. Photo courtesy of St. Bonaventure University. Holy Name Collection.

Black Saints and Sacred History

Just as with hagiographies, the religious orders employed the visual as key parts of their sacred histories. In both Portugal and Spain, efforts by Franciscans to incorporate Benedict into their larger pantheon of black saints have left traces,

Figure 4.7 *Ostenditvr Paradisvs, Cvivs Fructvs Incorrvptvs Perseverat*, seventeenth century, engraving in Pietro Tognolleto, *Paradiso Serafico del Regno de Sicilia*. Photo courtesy of St. Bonaventure University. Holy Name Collection.

particularly in the private spaces of Franciscan convents. Here, we see a series of oil-on-wood paintings in the convent's choir, featuring a line of Franciscan friars and nuns with their common attributes around the walls behind the choir chairs where the brothers would have gathered for meetings. The saints are depicted in similar desert-like landscapes, highlighting their asceticism. Benedict is located in this photo fourth from the left, holding the bloody rag. [Plate 69] The sameness of the size, shape, and wall position as well as the backdrops of the paintings emphasizes the common spiritual lineage joining the saints together. The image of Benedict stands within this lineage, undifferentiated in any way from the Franciscan men and women around him, except for his blackness.

Images of Benedict were not restricted to male convents. One rare example of a surviving reliquary was housed in Convento da Madre de Deus in Lisbon, a former Clarissian house, which today is part of the Museu de Azulejo. The Clarissian choir included dozens of reliquaries, which conservators believe had originally been arranged thematically in groups on separate altars. Today, they stand in rows behind the choir seats in glass cabinets. Among them is the bust of Benedict of Palermo, the relic unfortunately missing, which must have been part of a larger program of Franciscan saints' reliquaries in the nuns' possession. [Plate 70] Its presence suggests that the saint's relics were valued by the nuns, who had close connections to the royal family, as the monastery had been founded by Queen Leonor at the beginning of the sixteenth century. These two examples of extant images of Benedict in Franciscan houses in Portugal are relatively rare, as many were removed from the convents and their churches to parish churches following the disentailment of the religious houses. The dissemination of conventual images to parishes indicates that some found in parish churches today might have been moved there in the nineteenth century.[61]

In other cases, images of St. Benedict are located in parish churches as part of intentional altar design. For example, the main church of San Juan de las Cabezas (Andalusia), built the second half of the eighteenth century, includes a Chapel del Sagrario containing an altar dedicated to Our Lady of the Rosary (though the image that stands there today dates to the nineteenth century). The altarpiece contains a series of bas-reliefs of saints from the upper thighs (or knees) up, including Sts. Augustine of Hippo, Felipe Benicio (d. 1285, Order of the Servants of Mary), Diego de Alcalá (d. 1463, Franciscan), Nicholas of Bari (d. 343, bishop of Myra), Pedro de Alcántara (d. 1562, Franciscan), Inés (d. 301; martyr), Apollonia (d. 249, martyr), and Benedict of Palermo. Benedict appears in the top right corner, next to a center top relief of the Annunciation, and parallel with another Franciscan saint (San Diego or San Pedro); while Benedict's robes are darker, the gilding on their robes are parallel,

---

[61] In more than one case, while viewing an image of Benedict in a parish church, I was told by the custodian that the image had originally been in the local Franciscan convent.

emphasizing their shared place in the order.[62] Though the saints presented on the altarpiece are diverse, all the early modern figures were Franciscans, which places Benedict squarely in conversation with his fellow brothers. [Plate 71]

In Seville's Franciscan Iglesia de San Antonio de Padua, the main altar features four Franciscan saints clustered around central sculptures of the Nuestra Señora de la Palma (below) and St. Anthony of Padua, holding the Christ child (above). The present altarpiece was constructed in the early eighteenth century for the Oratorio de San Felipe Neri, from which it was relocated to the Iglesia de San Antonio de Padua in the early nineteenth century. Four saints flank the central two sculptures of the altarpiece: on the left stand St. Dominic (below) and Benedict of Palermo (above); on the right are St. Francis (below) and St. Colette (above). The parallel structure is striking – on the bottom, we see arguably the two most important friars in the premodern Church, while above sit the female saint and the black saint, both tertiaries and holding flowers in the folds of their habits.[63]

Carmelite authors and artists likewise sought to integrate their black saints into a larger pantheon of Carmelite saints. In addition to the brief descriptions of the location and appearance of images, Santana's *Chronicle of the Ancient and Calced Carmelites* included an expanded description of Lisbon's Carmelite church. Within, the images were located on the altarpiece dedicated to St. Simon Stock (d. 1265), an English Carmelite who had been a prior of the order. Elesban, Santana explains, was on the *"Evangelho"* (right side of the altar) while Efigenia's image was in the *Epistola* (left side), and that they were the same height and "equally perfect." He described Efigenia's image as holding the traditional burning convent, but provided no details about Elesban's.[64]

Santana did, however, describe the history of the images and their altars: the two Ethiopian saints had originally been placed on an altar with the Carmelite St. Maria Madgalena de Pazzi (d. 1607), shared jointly between two confraternities. Conflict ensued, and, as a result, the black brotherhood sought a new altar that could be for their exclusive use, and the two images were subsequently moved to Simon Stock's altar in 1737. Santana continued by remarking on a large celebration in honor of the altar's three saints in the following year, consisting of one

---

[62] Information on the Iglesia de San Juan Bautista was found: http://enclasedepatrimonio.blogspot .com/2010/02/finalizado-iglesia-de-san-juan-bautista.html [accessed December 20, 2017].

[63] The presence of flowers with Colette led me to wonder if it is possible that the saint is in fact Isabel of Portugal, especially considering that Colette was not beatified until 1740 (although of course it is possible that the sculpture was commissioned in celebration of her beatification).

[64] Santana, *Os dous atlantes*, 1:323; Santana, *Chronica dos Carmelitas da Antiga, e Regular Observancia*, 1:728–9.

Map 4.4 Images of Elesban and/or Efigenia in Algarve, Portugal

hundred "people of the purest blood and most virtuous."[65] Here he makes it clear to his readers that the Ethiopians saints were venerated by a large number of people, some of whom were probably members of the nobility, rather than restricted to the members of the confraternity.

Santana also described images of the Ethiopian saints at another convent in Lisbon – the Convent of Santa Clara for female Franciscans – where the two saints stood "beautifully decorated" in a "new chapel" built for them that had the nickname "The Hermitage of the Black Saints," although unfortunately, in this case, he did not include additional details.[66] The presence of the two saints outside Carmelite convents indicates a wide devotional base; Santana emphasized their numerous devotees, including many members of court who experienced miracles worked by Efigenia. When emphasizing the broad reach of devotion to the Ethiopian saints, Santana named places that housed their images, most of which were in the region surrounding Lisbon, central Portugal, and Andalusia. Yet one of the largest concentrations of surviving images of Elesban and Efigenia (particularly the latter) – unmentioned by Santana – is located in the Algarve, the southernmost region of Portugal, which borders on Andalusia to the east. [Map 4.4]

Like Benedict, images of the Ethiopian saints survive on Carmelite altars. One late eighteenth-century altarpiece in the Iglesia del Carmen in Écija, Spain, contains bas-reliefs on the main altar of Elesban and Efigenia. The two figures

---

[65] Santana, *Chronica*, 1:728–30.
[66] Santana, *Os dous atlantes*, 2:109–10. Santana's descriptions of these two churches are invaluable for modern scholars because both were destroyed by the devastating earthquake, fire, and tsunami in 1755 that damaged or completely eradicated much of Lisbon and the southwest corner of the Algarve.

immediately catch the eye for the rich blackness of their faces and hands. Their blackness is highlighted by the cream of their Carmelite mantles. [Plate 72] The two saints here are depicted as a matched pair – the pigments used for both habit and face, for example, appear identical; their facial expressions are also nearly identical, with eyes facing forward, mouths closed, expressions stern and forceful. They both wear gold crowns and hold attributes in their hands – in their left, cradled to their bodies, are books; Efigenia also holds a scepter in her right hand. [Plate 73] Elesban's right hand remains curled but empty, suggesting that it had at one time held a scepter as well. [Plate 74] The double representation of their royalty – crowns and scepters – is rare for the Ethiopian saints, and therefore an aspect of their cults that held particular significance to the sculptor.

Like the Benedictine bas-relief, the altarpiece in Écija includes a cluster of Carmelite friars and nuns, as well as a dramatic bas-relief of Elijah in his chariot being lifted up to the sun, represented as a circle surrounded by rays with the figure of God in the center. The reliefs of Elesban and Efigenia are below, in parallel to each other at the midpoint of the altar. Elesban, Efigenia, and Elijah, three ancient saints of the Carmelite order, create a visual and material triangle in the top half of the altarpiece. The rest of the images in the altarpiece are polychrome sculpture, including Teresa of Avila and Mary Magdalene de Pazzi. While the Ethiopian saints are about half the size of those below and above, they are easily visible by the viewer from the pews. Above Elesban and Efigenia are sculptures of the prophet Elisha (Elijah's successor) and St. Albert of Sicily (d. 1307).[67] In a straight vertical line, one sees Elijah, the founder of the Carmelite order, and the Virgin, presiding over all the Carmelite saints in the altarpiece.

A similar didactic use of Efigenia and Elesban for a lesson on Carmelite history can be found in the Museu do Escravos in Lagos, Portugal. The museum houses a giant painting, once hung in the church across the road (where a reproduction now stands). The Virgin Mary is positioned in the center wearing a Carmelite habit, holding the cloak with her arms outstretched; angels hold the edge of the mantle, creating a shelter for her children, who appear within, three male saints on the left and three female saints on the right. [Plate 75] The three female saints stand in a row; in the foreground is Teresa of Avila, followed by Efigenia, and lastly (closest to the Virgin) is Mary Magdalene de Pazzi, all easily recognizable by their various attributes. As we have seen, Mary Magdalene and Teresa were

---

[67] The inclusion of Albert of Sicily is less obvious than the other saints, but it is important to note that both Teresa of Avila and Mary Magdalene de Pazzi – the two most important early modern Carmelite saints – were devoted to St. Albert's cult.

important sixteenth-century Carmelites, beatified in the early seventeenth century, and with widespread cults.[68]

On the other side of the Virgin stand the male saints: the archangel Michael, Elesban, and John the Baptist. Elesban, unlike Efigenia, stands in the back, his body almost completely hidden by those of the other two saints. It is entirely possible that Elesban was added to the painting after the other two male saints, perhaps to create symmetry with the other side and to act as Efigenia's partner. John the Baptist was associated with the Carmelites through purported similarities in their habits, leading some Carmelite historians to argue that he, too, had been of their order; they further believed that his prophetic role aligned him with Elijah and the order's unique legacy. In a wonderful detail, Elesban and Michael both hold croziers. Because Elesban is slightly hidden behind Michael, it is by the eye following his spear downward that one sees the evil king, Dunaan, crumpled at Elesban's feet, the point of the crozier at his neck. [Plate 76]

Here, then, the Carmelite Virgin embraces her saints, past and present, from the earliest times of the New Testament all the way to Pazzi and Teresa of Avila. The divisions – sometimes bitter – between Calced and Discalced Carmelites are elided here, creating a unified Carmelite order. Elesban and Michael represent militaristic responses to evil, while the other saints depict asceticism, mysticism, and wisdom in the promotion of belief. The arrangement of the saints further reinforces the antiquity of the Carmelite lineage, which claimed its foundation from before the birth of Christ; here we see Elesban and Efigenia stand in central positions in this history, similar to their placement in the Écija altarpiece.

While Benedict's case provides the most detailed evidence for understanding the circulation of black saints throughout the Iberian world, we can create a similar "mapping" of images for Elesban and Efigenia in the eighteenth century. Joining together textual evidence of their images and the surviving images provides insight into the wide geographic spread of their cults. Carmelite authors, particularly Santana, began to promote their black saints aggressively by the early eighteenth century, just as hagiographies of Benedict began to kick into high gear. It is not an accident that the majority of sculptures and paintings of black saints date to this period – the chronology strongly suggests that in spite of ample evidence of devotion to black saints in the seventeenth century, Carmelites advertised their own black saints partly to compete with Franciscans as staking a claim to be representative of global Catholicism. Yet one must also keep in mind that although specific saints might be associated with specific orders, their

---

[68] The number of Carmelite altars in Portugal that included Mary Magdalene de Pazzi reminds us of her significance to early modern Calced Carmelites, in spite of the relative paucity of scholarship on her cult. For an important exception, see Copeland, *Maria Maddalena de'Pazzi*.

images can be found in a variety of churches, including parish, Jesuit, Mercedarian, and Dominican, which further emphasizes their devotional significance for the larger early modern spiritual landscape.

Sculpture, paintings, and engravings told interlocking stories about black saints, who they were, what they were famous for, and how widespread their cults were in the Iberian world. They spread multiple messages about blackness and sanctity. Black saints could be humble, ecstatic, one with Christ, royal, or military victors. Most of all, however, they were black – the darkness of the *encarnaciones* applied to their sculpture emphasized their blackness as a key attribute of their sanctity, rendering them visually striking within churches, distinguishable from white saints even in shadowy side chapels. The striking black pigment emphasized an idealized representation of their physical selves as well as the embodied nature of holiness. This holiness was beautiful, complex, and multifaceted; it communicated spiritual truths about penance and suffering, body and soul, and the lineages of religious orders. Black saints were present in churches and convents and in the streets, venerated by enslaved and free people of color, the religious orders to which they belonged, and the white laity. Most importantly, their presence in churches throughout the Iberian Atlantic offered black Catholics the ability to see themselves reflected in sacred art and history.

5 BRILLIANT BLACKNESS: HAGIOGRAPHIC METAPHORS OF LIGHT AND DARK

While the first printed account of the lives of Antonio da Noto and Benedict of Palermo appeared in Daza's history of the Franciscan order in 1611, the majority of hagiographies of black saints appeared between the mid-seventeenth and the mid-eighteenth centuries – more than fifty years after devotion to black saints had begun to spread across three continents. The gap between lay popularity and textual production underscores the informal (and grass roots) nature of the devotion to black saints, since the cults encompassed a wide geographic span even in the absence of official recognition or printed vidas. Yet the written accounts augmented cults of black saints by providing official support for their veneration, and, in some cases, textual persuasion aimed at achieving beatification, the first major step to canonization. The genre of hagiography in the early modern era tends to refer to a stand-alone printed work produced for wide circulation. Yet information about holy people could circulate through multiple sources, including vidas of saints that remained in manuscript (usually in convent libraries), entries in local sacred histories and histories of orders, and sermons preached in honor of the saints. All such material provided authors and preachers similar opportunities to espouse ideas about specific holy people to what can be found in vidas. The patterns that emerge from close analysis of hagiographies of black saints during this era, therefore, demonstrate a remarkable degree of continuity in rhetoric and approach, in spite of minor variations, which resulted in a widely dispersed discourse of black sanctity.

Hagiographies, sermons, and histories had different goals, but all worked to expand the devotional base for a saint. While the celebration of a feast day or commission of an image (including printed engravings) could publicize a new devotion among a broad swath of people, a hagiography or entry in a chronicle acted as an effective way of spreading information about a new saint. Although long printed texts were most likely to circulate among the elite, they were occasionally integrated into the liturgy, making their ideas available to a lay audience as well. Hagiographers might produce lives of contemporary holy people after their deaths in order to help promote the cult with an eye to formal recognition by the papacy, after a successful beatification or canonization to celebrate the saint's elevation, or to express devotion (local or personal) to a centuries-old saint. Authors frequently used older hagiographies as sources for writing new ones, copying themes and even entire passages from older work, with or without attribution. Saints' Lives, then, were palimpsests on which new texts were layered onto old.[1] Following this pattern, hagiographies of black saints drew from tropes developed in older medieval and early modern works, while developing new discourses of sanctity required by the racial difference of their subjects.[2]

Hagiographies of black saints exist in two types: those of sixteenth- and seventeenth-century holy people; and those of the ancient saints Elesban and Efigenia. Ancient saints generally enjoyed *de facto* status as saints even though they had not undergone a formal canonization process.[3] Such status might offer a partial explanation for the paucity of surviving hagiographies of Elesban and Efigenia; furthermore, the establishment of their sanctity had the potential to change the hagiographers' rhetoric, since they were not making cases for their subjects' worthiness for canonization.[4] The lives of contemporary holy people of color, however, necessitated a different approach, one that neutralized color difference and low status as a barrier to holiness. As a result, unpacking the hagiographies of black saints reveals how clerical authors discussed, understood, and provided spiritual meaning to black saints' color difference within the framework of Catholic theology. The hagiographers' task required universalizing the subject by folding the specific circumstances of the holy person's life and status into long-standing tropes about sanctity.[5] Almost all hagiographers of black saints included elaborate discussions on the heroic virtue of suffering and the

---

[1] Barbara Newman points out that hagiographies were layered, built upon oral traditions (including oral testimonies of the hagiographer or others who knew the saints in life) in addition to other saints' Lives: "which supply not only stylistic models and structural patterns, but also specific episodes that may be adapted or even borrowed verbatim": "Preface," xxix –xxx.

[2] For an example of the trope of humility in the life of a white holy woman, see Isabel de Jesús (d. 1648), who – along with her supporters – employed the language of "from the lowest to the highest" to support her claim to sanctity: "The Poor Pray More."

[3] Formal papal canonization was not established until the Middle Ages (included in canon law by 1234), and even then was unevenly employed, especially in cases of local holy people.

[4] Alison Knowles Frazier argues that disentangling hagiography from canonization also yields significant historiographical interventions: *Possible Lives*, 10–12.

[5] All hagiographers needed to defend any controversial aspects of potential saints in their works. For one example, see Francisco de Ribera's life of Teresa of Avila: Ribera, *Vida de Santa Teresa de Jesús*, 61–90. He argues here that "de Dios no hay hombre ni muger, todos son criaturas suyas" (p. 88), the exact Scripture cited by hagiographers of black saints. On the "problem" of femininity and holiness, see the important works: Weber, *Teresa of Avila*; and Schutte, *Aspiring Saints*.

light of universal salvation that infused all Christians. Yet hierarchies of color difference created tensions within the texts themselves as hagiographers consciously and unconsciously grappled with deep ambivalence regarding the relationships between color difference, ethnicity, status, and holiness.

The repeating themes in hagiography form a typology of a black saint. Saints had long been divided both hierarchically and typologically – in fact, typologies emerged along a hierarchy, organized by physical proximity to Christ and those who imitated his Passion: apostles, martyrs, doctors, confessors, and virgins. Liturgical celebrations for each holy person on his or her feast day were shaped by such categories, often using a general template based on type, rather than the specific details of individual lives. Additional informal "types" later developed, including mystics, royal saints, founders, and bishops, which gave rise to their own series of characteristics and tropes. Hagiographers of black saints followed these trends, developing similar themes that expressed a shared theological understanding of what characteristics a black saint should exhibit and how such characteristics should be explained to the audience.[6]

Color difference was often one of the first issues addressed by hagiographers in their vidas of holy people of color such as Benedict of Palermo, Antonio da Noto, Martín de Porres, Úrsula de Jesús, and Teresa Juliana de Santo Domingo.[7] By immediately engaging in discussions of blackness and sanctity, the authors attempted to defuse the audience's potential rejection of a black saint. As a result, such texts reveal valuable information about the clergy's view of the relationship between color difference and holiness, body and spirit, during a time when views of human difference were becoming increasingly entrenched, embodied, and racialized. While authors occasionally invoked places of origin to specifically locate the saints' difference, they overwhelmingly focused on skin color, which had the effect of defining difference solely through complexion. In spite of the early contributions on Benedict and Antonio by Antonio Daza and Alonso de Sandoval in the early seventeenth century, hagiographies of black saints largely peaked in the first half of the eighteenth century, though they began to appear with greater frequency beginning in the mid-seventeenth century. Such frequency coincided with the build up to and result of Benedict's beatification in 1743. Vidas printed in this period – particularly in the early-to-mid eighteenth century – largely focused on Benedict, but we also see a cluster of works on other holy people of color appear, most likely inspired by the

---

[6] This list represents something of an oversimplification. For more on categories of saints, see Bartlett, *Why Can the Dead Do Such Great Things?*, 150–205. See also Hahn, *Portrayed on the Heart*, which discusses specific topoi associated with martyrs, virgins, and confessors.

[7] Úrsula de Jesús and Teresa Juliana de Santo Domingo will be discussed in greater length in Chapter 6.

heightened visibility of Benedict's cult. Several of the vidas that appeared in the seventeenth and eighteenth centuries will be discussed together in order to compare and contrast the approaches taken by authors with differing subjects, geographies, and time periods. While differences emerge, this cluster of sources also reveals patterns – repeating themes overlaid onto the unique events of each subject's life and the various authors' aesthetic and theological preferences.

Color Difference

Scholars often pinpoint the mid-to-late eighteenth century as the period in which modern racism – with its ideas of entrenched bodily difference – took root, but the history of such ideas throughout the early modern period is complex. Throughout the seventeenth and eighteenth centuries, ideas of difference were in flux, with older ideas intermingling with emerging ones, overlapping and in contestation with each other. For millennia, Christian theorists adhered to the biblical account of the origin of life: God created the universe, and then He created man and woman. All human beings descended from Adam and Eve, in what scholars describe as a monogenetic theory of human origins – that is, that human beings shared one (mono) family tree. Yet proponents of monogenesis had to account for human diversity. Why, if human beings had a common ancestor, did people appear different from one another? Medieval Europeans had pondered differences in skin color and other physical characteristics; their theories largely drew from Greek physicians, who explained color difference as a result of what scholars refer to as climate theory.[8] This theory holds that different climates could result in physical characteristics; for example, an exceptionally strong sun could "burn" the skin black.

Climate theory emerged out of the Greek medical notion of the four qualities and four humors – substances that generated human traits such as physical strength or weakness, as well as health or illness.[9] Although humors gave rise to the physical and emotional features of human beings, they were substances that manifested themselves differently in different people. Humors were also in a near-constant state of flux and required frequent balancing. The humoral basis of physical appearance, including complexion, meant that some early modern

---

[8] Curran, *Anatomy of Blackness*, 80–130; and Ziegler, "Physiognomy, Science, and Proto-Racism," 181–99. Epstein discusses the ways color difference could be used as a shorthand for ethnicity in the Middle Ages: *Purity Lost.*

[9] Wheeler, *The Complexion of Race*, 23–8. For more on medieval understandings of qualities, humors, and difference, see Cadden, *Meanings of Sex Difference.*

Europeans believed that blackness and whiteness were neither permanent nor inevitable states of being but rather mutable.[10]

The interconnection of climate theory and monogenesis led to slippage in categories often seen in the modern world as fixed, especially gender, personality traits, and skin color. At the same time, the early modern period espoused rigid hierarchies of people, whether based on social status, religion, or skin color, deeply entrenched modes that co-existed with monogenesis and climate theory. For example, sixteenth-century Jesuits developed a civilizational hierarchy – that is, that the world could be categorized vertically based on the levels of civilization exhibited by its members, with the "most civilized" – i.e., elite Christian Europeans – at the top. Less "civilized" groups included unruly peasants, to whom some Jesuits referred as "Indians." Increased social control in Europe, then, fed and was fed by the reactions of Europeans to encountering different groups while traveling the globe.[11] The lower down the group, the more it required intervention from those on top in order to control it. Such interventions took place on a micro level in Europe with increased regulation of the poor by municipal governments, as well as on the macro level with the organization of imperial regimes and their coercive apparatus. Like social control within Europe, transatlantic slavery was never merely an economic system; it also required a variety of apparatus (legal, intellectual, religious) for its justification and reinforcement.

It is important to keep in mind, however, that there was no single way of thinking about the world and its people during this period. The Spanish, for example, erupted into a lively debate over empire, just war, and the treatment of the indigenous in Mexico and the Caribbean. The most well-known moment in this debate took place between Bartolomé de las Casas and Juan Ginés de Sepúlveda in front of the Spanish king Charles V in Valladolid. The Dominican friar Las Casas is most famous for his treatise, *The Destruction of the Indies* (1542), which launched a vehement attack on the treatment of the indigenous by the Spanish, accusing them of illegal slavery and mass murder. Much of the debate between Las Casas and Sepúlveda centered on the ability of native people to reason – if they could reason, they could not be enslaved. If they could not, they fit the Aristotlean definition of "natural slaves" – that is, individuals who required mastery from a superior group because of their inherent defects of reason.[12]

---

[10] Hill, "Entering and Exiting Blackness." See also, in the same volume, Hill, "Categories and Crossings."

[11] Selwyn, "'Procur[Ing] in the Common People,'" 4–34.

[12] Sixteenth-century Spanish beliefs about "natural slavery" were intertwined with their delineation of "just war." For more on Sepúlveda's theories of just war and slavery, see Castañeda, "La esclavitud natural."

Las Casas and Sepúlveda provide just one example of the angles from which we can view early modern ideas about difference, natural slavery, and just war. Different conversations emerged in northern (Protestant) Europe and in Italy over similar questions, even in comparable slaving powers like Britain. Moreover, Spanish American frameworks could differ significantly from peninsular ones, in spite of a continuous influx of Iberians to the Americas. Indeed, the gap between American and Iberian ideas grew with time, when, by the early eighteenth century, Creoles began to articulate more firmly their own political and social perspectives. Jorge Cañizares-Esguerra argues that Creoles in the Americas pushed back against climate-based theories that posited the degeneration of European bodies in tropical climates. Fearing the reduction of their position to the same "state" as indigenous people, Creoles attempted to "fix" or make stable European bodies.[13] Even within the same time frames and geographic locations, individuals engaged in acrimonious disputes over ideas like climate theory and bodily difference.

Throughout the seventeenth and eighteenth centuries, moreover, climate theory faced ever-sharpening critiques from natural philosophers, who began to question why, if bodily difference and humoral constitution were climate influenced, did the differences between people persist even in new environments after multiple generations? Neither monogenesis nor climate theory acted to halt oppressive regimes based on civilizational and color difference – it could promote the idea of potential equality grounded in a shared humanity, but it could also just as easily be placed within a framework of degeneration, as Cañizares-Esguerra notes for the Americas. Andrew Curran cautions against dividing eighteenth-century thinkers who espoused monogenesis versus polygenesis into the simple camps of "anti slavery" and "pro slavery." Yet increasing eighteenth-century interest in polygenesis was built on a fixed idea of difference, which in turn created not only observable variations in appearance and culture, but intellectual and moral ones that could not be transcended by any means.[14]

Yet for most Iberian clergy, one's "civility" was intimately connected to acceptance of Christianity. European theologians viewed Christianity as a "reasonable" religion, which meant that those who were endowed with reason

---

[13] Cañizares-Esguerra, "Demons, Stars, and the Imagination," 313–25. On the role of food in ideas of body and difference, see Earle, *The Body of the Conquistador*. Many scholars have also noted a fundamental pivot in the way natural philosophers discussed physical difference in the sixteenth century as a result of a European need to understand themselves in relationship to people in the Americas and Africa. See also Joseph Ziegler's essay in the same volume: "Physiognomy, Science, and Proto-Racism," 181–99, especially pp. 198–9.

[14] Curran, *Anatomy of Blackness*. Polygenesis posits distinct lines of human development, rather than one, diminishing the vestiges of "sameness" provided by monogenesis.

would hear the truth of Christianity when it was preached to them and accept it immediately.[15] Resistance, refusal, or backsliding into previous religious practice were considered not only insults to God, but acts of rebellion requiring a strong civil as well as ecclesiastical response. All subjects of the king were his children; as such, they required guidance and admonishment. Such beliefs were amplified in the cases of Amerindians and Africans, who were viewed as children because they had lived without Christianity, or were new to Christianity, in addition to coming from cultural environments considered less "civilized" than Europe.

The Problem of Black Sanctity in Early Modern Hagiography

Black saints stood at the crossroads of complex and evolving early modern theories about bodily and cultural difference. While all baptized Christians were theoretically spiritual equals, entrenched civilizational hierarchies militated against such equality in practice. Early modern hagiographers found themselves at the nexus of competing impulses – theological teachings about spiritual equality and ever-hardening views on the moral inferiority of non-European groups. Many clergy, therefore, were inclined to be deeply skeptical about the ability of non-Europeans to attain the required levels of virtue and devotion necessary for achieving sanctity. At the same time, however, others promoted holy people from a variety of geographic locations and ethnic backgrounds. Such efforts were integral to global missionary work and the Church's promotion of its universal dominion and evangelical successes. Scripture told them that before the Apocalypse, God's word would be transmitted throughout the globe. The success of this message found its most powerful evidence in the ability of a few people of color to attain holiness.

Hagiographers of black saints struggled with the problem of their subjects' ethnicity, which generally focused on the static universalism of color difference, though they occasionally referred to birthplace when the subject had been born in Africa. Some authors revealed their own ambivalence about how low-status people of color, with their inherent social and religious inferiority, could be God's chosen vessel. Even if not felt by the hagiographer himself, all authors recognized the ambivalence, even hostility, with which their texts might be greeted by their audience. They needed to persuade a potentially skeptical audience that black Christians were capable of attaining heroic virtue, which was

---

[15] The role of reason and conversion in Christian truth is most clearly articulated in Christian–Jewish debates of the High Middle Ages: Dahan, *The Christian Polemic*. Of course, most medieval theologians understood the limits of reason over revelation in knowing God.

only possible by addressing the meaning(s) of blackness. This tactic by hagiographers allows us to compare the arguments employed by some members of the clergy about the relationship between color difference and holiness.

There were three main discursive strategies developed by hagiographers: scriptural rhetorical about those of the lowest status becoming the most glorified, botanical metaphors, and allusions to climate theory. Antonio Daza explained the relationship between blackness and sanctity this way: "The viler the material and the less esteemed it is by men, the more skillful it credits the sovereign Artist [God], that He knows how to perfect . . . and to demonstrate the skills of His art, and quality of His genius." Daza described sinners who had become saints, describing Antonio da Noto as a black man (un Negro), black "like those from Guinea, Xalose, and Manicongo,"as well as a Muslim.[16] Daza's connection of the lowliest and most sinful of men with Antonio's skin color and Muslim birth links low status with blackness.[17] God's ability to transform the saints proved the greatness of divine power (here, God, as the ultimate artist), since to make something that is ugly into something beautiful is a more challenging task for an artist than to make something attractive even more beautiful. Here Antonio's vida linked color difference to his previous adherence to Islam, which had the effect of doubling his "vile" past.

Alonso de Sandoval's 1627 treatise repeated Daza's section on vile material bringing greater glory to God almost verbatim in his introduction to the two black Franciscan saints.[18] Such rhetoric had an extended legacy, as similar ideas appeared in Pedro de Mataplanes's 1702 hagiography of Benedict of Palermo. Before beginning his first chapter on Benedict's life – which outlined the good morals and piety of his parents – Mataplanes opened with a long panegyric. Here, he cited the Italian polymath Girolamo Cardano (d. 1576), "whose 'Book of Plants'" (part of a larger work, De subtilitate) "teaches us the color of true black comes from thick and coarse material: and the flowers produced [in such soil] are the most delicate and subtle of plants."[19] He then called Benedict a flower,

---

[16] Daza, Chronica de Quarta Parte, 155–6: "Quanto la material es mas vil, y de menos estima en los ojos de los hombres, tanto queda mas acreditado el primor del artifice, que la sabe perficionar y poner en su punto, mostrando en ella los primores de su arte, y las ventajas de su ingenio. Y como el hazer santos de pecadores, tenga en si tanta dificultad, que afirman los santos, serle a Dios mas dificultoso, que criar cielos y tierra; de aqui es, que considerando la vileza de la material, queda mas acreditado el primor de aquel soberano Artifice que la supo perficionar."

[17] Such discourses echo the ways in which hagiographers discussed female saints as well, relying on the subversion of traditional hierarchies as evidence of God's power.

[18] Sandoval expands from Daza's text by including a more general list of groups that could be elevated by God, including: "negros gentiles, barbaros, broncos, boçales, salvages": Naturaleza, 128.

[19] Mataplanes, Vida de fray Benito, Preface, n.p. "[S]egun la solida, y fundada razon, qu nos dà en su florido Libro de las Plantas el erudite Cardano; diziendo, que la color verdaderamente negra se engendra de material muy espesa, y crasa: y siendo que las Flores se producen del sumo màs

adding that his "fragrant, fresh, and sprightly" corpse had been preserved by the Franciscans for over a hundred years. Moreover, the holy man was a "rare" and "mystical" flower, rare because he was black, esteemed because he was unique. The rarity of Benedict's grace, therefore, was the source of his heightened holiness. God's ability to create a wondrous and admirable creature out of the coarsest material elevated Benedict's holiness as a particularly exceptional saint. The beginning of the text is ambiguous, because it is unclear if Benedict's blackness represents the coarse 'material' or the delicate and subtle flower – if his body was the source of beauty or the beauty itself, once transformed.[20]

Botanical metaphors were relatively common in the lives of the saints, since the beauty of the natural world connected the material and the spiritual. Sara Ritchey argues that the material world was "understood as holy matter – matter made sacred by the world's creation."[21] Because people were in and of the world, part of God's creation, they too could be re-created through divine power. As in the previous example, botanical metaphors played a heightened role in the hagiographies of black saints, as authors emphasized the saints' black skin. In 1747, Diego Álvarez turned to Song of Songs in the extended preface to his work, where he compared Benedict's body to the black cedars of the tabernacles: "I am black but beautiful, like the tents of Kedar, like the curtains of Solomon."[22] Cedar, a valuable and highly desirable wood throughout the Near East, had been used to build Solomon's temple. For Álvarez, then, Benedict acted as a beam that held up the roof of the Church. Moreover, Benedict-the-tree stood in the orchard of holiness, an aromatic and colorful display that "nature planted in the blackened earth of Ethiopia."[23] The phrase "blackened earth of Ethiopia" parallels climate theory, in that the bodies of those who lived there had been blackened by the sun.

---

delicado, y sutil de las Plantas ..." This passage from Mataplanes appeared, word for word, in a 1744 Portuguese hagiography written by Apolinário da Conceição: *Flor peregrina*, 2.

[20] It is worth noting the long history of "exceptionality" of people of color being used as part of Western white supremacy.

[21] Ritchey, *Holy Matter*, 11. She specifies later that trees played a particularly important role in medieval imagery because they "became ... emblematic of the work of re-creation, of the changes to be expected in the natural world as a result of God's remaking it in the incarnation" (18).

[22] In modern editions of the Bible, the word often appears as Kedar – as cited here – referring to a group of people, the Kedarites, but in the early modern era it was translated occasionally glossed as referring to the cedar tree.

[23] Álvarez, *Sombra Ilustrada*: "Como el Blanco de Cuerpo Negro, (sì Negro como los Tabernaculos Cedarenos, hermoso tambien como las Salomonicas Pieles) ... à que miran los empleos de Alma, y pluma en esta Historia, en cuyo campo se descubre para el gustoso recreo de la devocion Española un Huerto tan aromatico por sus Rosas, Lirios, y Azuzenas, que symbolizando à el Hybleo, es fragrante, y vistosa gala de aquellos Jardines amenos, que plantò naturaleza en el tiznado terreno de la Ethiopia" (n.f.).

The orchard implies multiplicity rather than singularity – that is, he is not a lone tree, but one of many born of Ethiopia. In another botanical metaphor, the anonymous author of the vida of seventeenth-century Afro-Peruvian tertiary Úrsula de Jesús described all the nuns in the convent as flowers with "fragrant virtues," while Úrsula was a "most humble plant . . . worthy to be included in this distinguished choir of Virgins."[24] The designation "most humble" here is ambiguous – while the author could be marking out Úrsula as lesser than her sisters, it is also plausible that the adjective (*humildissima*) was meant to convey her spiritual superiority. The authors of these hagiographies, then, employed the common trope connecting flowers or plants to holiness and virtue, although the example of Úrsula's vida provides a less embellished description.

As in the example of Medina, many hagiographers' discussion of blackness was most deeply grounded in Scripture, specifically passages that addressed the paradoxical nature of spiritual darkness and light. Yet the "dark" bodies of the saints could reveal ambivalence – that is to say, was their blackness a negative that was overcome? Or a neutral quality that did not impede holiness? Did its "vileness" signal a lesser worthiness of black Christians? The Pauline epistles were the most evocative meditations on light and darkness, life and death, in the Bible, which helped some hagiographers clarify the relationship between body, soul, color difference, and holiness. In his letter to the Ephesians, for example, St. Paul exhorted: "For you were once darkness, but now you are light in the Lord. Live as children of the light . . . and find out what pleases the Lord. . . . But everything exposed by the light becomes visible: and everything that it illuminates becomes a light" (Eph 5:8–14). In the Biblical language of light and darkness, light represented eternal life – promised to all Christians through baptism – while darkness ("*tenebrae*") represented sin and ignorance, the shadows to which those focused on worldly life were condemned.

The language of light and darkness here reflects the Christian doctrine that degraded the secular understanding of "life" – i.e., one's time as a breathing person on earth – as "false life" or life leading to eternal damnation (or "death," because the soul died). "True" life occurred at the moment of human death, when the saved soul experienced eternal life in Heaven. In 2 Timothy, St. Paul declared that Christ "has abolished death and has brought life and immortality to light through the Gospel (2 Tim 1:10).[25] Because the darkness of sin and the light of salvation were applied equally to all souls, such language provided the richest

---

[24] *Transcripción modernizada de la Vida,* 3–4.
[25] Antonio Castellano cited many examples from the Pauline epistles, including 2 Cor 4:6: "For God who said 'Let light shine out of darkness,' has shone in our hearts to bring to light the knowledge of the glory of God on the face of Christ."

ground for hagiographers seeking to act as a counterweight to their saints' color difference to potentially skeptical readers.

Bernardo de Medina, for example, writing from Lima in 1675 about Martín de Porres, declared: "Out of a night so dark was born a sun so resplendent in sanctity, because to God there is no difference between Hebrew or Greek, slave or free, man or woman, as the Apostle says."[26] The "apostle" in question was St. Paul, writing to the Galatians in one of the most famous passages in his epistles.[27] Here Medina joined two important elements of the black saints: the play on the traditional binaries of light and dark and a more oblique invocation of monogenesis. Martín was born of "a night so dark" – here, his mother's black body, and by extension his own skin.

At the same time, he was born not into darkness, but into a holiness that was "resplendent" or brilliantly beautiful. The adjective "resplendent" signifies light, a theme to which I will return below. Martín's interior blazed forth like the light of the sun with the holiness gifted to him from God Himself. Medina concluded that such a miracle is possible because the color of a person's skin was irrelevant to God. Like Medina, Álvarez described Benedict's lineage as "*obscurissimo*," ("most obscure") but insisted that such obscure blood produced a bright light that illuminated everything around it.[28] Here, Álvarez played on the word "obscure," a word that evokes darkness, contrasted again with the bright light of Benedict's sanctity (*respladores*).

The language of obscure and dark origins also drew inspiration from Scripture. Passages in the New Testament emphasized the paradox of low status and high status: One major theme of the Gospels' accounts of Jesus's life was his frequent condemnation of the wealthy, the powerful, and the religious elite in favor of those despised and condemned by secular society. In Christianity, the despised become the chosen and the elite are cast down. The rhetoric of lowliness and superiority, dark and light, provided Christian theologians a way to express that what appears on the outside is irrelevant to God, and even detrimental to the soul. Hagiographers of black saints, then, employed such passages and concepts to ground the vidas of black saints in traditional Christian rhetoric, to diffuse their readers' color prejudice, and to weave black saints into the fabric of Christian doctrine. Interior light and exterior darkness applied to all Christians

---

[26] Medina, *Vida prodigiosa*, 190.

[27] Galatians 3:28: "There is neither Jew nor Greek, there is neither slave nor free person, there is not male and female; for you are all one in Christ Jesus."

[28] Álvarez, *Sombra Ilustrada*, 2 "El linage de Benito fue obscurissimo; y esto tubo este Heroe Glorioso de mas admirable, pues naciendo de obscura sangre, supo ganar resplandores, como la luz, que con el caudal de su proprio lucir se manifiesta a sì misma, y lo ilumina todo, sin mendigar agenos lucimientos."

since they represented spiritual grace and sin (respectively); the hagiographers' use of such language was generally employed to chide their audiences that the same was true of holy people of color, despite society's view of black Africans.

Seventeenth-century hagiographers usually began their works about black saints by invoking widely known Christian ideas of light and dark, while eighteenth-century hagiographers often emphasized the concept of "accidents" in addition to Scripture. Aristotle had defined "accidents" as attributes that can be variable without changing a thing's essential nature. Spanish friar Juan Carlos Paniagua used the term "accidental" several times in 1745 to describe Teresa Juliana's skin color, as in "the accidental color of her skin."[29] Around the same time, Antonio Vicente de Madrid, author of a life of Benedict of Palermo, reminded his readers that color difference was the result of the humors, and that there was no substantial difference in human beings that could be discerned other than one's proximity to or distance from God.[30] In his eighteenth-century life of St. Elesban, the Portuguese Carmelite José Pereira Santana provided a climate-theory explanation for how Ethiopians became black, saying simply that it was the sun that blackened them rather than a "defect of nature."[31] Through the lives of black saints, hagiographers actively engaged in larger Enlightenment conversations about human development and degeneration, which were moving away from the Bible, and focusing on anatomy and "observation."

Nevertheless, the hagiographers could evince ambivalent views of blackness, occasionally connecting blackness with unbelief and savagery. For example, while Paniagua employed the word "accidental" to describe Teresa Juliana's skin color, he also described her birthplace Guinea in this way: "But however dark their faces, they were much blacker in their souls," an observation followed by a brief discussion of the region's pagan practices. The passage provides an excellent example of the frequent doubleness of hagiographic rhetoric. On the one hand, he labeled true blackness a state of the soul without God, implicitly arguing that those who experienced the truth of God lived in light rather than darkness, regardless of appearance. On the other hand, he established a clear connection between West Africans, pagan savagery, and dark complexions.[32] He further described her enslavement as ultimately an act of redemption, as she had been lifted out of pagan darkness into Christian light through her kidnapping.

---

[29] Paniagua, *Compendio de la vida*, 57–8.

[30] Antonio Vicente de Madrid, *El negro mas prodigioso*, 2.

[31] Santana, *Os dous atlantes*, 1:22: "effeito do Sol este denegrido accidente ... naõ defeito da naturea."

[32] Paniagua, *Compendio de la vida*, 2: "En sus dias festivos salia el Pueblo, Rey, y Reyna, con toda su familia, segun el rito de sus barbaras ceremonias" (p. 3).

The preface to Francisco Antonio Castellano's eighteenth-century hagiography of St. Benedict included a similar play on darkness, polytheism, and sin.[33] As part of this discussion, the two authors invoked climate theory, arguing that there were two ways of being black (*obscuro*): one was through nature, or how one was born, but through salvation one could become "very white in the Divine presence." Others were dark due to disgrace, "which leaves on the face the ugly mark of sin." Those in the second category needed to wash themselves in the "font of penitence in order to recover the whiteness that they had lost." Benedict's blackness, they insisted, was not due to sin; rather his soul had "the whiteness of snow."[34] The passage is ambivalent, as the second type of blackness could apply to *all* people, not just people of color – their use of the word "disgrace" (*desgracia*) indicates that those in this group had fallen into sin, rather than being born into unbelief. Yet the reference to the "ugly mark of sin" appearing on the face seems to inscribe sin (blackness) on the body.[35]

Hagiographers' attempts to explain to their (white) audience that a black person was capable of attaining heroic virtue, unimpeded by their skin color or place of birth, framed their spiritual biographies. The majority suggested that God did not care about color difference, that His priority was the state of a person's soul, not his or her appearance. Yet their texts cannot escape their early modern context, in which blackness was vilified, yoked to ideas about natural slavery, divine punishment, and unbelief. They did not address such potential objections explicitly, although such views can clearly be read as the flip side of the ideas they defended. Their own ambivalence, moreover, often leaks into the text, creating tensions and slippages.

Suffering, Slavery, and Blackness

The overarching rhetoric of lowliness and blackness permitted hagiographers to extend their arguments about suffering beyond slavery. In fact, only two early modern holy people of color had been enslaved – Antonio da Noto and Teresa

---

[33] Hagiographies, like most early modern books, included a variety of front matter before the main work (including approvals granting the printing licenses), which could be brief or extensive.

[34] "Unos, en quienes dispuso la naturaleza, se descubriesse en el semblante o obscuro de su origen; y otros, que por su desgracia, les sale al rostro el borron feo de la culpa ... Los primeros son Negros sin culpa por lo que pueden ser muy blancos en la Divina presencia; pero los que son negros por la obscuridad de sus pecados, necessitan lavarse en la fuente de la penitencia, para recuperar la blancura que perdieron con la gracia." Castellano, *Compendio de la heroyca, y maravillosa vida*, n.f.

[35] He did, as can be seen above, use the word "black" twice – once as an adjective for those with spiritual darkness and once as a proper noun describing the sub-Saharan Africans (*Negros*).

Juliana. In both cases, hagiographers portrayed them as serving their owners loyally and patiently. For Antonio, there was no suffering associated with his enslavement – he was simply described as living "in the world," caring for the poor, and serving his master, although his low social status was described as the origin of his immense pity for the poor. It is important to remember, however, that Antonio was hardly discussed in hagiographies or sacred histories in Spanish or Portuguese following Sandoval's 1627 text, and the eyewitness testimony taken in the sixteenth-century processes in Sicily drew from an environment where enslavement of Africans operated quite differently than the seventeenth- and eighteenth-century Iberian world.

The language of color difference intertwined with lowliness, which came together to form a third major element of the vidas of black saints: the immense suffering they experienced as a result of social prejudice. Such suffering in fact became a central focus of hagiography, which, like the rhetoric surrounding color difference, was steeped in ambivalence. On the one hand, the suffering that derived from slavery shone a spotlight on the injustice meted out against enslaved people. On the other hand, it had the potential to serve European and colonial hierarchies by reinforcing the need of slaves to suffer patiently and silently. While the latter was certainly a purpose to which such discourses could be put, the hagiographers themselves focused more on the closeness to Christ the saints experienced as a result of their spiritual martyrdoms at the hands of society.

In the seventeenth-century Iberian empires, however, the suffering of enslaved people was acute and could not be ignored by the clergy. Alonso de Sandoval criticized owners who treated their slaves badly, but also instructed enslaved people: "Your vocation is to obey not only masters who treat you mildly, but also masters who treat you harshly and who oppress you. Because Christ suffered for you, giving you an example so that you can follow in his footsteps."[36] In mid-seventeenth-century Brazil, Portuguese cleric Antonio da Vieira (d. 1697) echoed Sandoval: "Slaves, be submissive to all your Masters, not only to the good and modest ones, but also to the mean and unjust."[37] Vieira cited Sts. Paul and Peter in passages where the apostles advised obedience (Colossians 3:22–24; 1 Peter 2:18, 20–21). Yet both Sandoval and Vieira drew from the Christian exegetical tradition where Christ himself was called a slave, exemplified again in St. Paul's letter to the Philippians: "But he [Christ] emptied himself, taking the form of a slave, becoming as human beings are ... And for this God raised him high" (Phil 2: 7–9). In Christian rhetoric, then, voluntary acceptance of enslavement was not

---

[36] Sandoval, *Naturaleza*, 141: "Porque vuestra vocacion, es para obedecer, no solamente a los señores que os tratan con blandura, sino tambien a los que os tratan con aspereza, y os agravian. Porque Christo, dize, padecio por vosotros, dando os exemplo, para que sigays sus pisadas."

[37] Vieira, *Six Sermons*, 185.

solely a social-legal category – Christ himself had been a slave, obedient to his Father until his death. While neither Sandoval nor Vieira was "anti-slavery," both discussed Christ's slavery and obedience in order to elevate the dignity of enslaved people as fellow Christians.

Vieira used the parallel between Christ's enslavement and the enslavement of Africans as a way to offer solace. In one sermon, he assured the brothers of a black Rosary confraternity that while their bodies were in chains, their souls were free, and that their reward of eternal joy would come "easily" in the next life because the punishments from masters "are a martyrdom." He continued: "Because in that state in which God placed you, your vocation is similar to that of His Son, who suffered for us, leaving you the example you shall imitate."[38] A vocation is a calling from God, associated in Catholicism with the act of conversion – that is, turning one's back on the secular world and joining a religious order to live a life of simplicity and prayer. In this passage, then, Vieira compared living as a slave to the most important role in the early modern Church. This comparison was compounded by the "imitation of Christ," which was a specific spiritual practice followed by the religious in the premodern world and the most direct route to salvation.

Unlike Vieira and Sandoval, however, the hagiographers of black saints had to be careful about their condemnation of the suffering of their enslaved subjects. Teresa's hagiographer, Paniagua, described her owners as generous and Christian, perhaps because they were powerful members of the nobility – her owner's husband was the former viceroy of New Spain, Antonio Sebastián de Toledo Molina y Salazar, Marquis of Mancera (d. 1715). Paniagua's account of Teresa's life included the great suffering she endured as a slave, but this suffering occurred at the hands of servants and slaves in order to displace violence away from her white owners. The author instead insisted on her close relationship with the marquis and his wife (Doña Juliana Teresa de Meneses). A child when kidnapped and enslaved, Teresa found herself in a position of particular vulnerability in the marquis's household and was subject to significant physical violence.[39] Paniagua explained the theological meaning of the cruelty with which she was treated: "Heaven permits this ... to purify, to train Teresa." He emphasized the perfection of her response: "She remained quiet, suffering with patience and silence."[40] The ability to endure great suffering in the proper spirit

---

[38] Vieira, *Six Sermons*, 186.

[39] Bodily and emotional suffering were universal components to hagiography of early modern women. For a few examples of this vast historiography, see Myers, *Neither Saints Nor Sinners*; Coakley, *Women, Men, and Spiritual Power*; Zarri, "Living Saints"; and Bilinkoff, *Related Lives*.

[40] Paniagua, *Compendio de la vida*, 27.

of patient acceptance was a key spiritual virtue for holy women, since it elevated them to the crucial Catholic Reformation quality of heroic virtue.[41]

Both the punishments to which Teresa Juliana was subject and her silent acceptance of them elevated her virtue to the heights of humility. Passivity was the proper spiritual response to suffering, echoing that of martyrs about to be executed. The physical suffering Teresa experienced was crucial to Paniagua's account of redemption and spiritual gifts, so he made no effort to obscure or minimize the brutalities of her life as a slave; on the contrary, he employed vivid and condemnatory language in order to be clear that this was not suffering she deserved, although he placed the blame solely on the head of a "Turkish" servant. Whatever the source of violence, many heroic virtues of the saints came from their willingness to accept unmerited suffering and judgment, just as Christ had done, themes that clearly echoed throughout the Atlantic from the seventeenth to the eighteenth centuries.

Several authors connected low status, suffering, and penance. Paniagua mentioned the suffering Teresa Juliana felt when rejected by convents when seeking to become a nun as a result of her skin color. He remarked that never in her life had she cared whether her skin was white or black, but in this case, her black skin caused her a "great martyrdom" by preventing her from achieving her most cherished desire.[42] The hagiographer himself frequently called attention to Teresa Juliana's blackness by referring to her as "*esta Negra*." Each use of "*esta Negra*" served to remind the reader of the lowliness and suffering Teresa endured in her life. Moreover, there is a noticeable increase in Paniagua's usage of this epithet when discussing the problems that the holy woman encountered during her enslavement and attempts to find a convent that would accept her. Repeated references to the blackness of his subjects was fundamental to the text precisely because complexion acted as the source of her suffering.

The themes of humility and suffering of holy people of color could extend to those who had not been enslaved. The hagiographers of Benedict of Palermo and Martín de Porres emphasized that their subjects also faced cruelty and mistreatment, in spite of being free. Eighteenth-century hagiographer Antonio Vicente de Madrid discussed the resistance Benedict faced from the friars during an effort to elevate him to a position of authority within his convent. Vicente framed this

---

[41] Heroic virtue was a quality required of holy people for successful canonization bids in the post-Tridentine era: Ditchfield, "Tridentine Worship," 201–20. John Kitchen discusses the role of suffering as a method of reconciling femininity to holiness in Merovingian France: *Saints' Lives*, 120–2.

[42] Paniagua, *Compendio*, 57: "Nunca en la vida ajustada, que siempre llevò Teresa, le pudo dàr cuydado el accidente de que huviesse vestido naturaleza de color blanco, ò negro su rostro; pero en esta ocasion la sirviò de gran martyrio, por lo much que atrasò sus amantes deseos."

account in a passage from the Old Testament Book of Numbers, in which the members of Moses's household complained when the prophet decided to marry an Ethiopian woman. Vicente then claimed that the Franciscan brothers "murmured" against Benedict "for the same reason as the brothers of Moses."[43] Prejudice, therefore, defined the terms on which people of color were able (or not able) to enter religious houses.

Benedict and Teresa Juliana, like many people of color, faced racially based opposition to their efforts to join a convent (which included slurs and color prejudice). In Teresa's case, such opposition persisted even with the support of the marquis and the significant dowry he supplied. In fact, she had to leave Madrid and move to Salamanca before she could find a convent to accept her.[44] Such challenges are also reflected in the limitations of their entrance status: almost all religious people of color in the early modern period belonged to the lowest level of their respective religious orders, called the tertiary, or "lay" orders. If they received a full habit, it was almost always on their deathbeds, or in their imaginations. Hence, they were systematically marked as different and lesser by the communities in which they dwelt.[45]

Hagiographers, therefore, sometimes emphasized deep color prejudice faced by black saints instead of the misery of enslavement, primarily through verbal rather than physical abuse. Pedro de Mataplanes recounted a story in which Benedict experienced the rage of a gatekeeper because the holy man arrived back at the convent a few minutes late. Getting right into Benedict's face, the gatekeeper called him "black and a dog."[46] Mataplanes underscored the intensity (and irrationality) of the gatekeeper's anger for the reader. Calling someone a "dog" was a common – and serious – insult throughout early modern Europe.[47] Adding the adjective "black" compounded the insult by racializing it. In fact, most of the stories Mataplanes recounted of people insulting Benedict included adjectives like "slave" and "black man" as part of the slur.[48]

[43] Antonio Vicente de Madrid, *El negro mas prodigioso*, 18–19.

[44] Paniagua, *Compendio de la vida*, 57. Paniagua emphasized the great efforts made by the Manceras to convince convents to take Teresa by offering them large sums of money. Nevertheless, the nuns were often demeaning and cruel to her; see Paniagua, *Compendio de la vida*, 89.

[45] Teresa Juliana experienced a vision after the bishop refused her permission to become a nun. In the vision, St. Dominic handed her the black veil: "This was the profession invisible to mortal eyes, but very apparent to the angels, saints, and the blessed." Paniagua, *Compendio de la vida*, 77–8.

[46] Mataplanes, *Vida de fray Benito*, 36.   [47] Taylor, *Honor and Violence*, 38.

[48] Mataplanes, *Vida de fray Benito*, 36–9. Tognoletto, by contrast, tells a story in which Benedict refuses higher office in the convent because it was not fitting to have a "black slave" be in such a position: Tognoletto, *Paradiso Serafico*, 229.

Such insults recurred in the vidas of saints of color. Martín de Porres was subject to a nearly identical insult to Benedict – "*mulato* dog," in reference to his mixed-race heritage – that occurred in the course of an encounter with a white brother. Martín's hagiographer, Bernard of Medina, made clear that the torrent of insults resulted from the slightest of incidents. Martín's tormenter continued his verbal abuse, proclaiming that he (Martín) deserved to be a galley slave – one of the most grueling forms of slavery in the early modern world. Medina added that these insults were "an affront to [Martín's] *calidad*."[49] *Calidad* was a key component of colonial life – it referred to a person's social rank, which in turn was bound up in ideas about virtue and honor.[50] Here Medina insists that Martín maintained honor of his own; therefore, he did not deserve the insults levelled at him.

Such encounters were common for Martín during his time at the Dominican convent and hospital. Medina explained that God tried Martín's patience many times by subjecting him to verbal abuse from his brothers, one of whom "unleashed his tongue" with vehement insults and slanders.[51] When a superior arrived and, shocked by the brother's behavior, attempted to intervene on Martín's behalf, Martín insisted that his treatment was a deserved punishment for his sins. He proclaimed: "Today I am taking ashes even though it is not Wednesday," a reference to the penitential rite in which Catholics participated on Ash Wednesday, the day that marks the beginning of Lent, the traditional season of penance preceding Easter. The act of enduring verbal abuse with humility and patience transformed the suffering of black saints into penitential rites.

Hagiographers emphasized color prejudice in additional ways. Friars Francisco Payá and José Fernández Quevedo, authors of the "censure" of Castellano's life of Benedict, declared that "To be a slave, or a dark black man, is the greatest misfortune in the order of nature." Yet in the next phrase they added the paradoxical argument that it was also the "greatest fortune of grace," and meant that one so burned was "adorned with a most precious jewel." Such rhetoric echoed closely what we saw in sermons of Bernard of Clairvaux, where external ugliness helped to focus an individual on piety (which produced "true" beauty). On the next page, the authors admitted that although Benedict himself had not been a slave – the "stain" (*borrón*) he bore "was what nature put on his face." The following pages played on the brightness, beauty, and whiteness of his soul in contrast to his exterior blackness. The authors also connected the

---

49 Medina, *Vida prodigiosa*, 11v–13r.
50 The concept of *calidad* had increased use and significance in colonial Latin America than in peninsular Spain. For a discussion of its meaning, see Carrera, *Imagining Identity in New Spain*, 6–21; and Katzew, *Casta Paintings*, 45–6.
51 Medina, *Vida prodigiosa*, 14v–15r.

blackness of skin with the black clothes with which monks frequently adorned themselves; they chose black, the authors explained, because it signified penance. They declared: "He was a dark color by his origin, but rigorous penitence made him blacker."[52] The connection between skin color and the blackness of penitence – particularly as it was represented in the habits of the religious – also occurred in Medina's life of Martín de Porres, as the author described Martín's black parentage as a parallel to the black of the Dominican habit, which represented penance.[53]

Alternative tropes of humility appeared in hagiographic texts. Although it is often difficult to know the provenance of the statements, in several cases there is good evidence to suggest that the saint may have uttered the words in question, or something similar. Martín de Porres, for example, gained a great reputation for his healing. While he preferred to heal the poor, he was often called to minister to the mighty. In one case, a visiting archbishop asked for his services. The archbishop requested Martín give him his hand in order to help the ailing man up, to which Martín replied, "Why would your Grace wish to take the hand of a poor *mulato*, son of a slave?"[54] It is not easy to gauge to what extent Martín's humility was performative, but he clearly understood the power that could come with humility and occasionally used it subversively. In one case, he permitted a wounded indigenous man to enter his rooms so Martín could minister to the man's injuries, which the saint had been forbidden to do. When discovered, he was called to account for himself to his angry provincial. Martín fell on his knees in front of his superior; despite this gesture of submission, the saint replied that he did not understand how he sinned, because denying the poor man care would have contravened charity, a greater law than the provincial's. Here Martín substituted his own judgment and morals for that of his Dominican superior, and the superior was immediately chastened by Martín's holiness.[55] Subversive humility occurred sporadically in the vidas of saints, who frequently professed obedience while ignoring earthly authority in favor of the divine.

Humility, then, could have multiple meanings, and even act as leverage against hierarchical norms.[56] The relationship between gender and humility in the

---

[52] The censure was written by censors who read the work to make sure it did not have objectionable content. Their exact phrasing was: "El ser Esclavo, ò atezado Negro, es la mayor infelicidad en el orden de la naturaleza" ("To be a slave, or burned black, is the greatest misfortunate in the natural order"). Their collapse of slavery and blackness is telling. Castellano, *Compendio de la heroyca, y maravillosa vida*, n.p.

[53] Medina played on Martín's mixed race heritage and the Dominican habit – Martín had one white and one black parent, just as the Dominican habit was black and white:

[54] Manrique, "Marabilla perfecta," 241.   [55] Manrique, "Marabilla perfecta," 212–13.

[56] Here again, Martín's story echoes strategies of hyper-humility employed by female saints wishing to make space for themselves or subvert the authority of their confessors: Weber, *Teresa of Avila*.

context of early modern sanctity is complex, particularly in the case of low-status black men who had the potential to be feminized through the submission required of them by society. Yet we must be cautious before viewing these tropes in Martín and Benedict's life as a method of feminizing them. Humility and chastity were both heroic virtues that were associated with male saints as well as female saints, discussed in all their hagiographies. Jacqueline Murray has posited the possibility of a third gender in Catholic religious culture, inhabited by virginal men and manly women, while Ruth Karras suggests that rather than a third gender, clerical masculinity "was a model of masculinity distinct from those models found among the laity." She points out that humility and chastity were understood as a struggle, a heroic internal battle superior to the external military battles.[57] Benedict and Martín were consistently depicted as powerful, even virile, personalities: while Martín defied his prior, Benedict overturned the egg cart of an overzealous admirer in order to prevent her from praising him. Their gendering results from a multiplicity of hagiographic discourses, those applied to male as well as female saints.

But saints had to suffer, whether from bodily illness, oppression from evil rulers or temptation from the devil. The suffering the saints endured was test and trial, serving to purify them and elevate them to holiness. In early modern Catholicism, suffering bore spiritual fruit. For this reason, hagiographers often immediately segued from accounts of suffering to examples of the miraculous consolations offered to the saints by God, often in the form of visions or miracles. Paniagua recounted a story involving Teresa Juliana receiving comfort from a miraculous image of an Ecce Homo that hung in the house in which she lived.[58] "Ecce Homo" refers to the words spoken by Pilate when he presented Christ to the angry crowd, bleeding from his whipping and the crown of thorns. (The words are Latin: "Behold the man!") The image in Teresa's household inspired in her a desire to suffer "infinitely" for His sake while simultaneously being filled with consolation for her own suffering.[59] The analogy of Teresa's suffering to that of Christ casts her as a martyr, a trope that was repeated not only in Vieria, as we have seen, but throughout the hagiographies of black saints.

The vidas of Benedict and Martín also placed a strong emphasis on the saints' particular devotion to Christ's Passion and the martyrs. Benedict was described as being "transported" by spiritual ecstasy during a procession in which a float carried an image of Christ crucified. He was so consumed with contemplation that he emitted a bright light, neither seeing nor hearing the crowd around him.[60]

---

[57] Murray, "One Flesh"; and Karras, "Thomas Aquinas's Chastity Belt," 53–4. In the same volume, Lifshitz argues that clergy could use virginity as leverage for social power.

[58] Deslandres, "In the Shadow of the Cloister," 135.   [59] Paniagua, *Compendio de la vida*, 28.

[60] Castellano, *Compendio de la heroyca y maravilla vida*, 38.

Martín's hagiographer describes his extreme penitential practices in graphic language that explicitly compares his bodily suffering to that of the martyrs.[61] He made frequent use of whips, steel chains, and hairshirts, creating continual torment and rivers of blood; a belt of iron bit into his flesh until it reached the bone, much like the tortures to which the early martyrs were subjected by pagan authorities. The authors also linked together their saints' devotion to Christ and suffering for Christ by pointing out their Christ-like natures. Mataplanes, for example, remarked that Benedict's reaction to the cruel words of those tormenting him was silence, just like Teresa Juliana's; in this silence, Benedict acted "in imitation of the Redeemer of the World" – that is, Christ.[62] Bernardo de Medina likened Martín's response to ill-treatment to that of the martyrs: "but the Man of God, [was] wearing the expression of an Angel, [on his knees] like the Protomartyr Stephen."[63] [Fig 5.1] Here the author evoked the position of passive and peaceful acceptance of suffering so integral to the representation of the martyrs.

These clergy expressed the idea that blackness itself was a vehicle to holiness uniquely available to members of the African diaspora, not in spite of their lowly status but because of it. While we do not have direct evidence that hagiographers read texts across geographies, time period, or religious orders, the recurrence of similar themes in hagiographies and sermons from Lima and Salvador to Salamanca and Seville reveal how widespread such ideas were among Catholic clergy in the seventeenth and eighteenth centuries. Hagiographers and missionaries participated in a conversation that insisted on the inclusion of African converts in universal Christendom and offered them special access to redemption as consolation for their immense suffering. For early modern clergy, the point of earthly existence was salvation, a pilgrimage ending in eternal glory. The suffering of people of color, therefore, was an important spiritual opportunity that elevated them above others in keeping with the long history of Christian belief and doctrine. Yet outside the hagiographies of a handful of holy people of color, Christianity could be used throughout the Atlantic as method of containment and coercion, drawing from the teaching that a slave's "proper" place was humility and obedience no matter what violence and horror they experienced. While they did not deliberately set out to create justifications for brutality, the clergy's rhetoric enabled the maintenance of rigid hierarchies of colonial society. The rhetoric of redemptive suffering simultaneously offered liberation – either spiritual or practical, as in the cases of black confraternities freeing brothers – and strengthening of the chains binding blacks to their enslavement.

---

[61] Medina, *La vida prodigiosa*, 23v.   [62] Mataplanes, *Vida de fray Benito*, 36.
[63] Medina, *La vida prodigiosa*, 12r.

Figure 5.1 Juan de Juanes, *The Martyrdom of St. Stephen*, 1555–1562, oil on panel, 160 x 123 cm. Museo del Prado, Madrid.

And while hagiographers presented the harsh realities of the saints' situations, they did not critique those realities. Hagiographers recognized the prejudice encountered by holy people of color from everyone ranging from fellow servants to the senior ranks in the ecclesiastical hierarchy. As these texts demonstrate, friars and nuns were steeped in class and racial discrimination, and could cruelly mistreat slaves and servants of color. Through the hagiographic lens – which seeks to create a universalized and static vision – they read as the expected struggles encountered by early modern saints who often suffered ill-treatment by those in authority. Hagiographers understood the corruption and hardship faced by the saints as forces to be overcome or to be borne patiently, not overturned or transformed. It is not a genre that called for social change; it accepted and normalized the inequities and abuses of the status quo.[64] Because sanctity was intertwined with suffering, clerical discussions of the abuse experienced by people of color created slippage between the sacred and the secular. As a result, the texts read as deeply ambivalent – on the one hand, there is the normalization of slavery, and, on the other, an assertion of the spiritual inclusion of all baptized souls in universal Christendom. Perhaps most significantly, however, the promotion of black saints compelled hagiographers to highlight the spirituality equality and dignity of their souls, which at least implicitly extended to all baptized Africans, a powerful alternative to the Curse of Ham.

Royal Ethiopian Saints

Yet not all black saints were defined by their relationship to suffering, humility, and low status. In fact, two of the most visible black saints of the early modern period were the Ethiopian royal saints, Elesban and Efigenia. As a powerful king and princess respectively, they required different archetypes than the black saints of low status. The disparity between Antonio da Noto – enslaved, black, Muslim – and Elesban – emperor, defender of the faith – could not be starker. Elesban and Efigenia fit into the devotional archetype of Balthazar, the black magus, as all three were represented with a crown or wearing lavish and expensive clothing, marking them as wealthy and powerful. Examining the contrast between the typologies of slave and king highlights the diverse forms black sanctity could take in the early modern church. Blackness and African-ness were not inevitably associated with lowliness.

While the cults of Elesban and Efigenia were promoted in the late sixteenth century and spread in a limited fashion to Iberia through the martyrology and vernacular *flos sanctorum*, they did not spread significantly for another half century, by which point devotion to Benedict of Palermo had been widely established on several continents. While Efigenia appears to have been more popular than her counterpart, the earliest references to her patronage of a black confraternity date to the early seventeenth century, while the earliest surviving visual evidence (in Iberia) comes from a slightly later period. By the

---

[64] Catherine Sanok argues that beneath the seemingly static exterior, hagiographers developed nuanced historical and social arguments: *Her Life Historical.*

time Efigenia's cult began to spread widely, the Carmelites had adopted her, and mostly likely began promoting Elesban soon thereafter. Unfortunately, fewer hagiographies of the Ethiopian saints survive, creating challenges in our ability to trace what the breadth of specific discourses of royal blackness might have been.

Elesban and Efigenia's cults followed a distinct path from Benedict and Antonio. The Carmelite promotion of the Ethiopian saints in Iberia derived from the order's efforts at bolstering the controversial antiquity of their origins, which they dated back to the Old Testament prophets Elijah and Elias. The order's seventeenth-century historians spent much time and energy defending their long-held traditions against skeptical ecclesiastical historians like Baronius and rival orders like the Dominicans.[65] Elesban and Efigenia were not the only ancient saints adopted by the Carmelites, who had a habit of claiming early Christian saints from the Eastern Mediterranean and Middle East, such as Sts. Eugenia, Eufrasia, and Pelagia. Santana was still defending Carmelite history in his vida of Elesban in the eighteenth century.[66] The order's emphasis on the Carmelite origins of Elesban and Efigenia was circular – it both shored up Carmelite historiography and provided evidence for Elesban and Efigenia as Carmelites, making the promotion of these two saints an important feature of the early modern period Carmelite agenda.

Moreover, the Ethiopian saints were part of the saintly pantheon in the Calced branch of the order, which placed more emphasis on its ancient origins. The Discalced Carmelites tended to celebrate its early modern founders, Teresa of Avila and John of the Cross, who reformed the order in the sixteenth century. Teresa of Avila, in particular, was one of the most important and influential Spanish saints of the early modern period, whose fame eclipsed the pantheon of Calced saints. As a result, the aggressive promotion of the Ethiopian saints by the Calced Carmelites could have acted as a bid for increased fame during a period when they were marginalized by their Discalced sisters and brothers, in addition to their on-going competitions with other orders like the Dominicans and Jesuits.

Other than Sandoval and various *flos sanctorum*, however, there is little textual evidence about the Ethiopian saints, even by the Carmelites, before the early eighteenth century, with the exception of martyrologies and Sandoval's history. Sandoval, it is crucial to note, did not refer to either as Carmelites.[67]

---

[65] See for example Cartagena, *Dos tratados*, 26v-101v. Ethiopia as a mission field became a site of bitter contestation in the seventeenth century, as some Spanish Dominican authors fought with both Carmelites and Jesuits: Urreta, *Historia eclesiástica*.

[66] Santana, *Os dous atlantes*, 249–71.

[67] Sandoval's entry on Efigenia is the shortest of his section on Ethiopian saints, while his entry on Elesban was slightly more detailed; here he cited not the Martyrology but fellow Jesuit Pedro Sánchez and his *Libro del reyno de Dios*: Sandoval, *Naturaleza*, 126.

The visual evidence is older than most texts, suggesting that the saints circulated before being officially folded into the Calced Carmelites, possibly in the mid-seventeenth century. The documents I have been able to find include two Portuguese works by Santana dedicated to both saints, a sermon from Avila celebrating the introduction of the saints' images to the local church, and a novena from New Spain. Such textual paucity contrasts with the hundreds of eighteenth-century images that have survived, particularly of Efigenia, in addition to the many confraternities dedicated to them. Hagiographies and sacred histories, then, can present a limited picture of early modern devotional life.

The texts on the vidas of Elesban and Efigenia eschewed the models provided for other black saints in favor of older typologies that fit their life stories. As we have seen in sculpture, Elesban was a king-saint, a kind of specialist saint that mostly flourished during initial phases of Christianization in various regions of Europe.[68] Because medieval and early modern kingship focused largely on military defense/expansion and accumulation of power, often at the expense of the Church, kings were rarely candidates for sainthood. The few king saints that emerged in the medieval West were often those whose military skills were mobilized for the defense of the faith, such as St. Louis IX (d. 1270) who fought a crusade, or Ladislaus I of Hungary (d. 1095). A few were noted for their prayerful piety, such as Edward the Confessor (d. 1066), although the majority of king-saints were lauded for their military deeds, which was the source of Elesban's fame. Preacher Joseph de Navia hailed Elesban's victory as "among the greatest saints who fought against the most powerful monarch of the century," adding that the entire world applauded him for this victory.[69] Images of Elesban mirrored Navia's assessment, portraying him as a powerful figure, even in his humble Carmelite robes.

Efigenia, like Elesban, had been born into a royal family (her father was king), although she happily renounced this status in order to enter a convent after her conversion by the apostle St. Matthew. Her hagiographers also reached back into the past for saintly models around which to structure her vida: ancient virgin martyrs. Ancient virgins were inevitably beautiful princesses or noblewomen who converted to Christianity, usually desired in marriage by a cruel pagan. Her refusal of his advances generally led to suffering and death, although in Efigenia's case, there were differing accounts of whether or not she was killed in the fire set by Hyrtaco, and generally she was not considered a martyr. The trope of pagan king and virtuous virgin was echoed in some of the most popular female saints' lives in early modern Spanish devotions: Catherine, Agatha, Agnes,

---

[68] Bartlett, *Why Can the Dead Do Such Great Things?*, ch. 7.
[69] Navia, *Sermon panegyric-historico*, 14.

Úrsula, and Eulalie, among others.[70] In addition to royalty and persecution, these female martyrs were also praised extravagantly for their beauty. While hagiographers of black saints extolled the beauty of their subjects' souls, they rarely described their bodies as beautiful. Santana, however, did mention that images of Efigenia always portrayed her as "supremely beautiful" (*sumamente fermosa*), as well as black in her body, face, and hands.[71] The physical beauty required of ancient female martyrs, then, extended to Efigenia. Unlike these virgin martyrs, however, there is little evidence of surviving paintings depicting Efigenia during a scene from her vida.[72] As we have seen, surviving images are almost all polychrome sculpture – or paintings where she is presented in a pose similar to the sculptures –standing and holding attributes central to her iconography, which included either a virgin's palm or a cross, and a burning convent.

In spite of these significant differences between hagiographies of humble black saints and the royal Ethiopians, authors described the blackness of Elesban and Efigenia in almost exactly the same ways as hagiographers of lower-status black saints. Santana declared that Elesban's blackness had no negative connotations; derived from climate, it was not a punishment, and the saint was not "for this reason [his blackness] inferior to the other saints."[73] Like most defenses of black saints, Santana's work expressed ambivalence – on the one hand, he described blackness as neutral, exterior, unimportant. On the other hand, he pre-emptively defended the possibility of black sanctity, declaring that Elesban was "so clean, and clear of conscience that he never committed a sin so serious as to stain the brightness of his interior."[74] The play between the whiteness or brightness of the souls (interior selves) of black saints and the darkness or blackness of their bodies was central to their hagiographies, allowing authors to move away from a physical white–black binary to a spiritual one.

Light-Infused Blackness

Beyond general arguments about the neutral origins of black skin, assurances to their readers that black saints demonstrated profound divine gifts, and heroic

---

[70] Vincent-Cassy, *Les saintes vierges.*   [71] Santana, *Os dous atlantes*, 107.

[72] There is one important exception – in La Antigua Guatemala, a 1766 altarpiece survives that contains a sculpture of Efigenia, St. Matthew, and Balthazar. The sculptures stand vertically, and flanking their sides are four oil paintings depicting scenes from Efigenia's life: Melchor Toledo, "El arte religioso de la Antigua Guatemala," 280.

[73] Santana, *Os dous atlantes*, 1:21–22. On Elesban's lack of inferiority: "naõ fica por essa causa sendo inferior aos outros Santos."

[74] Santana, *Os dous atlantes*, 1:21–22.

virtue through suffering or resisting paganism, hagiographers assigned spiritual value to bodily blackness. It carried significance – not because blackness itself had theological weight per se, but because such blackness led to suffering in the secular world, and therefore to a heightened state of grace. Hence, rather than their bodies being seen in opposition to their white souls – as a defect to be overcome – the physical self opened up the soul to deeper spiritual evolution, in ways that echoed many early modern vidas.

One striking example of the relationship between blackness and whiteness came from accounts of the death of Benedict of Palermo in 1589, stories that circulated widely throughout the seventeenth and eighteenth centuries.[75] Benedict's niece, praying for her uncle's soul in a room across town because he was gravely ill, reported seeing a dove of dazzling whiteness ("*candida Paloma*") rising to Heaven and speaking to her in Benedict's voice.[76] She understood this miracle to mean that her uncle had died and his soul was rising to Heaven. Here it was not Benedict's physical body that manifested whiteness but a dove that represented his soul: it signaled the saint's entrance into Heaven.

Paniagua described a similar anecdote at the moment of Teresa Juliana's death: "Several prodigious events were noted at the time of her death, and after her death, because her life having been so oppressed, her departure was greatly celebrated in Heaven: the color of her face, naturally black, turned white before her death and remained so after her death for no short amount of time."[77] He elaborated that those caring for Teresa in her final illness noted the miraculous change before her death, proving that the event was not merely the physical effect of death on the human body. His emphasis on what happened to Teresa as fundamentally separate from natural processes of death followed the general pattern of hagiographers who nearly always described the dead bodies of the saints as transcending nature – they smelled beautiful, they did not decompose, their resting faces were particularly beautiful and peaceful. Her face whitened, Paniagua argued, because her soul shone forth, separating from the physical body. This emphasis ultimately served to contrast the adversity she faced in life as a black woman with the joy with which she was received in Heaven.

[75] Fiume, "Saint Benedict the Moor," 16–51.

[76] "En el mismo instante que espiró, vió una Negrita, sobrina suya, volar su dichosissima Alma à la Celestial patria, como candida Paloma": Castellano, *Compendio de la heroyca, y maravillosa vida*, 80r.

[77] Paniagua, *Compendio de la vida*: "Algunos prodigios se notaron al tiempo de fallecer, y despues de muerta Teresa porque aviendo sido, como fue, su vida tan ajustada, era forzoso festejasse el Cielo su partida: el color del rostro, por su naturaleza negro, antes de espirar se le puso blanco, y aun despues de muerta perserverò assi no poco tiempo" (p. 146).

Teresa was not the only saint of color who was described as turning white at the moment of death. When Catherine Tekakwitha (d. 1680), a holy Mohawk woman in New France, died, Jesuit witness Father Cholenec recorded seeing seeing her face ("so marked and swarthy") transformed into whiteness immediately following her death. Cholenec remarked: "I admit openly that the first thought that came to me was that Catherine at that moment might have entered into heaven, reflecting in her chaste body a small ray of the glory which her soul had taken possession."[78] His description is astonishingly similar to Paniagua's half a century later, even though it is unclear if Paniagua ever read the Spanish translation of Cholenec's hagiography.[79] Both authors connected the whiteness of their saints' countenance to the "glory" of the divine light. The miracles that occurred in the female saints in the moments before and after death reflected a belief that the brightness of the soul would replace or disappear the brownness of their bodies, if only temporarily.

Úrsula de Jesús, an Afro-Peruvian holy woman, employed similar language of whiteness and salvation in her spiritual diary, though she articulated a different understanding of the relationship between body and soul than white hagiographers. On Epiphany (the feast day that celebrated the three wise men's visit to the baby Jesus), Úrsula experienced a vision she had of María Bran, a deceased slave from the convent: "I saw her [María] in a priests' alb, [it was] the whitest of whites (*alba albissima*), beautifully embellished and gathered together with a short cord with elegant tassels. She also wore a crown of flowers on her head. The celestial beings arranged for me to see her from the back, although I could still see her face and she was quite lovely, her face a lustrous (*lustrosisimo*) black."[80] While Úrsula, like other hagiographers, connected María's presence in Heaven with dazzling light, she described light as irradiating María's black skin – rather than lightening it to white, divine brilliance illuminated her face in bright, beautiful blackness. Úrsula's account of a black woman's reception into Heaven and those of white hagiographers might seem quite similar, but her vision emphasizes the beauty of the black body and its ability to act as a locus for the divine.

Some white authors depicted a vision similar to Úrsula's of a black body irradiated with divine light. Andalusian Jesuit Martín de Roa (d. 1637) wrote a treatise on the afterlife – specifically, what it would be like in Purgatory and Heaven, which included questions about eating, drinking, people's relations with each other, etc. The work began by tackling the most pressing question revolving

---

[78] As quoted and translated by Greer, *Mohawk Saint*, 17.
[79] Cholenec's account of Catherine's life was printed in Paris in 1717 and less than a decade later translated into Spanish and published in Mexico: Greer, "Iroquois Virgin."
[80] Úrsula de Jesús, *Souls in Purgatory*, 80.

around the body and how it would appear after resurrection. Resurrection was generally understood as regenerating the body in its perfect wholeness, in spite of what might have happened to a person in her lifetime or to a corpse, including loss of limbs or dismemberment. As part of this discussion, Roa included a section on whether or not black Africans would remain black in Heaven.[81] Therefore, the question Roa posed was really – "is blackness a defect?" though he did not articulate it this way. His opinion was that, although the first people had been created white, black skin was *not* a defect, but rather a natural effect of the sun. It was "natural," and "no less admirable [in Heaven] as a pleasing variation."[82]

Roa further described black skin as infused with light, speaking of the lustrous ("*lustroso*") nature of blackness, a word that conveys shininess, or the reflection of light. He further described their black skin: "[It] will not be faded or dull, but alive, dazzling, like the color of a jet stone shot through with blood, completely penetrated with more light than the Sun, which it will have through the gift of brightness, and which will give them an incredible grace."[83] He further proclaimed that no one should deny the beauty of black people, which "does not consist so much in color as this sweetness, which will be equal in black men as well as white, and will give more pleasure to the eye." Similar to Úrsula, Roa argued that blackness could be "dazzling" with a light brighter than the Sun. Such light could make the countenance come to life (like "jet shot through with blood"). Here, Roa alluded to the fact that jet – an opaque stone – could be infused with life ("blood") in the same way black bodies could be restored perfectly in their original state in Heaven.

The language of light was a recurring theme in hagiographies of black saints. One early modern friar, for example, described Benedict as having an "*alma candidismo*": a soul of the most dazzling brilliance.[84] Castellano referred several

---

[81] Near the beginning of chapter 1, Roa asserts that everyone would be resurrected "in their youthful state, whole and robust, without any defect of the body that they had in the world": *Estados de los bienauenturados*, 4r. This work was reprinted several times, including 1645 and 1653.

[82] Roa, *Estados de los bienauenturados*, 7r-v.

[83] Roa, *Estados de los bienauenturados*, 7r-8v: "Serà el negro no deslavado, ni desluzido, sino vivo, resplandeciente, qual fuera el de un azabache quajado con sangre, penetrado todo de luz mas que de un sol, qual tendran por el don de la claridad, que les dara increible donaire, i gracia." I translated "vivo" as "bright" here, since the Spanish adjective has multiple meanings, and the more literal translation – lively – is awkward in English.

[84] As quoted in Ortega Sagrista, "La cofradía de los negros," 131. The citation comes from a petition to found a new confraternity, instigated by the Afro-Iberian Cristobal de Porras in 1627: "para que fundase en el dicho lugar la Cofradia de San Benito de Palermo de nuestra sagrada religión que por haber sido el santo de color morena (quenque el gran devoción y alma candidisimo)."

times to the *"candor de las virtudes"* (the brightness of Benedict's virtues), while Antonio Vicente de Madrid described Benedict's soul as *"muy candida."*[85] A Portuguese Carmelite used the adverb *"candidez"* when describing the Ethiopian saint Elesban and his inward virtue: "so very pure, and of clear conscience that he had already been wiped clean of every grave sin to cleanse his interior to *candidez."*[86] Pedro Contrares's funeral sermon for Magdalena de la Cruz, an Afro-Iberian nun in eighteenth-century Seville, also argued for the *candidez* of her soul: "This Ethiopian pilgrim, seen by the world as black, was for Heaven the most brilliant white [*albada candidez*]."[87] Here the term *candidez* emphasized the disparity between what the world saw and Magdalena's hidden but true and holy nature. All of these authors tied *candidez* to purity and holiness, to inward states inaccessible to the human eye but perfectly visible to God.

Such language circulated widely. The text of the Franciscan friar Francisco de Hoyo demonstrates the ways in which specific rhetoric could be picked up from one author to another. Hoyo composed a hagiography of Benedict of Palermo in celebration of his beatification in 1743. In this work, Hoyo cited the works of previous Franciscans who had written about Benedict, including Pedro de Mataplanes, Antonio Daza, and Franciscan historian Luke Wadding (d. 1657).[88] When describing Benedict's parentage, Hoyo remarked that Benedict inherited his blackness (*"negro color"*), adding that he was "most black in body and most white in soul." For this last phrase, Hoyo cited Luke Wadding, adding Wadding's original Latin to Hoyo's vernacular translation: "negro nigerrimus, anima candidissimus."[89] Thus, the word Hoyo translated as *"blanco"* had originally been *"candidus."* Hoyo's citation of this particular phrase from Wadding highlights the ways in which hagiographers drew specific concepts and words from each other's work.

The term *"candidez"* circulated abundantly in the lives of black saints. Even though the word is not echoed in Teresa's deathbed scene, where Paniagua chose

---

[85] Antonio Vicente de Madrid, *El negro mas prodigioso*, 92. He repeated the description of Benedict's soul on the next page, asserting: "Este, y otros efectos maravillosos, en prueba de su pura inocencia, y de la candidez de su Alma, se vieron claramente en este Siervo de Dios experimentados, por donde se llega à conocer lo que resplandeciò en esta hermosa Virtud" (p. 93).

[86] Santana, *Os dous atlantes*, 1:21: "mas taõ limpo, e claro de consciencia, que jà mais se atreveo culpa grave a mancharlhe a candidez do interior."

[87] Contreras, *Sermón fúnebre*: "una continua amada candidez en la amistad y gracia de le Señor: esta vence esse imposible grande, de que se pueda un Ethiope de albar, y que un Negro tenga blanco color. Creo, que este exordio nos lleva de la mano à aquella Ethiopisa peregrine, que siendo para el Mundo de negro color, fue para el Cielo de albada candidez" (p. 1).

[88] Daza, *Chronica de Quarta Parte.*

[89] Hoyo, *Doctrina mysticas, morales, fundadas, y elucidas de la vida del santo Negro, san Benedito de San Fratelo* [1744], BNE, MS 3418.

"white" (*blanca*), *candidez* occurred frequently in the hagiographies of holy people of color. The Spanish term "*candidez*" derives from the Latin adjective *candidus*. *Candidus* did not mean simple whiteness; the adjective white for description or physical description in Latin is *albus*. *Candidus*, on the other hand, transcended color, bringing together color and light – a shining, dazzling brightness that throughout classical antiquity was associated with moral worth and the divine.[90] The adjective evolved into medieval Latin, which connected *candidus* with the Christian divine. It is a term that appears, for example, in Dante's *Paradiso*, most famously in his description of the *candida rosa*.[91] Circulating back to Benedict's death, it is not a coincidence that the term "*candidez*" is employed to describe the miraculous transformation at the moment of death, as death represents the liminal moment when the chosen soul of a saint slips out of the body and reunites with God in Heaven, reflecting the brightness of the divine.

The *candidez* exhibited by saints of color transcended whiteness – that is, these hagiographers were not positing a return to the whiteness exhibited in the flesh by white Europeans, but rather the return to primeval purity as distinct from earthly whiteness as it was from earthly blackness. A mid-seventeenth-century Sicilian Franciscan hagiographer described Benedict as having "virginal *candidezza*," an example that highlights the relationship between *candidez* and purity that was both bodily and spiritual.[92] The dazzling brilliance of divine light shone more brightly in some human beings according to divine grace; these clerical authors, therefore, argued spiritual chosen-ness transcended human flesh or pigmentation.

Language of light permeated Christian scripture, as we have seen, particularly in the letters of St. Paul, who exhorted his followers to turn their backs on the darkness of sin and to embrace the light of God, adding: "everything exposed by the light becomes visible, and everything that is illuminated becomes a light" (Eph. 5:13). The particular phrasing – everything that is illuminated becomes a light (*omne enim quod manifestatur lumen est*) – underscores the rhetorical efforts of hagiographers. Rather than viewing darkness and light as binaries,

---

[90] Lewis, *An Elementary Latin Dictionary*, 106. (This includes the entries for *candidus*, as well as the noun *candor*, defined here as "a dazzling whiteness, lustre, clearness, radiance, brilliance.") For a discussion of *albus* and *candidus* specifically in terms of the evolution of European racial thought, see Alleyne, *The Construction and Representation of Race*, 44–54. Steven Epstein also discusses the use of the term in twelfth-century Europe: *Speaking of Slavery*, 18–19.

[91] Dante, *Paradiso*, Canto XXXII. In this canto, St. Bernardo describes the rose of brilliant light surrounding the Virgin Mary, made up of dazzlingly bright souls. It was also picked up in medieval love poetry: Dronke, "The Song of Songs," 209–36.

[92] Pietro de Palermo, *Vita, e miracoli del venerabile servo de dio F. Benedetto da S. Fradello (1652)*, BAV, Stamp. Barb. U. IX. 41, 35.

Paul's language provided another possibility: that anything can be a light once illuminated by divine grace. Although the hagiographers did not directly invoke this passage from Ephesians, as they did other Pauline passages, their use of adjectives and metaphors of light expresses the same theological idea, allowing them to sidestep the "problem" of color difference. Sometimes the language of light separated the body from the soul, and sometimes it worked in more complex ways that connected the suffering of the body to the brightness of the soul, as we have seen.

Works celebrating holy people of color resounded with the language of light – we see the repetition not only of *candidez*, but "resplendent" (*resplendente*), "illuminated" (*esclarecido*), and "flaming" (*encendido*). These words were common in accounts of the lives of holy people more generally, but recur with a striking intensity in lives of black saints from the earliest accounts by Daza and Sandoval. Sandoval used these terms in describing Antonio da Noto: "I say only that his face was resplendent like flames, his head alight like a globe of fire surrounded by a most beautiful star, and that in the altar of God there were flaming coals but also a resplendent carbuncle."[93] Here Sandoval crammed as many words associated with light as one sentence could contain: resplendence, flame, fire, star, coal, carbuncle. His pivot from *carbón* to *carbunco* was in keeping with early modern Spanish understanding of the word "*carbunco*," which Covarrubias's dictionary described as a "precious stone whose name comes from that of a flaming coal, because it has the color of fire and gives off flames, which without any other light can give enough light to aid reading a letter at night."[94]

Sandoval's description emphasized the purification of coal into a precious stone, which altered not only in appearance but substance, from a valueless object to a gem that produced light. He was not the only one who invoked coal; José Gómez de la Parra described the charity of the black Carmelite nun Juana Esperanza de San Alberto as "a burning coal alight with the fire of divine love."[95] Coal (*carbón*) was a common metaphor for describing black skin in the early modern period. It was particular useful in the context of black holy people because it paired the language of blackness with flame and fire; coal could be

---

[93] Sandoval, *Naturaleza*, 129r-v: "Solo digo viendo su rostro resplandeciente como unas llamas, y su cabeça encendida como un globo de fuego, cercada de una fulgentissima estrella, que en el altar de Dios no solo auia carbones encendidos, sino tambien resplandecientes carbuncos [gemstone], y finissimas piedras."

[94] Covarrubias, *Tesoro de la lengua castellana*, 268: "una piedra preciosa que tomó nombre del carbón encendido, por tener color de fuego y echar de sí llamas su resplandor, que sin otra alguna luz se puede con ella leer de noche una carta u aun dar claridad a un aposento."

[95] Gómez de la Parra, *Fundación*, 311: "un carbón encendido y abrasado con el fuego de divino amor."

transformed and purified, and it also gave light. In Sebastián Covarrubias's early-seventeenth-century dictionary, the entry for *"carbón"* informed its readers of the simile of coal to black skin, explaining that the word was often used to describe black or brown people.[96] The metaphor of coal resembles that of Úrsula de Jesús and Martín de Roa where the black body did not recede into whiteness, but transformed body and soul into both light and flame.

The relationship between body and soul could manifest in a more complex relationship, however, even in a coal metaphor, which could also suggest that the body burned away in the process of its purification. We see a similar idea (the burning away of the body) in an analogy sometimes invoked by hagiographers – that of the phoenix – particularly in works on Efigenia. Phoenixes were a relatively common Christian metaphor for explaining salvation and spiritual rebirth.[97] Luis Soler y Las Balsas, author of an eighteenth-century poem in honor of the Ethiopian princess, connected the "ashy" color of Guineans to the ashes left behind as the phoenix's own skin and body burned away, leaving only the purified soul.[98] Santana used similar language when describing Efigenia: "she, like a Phoenix, embraced the scented flames of her Divine love, raising up out of the same fire, reborn in the waters of baptism ... regenerated."[99] While Santana did not connect Efigenia's fire with the "ash" of her body the way Soler did, her role as a phoenix derived from her conversion from paganism. The playwright Felipe Godínez employed the comparison in the same way – Efigenia was the phoenix who resisted the horror of paganism.[100] The metaphors of the burning coal and the phoenix's rise reveal the complexity of body and soul in hagiographies of black saints – fires could consume black bodies, but did not destroy; rather, they gave new life to a purified spirit. But both the coal and the phoenix, for the most part, retained their materiality, rather than transforming into disembodied light.

[96] Covarrubias, *Tesoro de la lengua castellana*, 268–9.
[97] Van den Broek argues that the phoenix could symbolize a range of concepts, including the sun, time, resurrection, life in Heaven, Christ, Mary, virginity, and Christian virtue: Van den Broek, *The Myth of the Phoenix*, 9.
[98] Soler, *Vida de la Venerable Negra la Madre S. Teresa Juliana de Santo Domingo (1757)*, NYPL-Schomburg, Ms Sc Rare 81–6, 4r. In addition to the metaphor of the phoenix in Christian polemics, it is possible that the image was particularly chosen for these black saints. Margaret Olsen points out that Alonso de Sandoval discussed black Africans as coals from which the fire of Christianity could be stoked, a clear parallel to the phoenix myth: *Slavery and Salvation*, 87–8.
[99] Santana, *Os dous atlantes*, "quando a inclyta Princeza em religiosa observancia da Ley de Christo, deyxando-se abrazar como a Phenix nos odoriferous incendios de seu Divino amor, se levantasse do mesmo fogo renascida, e por beneficioda agua do Bautismo, regenerada: que naõ he ete incendio da condiçaõ do elementar, que com as aguas se apaga; he hum fogo Celestial, que com ventagens ao do Sol, illumine, e dá a vida" (p. 31).
[100] Godínez, "San Mateo en Etiopia," 374.

Plate 41 Unknown artist, *St. Efigenia*, polychrome wood sculpture. Iglesia del Carmen, Antequera, Spain.

Plate 42 Unknown artist, *St. Elesban*, polychrome wood sculpture. Iglesia del Carmen, Cadiz, Spain.

Plate 43 Unknown artist, *St. Efigenia*, polychrome wood sculpture. Igreja Matriz, Alte, Portugal.

Plate 44 Torcuato Ruiz del Peral, *San Miguel*, eighteenth century, polychrome wood sculpture. Iglesia de San Miguel Bajo, Granada, Spain.

Plate 45 Detail of King Dunaan, unknown artist, *St. Elesban*, polychrome wood sculpture, located on the Altar of la Virgen del Carmen (by Manuel Pérez da Vila, 1757), Cathedral of Tui, Spain.

Plate 46 Unknown artist, *Santo Elesbão Imperador da Abissina*, eighteenth century, oil on canvas, 110 cm × 75 cm. Courtesy of Museu de Arte Sacra de Arouca.

Plate 47 Unknown artist, *St. Elesban*, polychrome wood sculpture. Iglesia del Carmen, Antequera, Spain.

Plate 48 Unknown artist, *St. Elesban*, sculpture, polychrome wood, altarpiece of the Virgen del Carmen (by Manuel Pérez da Vila, 1757). Cathedral of Tui, Spain.

Plate 49 Unknown artist, *St. Efigenia* and *St. Elesban*, polychrome wood sculptures. Iglesia del Carmen, Cadiz, Spain.

Plate 50 Unknown artist, *St. Efigenia*, polychrome wood sculpture. Igreja do Carmo, Faro, Portugal.

Plate 51 Unknown artist, *St. Elesban*, polychrome wood sculpture. Igreja do Carmo, Faro, Portugal.

Plate 52 Detail, unknown artist, *St. Elesban*, polychrome wood sculpture. Igreja do Carmo, Faro, Portugal.

Plate 53 Detail of the robe and gilding, unknown artist, *St. Efigenia*, polychrome wood sculpture. Igreja do Carmo, Faro, Portugal.

Plate 54 Unknown artist, *St. Efigenia*, polychrome wood sculpture. Algarve, Portugal.

Plate 55 Pedro de Mena, *María Magdalena Penitente*, Spanish, late seventeenth century, polychrome wood sculpture. Museo Nacional de Escultura, Valladolid, Spain.

Plate 56 Detail, unknown artist, *St. Efigenia*, polychrome wood sculpture. Algarve, Portugal.

Plate 57 Juan Pascual de Mena, *St. Benedict of Palermo,* between 1770 and 1780, sculpture (statue), coniferous wood, oil, gold, glass, cord (fiber). Courtesy of Detroit Institute of Art, Museum Purchase, Jill Ford Murray Fund, 2017.21.

Plate 58 Unknown artist, *Santa Caterina da Siena,* Italian, fifteenth century. Pinacoteca di Brera, Milan, Italy.

Plate 59 Unknown artist, *St. Benedict of Palermo*, Altar of Cristo a la Columna, egg tempera on canvas, 52 × 29 cm, Granadian School. Iglesia de Nuestra Señora de la Cabeza, Ogíjares, Spain.

Plate 60 Unknown artist, *St. Benedict of Palermo*, polychrome wood sculpture. Central Portugal.

Plate 61 Unknown artist, *St. Benedict of Palermo*, polychrome wood sculpture. Convento de San Francisco, Pontevedra, Spain.

Plate 62 Unknown artist, *St. Benedict of Palermo*, polychrome wood sculpture. Cambados, Spain.

Plate 63 Unknown artist, *St. Benedict of Palermo*, polychrome wood sculpture. Andalusia, Spain.

Plate 64 Detail of Altar of St. Francis of Assisi, 1675–1725, *St. Benedict of Palermo*, oil on canvas, 40 × 40 cm, Cordoban School. Iglesia Conventual de San Francisco, Baena, Spain.

Plate 65 Detail, unknown artist, *St. Benedict of Palermo*, polychrome wood sculpture. Central Portugal.

Plate 66 Unknown artist, *St. Benedict of Palermo*, 1785, polychrome wood sculpture, Granadan school, 56 × 28 cm. Near Granada, Spain.

Plate 67 Detail, unknown artist, *St. Benedict of Palermo*, eighteenth century, polychrome wood sculpture, Granadan school, 1.42 × 0.57 × 0.51 m. Near Granada, Spain.

Plate 68 José de Mora, *St. Benedict of Palermo*, 1666–1724, Granadan school, polychrome sculpture, wood and gilded, 1.53 × 0.57 × 0.47 m. Convento de la Encarnación, Granada, Spain.

Plate 69 Unknown artist, series of paintings on the back of choir chairs, including St. Benedict of Palermo, eighteenth century, oil on wood. Central Portugal.

Plate 70 The reliquary bust in its current location. Unknown artist, *St. Benedict of Palermo*, eighteenth century (?), polychrome wood. Convento da Madre de Deus, Lisbon, Portugal.

Plate 71 Unknown artist, *St. Benedict of Palermo*, late eighteenth century, relief, polychrome and gilt wood. Altar of Nuestra Señora del Rosario, Iglesia de San Juan Bautista, Las Cabezas de San Juan, Spain.

Plate 72 The bas-relief of the two Ethiopian saints can be found on the right and left, a little more than half way up the altarpiece. *St. Elesban* and *St. Efigenia*, bas-relief, main altar, last half of the eighteenth century. Iglesia del Carmen, Écija, Spain.

Plate 73 Detail of *St. Efigenia*, bas-relief, main altar, last half of the eighteenth century. Iglesia Carmen, Écija, Spain.

Plate 74 Detail of *St. Elesban*, bas-relief, main altar, last half of the eighteenth century. Iglesia del Carmen, Écija, Spain.

Plate 75 Unknown artist, *Senhora do Carmo*, oil on canvas. Antiga Mercado do Escravos, Lagos, Portugal. Photo: © CMLagos/ Hélio Ramos.

Plate 76 Detail of St. Elesban, *Senhora do Carmo*, oil on canvas. Antigo Mercado do Escravos, Lagos, Portugal. Photo: © CMLagos/ Hélio Ramos.

Plate 77 *La negrita de Salamanca y su confesor el P. Suarez*, eighteenth century, oil on canvas. Courtesy of Museo de Salamanca, Spain. © JCyL, Photo by Santiago Santos.

Plate 78 *St. Efigenia*, polychrome wood sculpture. Fão, Portugal.

Plate 79 *St. Efigenia*, polychrome wood sculpture. Galicia, Spain.

The language of light could be connected to other kinds of bodies, especially celestial ones. Santana, for example, described Elesban as an "illustrious sun,"[101] while Joseph de Navia, preaching a sermon about Elesban and Efigenia in Avila, also employed planetary imagery. Navia's elaborate metaphor included calling Elesban the sun, ruling during the day (citing Gen. 1:16) before Ethiopia's subsequent descent into heresy. Efigenia, for her part, was the moon, who shone with the light of God when her land was darkened by the "shadows of ignorance." They were both "flaming lights" (*flamantes luminarias*) and "shining stars" (*astros refulgentes*) who should not be demeaned because of their bodily blackness, but rather admired for the beauty of their lights. "We have," he declared, "in this Carmelite church, a beautiful sky transformed by the adding of these excellent stars, a beautiful sky, completed and totally perfect."[102] While the first part created an implicit contrast between the lights of their souls – not just illuminated, but *illuminating* – and the darkness or shadows of unbelief that preceded them, Navia finished the metaphor not with a play on the blackness of their bodies against the brightness of their souls. Rather, he insisted that Efigenia and Elesban were part of the celestial kingdom, not just part but completing the Carmelite pantheon. He began the piece by chiding his audience that saints must not be ignored because of their skin color, and ended with a ringing declaration of their perfect inclusion in Heaven.

Precious stones, like the carbuncle discussed by Sandoval, were also frequently used as descriptors for black saints. Comparing the saints to jewels was common in early modern discourses of the holy – largely because they adorned Christ – and this was no less true for holy people of color. One of the most common stones was jet, which had been discussed by Martín de Roa in his discussion of blackness in heaven. Gómez de la Parra proclaimed: "Of this precious stone, even though it is often underrated because of its black color and taken as rustic, in the interior they enclose and contain divinity."[103] Jet appeared in several hagiographies. It is a shiny, black stone, and it was frequently used as a descriptor for African skin in early modern Spanish, in both popular culture and hagiography. In Covarrubias the word is defined as "a lustrous stone that is not very hard." He ended the entry by commenting: "Something very black is compared to it, and we say 'to be black like jet.'"[104] Rather than a word

[101] Santana, *Os dous atlantes*: "Esta Cidade [Aksum] pois, e corte da Ethiopia soy o illustre solar, e patria do esclarecido Elesbão" (1:2).

[102] Navia, *Sermon pangyrico-historico*, 4–5.

[103] Gómez de la Parra, *Fundación*, 310: "De esta piedra preciosa, que aunque por el color negro es despreciable y se tiene por rústica, en lo interior incierra y contiene algo de divinidad Jesus."

[104] Covarrubias, *Tesoro de la lengua castellana*, 145: "La cosa muy negra comparamos a él, y decimos ser negra como un azabache."

specifically related to humans and skin color, it was a common descriptor for black objects, although it was clearly extended as a simile for black skin. Gómez de la Parra invoked the simile of jet several times when describing Juana Esperanza, describing her as wearing a "crown of the finest jet, which illuminates her interior," while after death, he described her face as looking like a young girl, with a "sheen of jet," evoking shining, beautiful blackness.[105] In this simile, her blackness acted as an ornament to her holiness. Black saints, then, were associated not with jewels generally, as white saints were, but with black stones. Some of these – carbuncle, jet – were jewels, and some were common, like coal and lodestone, but all associated with light.[106]

Pedro Contreras's funeral sermon for an eighteenth-century Afro-Iberian holy woman, Madgalena de la Cruz, also invoked the metaphor of the precious gem. Eschewing the more common jet and coal, he instead chose topaz, calling her "The Ethiopian Topaz," "most precious Topaz," "most fine Topaz," and "Topaz polished with virtues." These are passing epithets rather than extended metaphors, but in the approbation before the sermon Luis Ignacio Chacòn provides a brief explanation for how Madgalena resembled topaz: "This Ethiopian stone, according to Saint Isidore, appears in all the variety of colors ... and all the varieties of virtue adorn our venerable Madgalena."[107] Such language calls attention to two facts: like jet and coal, the stone was most commonly dark yellow, therefore connecting the gem to Madgalena's skin tone; he also made it clear that topaz originated in Ethiopia, which underscored the same kind of sacred roots in ancient Christian Ethiopia that we see in discussions of black saints as cedar trees.

The vast majority of metaphors and analogies employed for black saints – botanical and stone – called attention to the blackness of their bodies. The language of light also originated in the holy people's color difference. The rhetoric of black sanctity, then, was both shaped and constrained by color prejudice in the early modern world. Color prejudice no doubt limited the imaginations of the hagiographers themselves, but they were also faced with the challenge of neutralizing the prejudice of their white audience in order to promote their saints more effectively. Moreover, holiness required perfect virtue, untainted by weakness or spiritual inferiority, both of which were frequently used to describe people of color. The very paradox that could make a white

[105] Gómez de la Parra, *Fundación*, 309: "for the color black that nature gave her body, the spiritual diadem illuminated her interior, en lio exterior, with another crown of the finest jet."
[106] Castellano, *Compendio*, n.f.
[107] Contreras, *Sermon funebre*, n.f.: "Esta piedra Ethiopisa, segun S. Isidoro, se adorna de toda la variedad de los colores ... y de toda la variedad de las virtudes se adorna nuestra Magdelena venerable."

audience skeptical about the potential of black Africans to achieve sanctity permitted hagiographers to subvert the readers' prejudice. In the process, they created new discourses of blackness and sanctity. None celebrated blackness as a distinct category of beauty and it is clear that most hagiographers shared the contemporary attitudes of blackness as an inferior complexion. Yet their construction of archetypes of black sanctity led to the creation of new ways to re-imagine scriptural dictates about dark and light, enslaved and free, body and soul, in ways that challenged entrenched views on people of color and their place in the Hispanic world.

6 THE PRACTICE OF HUMILITY AND SPIRITUAL AUTHORITY IN THE LIVES OF BLACK HOLY WOMEN

The creation by early modern clergy of the typology of black sanctity and its illuminated brilliance helped to shape a new archetype that blended enslavement, racism, humility, divine gifts, and heroic virtue. The archetype that predominantly evolved for Benedict could be applied to other people of color who took vows or lived in convents across the Iberian Atlantic, facilitating the recognition of other black saints. From this perspective, the official successes of the cults of Benedict of Palermo and Martín de Porres were less exceptional than they might appear on the surface. Moving beyond both "successful" cults and hagiographic discourses reveals that a number of holy people of color lived throughout the Iberian Atlantic from the late sixteenth to the mid-eighteenth centuries. Rather than continuing to assess black sanctity as a hagiographic discourses as I did in the previous Chapter, here I turn to the vidas of black women in early modern convents to examine more carefully their spiritual practices and effect on the larger community. Doing so enriches our view of black holy people, as it returns a measure of their subjectivity, manifested most dramatically in the spiritual autobiography of the Afro-Peruvian woman, Úrsula de Jesús. Humility remains at the center of the stories of holy black women, yet their humility acted as part of their spiritual practice, allowing us to glimpse how black women might have understood and employed clerical discourses of saintly behavior.

Many individuals in the early modern Catholic world gained local reputations for holiness during their lifetimes. Called "living saints," such people were venerated for a period of time after their deaths, yet eventually faded from communal memories. In communities constantly searching for access to the divine, living saints played a vital role in Iberian spiritual economies, acting as conduits on behalf of their monasteries and communities. Living saints provided examples of spiritual devotion that imbued their town with a reputation for holiness; they performed healing miracles; and they interceded on behalf of the community's dead. In short, they mimicked the saints in most ways, except they failed to maintain prominence after their deaths. Because they ultimately faded from the devotional landscape, they can appear of minor significance to modern scholars; yet, to contemporaries, living saints were beloved and reified. People of color could be living saints just as whites could, and studying the presence of black living saints throughout the Iberian world expands our view of how black women cultivated devotional practice, defended themselves, and made claims to authority and leadership.[1]

Donadas and Slaves in Early Modern Lima

Black holy people fall into one of three general categories: formerly enslaved people who entered into religious life upon manumission, those who lived in monasteries as slaves but were eventually freed, and those who were born free and able to enter into religious life as free people. In the cases I study here, the women were, for some period of their lives, enslaved. As a result, their experiences were defined through their legal status as well as skin color and gender. The examples of the previous Chapter demonstrate the prejudice encountered by people of color in early modern convents, the majority of whom were incorporated into the lowest ranks of convent hierarchies as tertiaries or, more commonly, the lowest status as *donados*. *Donados* wore a habit and took vows, but generally functioned as servants within monasteries.[2] In the Americas, *donados* lived and worked alongside enslaved people in convent kitchens and halls, and the lines between the two groups could be blurry. Convents mirrored social and colonial hierarchies, privileging those from elite (white) backgrounds and demeaning, or outright banning, those considered of low *casta* status. Convents housed women from a variety of social, racial, and religious statuses, from the most elite daughters of Lima's powerful families who went by the title of "doña" (lady) to their enslaved women. The joining of the convent's spiritual mission with its replication of secular hierarchies led to the creation of particularly colonial religious ecosystems.

[1] My study restricts itself to women who were widely considered orthodox by their contemporaries, and did not run afoul of ecclesiastical authorities. Other scholars examine women of color accused of false sanctity or witchcraft by the Inquisition: Jaffrey, *False Mystics*, which traces the trial of Ana Rodríguez de Castro y Aramburu, a *parda* (of mixed African and indigenous descent); Mott, *Rosa Egipcíaca*; Spaulding, "Covert Afro-Catholic Agency"; and Thornton, *The Kongolese Saint Anthony*. Rosa's entire trial is conserved by the ANTT, and can be found online.

[2] Nancy van Deusen describes *donadas* in Lima as "nearly always unmarried and of African or native Andean descent": *Embodying the Sacred*, 100.

Lima, as a viceregal capital, was a major locus of sanctity. Its prosperous Spanish and creole citizens zealously pursued universal recognition of their local saints, as did many Iberian and Iberian American cities, and it achieved a stunning success with the canonization of Rose of Lima, the first American-born saint, in 1671, as well as Toribio Alfonso Mogrovejo (beatified 1675) and Francisco Solano (beatified 1675), both of whom were born in Spain, but died in Lima after long careers in the Peruvian church.[3] A beatification cause was likewise launched on behalf of Martín de Porres in the seventeenth century, and gained much traction before stalling out as the century ended.[4] In addition to Martín, prominent black holy people in Lima gained reputations for sanctity, including Úrsula de Jesús, a Franciscan tertiary; Estefanía de San Joseph, another Franciscan tertiary; Francisco de la Concepción, a *donado* renowned for prophecy; and Francisco de Santa Fé, another *donado* who lived in the same convent as Martín de Porres, his close friend.[5] These black living saints were joined by several *mestizo* and indigenous holy people, including Estefanía de San Joseph's companion Isabel Cano, and Nicolás de Ayllón.[6]

While the specific environment of Lima cannot be considered a template for the diverse urban spaces of the Iberian Atlantic, it does provide striking evidence for ways women of color could experience female religious life. For example, the holy women who lived in Lima's many convents benefited from what Van Deusen has described as horizontal circuits, through which they had access to information about holiness and devotional practices, shared formally and informally by the white sisters around them.[7] While spiritual knowledge might circulate horizontally, colonial convents were structured along rigid hierarchies. Archival sources for *limeño* convents are replete with documents relating to the nuns' slave ownership, including requests for the entry or sale of slaves, or complaints against the nuns in matters surrounding slavery.[8]

[3] Both men were canonized in 1726, just decades before Benedict of Palermo's beatification. For an important study on efforts to canonize New Spanish saints, see Rubial García, *La santidad controvertida*.

[4] The local demand for living saints in the early modern Catholic world was fierce. As Pearson explains, "The local holy person was made through the combined forces of tradition, the colony, audience, and the self in the give and take between conservative notions of sanctity and local demands": "'I Willingly Speak to You,'" 333.

[5] Van Deusen, "The World of Úrsula de Jesús," in *The Souls of Purgatory*.

[6] Lives of indigenous women and *mestizas* also appear in local chronicles and histories. For one example, see Rice, "La 'Teresa Indiana.'"

[7] Van Deusen, "Circuits of Knowledge."

[8] There are too many examples of petitions regarding the entrance and exits of enslaved women to cite, but for a couple of examples, see Archivo Arzobispal de Lima (hereafter AAL), Monasterio de Encarnación, VI: 23 (1643) (license to permit the departure of a slave, due to illness); AAL, Monasterio de Santa Clara, XII: 106 (1667) (license to sell a "disobedient" slave); and AAL,

Nuns frequently requested permission to admit their personal slaves into the convents, including requests to "exchange" one slave for another, usually on the grounds of illness.[9] For example, in Santa Clara, nun Petronilla de Castro petitioned to be able to switch out one enslaved woman (Catalina the Angolan) for another (unnamed) because Catalina suffered from a prolonged illness rendering her unable to serve properly.[10] Several documents from the Monasterio de Santa Catalina noted specific "donations" of enslaved women to the monastery as servants, with particular service to the donating nun.[11] The majority of enslaved women in religious houses remained the property of individuals, rather than of the convent collectively, even if they performed labor for all the nuns. In spite of some oversight into the arrival and departure of slaves, slave ownership was an entrenched practice within *limeño* convents.

On the other side of the legal coin, enslaved people engaged in several types of legal actions against nuns in their role as slave owners. One enslaved man sued a nun of Santa Clara to prevent her from selling his wife, Mariana Solupa, out of the city, which violated a precept of canon law that stipulated that married enslaved people could not be forcibly separated. Margarita Muñoz, a free *parda*, sued the abbess of Santísima Trinidad and accusing the nun of stealing ("violently") her son Miguel because the abbess claimed the child as her property.[12] Enslaved women launched lawsuits against their owner-nuns for mistreatment as well as general petitions for manumission.[13] For example, the archbishop sued Ana María de Fría, a nun at the Monasterio de la Encarnación, for having injured Pascuala, an enslaved woman.[14] Such lawsuits emphasize that there were few differences between the treatment of slaves by nuns and the treatment of slaves by lay owners in Lima. In many ways, then, life as a slave or person of color inside a convent could be almost identical to life outside.

Donadas likewise could struggle within convents. In 1667, Ana de Mora ("*negra libre*") petitioned that her niece Isabel not be sold because she (Isabel) was, in fact, free, and Ana had already paid Isabel's dowry to become a *donada* in

---

Monasterio del Prado, II:32 (1622) (donation of two female slaves to the monastery). There are also many references to enslaved indigenous women as well as indigenous and *mestiza donadas*.

[9] For example, a record for the Monasterio de Santísima Trinidad is a transcription of a donation of María, an Angolan slave, to the daughter of the owner; the daughter, María de Salazar, was a nun in the convent: AAL, I:34 (1626), s.f.

[10] AAL, Monasterio de Santa Clara, I:33 (1611): "esta presenta mala de enfermedades prolijas que no la han dejado ni dejan servir ni acudir a lo necessario."

[11] For a few examples, see AAL, Monasterio de Santa Clara, II:2 (1615); I:48 (1614); and III:34 (1630). Occasionally one finds a reference to an enslaved woman who was permitted to become a nun "with time" or "when she is older": AAL, Monasterio de Santa Clara, VIII:78 (1648).

[12] AAL, Monasterio de Santa Clara, VII:43 (1644); and AAL, Santísima Trinidad, IV:7 (1646), s.f.

[13] AAL, Monasterio de Santa Clara, XI:9 (1661); and ibid., XI:71 (1663).

[14] AAL, Monasterio de la Encarnación, 1:45 (1622/1640).

the Monasterio de Santa Clara.[15] Ana's financial backing enabled Isabel to enter Santa Clara. Numbers of *donadas* could be quite large in *limeño* convents: In Santa Clara, a visitation in 1633 noted the presence of 157 nuns ("of the black veil"), 63 *donadas*, and 22 tertiaries ("of the white veil").[16] Accounts of enslaved women in *limeño* convents tell us little about possible spiritual vocations for women of color. The most common way for a woman of color to join a convent as a member, rather than a slave or servant, was to become a *donada*. Women of color were never granted the full status of nun, except occasionally on their deathbeds. Even the numbers of tertiaries of color remained few; this left the lowest position for women of color, that of *donada*. The concept of a *donado* might have had European antecedents, but it only became a thriving aspect of conventual life in the Americas, likely a response to the need for a special position for women of color with vocations.

Looking deeper into the *casta* designations provided for women requesting entrance into *limeño* convents, we see more licenses for mixed-race women over black and indigenous women. The majority of requests were made by *parda* or *cuaterona* women ("*cuaterona*" referred to a woman with one black grandparent). A number of *donadas, pardas*, and *cuateronas* entered Santísima Trinidad between 1689 and 1701 – at least nine, including six *cuateronas*, two *parda*, and one "*samba*," a term for an individual of African and indigenous parentage.[17] More research needs to be undertaken to understand the full scope of the black and indigenous presence in American religious houses, but the overall trends are clear: Female religious houses in Lima consistently replicated the entrenched hierarchies of the secular world, while simultaneously creating shared spiritual and social environments.

The Practice of Humility

The key site of overlap between hagiographic tropes of submission and humility as a deliberate spiritual practice centers on work. For example, the lives of Benedict and Martín de Porres were defined by work – Benedict in the kitchen, and Martín in the kitchen and the hospital. Their cheerful acceptance of menial work acted as a form of heroic humility, partly because of the low status

[15] AAL, Monasterio de Santa Clara, XII:120 (1667).

[16] AAL, Monasterio de Santa Clara, IV:42. For a broad overview of *donadas* in Lima, see Van Deusen, *Embodying the Sacred*, 95–116.

[17] There was a slight surge of in 1665–1667 when eleven *donadas* of color entered Santa Clara, almost all *parda* and *cuaterona*, with the exception of one black and one indigenous woman: AAL, XII: 71, 74, 83, 89, 96, 98, 99, 112, 127, 129, 131.

associated with the work in question and partly because the act of working was considered a path to living spiritually. Benedict's and Martin's physical labor, then, became cornerstones of their reputations for sanctity. We see the same themes emerge in the vidas of black holy women, as the status of a *donada* and the ceaseless labor it required transformed into a unique brand of humility only available to women of color.

Juan Gómez de la Parra's short life of Juana Esperanza de San Alberto (d. 1679), which appeared in his *Chronicle of the First Convent of the Discalced Carmelites in Puebla*, provides a framework for analyzing black women's humility.[18] Esperanza had been born in West Africa, enslaved as a five- or six-year-old child. Upon arrival in Veracruz, Esperanza was purchased by a wealthy noblewoman, and then willed to the convent when her owner died.[19] She thus initially entered religious life unwillingly and spent the rest of her life within the convent's walls. Gómez described her as spiritually perfect, but a major component of her extraordinary holiness was that she was "a poor black woman, *bozal*, ignorant, and rustic."[20] Gómez's emphasis on the negative characteristics associated with her race and gender reflected common hagiographic discourses which, as we have seen, proclaimed that the least and the worst could be transformed by God's grace into perfection. Esperanza, Gómez asserted, represented the lowest. Yet she became the "spiritual diadem" that rested on the collective body of the convent. The metaphor, then, calls attention to her supremacy but simultaneously undermines it, as Esperanza functions as an object that decorates the body (i.e., the community of nuns).[21]

But Gómez provided further details that complicate his objectification by explaining that Esperanza was renowned for her complete obedience and silence. These qualities, he informed the reader, were not because she was enslaved. In fact, she was not compelled by her *calidad* (i.e., what he might have considered her "natural" state of obedience); rather, silence and obedience formed a deliberate spiritual practice. We can see this, Gómez insisted, because she acted the same way with people of all stations, even those who worked with her in the kitchen.[22] Even though obedience and submission were the "proper" behavior of enslaved people, Esperanza's obedience was not typical, because it

---

[18] Gómez, *Fundación*, 310. Gómez provides her whole name at the beginning of the entry, but proceeds to refer to her solely as "Esperanza."

[19] Agustín de Vetancurt inserted brief accounts of the lives black *donados* Diego de Santa María and Cristobal de Santa María in his religious history of Mexico: *Teatro mexicano*, 2:78, 110–11.

[20] Gómez, *Fundación*, 310.

[21] Joan Bristol has emphasized the ways in which this text underscores the "impossibility of black sanctity": "'Although I am Black, I am Beautiful.'"

[22] Gómez, *Fundación*, 313.

was chosen rather than coerced. For Gómez, this meant that Esperanza's virtue was heroic. But we can also read his description as a window into Esperanza's chosen practices: she remained silent as much as possible, rarely speaking, even moving around the convent quietly so as not to disturb anyone. From her behavior and spiritual gifts, the nuns were provided a daily lesson in virtue that prevented them from falling into negligence and sins of omission.[23]

Gómez included another telling anecdote: When the mother prioress suggested that Esperanza finally profess as a nun, Esperanza refused, much to the astonishment of the prioress. Here Gómez cited the prioress's own account of the event, in which she expressed her amazement at being confronted with a soul so pure it would refuse the habit in spite of the fact that Esperanza followed the strictures of the rule more faithfully than even she herself (the prioress) did. Assuming that the event occurred in the way described by Gómez and prioress, Esperanza's response might be as puzzling to the reader as to the prioress. Was Esperanza responding with a kind of internalized self-hatred enforced by years of colonial racism and her status as enslaved? Or had she embraced silence and obedience as a practice of deep and personal spiritual meaning? In some ways, the tension at the heart of this moment refracts the larger tensions at play when thinking about black people in early modern Catholicism. Understanding the relationship between meaningful engagement with Christianity and the hierarchical and often hostile environment of the convent presents a challenge, especially in absence of more direct accounts of black voices.

Incredibly, at least one spiritual autobiography by a black woman survived early seventeenth-century Lima, more than a century before Phillis Wheatley began to write her religious poetry in colonial New England. In addition to Úrusla's spiritual diary, a more traditional vida survives, as well as her portrait, which still hangs in the convent. The opportunities provided by Úrsula's diary are extraordinary – an early seventeenth-century account of a black woman's life in her own words. Úrsula was born enslaved in 1604, the legitimate child of Juan de Castilla and Isabel de los Rios. Isabel had been a black native (criolla) of Lima, the slave of Doña Jerónima de los Rios. When Úrsula was seven, her owner died and she went to live with Luisa de Soto Melgarejo for five years, after which, Úrsula entered Santa Clara as the slave of a nun who had been the niece of Doña Jerónima.[24] Úrsula's spiritual diary itself tells us nothing about her early life; the work is episodic, like a chronicle, in which events were described without being

---

[23] Gómez, *Fundación*, 309, 320–21.

[24] The Spanish edition of *Las almas* includes a modern transcription of the anonymous life. It appears on a supplementary CD provided with the book. I will cite this addition as *La vida* with the corresponding page numbers. *La vida*, 5–6.

organized.[25] As a result, it begins in the middle of Úrsula's life and ends abruptly, how close to her death we do not know. Like Esperanza, humility stands at the center of her spiritual life, winding around the mundane part of her life (work) and the divine (her visions).

Úrsula's text begins suddenly with a story of a vision, in which the soul of a Franciscan friar who committed suicide appeared to her and requested her aid. We begin, therefore, with an inversion – Úrsula, a lowly black *donada*, is called upon by a white friar to help him achieve salvation.[26] It further introduces the reader immediately to Úrsula's spiritual gifts: her ability to see and speak to the souls of the dead as they suffered in Purgatory. The next vision she recounted was of the soul of María Bran, a former slave of the convent. This story is strikingly different from the previous one, not only because of the disparities in race and status between the friar and María. In the second example, the two women engaged in an intimate conversation about salvation and Purgatory. Black woman to black woman, Úrsula asked a pressing question: "I asked if black women went to heaven and she said if they were thankful and heeded His beneficence." Among other things, Úrsula's doubt here reveals the corrosive qualities of white supremacy on the spiritual lives of black Catholics. Despite that fact that she had dedicated her life to God, she was still unsure of whether or not she could achieve salvation. María Bran offered hope and comfort.

The pattern of Úrsula seeking solace or advice from the souls of black women, especially formerly enslaved women, recurs in the text. In another case, she repeated the question about whether or not black people could go to heaven, and this time the dead woman, Luisa, responded that "yes, they remain separated to one side, and everything there occurs in great concord." This anecdote is ambivalent about whether or not the separation between black and white souls was imposed by the white hierarchy, or if it reflected a preference for the black women to be only with each other.[27] Úrsula experienced another vision of Luisa "the Angolan," who had been a servant – probably enslaved – in the convent,

[25] Greenspan, "Autohagiography," pp. 218–19: "Autohagiography is an account of a holy person's life written or told by its subject. It shares with traditional hagiography the intention to represent the life as 'more exemplary than real.'"

[26] Nancy van Deusen discovered Úrsula's diary and translated the document into English. More recently, she transcribed it for publication in the original Spanish: Úrsula de Jesús, *Souls of Purgatory* and Úrsula de Jesús, *Las almas*. Because of van Deusen's expertise on Úrsula, I will rely on her English translations when quoting directly, but I include the reference in the Spanish edition so that those who wish to read the original know where to find it. I cite solely the Spanish edition when not quoting directly, as it was the source for my analysis. Úrsula de Jesús, *Las almas*, 163–4. Úrsula recounted several visions of deceased clergy. For two more examples, see *Las almas*, pp. 189–90 and 219.

[27] Úrsula de Jesús, *Souls of Purgatory*, 84; *Las almas*, 172.

commenting: "Luisa had served this community in good faith, but sometimes they had accused her of certain things ... Before Luisa died, she had endured awful hardships, and because of them they had discounted much of the punishment."[28] What Úrsula meant here was that Luisa's earthly suffering earned her less time in Purgatory; this important idea also repeats throughout Úrsula's diary.

The black women in her convent were low status, mistreated, abused – tormented by the nuns with whom they lived and worked. Úrsula framed accounts of dead and living black women in the convent with tales of her own ill-use. One of the nuns "scolded her" to the point of despair: "Sometimes I feel – I do not know what – toward my companion, with all her scolding. Nothing seems to suit her." Úrsula found no compassion from the rest of the nuns; she recounted that they "tell me to suffer all that happens without complaints or criticism, not letting anyone know how I really feel, as though I were a stone."[29] The last phrase in particular is tinged with bitterness at the nuns' lack of compassion rather than resignation. Úrsula provided additional examples of the nuns' hostility toward her, particularly their skepticism about her spiritual gifts. At one point, she commented that she "went into the confessionals to hide from the nuns."[30] This is not the only time Úrsula sought refuge in a confessional. A confessional during this period would have been a small wooden box, with a door or curtain. Since priests came only at specific times to hear the nuns' confessions, the confessional itself would have remained empty for long stretches of time, and therefore could function as one of the only spaces of privacy available to Úrsula within the convent.

But Úrsula's spiritual practice centered largely on conversations with individuals to whom she referred sometimes as "voices," and sometimes as Christ or one of the saints. Even when she used the term "voices," it is evident from the context that the speaker was Christ, and they frequently discussed suffering and oppression as an area of communality between the two. The voice told her, "In the thirty-three years I spent in this world, I endured a tremendous amount of work and oppression." The voice continued describing His crucifixion as something that would be done to a "vile slave and thief." Work, oppression, vile enslavement: These are all major elements to Úrsula's life as a black slave and *donada*.[31]

---

28 Úrsula de Jesús, *Souls of Purgatory*, 82; *Las almas*, 168.
29 Úrsula de Jesús, *Souls of Purgatory*, 104; *Las almas*, 204–5.
30 Úrsula de Jesús, *Souls of Purgatory*, 86–7 ("They just wear me out, so I leave them"); *Las almas*, 217. For another example of Úrsula hiding in a confessional, see *Las almas*, 275.
31 Úrsula de Jesús, *Souls of Purgatory*, 98; *Las almas*, 193–4. Nancy van Deusen argues that "such toil [female labor] could easily resonate with the heroic virtues of charity, poverty, and devotion to God": *Embodying the Sacred*, 28. See also ibid., 32–4.

In the genre of hagiography, the suffering of holy women nearly always stemmed from physical illness and ascetic practices. Neither of these traditional elements appear with any frequency in Úrsula's diary; rather, her suffering stemmed from her misery over the exhausting and often demeaning work she performed at the convent. One day during Holy Week, Úrsula talked with an unnamed *mulata* in the kitchen, who recounted the miseries she endured at the hands of her owner's mother. Úrsula turned to God later that day demanding to know why He, God of mercy, did not assuage the *mulata*'s suffering. The voices responded: "I am pleased when some suffer from what others do to them."[32] In another moment, Christ reminded Úrsula that He could have easily cast His tormentors into hell. He did not do so in order to "teach you to follow His will . . . When someone humiliates himself, prostrating himself at everyone's feet . . . he improves and makes progress."[33] Christ later reminded Úrsula, "[w]hen someone loves, the more they suffer, the more they love."[34] The cycle of love and suffering were critical to Úrsula's understanding of her own spiritual life. Her suffering, like Christ's, was not a matter of passive endurance – it was transformative, a profound meditation leading to spiritual growth and salvation.

But Úrsula's text also revealed multiple ways she gained revenge against her cruel sisters. For example, during a vision of hell, she was told by her voices that those suffering were punished for their lack of faith and that they were "not able to see God." She further noted: "It also seemed to me that I saw some nuns there." She likewise witnessed nuns suffering in hell several times, including one vision where a nun was on her back "on something like a barbecue," with flames "erupting through her mouth, eyes and ears." The voices accused the tormented woman of having "[fed] her appetites" like other "lazy and indulgent ones" who "[spend] their time jeering and causing a ruckus."[35] The reference to the laziness of the nuns in hell is telling, as it reflected Úrsula's own criticism of the nuns, as well as her belief that they would suffer for living easily while Úrsula toiled. In another vision, Úrsula spoke with St. Francis about her desire to please God. St. Francis, renowned for his ascetic piety, poverty, and humility, responded: "Suffer a lot, be humble like the earth, and have faith in God, who does not neglect His own."[36] Here, the founder of Úrsula's order affirmed that she lived the virtues espoused by the order while many of the nuns betrayed them by their worldly existence.

---

[32] Úrsula de Jesús, *Souls of Purgatory*, 91; *Las almas*, 184.
[33] Úrsula de Jesús, *Souls of Purgatory*, 106; *Las almas*, 208.
[34] Úrsula de Jesús, *Souls of Purgatory*, 156; *Las almas*, 296.
[35] Úrsula de Jesús, *Souls of Purgatory*, 85; *Las almas*, 173.
[36] Úrsula de Jesús, *Souls of Purgatory*, 141; *Las almas*, 101: "que hare para agradar a dios sufrir mucho y umilde como la tierra y mucha confiansa en dios que no puede faltar a los suyos."

Úrsula highlights the connection between her low status and the nuns' poor behavior in another conversation with her voices. Christ reminded her: "Throughout my life, I never rested. Have you not heard them say, 'The labors of Christ?'" Úrsula responded: "Why do some find it so repugnant?" The larger conversation makes it clear that Úrsula's "some" referred to the nuns. Christ concluded: "Have you not heard the Angolan slave say, 'My owner orders it'? Do everything in the same way: with the desire to follow My will." By requiring that all His followers treat Him metaphorically as a slave owner who must be obeyed, Christ erased all distinctions of rank and race; at the same time, Christ's advice suggested that Úrsula – and all enslaved people – was spiritually more advanced than the nuns precisely because she practiced obedience in ways that they did not.[37]

Úrsula mentioned a deceased nun who had failed to pay attention during the Divine Office, and even interrupted the priest, concluding: "All must account for themselves according to their capacities, *donado* like a *donado*, black person like a black person, and whether they have upheld the Ten Commandments. The religious are judged more harshly because they have great obligations."[38] In another instance, Úrsula recounted meeting with a deceased formerly enslaved woman, Marucha, who explained to Úrsula that people in Purgatory were separated from each other and punished "according to their social positions." She then listed the categories by which they were divided, beginning with nuns and male religious first (though she added that they were in different areas), then the laity, specifying that all were punished "according to their conditions and distinct responsibilities."[39] The hierarchies of punishment in the afterlife, then, were direct inversions of those in earthly life.

Status and hierarchy conferred privilege on white men and women who were permitted access to religious orders and the priesthood, yet in return for such privileges they were held to a higher standard than the laity. Divine requirements for people of color were the lowest because they lacked access to education and – more importantly – the leisure required to dedicate themselves to continual prayer. Úrsula turned to St. Francis once more for advice: "'What is this? They say that the profession of donadas has no value?' The saint replied, 'There is a difference because the nuns are white and of the Spanish nation, but with respect to the soul, all is one: Whoever does more, is worth more."[40] Later,

---

[37] Úrsula de Jesús, *Souls of Purgatory*, 137–8; *Las almas*, 264.

[38] Úrsula de Jesús, *Souls of Purgatory*, 116; *Las almas*, 226: "que cada uno le pedian cuenta conforme al talento que se le a dado; que al donado como a donado; que al negro como a negro se le pide quenta de los dies mandamientos, mas al relijioso le corrian muchas mas obligasiones."

[39] Úrsula de Jesús, *Souls of Purgatory*, 108; *Las almas*, 212.

[40] Úrsula de Jesús, *Souls of Purgatory*, 121; *Las almas*, 235: "quien mas ysiere baldra mas."

a voice reminded her that "the more you lower your head, the higher you can ascend."[41] In these passages, the complex, intertwining themes of work, suffering, low status, and humility reach their clearest expression. Here, Úrsula's work enabled her to claim increased holiness and status compared to the elite whites who surrounded her. Humility, then, acted as a path to spiritual authority and privilege.

The performance of humility had been a powerful way for holy women to make claims to spiritual power and authority throughout premodern Christianity, perhaps most visible in the writings of Catherine of Siena and Teresa of Avila. An exaggerated discourse of abasement, which hinged in part on the inferiority of femininity, allowed holy women to seize the central paradoxes in Christian theology, in which the humble, outcast, and poor – manifest through Christ's humanity itself – could be raised above the politically and socially powerful. Alison Weber notes how Teresa's protestations of unworthiness were ancient literary tropes, methods of making claims to authority in ways that are viewed as non-threatening to officials and higher-ranking people.[42] In Úrsula's text, low *casta* status replaced gender. Although gender no doubt enhanced the rhetoric of humility used throughout the diary, Úrsula made no references to herself as a "little woman" or an "ignorant woman"; her self-portrayals focused on aspects related to race – enslaved, unworthy, etc. Yet Úrsula clearly understood her spirituality in conversation with saints famous for their humility, like Francis and Teresa: Christ reminded Úrsula that she should receive the Eucharist "in a humble, obliging, and thankful manner: that is how St. Teresa of Jesús did it."[43] And like Teresa, Úrsula leveraged humility and low status as ironic paths to assuming a position of spiritual authority over her sisters.[44]

Subtle additions are made to these themes through the text, such as when Úrsula mentioned that book learning is unnecessary to spiritual practice. The voices told her that "God is the true teacher. What can the priest or books teach me that would do me as much good as what they teach me there?" Later she repeated this idea: "Even if I read many books, I would learn nothing of what they [the voices] teach me here."[45] Úrsula also gave an account of situations in

---

[41] Úrsula de Jesús, *Souls of Purgatory*, 133; *Las almas*, 87: "Despues dije: 'Señor yo soy una esclavita de mi madre Santa Clara. Acordaos de mi.' Dizenme: 'Quanto mas se abajaren aca, tanto mas subiran alla.'"

[42] Weber, *Rhetoric of Femininity,*" 50: "In this sense all of Teresa's work are extended prologues because, in her circumstances, the act of disavowing the privilege to write was of necessity conterminous with the act of claiming the privilege to write."

[43] Úrsula de Jesús, *Souls of Purgatory*, 89; *Las almas*, 180.

[44] Teresa of Avila looms large in the hagiography of Teresa Juliana de Santo Domingo, who visited Teresa's sepulcher in Alba de Tormes to venerate her relics: Paniagua, *Compendio*, 66.

[45] Úrsula de Jesús, *Souls of Purgatory*, 90, 92; *Las almas*, 182, 185.

which she was sought out by other nuns for her wisdom and authority. In one case, God had told Úrsula to tell the nuns that their bad behavior angered Him. With the abbess's permission, Úrsula wrote a paper remonstrating them for their lack of preparedness for the sacrament, which the abbess read aloud to the sisters, "saying it was from God." Here the abbess considered Úrsula a conduit for God, and Úrsula immediately verified the efficacy of her intervention by claiming that afterwards the nuns' behavior improved.[46]

In spite of Úrsula's rejection of book learning, she clearly maintained a body of knowledge about spiritual practices and the lives of important saints, including Teresa of Avila and St. Francis. This is unsurprising, given how often the lives of the saints would have been read out loud during meals and other times at the convent, or included in the liturgies for specific feast days, and shared informally among nuns. But she spent time with Luisa de Soto Melgarejo before arriving at Santa Clara, which most likely had an effect on her spiritual development. The author of Úrsula's vida provided no information about Melgarejo except a brief description of her as a "holy lady," but Melgarejo had, in fact, been a person of great significance in the spiritual landscape of early seventeenth-century Lima. A disciple of Rose of Lima, Melgarejo was widely venerated for her visions and ecstasies. She maintained a household filled with devout women from a variety of social and ethnic origins until she and the members of her circle were arrested by the Inquisition and tried for false sanctity.[47] Melgarejo's subsequent trouble with the Inquisition probably accounts for the hagiographer's silence about Úrsula's time with the famous mystic, but it no doubt shaped her knowledge and life.

While the themes of mistreatment over status and color difference permeated hagiographies of saints of color, Úrsula's text added immediacy and poignancy. It also revealed the deep spiritual and psychological ramifications of such abuse. She was not in and among the white sisters, but always separate, allied with the other black women who circulated in and out of the convent. The perpetual distance between black religious from their white-dominated environments caused suffering and spiritual doubt. The poignancy of Úrsula's diary is thrown into relief by the hagiography written about her by an anonymous Franciscan friar. The friar relied extensively on Úrsula's diary as his source, but his text followed standard hagiographic conventions. Yet its chronological organization permitted the author to provide important context to particular elements of Úrsula's life.

---

[46] Úrsula de Jesús, *Souls of Purgatory*, 124–5; *Las almas*, 240–41.
[47] Schlau, "Flying in Formation"; Iwasaki Cauti, "Mujeres al borde de la perfección"; and Iwasaki, "Luisa Melgarejo de Soto."

For example, the author recounted the story of how Úrsula ended up taking vows as a *donada* after having lived for many years at the convent as a slave. Apparently, Úrsula had desperately desired to escape the convent (and bondage, presumably). After she was freed, Úrsula was faced with a choice – she could leave the convent as a free woman, or she could remain and take vows as a *donada*. The friar explained that Úrsula struggled with her choice, because she had "gained her liberty and free will with which she could not take the habit." Because religious vocation required complete submission to God, she would have to surrender again the liberty she had just gained through legal emancipation. Úrsula's inner conflict was resolved by divine intervention. The author described a fire in the convent's chapel that led to the destruction of many of its images, which occurred on the feast of St. Úrsula. Úrsula was devastated and asked God why he did not burn her up instead of the holy images. God responded, with a hint of amusement, that perhaps she could do something smaller than being burned alive for His sake, like become a *donada*? And so she did.[48] But her profound struggle between spiritual vocation where she would be constrained by several different types of unfreedom and life outside the convent speaks to the specific experiences of black women in religious service. Yet it also emphasizes that, even within tight constraints, Úrsula's life as a *donada* was the result of her own choice, much as Esperanza's refusal of the habit was.

A similar account appeared in Úrsula's diary, although the context is less clear because the diary does not have a chronological structure. Yet the Franciscan's authorial process of giving shape to a series of disconnected spiritual meditations erases the emotional impact of Úrsula's experiences, even though he did not omit or misrepresent Úrsula's stories. What changes between the two texts is subjectivity – from inner thoughts to exterior organization, the chaos is smoothed away and the theological relationship between ideas is clarified by the anonymous friar. In the process, the black women so important to Úrsula's day-to-day life remain unnamed in the vida, all but erasing them from the text. In contrast, one of the most surprising features of Úrsula's diary is how emotionally candid it appears. While it is possible that she engaged in self-censorship, the text does not demonstrate the caution of, say, Teresa of Avila's spiritual autobiography. As a result, we are left an emotional rawness not often seen in such works, expressing the great suffering and spiritual doubt caused by white supremacy in the convent. In the gaps between the vida and the diary, the paradox of black religiosity in seventeenth-century Lima emerges.

---

[48] *La vida*, 7–8. Úrsula reflected on her days before taking vows, remarking on how much she liked to dress well.

But outside the texts, it is important to remember the sheer number of people who come to Úrsula asking for aid – supplicants both living and dead. The perception of her successful ability to intercede for those in Purgatory made her famous both inside and outside the convent. Úrsula's voices assured her of her superiority to the nuns around her, just as Esperanza taught the rest of her community how to practice their rule properly.

Estefanía de San Joseph (d. 1645) was another enslaved *limeña* who achieved fame for sanctity in her community. A Franciscan tertiary, her vida was part of Diego de Cordova y Salinas's lengthy tome celebrating the spiritual wealth of late-sixteenth- and seventeenth-century Peru. Not surprisingly, the largest vida in the book was dedicated to Francisco Solano (d. 1610), the friar and missionary whose beatification campaign was a major Franciscan cause in the seventeenth century.[49] Nevertheless, Cordova's chronicle provides a plethora of spiritual biographies of varying lengths, some several pages, and some only a few short paragraphs. Book Five of his chronicle consisted of two parts, one on Third Order Franciscans (male tertiaries), and the other on Clarissian houses, where the vida of Estefanía de San Joseph is located.[50]

Estefanía was the daughter of a black slave (later referred to as Isabel la Portuguesa) and a white father ("español") in Cuzco. Isabel was a devout woman who entered the Clarissan convent in Cuzco as a tertiary upon the death of her owner. Like her mother, Estefanía's owner freed her upon his death but in this case the owner's family members adamantly refused to let her go. Estefanía ended up fleeing to Lima, where her freedom was eventually ratified by the Real Audiencia in order that she be able to fulfill her vocation. Her Franciscan spiritual advisor, Dávila, described the Audiencia's decision as God's will to liberate Estefanía's body so that her soul could be dedicated to prayer.[51] The anecdote echoes ancient hagiographic themes in which devout young girls wishing to become nuns had to struggle against their families who wished them to marry, a trope that would have been recognizable to readers. It also echoes the dynamics at play in both Esperanza's and Úrsula's lives where tensions emerged between earthly liberation and spiritual submission, and the deliberate choice to submit enhanced their reputations for heroic virtue.

At some point, Estefanía professed as a tertiary and joined the Clarissan convent where she lived out the rest of her days. Like Úrsula and Esperanza before her, Estefanía engaged deeply with the spiritual practice of abasement. In

---

[49] Cordova y Salinas, *Crónica franciscana*, 949–52. The Franciscans were unsuccessful in their efforts to beatify the first Peruvian holy person (though Solano was Spanish-born) Dominican tertiary Rose of Lima, who had already been canonized by the time Solano was beatified in 1675.

[50] Another scholarly discussion of Estefanía can be found in Wood, "Religious Women of Color."

[51] Cordova, *Crónica franciscana*, 950.

one instance, Estefanía expressed a desire for everyone to think that she was "a terrible and vile sinner, scourge of the world, so that they would despise her."[52] In another, when a nun chastised Estefanía for wearing a torn and patched habit, the holy woman responded: "It would be pleasing to God if I were so despicable that men threw stones at me in the streets and plazas of the city."[53] Estefanía's desire to prevent visible admiration was a crucial trope of hagiography: holy people could cultivate divine gifts only if they expressed unworthiness. Estefanía's declaration echoes the moment when Benedict of Palermo overturned the egg cart of an admirer so she would despise him.[54] Both Estefanía's comment about having rocks thrown at her and Benedict's overturned cart revealed their formidable personalities, and how humility could be performed (whether deeply felt or not).

Estefanía also moved around the city outside the convent walls, which created increased opportunities for her performance of spiritual authority. For example, she encouraged local children to own and pray the rosary by rewarding them with little packets of raisins for those who showed her their rosaries. Dávila proclaimed that her methods were so successful that of the children she taught one became a Jesuit and another a cleric, while several girls became nuns. In addition to teaching children, Estefanía ministered to (white) adults with insight and tact, careful not to disturb racial, social, and gendered expectations while pursuing her divine calling. Estefanía would visit wealthy ladies and ask them to read to her. She would then choose devotional books based on what she felt the women in the room needed to hear; after the reading, they would discuss the texts. Dávila referred to these conversations as "preaching," indicating it was Estefanía who guided the discussions. She might do such directed readings four to six times per day. Here we see that Estefanía's protestations of illiteracy allowed her to express her spiritual authority while maintaining an outward appearance of modesty and humility; in return, she gained widespread respect and admiration.[55] She was able, therefore, to transform her reputation for sanctity

---

[52] Cordova, *Crónica franciscana*, 950: "abominable pecadora y la vileza y scoria del mundo, para que la menospreciassen."

[53] Cordova, *Crónica franciscana*, 949.

[54] A short vida of Isabel Cano, a *mestiza* disciple of Estefanía, followed Estefanía's life. At the end of Isabel's vida, Cordova cited Proverbs, chapter 31: "Manum suam misit ad fortia." In the Revised Catholic Standard Version, Proverbs 31:19–20 reads: "She puts her hands to the distaff, and her hands hold the spindle. She opens her hand to the poor, and reaches out her hands to the needy." Cordova concluded: "es gran valentía cumplir uno las obligaciones de su estado, aun en cosas pequeñas ... Assí estas santas mujeres, con las virtudes proporcionadas a su estado": *Crónica franciscana*, 958. It is striking that Cordova did not describe Estefanía in such terms in her own vida.

[55] Cordova, *Crónica franciscana*, 951.

into a position of power within the larger community even as she outwardly performed normative gendered and racialized roles.

As a result of Estefanía's reputation for sanctity, the most important people in the city admired and visited her. For example, she also had a chance encounter with Pedro Álvarez de Toledo, Marquis of Mancera, viceroy of Perú (1639–1648), and his wife during a routine visit to the hospital, where Estefanía lay ill. Estefanía asked them to pray and offer alms for the sick; in return, she offered to pray for their souls. They kissed her and asked for her blessing, whereupon she made the sign of the cross over them.[56] Dávila concluded by praising her ability to speak to powerful people with "such valor and humility" that even though she had been a slave, the viceroy was able to recognize her holiness. The wedding of humility with valor tells us something significant about how early modern people understood humility – the denial of one's free will was an act of courage that, in fact, conveyed spiritual authority.

Influential members of the nobility both recognized and enhanced the reputations of certain holy people; in the colonies, viceroys appear in several texts about holy women of color. Estefanía's encounter with the viceroy appears to have been a happenstance, but others were sought out. For example, the Marquesa de Mancera, the viceroy's wife, visited Esperanza's convent, "because of the news she had heard of [Esperanza's] virtue." Networks of information bound convent communities not only to the larger towns or cities around them, but to larger spaces – Esperanza lived in Puebla, while presumably the viceregal couple lived in the capital, Mexico City. Tracing the networks of information that circulated about holy women is not always easy, but their vidas occasionally provide glimmers. Gómez, for example, described two Discalced Carmelite priests who visited the convent on their journey from Spain to the colonies. They spoke at length with the prioress, who told the friars about Esperanza and her virtues. The prioress eventually invited Esperanza into the room to speak to them.[57] Presumably, they continued on their travels taking their knowledge of the *santa morena* with them. Circuits of sanctity, then, need not be textual, and, in most cases, they were likely powered by personal contact and anecdotes.

Iberia

People of color who were renowned for their virtue or holiness were venerated in Iberia as well as the Americas, although, like their American brethren, they often

---

[56] Cordova, *Crónica Franciscana*, 952. Dávila says "la besasen la mano y pidiesen la bendición."
[57] Gómez, *Fundación*, 315–17.

appear only in tantalizing glimpses.[58] Domínguez Ortíz mentioned the case of an enslaved black man, Salvador de la Cruz, who had been buried in his confraternal chapel (he had been the mayordomo for the confraternity) in Seville. Salvador gained a reputation for virtue, which led to a close relationship with Cardinal Solís, an archbishop of Seville who was elevated to the rank of cardinal in the mid-eighteenth century.[59] Francisco Bermúdez de Pedraza's *Antigüedades y excelencias de Granada* noted among three of the city's "famous blacks" a Dominican friar named Cristóbal de Meneses, the son of black woman and a white nobleman.[60] Another woman, María Escovara, appears in a nineteenth-century catalogue, from a work entitled "La esclava menos esclava María Escovara, sus penitencias y virtudes con las de otras dos hermanas de la Tercera Orden" (The Slave the Least Enslaved María Escovara, Her Penances and Virtues, along with Two Other Sisters of the Third Order.) Vicente Barrantes, the compiler of the catalogue, provided some basic biographical information, stating that María was born in Fregenal de la Sierra (between Mérida and Seville, close to the Portuguese border) in 1602 and died in 1653, and that she took the veil as a tertiary after living with Doña Catalina de Aponte, most likely as Aponte's slave.[61]

Two additional holy women of color also emerge from the records of eighteenth-century Spain: Teresa Juliana de Santo Domingo (1676–1748) and Magdalena de la Cruz (d. 1735).[62] Their experiences overlap with their earlier American counterparts in many ways. They too were enslaved women; like Esperanza, both women had been enslaved as young girls. Yet the environments they encountered were far different from colonial convents,

---

[58] It is possible that women of color lived in convents or gained reputations for sanctity in other European countries, including a famous case in France – Louise Marie Thérèse (d. 1732), most likely the illegitimate daughter of Louis XIV, who became a nun. Sources on Louise Marie can be found in memoirs of the Duchess of Montpensier, Madame de Montespan, and the Duke of Saint-Simon. Another woman, Pauline, fought to enter a convent in Nantes rather than return to the West Indies where she would be re-enslaved. The account of Pauline's life comes from Harms, *The Diligent*, 6–11.

[59] Domínguez Ortíz, *Esclavitud en Castilla en la edad moderna y otros estudios*, 27. Solís was a powerful man, the son of Gabriel Álvarez de Toledo, royal librarian, knight of Santiago, and a co-founder of the Real Academia Española.

[60] Bermúdez de Pedraza, *Antigüedades y excelencias de Granada*.

[61] Barrantes, *Catálogo*, 144. The vida of Escovara is also mentioned in Díaz y Pérez, *Diccionario histórico*, Vol.1, 238. The Aponte family appears to have been prominent in Fregenal de la Sierra. Brief mentions of their lineage with a family tree bearing several women named Catalina de Aponte can be found in Caso Amador, "El origen judeoconverso," 1684.

[62] Teresa Juliana has received recent attention from scholars. See Melián, "Chikaba"; Jiménez de Baéz, "Sor Teresa de Santo Domingo"; Maeso, *Sor Teresa Chikaba*; Benoist, "La doble identidad de Sor Chicaba"; Ferrús Antón, "Sor Teresa Juliana de Santo Domingo"; and Houchens and Fra Molinero, *Black Bride of Christ*.

especially those in Lima that housed many women of color. Neither Teresa nor Magdalena appear to have interacted at length with other black women, although their perspectives are muffled by the mediated vidas that tell their stories. The demographics of eighteenth-century Madrid and Seville suggest that both women would have known other enslaved people of color, but it is possible that their religious houses only included whites, even as servants.

Teresa's and Magdalena's lives mirror those of colonial living saints in another crucial way: noble patronage. Teresa Juliana de Santo Domingo had been born in Guinea where her parents named her Chicaba. Kidnapped as a young child, she was carried to Cadiz and then to Madrid; during her journey, she was baptized and renamed Teresa. In Madrid, she became the slave of the Marquis of Mancera, Antonio Sebastián de Toledo (d. 1715), and his second wife, Juliana Teresa de Meneses, around 1685. The marquises' role in Teresa's early life is worth a brief mention, because it illustrates a broader Atlantic context for the networks discussed in colonial lives. Mancera served as viceroy of New Spain from 1663 to 1673 while married to his first wife. In New Spain, the couple became important patrons to prominent mystic Sor Juana Inés de Cruz; around the same time, the virreina visited Juana Esperanza de San Alberto, as we have seen.[63] Moreover, the marquis's father, the first marquis of Mancera, Pedro Álvarez de Toledo, served as the viceroy of Peru from 1639 to 1648. The marquis's son – Teresa Juliana's future owner – accompanied his parents on this sojourn in Lima, where he must have known Estefanía, at least by reputation. The Mancera family's interest holy women of color spanned three countries separated by thousands of miles, and two generations. We can only speculate what effect such experiences might have had on the precocious spirituality of the young enslaved girl in the Mancera's Madrid household.

Teresa's hagiography illustrates another important aspect of early modern spiritual economy – the relationship between confessor and holy woman. Paniagua had known Teresa Juliana in life, and based his texts on his personal conversations with her as well as her own writing. He further had access to one of Teresa's confessors, Jerónimo Abarrategui. Paniagua and Abarrategui were both Theatines, which maintained a house near the Dominican convent where Teresa lived. Although Abarrategui died decades before Teresa, he was the subject of a biography penned by Diego Torres y Villarroel in the mid-eighteenth century; Torres and Paniagua knew each other, creating another current of knowledge exchange.[64] The link between Abarrategui and Teresa Juliana was widely

---

[63] Gómez, *Fundación*, 315–16.

[64] Jerónimo Abarrategui died in 1719, sixteen years after Teresa Juliana's entrance into the convent. Paniagua appears to have known Teresa Juliana near the end of her life: Torres y Villarroel, *Vida*

acknowledged and became the subject of a painting, today housed in the Museo de Salamanca. [Plate 77] Although the painting has been poorly conserved, the two figures are clearly discernable – Abarrategui in his Theatine habit on the left of a central altar, with Teresa Juliana in the garb of a Dominican tertiary on the right. Above the altar floats a monstrance with the Eucharist. The inscription of the painting, almost completely illegible, names Abarrategui as the figure with Teresa. Teresa's eyes gaze upward at the Eucharist, her hands folded in prayer. Abarrategui, also on his knees, gazes downward at his hands, which appear to hold a book. On top corners are two saints floating the sky, standing on clouds and surrounded by light – presumably these are St. Cayetano and St. Dominic, the founders of the two orders represented. The provenance of the painting is unclear, although its obvious celebration of the relationship between the Theatines and Teresa Juliana suggest that it was commissioned by the Theatines to hang in their house.[65] Teresa's reputation for holiness was significant enough that the Theatines wanted to promote and to commemorate their relationship to her.

Paniagua's hagiography of Teresa was rooted in his conversations with her as well as her own writing. He noted early in his work that nothing could be known about Teresa's childhood in Guinea except what the nun herself remembered: "without having been provided [biographical details] from Mother Teresa, all these would have been hidden from our eyes."[66] Like the diary of Úrsula de Jesús, Paniagua presented some passages in Teresa's vida as direct quotations.[67] While the strength of Teresa's voice throughout this text distinguishes it from one written by a stranger, untangling Teresa's voice from Paniagua's is complicated. This vida does not contain the raw specificity of Úrsula's diary, but it follows a pattern of an anecdote from Teresa's life followed by analysis – a pattern that echoes an interview, which we know Paniagua conducted with the holy woman. The stories, therefore, are likely hers, while most of the analysis is his.

Teresa Juliana's hagiography tells an African Atlantic story that other hagiographies of black saints do not. Paniagua described Teresa's great sorrow and confusion at being taken on a Spanish ship and sailing away from her homeland.

---

exemplar, 75–6: "[Paniagua] quien en esta ultima enfermedad la assistiò repetidas veces, leeràn los devotos un compendio angustiado de la vida, y virtudes de esta dichosa Beata."

[65] The current Dominican convent, Las Dueñas, houses its own eighteenth-century portrait of Teresa Juliana, in a nearly identical presentation, except that she is alone. In Paniagua's funeral sermon, he mentioned that Teresa had interceded on behalf of a fellow Theatine in Purgatory, Gaspar de Olinden, who was a well-respected theologian, author, and rector of the Theatine house in Salamanca: Olinden, *Dialogos del Purgatorio*; Paniaga, *Sermón fúnebre*, 17.

[66] Paniagua, *Compendio*, 1. Paniagua's hagiography has recently appeared in an English edition: Houchins and Fra-Molinero, *Black Bride of Christ*.

[67] Houchins and Fra-Molinero, "The Saint's Life of Sister Chicaba."

Onboard, Teresa recounted two miracles that she claimed saved her life. She described being tormented by overwhelming thirst and exhaustion, which made her despair for her life. But then appeared a miraculous cup filled with water, which immediately restored her to life.[68] Next, in her despair over losing her beloved parents and the fierce desire to free herself from the horrors of slavery, the child vowed to jump overboard and swim to shore, although she did not know how to swim, as many enslaved people had done before her. At this moment, Teresa experienced vision of the Virgin Mary, who comforted and "caressed" the child into relief and calm.[69] The specificity of the description of Chicaba's experience on the slave ship echoes many accounts of the horrors of the Middle Passage and clearly represents Teresa's own memories of the event, rather than Paniagua's invention.

Atlantic crossings emerged again later in her vida in Teresa's young adulthood as she began to think about becoming a nun. Her owners expressed general support for her desire to enter a convent, but they counseled patience.[70] While she was waiting, her uncle from Guinea suddenly appeared at the Manceras' palace looking for her. Apparently, male members of her politically important family traveled to Spain on a diplomatic mission; in Madrid, they heard about Teresa Juliana. Thinking that the girl might be their long lost relative (although on what evidence it is unclear) they proceeded to the Manceras' house. There, they assured Teresa of her parents' conversion to Christianity before their deaths, relieving her long-held fear of their damnation. They further tried to convince Teresa to return with them to her homeland, which she refused.[71]

After their visit, Teresa was finally freed and provided with a dowry to enter La Penitencia. But life at the convent proved as challenging for Teresa as it had been for Úrsula. Teresa claimed that the nuns treated her "as if she were a slave," and that they would not, among other things, permit her to sleep in their dormitory. She began to wonder if it would have been better for her to accept her uncle's offer to return to her homeland. There she would have been respected as a member of a noble family and could have worked to spread Catholicism.

---

[68] The torture of terrible thirst on slave ships was widely remarked by contemporaries. Sandoval discussed the need to provide copious amounts of water in order to revive newly arrived enslaved people: Sandoval, *Naturaliza i policia*, 215: "Tanta como esta es la sed, con que desembarcan, y estan en las armazones, assadas las entrañas de la mucha salada que han bevido . . . se dexaran morir transidos de sed, principalmente mugeres y niños."

[69] Paniagua, *Compendio*, 19.

[70] Paniagua, *Compendio*, 56–61; Melián, "Chikaba, la pimera monja negra," 573–4.

[71] Paniagua, *Compendio*, 50–1; 55–6. Paniagua provided a few additional details in his funeral sermon: The uncle had been traveling to France, and ended up in Madrid in the household of the dukes of Pastrana, who were friends with Mancera, which is how the uncle heard about Teresa: *Sermon fúnebre*, 13.

Such doubts acted as a continual torment to Teresa, as she seethed over being treated poorly by her sisters.[72] This story echoes Úrsula's struggle over taking vows as a *donada* – in both cases, the holy women were offered earthly freedom that would take them out of the convent to a life of greater comfort and respect. Yet both chose to remain in spite of doubts and suffering. There are multiple ways to read these choices, but they can be seen as forms of resistance – a refusal to accept exclusion from religious life. And if success is the best revenge, it was, of course, they and not their sisters who ended up dying in the odor of sanctity, respected and venerated.

Paniagua's funeral sermon for Teresa repeated accounts of her childhood and life that appeared later in the hagiography. But the sermon's rhetoric was richly metaphorical, dramatic, and lavish, following a specific vision of black sanctity unique to Iberian holy women. Unlike other sermons about black saints, Paniagua eschewed the Song of Songs for the scriptural theme; instead, he chose the Gospel of St. Matthew and 1 Kings. These specific passages discussed the adoration of the black magus and Saba, the Queen of Sheba, both of whom were associated with Ethiopia in the early modern period. Paniagua's placement of these scriptural passages alongside the story of Teresa's life creates a parallel – Teresa was also the daughter of a king and traveled great distances to cultivate perfect Christian virtue.[73]

Paniagua also described her as "a rose" throughout the sermon, declaring that the rose was the "queen" of all flowers, the most beautiful and perfect. Later, Paniagua praised Teresa again as the "Rose Queen" who had been "transplanted" to Spain where she "exhaled such fragrant aromas in her prodigious virtues."[74] He connected her as the rose with the gifts of the three kings: "The Rose, because of her bright color is the symbol, like gold, of a birth regally elevated. Her scent tells, like Incense, a life full of the fragrances of its deeds and virtuous works. In the thorns that surround it, the bitter myrrh of penance."[75] Queen of Sheba also brought lavish gifts when she journeyed to visit King Solomon to praise his virtuous rule. Teresa, then, was clustered together with Balthazar and Saba, but not as a fellow traveler – instead, she was the gift they brought with them, the rose. Here, Paniagua underscored Teresa's lack of agency, since she had been taken against her will. Once in Spain, however, she exuded the powerful odor of sanctity and shone with the

---

[72] Paniagua, *Compendio*, 71–2.   [73] Paniagua, *Sermón fúnebre*, 1.

[74] Paniagua, *Sermón fúnebre*, 9, 20.

[75] Paniagua, *Sermón fúnebre*, 2–3. "La Rosa por su color encendido, es symbol, como el oro, de un nacimiento regiamente elevado. Su olor explica, como el Incienso, una vida lleno de fragrancias, por sus empleos, y obras virtuosas. En las espinas que la rodean, la Myrrah amarga de la penitencia."

beauty of virtue, to the extent that she herself became a queen. Here, humility dropped out of the vision of black sanctity altogether, instead permitting early modern women of color to be connected to ancient Ethiopian royalty, including Efigenia.

Bernardo Dorado's history of Salamanca briefly mentioned Teresa's life, and included her epitaph, which echoed Paniagua's rhetoric: "Here lies the chaste, pure innocent, and mortified Dove ... born Queen, died Slave, but as a Slave a Queen, a Queen because she reigned over herself."[76] Because Teresa had been freed long before her death, the epitaph's reference to her as dying a slave referred to her as a slave for Christ – a slave by choice rather than by violence. Because she chose her spiritual enslavement, she was elevated to queenship. A royal saint is quite a different thing than a slave saint, although the lives of Úrsula, Estefanía, and Esperanza developed similar ideas about the deliberate acceptance of low-liness as a path to spiritual ascension, represented by a position of authority (queenship). Of course, Teresa Juliana's birth in West Africa to noble parents placed her in the company of Efigenia, Elesban, Balthazar, and the Queen of Sheba.[77] Significantly, by connecting Teresa's nobility to the metaphor of the rose, Paniagua placed her femininity and beauty at the center of the funeral sermon, a rare example of an extravagantly feminine discourse in a vida of a black holy woman.

Strength developed through heroic virtue acted as the foundation of the funeral sermon for Magdalena de la Cruz, who died in 1735 in Seville, written by Pedro Contreras, a Mercedarian preacher.[78] The printed sermon contains two appro-bations (official endorsements of the work's publication); while all printed texts contained approbations or/and censures before them, the ones attached to Contreras's sermon are unusually full of rhetorical flourishes. The authors of these two pieces were Friar Juan Bermejo and Doctor Don Luis Ignacio Chacón, marques de la Peñuela and archdeacon in the nearby town of Nieblas. Chacón was himself a prolific author of funeral and festival sermons in Seville, while Bermejo was a Franciscan often employed as a "censure" on printed works in eighteenth-century Seville. These two pieces of frontmatter echoed themes in Contreras's sermon; as a result they read like interlocking texts, although they

---

[76] Dorado, *Compendio histórico*, 400: "Aqui yace la casta, la pura, la inocente, y mortificada Paloma en el alma, naciò Reina, y muriò Esclava, pero por Esclava Reina, Reina por que reinò en si propia."

[77] The idea of noble Africans as exceptional, making them worthy of freedom and sympathy recurs in early modern rhetoric. For one well-known example, see Aphra Behn, *Orinooko, or the Royal Slave: A True History* (London: Will. Canning, 1688).

[78] Contreras, *Sermón fúnebre*. Contreras also wrote at least two additional printed prayers – one on the Virgin's seven sorrows and one in honor of the death of Philip V.

each put their individual perspectives on the major themes. All three focused on the black/white synergy discussed in the previous Chapter. The entire document can in fact be read as a complex meditation on sacred blackness and its justification.[79]

Contreras's sermon moved quickly through Magdalena's life, providing only bare-bones biographical information: Magdalena had been born in Cabo Verde, kidnapped at the same age as Teresa (eight or nine), enslaved, brought to Cadiz and then on to Seville, where she lived the remainder of her life.[80] Contreras said next to nothing about her period of enslavement, manumission, and entrance into the convent, except for a brief mention of her owner's mother (the Countess of Santa Gadea), for whom Magdalena was an "inseparable companion." In place of a detailed biography of Magdalena, Contreras flattered Magdalena's owner, who most likely was Luis González de Aguilar de Torres de Navarra, count of Santa Gadea, which was an earldom created by Philip II at end of sixteenth century.[81] Much like Paniagua, Contreras described the enslaved girl as "servant" and "companion" to a virtuous and devout family, accentuating ties of affection rather than bondage. The priest spent some time comparing Magdalena and her owners to Jacob, his mother Rebecca, and Rebecca's slave, Deborah (Genesis 24:59, 35:8). The vidas of both Teresa Juliana and Magdalena demonstrate how strong ties to noble families provided opportunities for women of color to enter religious life in Spain, a significantly different track than what we see in Lima. The sanctity of Teresa Juliana and Magdalena reflected back on the families who had owned them and who were perceived as having been partly responsible for their holiness.

While Magdalena's enslavement was minimized in the funeral sermon, her blackness was omnipresent. Bermejo, for example, claimed that Hugh of St. Clair declared black to be the color of "human divinity" because, while it signaled human debasement, it also represented the theological virtues of mortification and penance. Just as Bernardo de Medina described Martín de Porres's black skin as representing the black of the Dominican habit, Bermejo understood the double meaning of blackness in premodern Catholic symbology – both vice and virtue, the

---

[79] There is an almost a bewildering range of footnotes and authorities cited throughout the sermon. In addition to others I specify in notes, one can find: Ovid, Plato, Cassaneus, (Cardenal) Hugh of St. Cher (d. 1263), St. Jerome (d. 420), Jean la Haye (d. 1661), Paulus Scherlogus, Gaspar Sánchez (SJ, d. 1628), Padre Orozco, Thadeus Perusimo, St. Cayetano, Philip Neri, and Ignatius of Loyola. Its scriptural exegesis further included discussions not only of the bride from the Song of Songs, but Jael, Jethro, Moses, Deborah, Jacob, Ezekiel, Candace, and Sephora.

[80] Contreras, *Sermón fúnebre*, 7.

[81] The marquesado of Campo Verde was also an early modern creation granted by Charles II specifically for Don Luis's father. González's mother was most likely María Josefa Torres de Navarra y Monsalve.

self-harming suffering of sinfulness and the redemptive suffering of those offering it freely.[82] Contreras picked up a similar theme, declaring: "This is the color that, according to Cassaneo, exceeds all the rest of the colors in virtue."[83] Because the color black was unchangeable, it could not be corrupted. Chacón chose a different play on black/white, describing the day of Magdalena's death as "dark, black, full of bitterness"; this was both a commentary on grief and a rhetorical subversion of body and soul – it is not Magdalena who was black, since she herself had been lifted to divine light, but her loved ones, left behind in darkness.[84]

Contreras returned to the exterior appearance of blackness, reminding his readers that Ethiopians – like Magdalena herself, "la Ethiopisa" – had been burned black by the sun and questioning how it would be possible to change such a dark color. "In nature," he answered his own query, "it is impossible ... but what is impossible in nature, is made possible by the marvels of grace."[85] In early modern Spain, "can the Ethiopian change his skin?" was a common aphorism; it originated from the Book of Jeremiah 13:23, and was frequently invoked to describe something that cannot be changed. Yet Contreras subverted this aphorism by reminding his readers of the limits of worldly thinking, and that through grace anything was possible. He further chided that beauty was not found in skin color, but in virtue (citing Plato), and later quoted a passage from Leviticus (13:37) that states if a leprous sore has a black hair growing in it, then it is ritually clean.[86] A blond hair (*cabello pajizo*), on the other hand, is a bad sign. Therefore, Contreras concluded, blond hair represents love of self, and black hair obedience. Here again we see an inversion, not only of status, but of power itself, in which the somatic trait associated with whiteness (yellow hair) is corrupt, whereas blackness represents spiritual purity.[87]

[82] In the margins, the citations appear: "Hug. In Pro oh. Super Luc. Ngredo and Berch. D[?]ict. Mor, Verb. Nigredo." The latter most likely refers to Bercharius's important work, *Reductorium morale*, which appeared in early modern print.

[83] This appears to be a reference to Bartholomeus Cassaneus (a.k.a. Barthélemy de Chasseneuz), *Catalogi gloriae mundi [1506]*. The first line of the paragraph on the color black reads: "Et licet color niger videatur laudabilior & principalior, cum per nullum alium colorem possit transmutari, incorporari, seu confundi," 384v.

[84] Chacón also reminded readers that virtue or sinfulness determined true whiteness or blackness. He contrasted the Nazarenes (the virtuous) to the Gentiles (the deformed and sinful): *Sermón fúnebre*, n.f.: "Los Nazarenos quando con sus cultos, e integridad de costumbres agradaban a Dios, merecieron el elogio de ser mas albos que la nieve; pero habiendose inficionado en los vicios de los Gentiles, dice el Divino Oraculo, que su deformidad, y negregura execida a la de los carbones ... Fuerte amenaza por haver cenizado, y obscurecido el candor de su Fe, la pureza de su vida, con las culpas, e idoltaria."

[85] Contreras, *Sermón fúnebre*, 1.

[86] He cites the Latin in full: "Si capilli fuerint nigri, noverit hominem esse sanatum, & confidenter eum pronuntiabit mundum."

[87] Contreras, *Sermón fúnebre*, 10.

Contreras engaged in additional word play when providing exegesis on the first lines of the Song of Songs. The line "I am black but beautiful" is followed by two similes of darkness, "as the tents of Cedar, as the curtains of Solomon."[88] He informed his readers that Magdalena was like the Cedarites, who were warlike and strong, because she also fought intense battles. Her weapons included crosses, hairshirts, and discipline "in order to command the passions and suppress the appetites."[89] Later, he praised her for triumphing over the cruel blows and horrifying visions of devils that came to tempt and torment her. She demonstrated heroic patience through silence when she was treated badly because she was black (here, Contreras cited the same story about Moses and his wife discussed in Benedict's vida).[90] Silence, then, constituted a form of bravery.

Contreras used the analogy of the Cedarites to situate Magdalena in the topos of the manly woman, so common in hagiographies of female saints. While the language of spiritual arms had ancient roots in Christian rhetoric, it took on new intensity in the early modern period in hagiographies of holy women.[91] In keeping with this tradition, Contreras concluded that Magdalena was "a powerful, heroic warrior who conquered the horror of sin," and praised her as "going out in such forceful battles, a heroic and victorious warrior, earning the triumphant laurel of the title of strong woman."[92] One of the biggest impediments to female sanctity was feminine weakness – because women were less rational than men, they were more susceptible to diabolic temptation. To counter such powerful cultural beliefs about women, holy women and their hagiographers described women as fully capable of picking up and bearing spiritual arms. The military language allowed women to slip free of accusations of weakness and highlight their moral virility.

While such gendered language permeated vidas of white holy women, they appear much less frequently in the lives of women of color. The topos of the manly woman also appears in Santana's vida of Efigenia, where the Carmelite described how the Ethiopian princess rallied her fellow nuns to "fight for Christ" against Hyrtaco's efforts to destroy their convent. They engaged in the most fundamental battle against temptation and evil when confronted with the pagan king's efforts to destabilize their faith. Santana declared the nuns

---

[88] On the curtains of Solomon, Contreras cites Pagnino and Agathio as indicating "per pelles Salomonis intelligitur vestis candidissima": *Sermón fúnebre*, 19. The two authors cited were both Christian Hebraists and authors of commentaries on the Song of Songs: Santes Pagnino (d. 1541) and Agathius Guidacerius (d. 1540).

[89] Contreras, *Sermón fúnebre*, 13.   [90] Contreras, *Sermón fúnebre*, 15–16.

[91] Perry, "The Manly Woman"; and Rowe, *Saint and Nation*, 117–19.

[92] Contreras, *Sermón fúnebre*, 17.

"brave combatants," and "bellicose Amazons," while Efigenia stood as their "Generalissima."[93] Another devotional work described Efigenia, like her Ethiopian counterpart Elesban, as a "defender of the faith," while a third compared her to the biblical hero Deborah.[94] The Amazons, the prophet Deborah, Moses's wife, and the desert ascetics who engaged in epic battles with devils – all existed in ancient, primitive Christianity. While the trope of the manly woman could be applied to women of any time period, it hardly seems coincidental that we find such rhetoric echoed in Contreras's sermon, as he consistently referred to Magdalena as an Ethiopian woman (Ethiopisa). Magdalena changed her sex as she changed her skin – two powerful transformations that removed the characteristics considered problematic or impediments to sanctity.

Contreras's sermon focused on the tensions between being and seeming, highlighting all the ways in which Magdalena transformed ideas of what she seemed into recognition of her true (spiritual) self. She confounded expectations, a living example of divine grace. Though poor, she was rich in virtue; elevated in divine gifts, she remained humble; an ignorant person, she evinced great wisdom. "It was," Contreras declared, "astonishing when she explained Scripture: to see an ignorant black woman, without knowing how to read, explain Scripture like a wise Doctor."[95] In keeping with his efforts to ground Magdalena's virtues in ancient and scriptural authorities, Contreras reminded his readers that one of the learned men of the Church of Antioch was called Simon the Black (Acts 13). In this comparison, Contreras created a lineage for Magdalena of wise black leaders dating from the apostolic era. He mentioned elsewhere that Magdalena, like Estefanía, would preach in the streets and plazas, calling people to repentance; during these moments, she was capable of transforming someone's "heart of bronze" into "soft wax," channeling the divine grace granted to her into converting others.[96]

The tension between inner and outer remained a consistent theme in the hagiography of black saints whether male or female. It functioned on two levels – the first as part of the hagiographer's effort to remind his readers that color difference did not matter to God, and the second as an explanation of how the

---

[93] Santana, *Os dous atlantes*, 2:72–3.

[94] *A inclyta Virgem Santa Ifigenia Princeza do Reyno de Nubia, e religiosa Carmelita, de cor preta,* Biblioteca Nacional de Portugal, RES. 1353, c. 1701. The work is printed, but without any publication information. See also, Navia, *Sermón panegyrico-historico,* 55. Navia also compared her to Abigail, Ifigenia daughter of Agemenon, and Diana (p. 57).

[95] Contreras, *Sermón fúnebre,* 22: "ver una negra ruda, sin saver leer, explicar los Evangelios como savio Doctor. En essa Santa Sacristia explicò la parabola del Thesoro Escondido como un Santo Padre de la Iglesia."

[96] Contreras, *Sermón fúnebre,* 12.

cultivation of spiritual practice opened the soul to divine gifts. In some ways, the experiences of women of color paralleled white women – both were viewed with skepticism by the male clergy, subject to more scrutiny, and more likely than their male counterparts to be silenced. But women of color faced significantly greater obstacles than white women in efforts to gain footholds into religious life. Most black women in Spanish America who lived in convents did so as slaves and servants; those who achieved higher status were almost all relegated to the lower status positions. And all were subject to prejudice, exclusion, and abuse by the nuns of the convent. Yet such obstacles did not prevent some women of color from attaining reputations for heroic virtue and enhanced sanctity that continued long after their deaths. The elevation of official black saints and their images helped to normalize living black saints, despite the fact that rigid hierarchies and racial prejudice created obstacles that could not be overcome, and the white reception of black holy people could not be separated from white supremacy. Yet the presence of obstacles and racist ideology should not elide the remarkable individuals who died in the odor of sanctity and the traces they have left us of their own subjectivities.

Violets and Crows

One of the most powerful proclamations of the dignity and beauty of African-descended people in Iberia comes from a manuscript letter written by an anonymous black author to the nuns of a convent, which today survives in the Biblioteca Nacional de España.[97] It provides another glimpse into ways a black person could defend the human dignity of Afro-Iberians, in a much more direct way than what we find in Úrsula's diary. Name, place, and date are unrecorded in the document, although it is tentatively dated to the seventeenth century. It is an odd text, written by a person of education – it contains more classical references than Christian ones – but its ultimate audience and intention are unclear, since the only discernable motivation to write it seems to be to denounce the nuns for their mistreatment of the (black) author.[98]

Glyn Redworth suggests through paleographic evidence that the author of the piece was a man, in spite of its listing in the catalog as being by a woman. Yet it is difficult to see what relationship an educated black man would have had with

---

[97] BNE, MS 6149 "Papeles históricos-políticos" (Siglos XVI-XVII), n. 83, f. 236r-37v.

[98] Glyn Redworth supplies a short study of the letter, addressing issues of authorship and audience: "Mythology with Attitude." Redworth includes a transcription of the original as well as an English translation in the appendices of the article. As with Úrsula's diary, my analysis of the letter comes from the BNE MS 6149 original, but I will cite Redworth's English translation.

cloistered nuns. In the unlikely event the male author was a member of the clergy, the content of the letter would be quite unusual. The problem to be resolved, then, is not merely one of whether or not Spanish nuns would have had black slaves or servants, but which black individuals might have had both proximity to nuns and to some form of literary and scriptural education. The author's social and legal status is unknown, but the early discussion of the nuns' "kindness" suggests a relationship of some intimacy.[99] The question of gender might never be completely resolved. As a result, in the discussion below I make use of the gender-neutral pronouns "they" and "their" in reference to the author.

The letter manifests both rhetorical sophistication and lack of refinement. For example, the composition mirrors central rhetorical features of early modern polemics, including a self-effacing preface and the movement from classical to natural to scriptural evidence. Yet within that progression, the author occasionally veers from one subject to another in ways that interrupt the flow of the argument.[100] While the author proclaimed that the purpose of the letter was to decry mistreatment from the nuns, they did not complain or lament – instead, they mounted a rigorous defense of black as a color and of black people as a demeaned group of people. In spite of the required protestations of unworthiness and ignorance that were the standard beginning of early modern works, the authorial voice here is strong. They declared that the corrective provided in the letter was "sunlight" that would prove painful for "dim eyes."[101]

Like the authors for Magdalena's funeral sermon, this author reminded their readers that black was the most prestigious of all colors. They then launched into a series of examples of black objects and individuals that were esteemed and valorized in classical mythology, including the horses that drove the chariot of the Moon goddess, the son of the goddess of dawn, whom the author claimed was black, and the god Pluto himself. In contrast, the only biblical black people they highlighted were Moses's wife – described here only as "Ethiopian" – and the bride from the Song of Songs. Yet the bulk of their defense of blackness centered on comparing black people to animals, fruit, and other objects.

They began the portion on flowers by comparing white and black violets. The white is poisonous, while the black, with its sweet fragrance, could be made into

---

[99] As we have seen, Bermúdez mentioned a *mulato* Dominican, Cristóbal de Menses, whom Bermúdez calls "father," that is, priest, in his work published in 1608. The possibility of the author as a male clergy – either secular or religious – must, therefore, be considered as well.

[100] Redworth discusses a few of the errors and rhetorical skill in the letter: "Mythology with Attitude," 55–9.

[101] Redworth, "Mythology with Attitude." For the original, see BNE, MS 6179, 236r.

medicine. The black, they concluded, was the antidote to the poison of the white. Rather than merely being prettier or sweeter-smelling, the black flower heals what the white flower destroys. The author not only praised blackness, but denounced whiteness as a kind of poison. In a similar way, the author described black mulberries as delicious, while the white and red berries were dangerous to people, "fit only for pigs and animals." In both the examples of berries and of violets, blackness is a marker for beauty, health, and healing. It is not only worthy in its own right, but superior to whiteness.[102]

Other examples of the natural world included a black ram sacrificed, burning coals, a crow (appearing three times), smoke, dark wine, and enameling on gold jewelry. In most of these examples, the black object or animal acts as the vehicle that enacts a miracle. In the case of coal, for example, the author explained that Isaiah's scabrous lips were healed by a piece of burning coal. Here again, we see the healing power of blackness; it cures, and eases suffering. Perhaps more importantly, the author explained that a black object illuminated with divine power had the power to aid a prophet in his ability to speak God's word. But then the author pivoted. While elsewhere, they proclaimed black as a "majestic" color, at the end of the letter they pointed out instead that outward beauty was not a marker for interior virtue. Here they provided a series of examples where what one sees on the outside does not correspond to the inside: a tomb with a rotting corpse within, a pretty but venomous snake, a chestnut in a prickly husk, and a simple shell holding a pearl.[103]

Although it seemed like a change of approach in the last section, to suggest that it was only the interior that mattered, sidelining blackness – the author had a more complex purpose. Following the logic of the author's denunciation of the nuns' disparagement, they provided the examples of corpses and snakes as subtle reminders to the nuns that their own exterior whiteness and status did not render them inherently virtuous. The lack of consistency between inside and outside destabilizes white supremacy, and acts as a lesson to the nuns to adjust their perceptions, rather than an expression of the author's own doubts or uncertainties about their worthiness. Here we see plainly the presentation of rhetorical tropes circulating in hagiographies of black saints and holy people throughout the same period. Yet the author does not engage in apologetics as hagiographers did. On the contrary, they mount a vigorous and powerful defense of hirself as worthy of respect and dignity. Reading this letter alongside Úrsula de Jesús's diary provides us startling and important glimpses at what a black-authored early modern hagiography might have looked like, in sharp contrast to the examples we have examined from white writers.

---

[102] BNE, MS 6179, 237r.   [103] BNE, MS 6179, 237v.

Conclusion

The rapid circulation of cults of black saints in the Iberian Atlantic through confraternal devotion and prominent images disseminated ideas about blackness and sanctity connected to slavery and universal salvation. While such discourses from the clergy could encourage passivity and proper service to a master (particularly in the accounts of Antonio da Noto's life), they also provided official recognition of black sanctity, as well as complex intersections of blackness and holiness. Clerical grappling with the "problem" of explaining how a black person could become a saint exposes their entrenched prejudice and reveals the polysemous nature of blackness in early modern European discourses. As hagiographers of black saints reshaped ideas about blackness, the soul, and the body, enslaved and free people could also adopt them in order to claim public space, ecclesiastical privileges, and even certain kinds of civic and legal opportunities. Beyond the social and cultural aspects of Christianity, Afro-Iberians occasionally practiced intense piety that gave meaning to their lives, for which they could be recognized by those around them as infused with divine grace.

Through their devotion to Benedict, enslaved and free people of color in the Iberian Atlantic supplied the most persuasive arguments in favor of Benedict's beatification by the turn of the eighteenth century, contributing to its success in 1743. Introduced as a method of encouraging devotion among newly enslaved Africans, cults of black saints spread widely and quickly in a Church straining for global reach and new sources of holiness. Though black saints were promoted for and by black Catholics, their appeal extended to white clergy and laity. The laity in particular were happy in many places to venerate black saints and to participate in important black confraternities, while simultaneously appropriating both, depriving them of their radical potential. The knot at the center of the entangled histories of black saints and sanctity was created by the idealization of black saints and the horrors of slavery and entrenched racism that people of color experienced daily. They cannot be separated from one another, and both demand recognition, just as the works of extraordinary art that they brought forth demand to be seen at last.

AFTERLIFE

"The hereafter is a hustle." – *Jesse Williams*

The memory of black confraternities has faded into obscurity in both Spain and Portugal. The surviving images, like the history of peninsular slavery itself, have gone largely unseen and unevenly studied, particularly in Portugal; parishioners worshipping in churches containing black sculptures often do not see them, let alone venerate them. Even when an image is recognized as being black, local traditions sometimes emerged to explain away the saint's blackness. In northern Portugal, for example, a church in the town of Fão houses a sculpture of Efigenia in a small museum, which also sold a guide to the church's sacred art. The author of this guide knew nothing about the saint – even misspelling her name ("Frigénia") – so he appealed to local residents for information, which resulted in the following account: The saint had been a beautiful young woman, pursued by many men, but she wanted to become a nun instead of getting married. Like so many holy women before her, the young woman appealed to God to help her by making her ugly; God granted her prayer by making her black, thus "disfiguring her beautiful face."[1] [**Plate 78**] The guide, published in 2000, tells us something significant about contemporary ideas about blackness circulating in Portugal and Spain, and opens up many questions about what contemporary Iberians see – or do not see – when they look at the sacred images of black saints in their midst. Or do not see, as was also commonly the case in my travels.

One region with a contemporary devotion to black saints in Iberia is Galicia, where one can find vibrant devotion to Benedict in small towns in the west and south. One Galician woman in Santiago de Compostela told me that Benedict was "beloved [*muy querido*] in Galicia." In many of these towns, Benedict's feast is regularly celebrated in early May or during Holy

---

[1] Mariz, *A Santa Casa*, 53. I imagine that the author was unable to find information about the saint because he was looking for "Frigénia" rather than Efigénia.

Week, during which his image is taken out on procession.[2] [Fig. A.1] Galicia's enduring connection to black saints is mysterious, but it is most likely no accident that devotion to black saints among white laity persisted in an Iberian region where there were few enslaved people or free people of color (as best we know). The cults of black saints might then have disentangled the saints from the legacy of slavery.

Efigenia's feast day is also celebrated by a cluster of towns on the western coast of Galicia. In this case, the image is housed in a private chapel on an estate, called a *pazo*. This tiny chapel is open to the public only one day per year when her image is taken out on procession for her feast day, which is attended by hundreds of people from nearby villages. The origins of the sculpture are murky; its provenance is eighteenth century but whether or not veneration of the image has been consistent over time is less clear. But today her cult is vibrant, evinced both by the annual procession and the ex-voto chains that hang on her arm, largely silver fish, reflecting the local fishing economy. [**Plate 79**] When I first approached someone about viewing the image, I was told that St. Efigenia was not black – meaning racially black – but that she was painted black as a symbol of the smoke from the fire in the convent. The custodian who showed me around the chapel, however, knew that Efigenia was an Ethiopian princess, suggesting that local knowledge about the saint was accurate. But we can also see how communal memories can fashion and refashion the meaning of the saints.[3]

Such instances highlight why it is so important to tell the story of black saints in Iberia, where communities (and national narratives) struggle with their history of slavery and the vibrant black communities that have existed from the late Middle Ages to present day. Portugal's participation in the UNESCO initiative, "The Route of Slavery," manifests largely in museums with objects connected to or representing black Africans with a tag labeled "*Rota do Escravo*." While bringing to light the long history of slavery throughout Europe remains a vital task, the presence of this initiative in the absence of diverse representations of people of color leaves the (white) viewer with the impression that all black Africans were enslaved, erasing the presence of free people of color and their contributions. More awareness is needed regarding

---

[2] I learned about these processions from Galician newspapers reporting about them: www.paxinasga legas.es/fiestas/san-benito-de-palermo-ponteareas-9158.html (Ponteareas); www.farodevigo.es/comarcas/2017/05/07/angoares-celebra-fiestas-san-benito/1674259.html (Angoares); and www.plataformadigitaldefiestas.com/fiestas-meano/5341-fiestas-san-benito-palermo-covas.html (Covas).

[3] I heard similar anecdotes of Benedict's blackness resulting from the (presumably white) saint's work in the kitchen from several people regarding Brazil.

Figure A.1 Standard of St. Benedict. Cambados, Spain.

the many impact Afro-Iberians have had on language, music, dance, cuisine, and religious practice.[4]

---

[4] There are important grassroots efforts in Portugal to advocate for the past, present, and future of Afro-Portuguese communities, including Djass – Associação de Afrodescendentes and the Museu Digital Afroportugues. See https://museudigitalafroportugues.wordpress.com/. See also recent important scholarly contributions: Goldberg, *Sonidos Negros*.

Not surprisingly, the most vibrant surviving cults of black saints exist in present-day Latin America. They are particularly widespread in Brazil and Venezuela, and more limited in Peru (focused particularly on Cañete, where she is celebrated as the patron saint of Afro-Peruvians). With the exception of the United States, places that today maintain vibrant African-diasporic communities sometimes channel their expression of that identity through Catholicism, particularly a Catholicism deeply intertwined with African ideas, practices, and music, which in turns creates and recreates unique cultural forms.[5]

Upon receiving the BET Humanitarian Award of 2016, actor and activist Jesse Williams delivered a powerful speech to his predominantly black audience, addressing the struggle for justice in the midst of the Black Lives Matter movement and in the wake of high profile deaths of African-American men and women at the hands of law enforcement. In spite of the centuries separating Williams's words from the events discussed in this book, his words about repeated promises to the black community resonated like the perfect coda for the history of black saints: "Freedom is always coming in the hereafter. But, you know what, though, the hereafter is a hustle."[6] The saints, of course, represent the highest spiritual ideals, and early modern clergy insisted to its enslaved audience that their suffering would be the vehicle for real salvation, achievable only after death. Members of clergy did not think of themselves as hustlers – they deeply believed that the miseries of the present would be healed only by the eternal embrace of God in the afterlife. Yet their beliefs and deeds informed the very foundations of colonialism and structural racism.

Black communities, however, were not the passive listeners clergy imagined they should be. The second half of Williams's declaration "The hereafter is a hustle" was "We want it now." Members of black confraternities never accepted an image of patient waiting for the hereafter. They freed and defended the enslaved in their midst, actively working to ameliorate the lives of themselves and their living brothers and sisters (as well as their dead, through dignified burial and memorialization). Many found their own comfort and meaning in Christianity while elevating saints of color to universal cults, and others turned their backs on Christianity altogether, forging new religious practices out of cultural memory and the crucible of slavery.

---

[5] Suárez, *El culto de San Benito de Palermo*; Luna Obregón, *Efigenia, la negra santa*; and, for an examination of Afro-Catholic music and dance in Brazil, Iyanaga, "Why Saints Love Samba."

[6] www.bet.com/video/betawards/2016/acceptance-speeches/jesse-williams-receives-humanitarian-award.html.

Black saints stand in the ambivalent space between the Church's vision of sacrifice and continuing Afro-Iberian resistance to their enslavement and discrimination. Black saints did not substantially transform the lives of early modern black people, enslaved or free. They did not upend colonial hierarchies or end the slave trade, which thrived in Brazil well into the nineteenth century, nor did they mitigate the entrenched color prejudices that persist in Iberia and throughout Latin America. Yet cults of black saints did provide channels for deep spiritual expression, protection, cultural and linguistic preservation, and acts of profound creativity. They further helped to produce a discourse of the equality of souls that could be mobilized by Afro-Iberians as they sought to fight for their rights to civic life, justice, and freedom.

BIBLIOGRAPHY

Archives Consulted

Madrid
Biblioteca Nacional de España (BNE)
Archivo Histórico Nacional (AHN)

Seville
Archivo General de Indias (AGI)
Archivo Arzobispal de Sevilla (APAS)
Archivo Catedralicio de Sevilla (ACS)

Cadiz
Archivo Diocesano (ADC)
Archivo Municipal (AMC)

Rome
Archivio Segreto Vaticano (ASV)
Biblioteca Apostolica Vaticana (BAV)
Archivio Storico di Propaganda Fide (APF)
Archivum Romanum Societatis Iesu (ARSI)

Palermo
Biblioteca Comunale di Palermo (BCP)
Bilbioteca Centrale della Regione Siciliana (BCRS)

Lisbon
Arquivo Nacional da Torre do Tombo (ANTT)
Biblioteca Nacional de Portugal (BNP)
Arquivo Histórico Ultramarino (AHU)

Lima
Archivo Arzobispal de Lima (AAL)

Washington, DC
Oliveira Lima Library, Catholic University of America

New York City
New York City Public Library, Schomburg Center for Research in Black Culture (NYPL-
Schomburg)

Printed Primary Sources

"A Black *Irmandade* in Bahia Brazil," in *Colonial Latin America*, ed. Kenneth Mills,
William B. Taylor, and Sandra Lauderdale Graham (Wilmington, DE: Scholarly
Resources, 2002), 280–89.

Aixalà i Gassol, Jaume, *Vida portentosa, heroicas virtuts, y estupendos Miracles
del molt insigne Sicilà: lo Beato Benet de Palermo, dit vulgarment lo Santo
Negro, fruyt molt preclar de la Religiò Franciscana* (Gerona: Juame Bròo,
1757).

Ajofrín, Francisco de, *Diario del viaje que por orden de la Sagrada Congregación de
Propaganda Fide hizo a la America septentrional en el siglo XVIII)*, ed.
Vicente Castañeda y Alcocer and Bonifacio Castellanos, 2 vols. (Madrid: Maestre,
1958).

Anguiano, Mateo de, *Misiones capuchinas en África*, 2 vols. (Madrid: Consejo Superior
de Investigaciones Científicas, 1950–1957).

Alacoque, Margaret Mary, *Letters*, trans. Clarenca A. Herbst and intro. J. J. Doyle
(Chicago: Henry Regnery Company, 1954).

Alegambe, Philippo, *Mortes ilustres et gesta eorum de Societate Iesu...* (Rome:
Typographia Varseli, 1657).

Alegambe, Philippo, and Pedro de Ribadeneira, *Bibliotecha Scriptorum Societatis Iesu*
(Antwerp: Ioannem Meursium, 1643).

Alegre de Casante, Marco Antonio, *Paradisus Carmelitiei decoris* (Leiden: Iacobi and
Petri Prost, 1639).

Almeida, Manoel de, and Baltasar Tellez, *Historia geral de Ethiopia a Alta ou Preste
Ioam, e do que nella obraram os Padres da Companhia de Iesus...* (Coimbra:
Manoel Dias, 1660).

Álvarez, Diego, *Sombra ilustrada con la razon, demonstracion, y verdad, admirable vida,
virtues, y milagros de el Beato Benito de San Fradello* (Alcala: Maria Garcia
Briones, 1747).

Andrade, Alonso de, *Vida del venerable y apostolico Padre Pedro Claver de la Compañia
de Iesus* (Madrid: Maria de Quiñones, 1657).

Andrés de Guadalupe, *Historia de la Santa Provincia de los Ángeles (1662)*, intro. and ed.
Hermenegildo Zamora Jambrina (Madrid: Editorial Cisneros, 1994).

Anguiano, Mateo de, *Misiones capuchinas en África*, 2 vols. (Madrid: Consejo Superior
de Investigaciones Científicas, 1950–1957).

Antonio Vicente de Madrid, *El negro más prodigioso: vida portentosa del Beato Benito de
San Philadelphia, ó de Palermo* (Madrid: Antonio Sanz, 1744).

Apolinário da Conceiçao, *Flor perigrina por preta ou nova maravilha da gracia.
Descuberta na prodigiosa vida do B Benedicto de S. Philadelfio* (Lisbon, 1744).

Arenal, Electa, and Stacey Schlau, ed., *Untold Sisters: Hispanic Nuns in Their Own Works*, rev. ed. (Albuquerque: University of New Mexico Press, 2010).

Aristizábal Giraldo, Tulio, and Anna María Splendiani, eds., *Proceso de beatificación y canonización de San Pedro Claver* (Bogota: Universidad Javeriana, 2002).

Barbado de la Torre y Angulo, Manuel, *Compendio historico, lego seraphico. Fundacion de la Orden de los Menores* (Madrid: Joseph Gonzalez, 1745).

Bayão, José Pereira, *Historia das prodigiosas vidas dos gloriosos sanctos Antonio e Benedicto, maior honra e lustre da gente preta* (Lisbon: Pedro Ferreira, 1726).

Beckford, William, *The Journal of William Beckford in Portugal and Spain, 1787–1788*, ed. and intro. Boyd Alexander (London: Hart-Davis, 1954).

Benegasi y Luján, José Joaquín, *Vida del portentoso negro, San Benito de Palermo* (Madrid: Juan de San Martín, 1750).

Bermúdez de Pedraza, Francisco, *Historia eclesiástica de Granada [1608]*, ed. facs (Granada: Servicio de Publicaciones, Universidad de Granada, 1989).

Bernard of Clairvaux, *Sermons sur le Cantique*, ed. and trans. Paul Verdeyen and Raffaele Fassetta, 2 vols. (Paris: Éditions du Cerf, 1998).

Brásio, António, ed., *Monumenta missionária Africana*, 12 vols. (Lisbon: Agência Geral do Ultramar, 1958–1989).

Budge, E. A. Wallis, ed., *The Sayings and Stories of the Christian Fathers of Egypt: The Paradise of the Holy Fathers*, vol. 2 (London: Kegan Paul, 2002).

Cadornega, António de Oliveira de, and José Matias Delgado, *História geral das guerras angolanas [1680]* (Lisbon: Agência-Geral do Ultramar, 1972).

Cartagena, Juan de, *Dos tratados de la sagrada antiguedad del Orden de la Bienuenturada Virgen Maria del Monte Carmelo*, trans. Geronimo Pancoruo (Sevilla: Iuan Serrano de Vargas y Vreña, 1623).

Cassaneus, Bartholomeus, *Cassaneus Catalogi gloriae mundi (1506)* (Frankfurt: Sigismundi Feyerbendij, 1579).

Castellano, Francisco Antonio, *Compendio de la heroyca, y maravillosa vida, virtudes excelentes, y prodigiosos Milagros del major negro por naturaleza* (Murcia: Felipe Diaz Cayuelas, 1752).

Catalogus generalis sanctorum qui in Martyrologio Romano non sunt (Venice: Jo. Guerilium, 1625).

Cieza de León, Pedro de, *Crónica del Perú, tercera parte*, ed. Francesca Cantú (Lima: Pontificia Universidad Católica del Perú, 1989).

Colmenero, Francisco, *El Carmelo ilustrado con favores de la Reyna de los Angeles* (Valladolid: Athansio y Antonio Figueroa, 1754).

Contreras, Pedro de, *Sermón fúnebre en las honras de la venerable Magdalena de la Cruz, negra de nación, que se celebraron en el real convento, Casa Grande, de el Real, y Militar Orden de nuestra señora de la Merced, Redempcion de Cautivo* (Seville: Los Gómez, 1735).

Córdova y Salinas, Diego de, and Lino Gómez Canedo, *Crónica franciscana de las provincias del Perú (1651)* (Washington: Academy of American Franciscan History, 1957).

Covarrubias Orozco, Sebastián de, *Tesoro de la lengua castellana, o española [1611]*, ed. Felipe Maldonado and Manuel Camarero (Madrid: Editorial Casalia, 1994).

Croiset, Jean, *La devocion al Sagrado Corazon de Jesus: medio no menos poderoso que suave para assegurar la salvacion en todo genero de estados* (Pamplona: Joseph Joachin Martinez, 1734).

Daza, Antonio, *Quarta parte de la chronica general de Nuestra Padre San Francisco y su Apostolica Orden* (Valladolid: Juan Godinez and Diego de Cordoba, 1611).

Defensa juridica por la cofradia de N. Sra de la Salud, San Benedicto de Palermo, y Santa Efigenia, sita en la auxiliar Iglesia del Rosario de Cadiz, en los Autos con los curas, y mayordomos de fabricas de ella, sobre restitucion de unas Alhajas (Seville: Imprenta de la Universidad, 1760).

Devoto aparato, en el que desea manifestar su veneracion, y afecto a la serenissima reynos de los cielos Maria Santissima del Rosario nuestra Señora y Madre en la solemne procession, que su ilustrissima Confraternidad... de la muy Noble, y muy leal Ciudad de Eciha (Cordoba: Antonio Serrano y Diego Rodríguez, 1761).

Diamante, Juan Bautista, *Comedias de Fr. Don Iuan Buatista Diamente: El negro más prodigioso* (Madrid: Poque Rico de Miranda, 1674).

Don Christoval de Pastor, presbytero, Notario, mayor, Secretario de el Oficio de Apelaciones, Breves, y Comissiones Apostolicas en esta Ciudad de Sevilla, y su Arzobispo: Certifico, que Autos se han seguido en tercera instancia ante el Sr. Doctor D. Joseph Ignacio Delgado y Ayala, ...entre la Hermandad de Nuestra Señora de la Salud, San Benedicto, y Santa Efigenia (Seville, 1762).

Diogo do Rosário, *Flos sanctorum, historia das vidas de Christo N.S. e de sua Santissima Madre. Vidas dos santos e suas destas* (Lisbon: Antonio Craesbeeck de Mello, 1681).

Dorado, Bernardo, *Compendio historico de la ciudad de Salamanca: su antigüedad, de la de su Santa Iglesia, su fundación y grandezas, que la ilustran* (Salamanca: Juan Antonio de Lasanta, 1776).

Espinosa, Isidro Félix de, *El lunar agraciado del rostro de la Iglesia el Negro Hermoso entre las candidezes de los santos, el milagroso y poco conocido portento San Benito de Palermo...* (Mexico: Viuda de don J. B. de Hoal, 1745).

Feijoo, Benito Jerónimo, *Theatro Crítico Universal o discursos varios en todo genero de errores communes*, 9 vols. (Madrid: Los herederos de Francisco Hierro, 1726–1740).

Fernández, Joseph, *Apostolica y penitente vida de el VP Pedro Claver de la Compañía de Iesus* (Zaragoza: Diego Dormer, 1666).

Ferrari, Filippo. *Catalogus generalis sanctorum qui in Martyrologio Rom. non sunt* (Venice: Guerilium, 1625).

Fiume, Giovanna, and Marilena Modica, eds., *San Bendetto il Moro: santità, agiografia e primi processi di canonizzazione* (Palermo: Biblioteca Comunale, 1998).

Francisco José de Jaca, *Resolución sobre la libertad de los negros u sus originarios, en estado de paganos y después ya cristianos: la primera condena de la esclavitud en el pensamiento dispano*, ed. Miguel Anxo Pena González (Madrid: CSIC, 2002).

Frías de Albornoz, Bartolomé, *Arte de los contratos* (Valencia: Casa de Pedro de Huete, 1573).

Gardellini, Aloisio, *Sacra Rituum Congregatione... ponente Panormitana canonizationis Beati Benedicti a San Philadelphio...* (Rome: Rev. Camerae Apostolicae, 1780).

Gerónimo de la Concepción, *Emporio del Orbe. Cádiz Ilustrada* (Amsterdam, 1690).

Giordano, Rosalia Claudia, ed., *San Benedetto il Moro: il Memoriale del Rubbiano e l'Ordinaria inquisitio del 1594* (Palermo: Città di Palermo Biblioteca Comunale, 2002).

Giovanni, Vincenzo di, *Palermo restaurato [1614]* (Palermo: Sellerio, 1989).

Godínez, Felipe, "San Mateo en Etiopia: Comedia famosa del doctor Felipe Godínez," in *Part Veinte y ocho de comedias nueuas de los mejores ingenios deste corte* (Madrid: Viuda de Francisco de Robles, 1667).

Gómez de la Parra, José, *Fundación y primero siglo: Crónica del primer convento de carmelitas descalzes en Puebla, 1604–1704*, intro. Manuel Ramos Medina (Mexico City: Universidad Iberoamericana, 1992).

Gubernatis, Domincus, *Orbis seraphicvs. Historia de tribvs ordinibvs a seraphico patriarcha S. Francisco institvtis... [1689]*, ed. Teofilo Domenichelli (Rome: S. Caballi, 1886).

Guijo, Gregorio M. de, *Diario, 1648–1664* (Mexico City: Editorial Porrúa, 1952).

Gumilla, José, *El Orinoco ilustrado: historia natural, civil y geographica de este gran rio, y de sus caudalosas vertientes* (Madrid: Manuel Fernandez, 1741).

Henríquez de la Jorquera, Francisco, *Anales de Granada: descripción del Reino y Ciudad de Granada: crónica de la Reconquista [1646]* (Granada: Universidad de Granada, 1987).

Horozco, Agustín de, *Historia de Cádiz [1598]*, ed. and intro. Arturo Morgado García (Cadiz: Universidad de Cádiz, 2000).

Houchins, Sue E., and Baltasar Fra-Molinero, eds. and trans., *Black Bride of Christ: Chicaba, an African Nun in Eighteenth-Century Spain* (Nashville: Vanderbilt University Press, 2018).

Hudson, William V, *Theatine Spirituality: Selected Writings* (New York: Paulist Press, 1996).

Jerónimo del Concepción, *Emporio de el Orbe, Cádiz Ilustrada, investigaciones de sus antiguas Grandezas discurrida en Concurso de el general Imperio de España...* (Amsterdam: Joan Bus: 1690).

José de Santa Teresa, *Flores del Carmelo: vidas de los santos de Nuestra Señora del Carmen* (Madrid: Antonio Gonçalez de Reyes, 1678).

Juan de Loyola, *Thesoro Escondido en el ... Corazon de Jesus, descubierto a nuestra España en la breve noticia de su culto* (Madrid: Manuel Fernandez, 1736).

Vida de el dulcissimo director de las almas S. Francisco de Sales, obispo y principe de Géneva, y fundador de la orden de la Visitacion de Santa Maria (Madrid: Manuel Fernandez, 1735).

Konetzke, Richard, ed., *Colección de documentos para la historia de la formación social de hispanoamerica, 1493–1810*, vol. 2 (Madrid: CSIC, 1958).

Languet de Gergy, Jean-Joseph, *Historia de la devoción al Sagrado Corazon de Jesus, en la vida de madre Margarita Maria, religiosa de la Visitacion* (Salamanca: Villagordo, 1738).

Leon Pinelo, Antonio de, *Epitome de la Biblioteca Oriental i Occidental, Nautica i Geografica* (Madrid: Juan González, 1629).

Lobo, Jerónimo, *The Itinerário of Jerónimo Lobo*, ed. Charles Beckingham and trans. James Lockhart (London: The Hakluyt Society, 1984).

Maffei, Giovanni Pietro, *Historiarum indicarum libri XVI* (Antwerp: Martini Nuntii, 1605).

Manrique, Alonso, "Marabilla de la cardidad perfecta," in *Retrato de perfeccion cristiana en las vidas de los Ves. P. Fr. Vicente Bernedo, Fr. Juan Macias y Fr. Martin de Porres* (Venice: Fr. Gropo, 1696).

Manoel de Esperança, *Historia serafica da Ordem dos frades menores de S. Francisco na provincia de Portugal* (Lisbon: Craesbeeck de Melo, 1656).

Martínez Delgado, Francisco, *Historia de la ciudad de Medina Sidonia* (Cadiz: Revista Medica, 1875).

Martínez López, Enrique. *Tablero de ajedrez: imagenes del negro heroico en la comedia española y en la literatura e iconografía sacra del Brasil esclavista* (Paris: Centre culturel Calouste Gulbenkian, 1998).

Martyrologio romano: reformado conforme a la nueua razon del kalendario y verdad de la historia ecclesiastica (Salamanca: Diego Fernandez de Cordoua, 1586).

Martyrologium romanum: ad nouam Kalendrii rationem et ecclesiasticae historiae veritatem restitum (Antwerp: Christophori Plantini, 1589).

Marzo, Gioacchino, ed., *Diario della Città di Palermo da' manoscritti di Filippo Paruta e di Niccolò Palmerino, 1500–1613*, Biblioteca storica e letteraria di Sicilia ossia raccolta di opere inedite o rare di scrittori siciliani da secolo XVI a XIX, vol. 1 (Palermo: Luigi Pedone Lauriel, 1869).

Mataplanes, Pedro de, *Vida de Fray Benito de S. Fradelo religioso recolto de la orden de S. Francisco, comunmente nombrado el santo Negro* (Madrid, 1702).

Matos, Diego de, *Copia de una carta que el Padre Diego de Matos de la Compañía de Jesús... en que da cuenta á su Paternidad del estado de la conversión á la verdadera Religión Christiana... del gran Imperio de Etiopia...* (Madrid: Luis Sánchez, 1624).

McKnight, Kathryn Joy, and Leo Garofalo, eds., *Afro-Latino Voices: Narratives from the Early Modern Ibero-Atlantic World, 1550–1812* (Indianapolis, IN: Hackett, 2009).

Medina, Bernardo de, *Vida prodigiosa del Venerable Siervo de Dios Fr. Martin de Porras; natural de Lima, de la Tercera Orden de No. P. Santo Domingo* (Lima: Juan de Queuedo, 1673).

Mendel Bernardo and Antonio Santamaría, *Novena del prodigioso San Benito de Palermo, llamado comunmente el Santo Negro...* (Buenos Aires: Real Impr. De los Niños Expósitos, 1782).

Mercado, Tomás de, *Suma de tratos y contratos* (Seville: Hernando Diaz, 1571).

Mesa Xinete, Francisco, *Historia de la muy noble y muy lead ciudad de Tarteso, Turdeto, Ásta Regia, Asido Cesariana, Asidonia Gera, Jerez Sidonia, hoy Jerez de la Frontera*, 2 vols. (Jerez: Melchor Garcia Ruíz, 1888).

Monumenta Historica Societatis Iesu (MHSI), *Litterae quadrimestres ex universis praeter Indiam et Brasiliam locis...*, 7 vols. (Madrid: Augustinus Avrial, 1894–1932).

Mills, Kenneth, William B. Taylor, and Sandra Lauderdale Graham, eds., *Colonial Latin America: A Documentary History* (Wilmington, DE: Scholarly Resources, 2002).

Muñoz de Gálvez, Juan, *Carta del Padre Iuan Muñoz de Galvez para los superiores y religiosos sobre la muerte y virtudes del P. Diego Ruiz de Montoya* (Seville, 1632).

Myers, Kathleen, ed. and intro., *Word from New Spain: The Spiritual Autobiography of Madre María de San José (1656–1719)* (Liverpool: Liverpool University Press, 1993).

Natalibus, Petrus de, *Catalogus sanctorum: vitas, passiones et miracula commodissime annectens....* (Lyons: Nolaum Petit & Hectorem Penet, 1534).

Navia, Joseph de, *Sermon panegyrico-historico en la solemne colocacion de los dos santos negros carmelitas San Elesban, Emperador de los Abysinos... llamada vulgarmente Preste Juan... y Sta Ifigenia, Princesa de Nubia... que celebrò el Convento de Carmelitas Calzados de la Ciudad de Avila...* (Salamanca: Eugenio Garcia Honoratio, 1753).

Newitt, M. D. D, ed., *The Portuguese in West Africa, 1415–1670: A Documentary History* (Cambridge; New York: Cambridge University Press, 2010).

Novena al portentoso negro del major amo, blanco que debe ser de la christiana devoción S. Benedicto de Filadelfio, o de Palermo (Mexico: los Herederos de Doña Maria de Riberia, 1767).

Novena en honra de la gloriosa Virgen, y esclarecida Emperatriz de la Etiopia Santa Efigenia, para impetrar por sus meritos el alivio, y socorro de nuestras necesidades (Mexico: Herederos del Lic. D. Joseph de Jaureni, 1784).

"Novena de los gloriosos etíopes San Esteban, emperador de Aquitania, y Santa Efigenia, Princesa de Ethiopía," in *Bibliografía de autores españoles del siglo XVIII, Tomo IX (Anónimos I),* ed. Francisco Aquilar Piñal (Madrid: CSIC, 1999), 549.

Oliden, Gaspar de, *Dialogos del Purgatorio, para examen de un libro, publicado con el titulo: Defensa de doctos, y armas contra Imprudentes* (Alcalá, 1732).

Ortiz y Zúñiga, Diego, *Anales eclesiásticos y seglares de la muy noble, y muy leal ciudad de Sevilla* (Madrid: Juan Garcia Infançon, 1677).

Owens, Sarah E., ed. and trans., *Journey of Five Capuchin Nuns* (Toronto: Center for Reformation and Renaissance studies, 2009).

Pacheco, Francisco de, *El arte de la pintura*, ed. Bonaventura Bassegoda i Hugas, 2nd ed. (Madrid: Catedra Ediciones, 2001).

Paniagua, Juan Carlos, *Compendio de la vida exemplar de la venerable madre Sor Teresa Juliana de Sto. Domingo, tercera professa en el convento de Santa Maria Magdalena, vulga de la Penitencia...* (Salamanca: Eugenia Garcia de Honora y S. Miguel, 1752).

   Oración fúnebre en las Exequias de la Madre Sor Teresa Juliana de Santo Domingo, de feliz memoria, celebradas en el día nueve de enero en el Convento de Religiosas Dominicas, vulga de la Penitencia (Salamanca: Eugenia Garcia de Honora y S. Miguel, 1749).

Pineda, Juan de, *Los treynta libros de la Monarchia Ecclesiastica, o Historia Universal del mundo, diuididos en cinco tomos* (Salamanca: Casa de Juan Fernandez, 1588).

Pirri, Rocco, *Notiae Sicilensium ecclesiarum Philippo IIII Hispaniarum et Siciliae regi Catholico dicatae,* 2 vols. (Palermo: Ioannis Baptistae Maringhi, 1630–1633).

   Sicilia Sacra, seu Notitae Siciliensium Ecclesiarum, Abbatiarum, Prioratuum, etc., 3 vols. (Palermo: Joannis Baptistae Maringhim, 1630–1644).

Ramos, Alonso, *Primera parte de los prodigios de la omnipotencia y Milagros de la gracia en la vida de la venerable sierva de Dios Catarina de San Juan* (Puebla: Diego Fernandez de Leon, 1689).

Ribadeneira, Pedro de, *Flos sanctorum o libro de las vidas de los santos* (Madrid: Luis Sánchez, 1604).

Ribera, Francisco de, *Vida de Santa Teresa de Jesús (1590),* intro. P. Jaime Pons (Barcelona: Gustavo Gili, 1908).

Roa, Martín de, *Estados de los bienauenturados en el Cielo: de los niños en el Limbo, de las almas en el Purgatorio, de los condenados en el infierno, y de todo este uniuerso despues de la resurreccion y juizio uniuersal* (Madrid: Juan Sanchez, 1628).

Ruiz de Montoya, Diego, *Instruccion para remediar, y assegurar, quanto con la divina gracia fuere possible, que ninguno de los negros que viene de Guinea, Angola, y otras provincias de aquella costa de Africa, carezca del sagrado Baptismo* (Seville, 1614).

Santana, José Pereira de, *Os dous atlantes da Ethiopia, Santo Elesbaô Emperador XLVII da Abessina, e Santa Ifigenia Princeza de Nubia ambos Carmelitas*, 2 vols. (Lisbon: Antonio Pedrozo Galram, 1735–1738).

Sermão dos Santos pretos Carmelitas, Elesbaõ emperador da Abessina, e Ifigenia, Princeza da Nubia, que na solemne festa da collocacam das suas Sagradas Imagens, celebrada na Igreja do Real Convento de Nossa Senhora do Carmo de Lisboa Occidental... (Lisbon: Antonio Pedrozo Galram, 1735).

Chronica dos Carmelitas da antiga, e regular observancia nestes reynos de Portugal, Algarves e seus dominios (Lisbon: Officina dos Herdeiros de Antonio Pedrozo Galram, 1745–1751).

Sánchez, Pedro, *Libro del reyno de Dios, y del camino por do se alcança* (Madrid: Luis Sanchez, 1599).

Sandoval, Alonso de, *Naturaleza, policia sagrada i profana, costumbres i ritos, disciplina i catechismo evangelico de todos los etiopes* (Seville: Francisco de Lira, 1627).

De instauranda aethiopum salute. Historia de Aethiopia, naturaleza, policia sagrada y profana, costumbres, ritos y Cathecismo Evangelico, de todos los Ethiopes con que se restaura la salud de sus almas (Madrid: Alonso de Paredes, 1647).

Sozomen, *The Ecclesiastical History of Sozomen: Comprising a History of the Church from AD 324 to AD 440*, trans. Edward Walford (London: Henry G. Bohn, 1855).

Splendiani, Anna María, and Tulio Aristizábal Giraldo, eds. and trans., *Proceso de beatificación y canonización de San Pedro Claver* (Bogotá: Pontificia Universidad Javeriana, 2002).

Theophanes, *The Chronicle of Theophanes Confessor: Byzantine and Near Eastern History, AD 284–813*, trans. Cyril A. Mango and Robert Scott (New York: Oxford University Press, 1997).

Tognoletto, Pietro, *Paradiso serafico del fertilissimo Regno di Sicilia overo Cronica ove si tratta della origine della Riforma de' Minori* (Palermo: Domenico d'Anselmo, 1667).

Tormes, Lazarillo de, *La vida de Lazarillo de Tormes y de sus fortunas y aduersidades [1554]* ed. and intro. Julio Cejador y Frauca (Madrid: Espasa-Calpe, 1962).

Torquemada, Juan de, *I°-III° parte de los veynte y un libros rituales y monarchia Indiana: con el origin y guerras de los indios occidentales, de sus poblaciones, descubrimiento, conquista, conuersion y otras cosas marauillosas de la mesma tierra* (Seville: Mattias Clauijo, 1615).

Torres, Alonso de, *Chronica de la santa provincial de Granada, de la Regular Observancia de Nuestra Serafico Padre San Francisco* (Madrid: Iuan Garcia Infançon, 1683).

Torres y Villarroel, Diego de, *Vida exemplar del venerable padre D. Geronymo Abarrategui y Figeroa, clerigo regular theatino de S. Cayetano* (Salamanca: Antonio Villaroèl y Torres, 1749).

Urreta, Luis, *Historia eclesiástica, política, natural, y moral de los grandes y remotos reynos de la Etiopía, monarchia del Emperador llamado Preste Iuan de las Indias* (Valencia: Pedro Patricio Mey, 1610).

Úrsula de Jesús, *The Souls of Purgatory: The Spiritual Diary of a Seventeenth-Century Afro-Peruvian Mystic, Ursula de Jesús*, intro. and trans. Nancy E. Van Deusen (Albuquerque: University of New Mexico Press, 2004).

    Las almas del purgatorio: El diario spiritual y vida anónima de Úrsula de Jesús, ed. and trans. Nancy E. van Deusen (Lima: Fondo Editorial Pontificia Universidad Católica de Peru, 2012).

Vega, Lope de, *Comedia famosa de el Santo Negro Rosambuco de la Ciudad de Palermo* (Madrid, 1613).

Vetancurt, Agustín de, *Teatro Mexicano, descripción breve de los sucesos ejemplares, históricos, políticos, militares, y religiosos del nuevo mundo de las Indias* (Mexico: Doña de Benavides viuda de Iuan de Ribera, 1697).

    Vida y milagros del Principe de los anacoretas y Padre de los cenobiarcas, nuestro Padre San Antonio Abad el Mahno... (Barcelona: Maria Angela Martí Viuda, 1747).

Vieira, António, *Six Sermons*, ed. and trans. Mónica Leal da Silva and Liam M. Brockey (Oxford: Oxford University Press, 2018).

Vorágine, Jacobo de, *Leyenda de los Santos (que vulgarmente Flos Santorum llaman): agora de nuevo empremida, y con gran studio y diligencia extendida y declarada, ya a la perfeción de la verdad trayda, y aún de las siguientes leyendas augmentada) [1520–21]* (Madrid: Universidad Pontificia Comillas, IHSI, 2008).

Wadding, Luke, and Josephus Maria de Ancona, *Annales minorum seu trium ordinum a S. Francisco institutorum, t. XIX [1554–1564]* (Quaracchi: Claras Aquas, 1933).

Ward, Benedicta, ed. and trans., *The Sayings of the Desert Fathers* (London: Mowbrays, 1975).

Wortley, John, ed., *The Book of the Elders: Sayings of the Desert Fathers: The Systematic Collection* (Collegeville, MN: Liturgical Press, 2012).

    Palladius of Aspuna: The Lausiac History (Collegeville, MN: Liturgical Press, 2015).

Yepes, Diego de, *Discursos de varia historia que tratan de la Obras de Misericordia, y otras material morales: con exemplos, y sentencias de Santos, y grauissimos autores* (Toledo: Pedro Rodriguez, 1592).

Secondary Sources

Os negros em Portugal, sécs. XV a XIX (Lisbon: Comissão Nacional para as Comemorações dos Descobrimentos Portugueses, 1999).

Aguiar, Marcos Magalhãs, "A evolução da vida associativa em Minas Colonial e a sociabilidade confrarial negra," *Anais da Sociedade Brasileira de Pesquisa Histórica* 21 (2002), 225–36.

Aguirre, Carlos, *Breve historia de la esclavitud en el Perú: una herida que no deja de sangrar* (Lima: Fondo Editorial del Congreso del Perú, 2005).

Alcalá, Luis Elena, "Blanqueando la Loreto mexicana: Prejuicios sociales y condicionantes materiales en la representación de vírgenes negras," in *La imagen religiosa en la monarquía hispánica: usos y espacios*, ed. María Cruz de Carlos Varona, Pierre Civil, Felipe Pereda, and Cécile Vincent-Cassy (Madrid: Casa de Velázquez, 2008), 171–96.

Alden, Dauril, *The Making of an Enterprise: The Society of Jesus in Portugal, its Empire, and Beyond, 1540–1750* (Stanford: Stanford University Press, 1996).

Alleyne, Mervyn C., *The Construction and Representation of Race and Ethnicity in the Caribbean and the World* (Barbados: University of the West Indies Press, 2002).

Almeida Mendes, António de, "Africaines esclaves au Portugal: dynamiques d'exclusion, d'intégration et d'assimilation à l'époque moderne (XV-XVI siècles)," *Renaissance & Reformation/Renaissance et Reforme* 31:2 (2008), 45–65.

Álvaro Rubio, Joaquín, *La esclavitud en Barcarrota y Salvaleón en el período moderno (siglos XVI-XVIII)* (Badajoz: Diputación de Badajoz, 2005).

Andrews, Frances, *The Other Friars: The Carmelite, Augustinian, Sack and Pied Friars in the Middle Ages* (Rochester, NY: Boydell, 2006).

Andrews, George Reid, *Blackness in the White Nation: A History of Afro-Uruguay* (Chapel Hill: University of North Carolina Press, 2010).

Aram, Bethany, "Three Kings between Europe, Africa, and America, 1492–1788," *Jahrbuch für Geschichte Lateinamerkias* 49 (2012), 41–57.

Ares Queija, Berta, "La cuestión del bautismo de los negros en el siglo XVII: la proyección de un debate americano," in *Mirando las dos orillas: intercambios mercantiles, sociales y culturales entre Andalucía y América*, ed. Enriqueta Vila Vilar and Jaime K. Lacueva Muñoz (Madrid: Fundación Buenas Letras, 2012), 469–85.

Ares Queija, Berta, and Alessandro Stella, eds., *Negros, mulatos, zambaigos: derroteros africanos en los mundos ibéricos* (Seville: Consejo Superior de Investigaciones Científicas, 2000).

Armenteros Martínez, Iván, "De hermandades y procesiones. La cofradía de esclavos y libertos negros de Sant Jaume de Barcelona y la asimilación de la negritud en la Europa premoderna siglos XV-XVI)," *Clio revista de Pesquisa Histórica* 29:2 (2011), 1–23.

"Un precedente ibérico de las hermandades de negros: la cofradía de Sant Jaume de Barcelona (1455)," in *Sociedades diversas, sociedades en cambio. América Latina en perspectiva histórica*, ed. Gabriela Dalla Carte, Pilar García Jordán, Javier Laviña, et al. (Barcelona: University of Barcelona, 2011), 123–42.

Asad, Talal, "Thinking about Religion, Belief, and Politics," in *Cambridge Companion to Religious Studies*, ed. Robert Orsi (Cambridge: Cambridge University Press, 2012), 36–57.

Aurell, Jaume, and Alfons Puigarnau, *La cultura del mercader en la Barcelona del siglo XV* (Barcelona: Ediciones Omega, 1998).

Bailey, Gauvin Alexander, *Art of Colonial Latin America* (New York: Phaidon, 2005).

Art on the Jesuit Missions in Asia and Latin America, 1542–1773 (Toronto: University of Toronto Press, 1999).

"Creating a Global Artistic Language in Late Renaissance Rome: Artists in the Service of the Overseas Missions, 1542–1621," in *From Rome to Eternity: Catholicism and the Arts in Italy, ca. 1550–1650*, ed. Pamela M. Jones and Thomas Worcester (Boston: Brill, 2002), 225–51.

Ballbè i Boada, Miquel, *Las Vírgenes negras y morenas en España* (Barcelona: Terrassa, 1991).

Banchoff, Thomas, and José Casanova, eds., *The Jesuits and Globalization: Historical Legacies and Contemporary Challenges* (Washington, DC: Georgetown University Press, 2016).

Banker, James R., *Death in the Community: Memorialization and Confraternities in an Italian Commune in the Late Middle Ages* (Athens: University of Georgia Press, 1988).

Barasch, Mosche, *Light and Color in the Italian Renaissance Theory of Art* (New York: NYU Press, 1978).

Barber, Malcolm, Peter W. Edbury, Keagan Joel Brewer, and Peter Jackson, eds., *Prester John: The Legend and Its Sources* (Aldershot: Ashgate, 2015).

Barbour, Daphne, and Judy Ozone, "The Making of Seventeenth-Century Spanish Polychrome Sculpture," in *The Sacred Made Real: Spanish Painting and Sculpture, 1600–1700*, ed. Xavier Bray (London: National Gallery, 2009), 59–72.

Barcellona, Francesco Scorza, "I santi neri di Sicilia," in *Schiavitù, religione e libertà nel Mediterraneo tra Medioevo ed età moderna*, ed. Giovanna Fiume (Cosenza: L. Pellegrini, 2008), 215–39.

Barquilla, J. B., and Ó. Mayorga, eds., *La Orden de Predicadores en Iberoamérica en el siglo XVII: actas del IX Congreso Internacional de Historiadores* (Mexico City: Editorial San Esteban, 2010).

Barrantes, Vicente, *Catálogo razonado y critico de los libros, memorias, y papeles, impresos y manuscritos que tratan de las provincias de Extremadura* (Madrid: M. Rivadeneira, 1865).

Barrios, Olga, "Entre la esclavitud y el ensalzamiento: La presencia africana en la sociedad y en el teatro del Siglo de Oro español," *Bulletin of the Comediantes* 54:2 (2002), 287–311.

Bartlett, Robert, "Medieval and Modern Concepts of Race and Ethnicity," *Journal of Medieval and Early Modern Studies* 31:1 (2001), 39–56.
  Why Can the Dead Do Such Great Things? Saints and Worshippers from the Martyrs to the Reformation (Princeton, NJ: Princeton University Press, 2013).

Bassett, Jane, and Mari-Tere Alvarez, "Process and Collaboration in a Seventeenth-Century Polychrome Sculpture: Luisa Roldán and Tomás de los Arcos," *Getty Research Journal*, 3 (2011), 15–32.

Bastide, Roger, *African Religions of Brazil: Toward a Sociology of the Interpenetration of Civilizations*, trans. Helen Sebba (Baltimore: Johns Hopkins University Press, 1960).

Bauer, Ralph, "The Hemispheric Genealogies of 'Race': Creolization and the Cultural Geography of Colonial Difference across the Eighteenth-Century Americas," *Hemispheric American Studies* (2008), 36–56.

Beckingham, Charles F., "European Sources for Ethiopian History Before 1634," *Paideuma* 33 (1987), 167–78.

Bechtloff, Dagmar, *Las cofradías en Michoacán durante la época de la colonia: La religión y su relación política y económica en una sociedad intercultural* (Zinacantepec, MX: Colegio Michoacán, 1996).

Beezley, William H., Cheryl English Martin, and William E. French, eds., *Rituals of Rule, Rituals of Resistance: Public Celebrations and Popular Culture in Mexico* (Wilmington, DE: Scholarly Resources, 1994).

Begg, Ean C. M, *The Cult of the Black Virgin*, 3rd ed. (Wilmette, IL: Chiron Publications, 2006).

Beidler, Philip D., and Gary Taylor, eds., *Writing Race across the Atlantic World: Medieval to Modern* (New York: Palgrave Macmillan, 2005).

Bennett, Herman L., *Africans in Colonial Mexico: Absolutism, Christianity, and Afro-Creole Consciousness, 1570–1640* (Bloomington: Indiana University Press, 2003).
  African Kings and Black Slaves: Sovereignty and Dispossession in the Early Modern Atlantic (Philadelphia: University of Pennsylvania Press, 2018).

Colonial Blackness: A History of Afro-Mexico (Bloomington: Indiana University Press, 2009).

Benoist, Valérie, "La doble identidad de Sor Chicaba/Teresa," in *Actas del III Congreso Ibero-Africano de Hispanistas*, ed. Noureddine Achiri, Álvaro Baraibar Etxeberria, and Felix K. E. Schmelzer (Pamplona: Grupo de Investigación Siglo de Oro Universidad de Navarra, 2015), 147–56.

"El 'blanqueamiento' de dos escogidas negras de Dios: Sor Esperanza la negra, de Puebla y Sor Teresa la negrita, de Salamanca," *Afro-Hispanic Review*, 33:2 (2014), 23–40.

Berco, Cristian, "Perception and the Mulatto Body in Inquisitorial Spain: A Neurohistory," *Past and Present*, 231 (2016), 33–60.

Beresford, Andrew M., "Sanctity and Prejudice in Medieval Castilian Hagiography: The Legend of St. Moses the Ethiopian," in *Medieval Hispanic Studies in Memory of Alan Deyermond*, ed. Andrew M. Beresford, Louise M. Haywood, and Julian Weiss (Rochester, NY: Tamesis, 2013), 11–37.

Berg, Maxine, ed., *Writing the History of the Global: Challenges for the 21st Century* (Oxford: Oxford University Press for The British Academy, 2013).

Bethencourt, Francisco, *Racisms: From the Crusades to the Twentieth Century* (Princeton: Princeton University Press, 2013).

Bethencourt, Francisco, and Diogo Ramada Curto, eds., *Portuguese Oceanic Expansion, 1400–1800* (New York: Cambridge University Press, 2007).

Bethencourt, Francisco, and Adrian J. Pearce, eds., *Racism and Ethnic Relations in the Portuguese-Speaking World* (New York: Oxford University Press, 2012).

Beusterien, John, *An Eye on Race: Perspectives from Theater in Imperial Spain* (Lewisburg, PA: Bucknell University Press, 2006).

Bezerra, Janaina dos Santos, and Suely Creusa Cordeiro de Almeida, "'Pompa e circunstância' a um santo pardo': São Gonçalo Garcia e a luta dos pardos por inserção social no XVIII," *História Unisinos*, 16:1 (2012), 118–29.

Bilinkoff, Jodi, "Francisco Losa and Gregorio López: Spiritual Friendship and Identity Formation on the New Spain Frontier," in *Colonial Saints: Discovering the Holy in the Americas, 1500–1800*, ed. Allan Greer and Jodi Bilinkoff (New York: Routledge, 2003), 115–28.

Related Lives: Confessors and Their Female Penitents, 1450–1750 (Ithaca, NY: Cornell University Press, 2005).

Biller, Peter, "Words and the Medieval Notion of 'Religion,'" *The Journal of Ecclesiastical History* 26:3 (July 1985), 351–69.

Bitel, Lisa, and Felice Lifshitz, eds., *Gender and Christianity in Medieval Europe: New Perspectives* (Philadelphia: University of Pennsylvania Press, 2008).

Black, Christopher F., *Italian Confraternities in the Sixteenth Century* (New York: Cambridge University Press, 1989).

Black, Christopher F., and Pamela Gravestock, eds., *Early Modern Confraternities in Europe and the Americas: International and Interdisciplinary Perspectives* (Burlington, VT: Ashgate, 2006).

Blakely, Allison, "The Emergence of Afro-Europe: A Preliminary Sketch," in *Black Europe and the African Diaspora*, ed. Darlene Clark Hine, Trica Danielle Keaton, and Stephen Small (Urbana: University of Illinois Press, 2009), 3–28.

Bleichmar, Daniela, and Peter C. Mancall, eds., *Collecting Across Cultures: Material Exchanges in the Early Modern Atlantic World* (Philadelphia: University of Pennsylvania Press, 2011).

Blumenthal, Debra, *Enemies and Familiars: Slavery and Mastery in Fifteenth-Century Valencia* (Ithaca, NY: Cornell University Press, 2009).

"La Casa dels Negres: Black African Solidarity in Late Medieval Valencia," in *Black Africans in Renaissance Europe*, ed. T. F. Earle and K. J. P. Lowe (New York: Cambridge University Press, 2005), 225–46.

Bolaños Donoso, Piedad, *La obra dramática de Felipe Godínez: trayectoria de un dramaturgo marginado* (Seville: Excma. Diputación Provincial de Sevilla, 1983).

Bollbuck, Harald, "Testimony of True Faith and the Ruler's Mission: The Middle Ages in the Magdeburg Centuries and the Melanchthon School," *Archiv für Reformationsgeschichte* 101:1 (2010), 238–62.

Bono, Salvatore, "Due santi negri: Benedetto da San Fratello e Antonio da Noto," *Africa: Rivista trimestrale di studi e documentazione dell'Istituto italiano per l'Africa e l'Oriente*, 21:1 (1966), 76–9.

Borges, Célia Maia, *Escravos e libertos nas Irmandades do Rosário: Devoção e solidaredade em Minas Gerais, séculos XVIII e XIX* (Juiz de Fora: Editora UFJF, 2005).

Borja Medina, Francisco de, "La experiencia sevillana de la Compañía de Jesús en la evangelización de los esclavos negros y su representación en América," in *La esclavitud negroafricana en la historia de España, siglos XVI y XVII*, ed. Aurelia Martín Casares and Margarita García Barranco (Granada: Comares, 2010), 75–94.

Bornstein, Daniel Ethan, and Roberto Rusconi, eds., *Women and Religion in Medieval and Renaissance Italy* (Chicago: University of Chicago Press, 1996).

Borucki, Alex, David Eltis, and David Wheat, "Atlantic History and the Slave Trade to Spanish America," *American Historical Review* 120:2 (2005), 433–61.

Boschi, Caio César, *Os leigos e o poder: Irmandades leigas e política colonizadora em Minas Gerais* (São Paulo: Editora Atica, 1986).

Bowser, Frederick P., *The African Slave in Colonial Peru, 1524–1650* (Stanford: Stanford University Press, 1974).

Boxer, Charles Ralph, *Race Relations in the Portuguese Colonial Empire, 1415–1825* (Oxford: Clarendon Press, 1963).

Boxer, C. R., *The Church Militant and Iberian Expansion, 1440–1770* (Baltimore: Johns Hopkins University Press, 1978).

Brading, D. A., *Church and State in Bourbon Mexico: The Diocese of Michoacán, 1749–1810* (New York: Cambridge University Press, 1994).

Brandão, Carlos Rodrigues, *A festa do santo de preto* (Rio de Janeiro: Fundação Nacional de Arte, Instituto Nacional do Folcore, 1985).

Braude, Benjamin, "The Sons of Noah and the Construction of Ethnic and Geographical Identities in the Medieval and Early Modern Periods," *The William and Mary Quarterly* 54:1 (1997), 103–42.

Braun, Harald E., and Lisa Vollendorf, eds., *Theorising the Ibero-American Atlantic* (Leiden: Brill, 2014).

Bray, Xavier, et al. eds., *The Sacred Made Real: Spanish Painting and Sculpture, 1600–1700* (London: National Gallery, 2009).

Brewer-Garcia, Larissa, "Black Skin, White Soul: The Ambivalence of Blackness in the *Vida prodigiosa of Fray Martín de Porras* (1663)," *Cuadernos del CILHA* 13:2 (2012), 113–46.

"Imagined Transformations: Color, Beauty, and Black Christian Conversion in Seventeenth-Century Spanish America," in *Envisioning Others: Race, Color, and the Visual in Iberia and Latin America*, ed. Pamela Patton (Leiden: Brill, 2016), 111–41.

Bristol, Joan Cameron, "Afro-Mexico Saintly Devotion in a Mexico City Alley," in *Africans to Spanish America: Expanding the Diaspora*, ed. Sherwin K. Bryant, Rachel Sarah O'Toole, and Ben Vinson (Urbana: University of Illinois Press, 2012), 114–35.

"'Although I Am Black, I Am Beautiful': Juana Esperanza de San Alberto, Black Carmelite," in *Gender, Race and Religion in the Colonization of the Americas*, ed. Nora E. Jaffary (Burlington, VT: Ashgate, 2007), 67–80.

Christians, Blasphemers, and Witches: Afro-Mexican Ritual Practice in the Seventeenth Century (Albuquerque: University of New Mexico Press, 2007).

Brockey, Liam Matthew, "Books of Martyrs: Example and Imitation in Europe and Japan, 1597–1650," *The Catholic Historical Review*, 103:2 (2017), 207–23.

Journey to the East: The Jesuit Mission to China, 1579–1724 (Cambridge, MA: Belknap Press of Harvard University Press, 2007).

Broek, R. van den, *The Myth of the Phoenix, According to Classical and Early Christian Traditions*, trans. I. Seeger (Leiden: Brill, 1972).

Brown, Jonathan, and Carmen Garrido, *Velázquez: The Technique of Genius* (New Haven: Yale University Press, 2003).

Brown, Peter, *The Cult of the Saints: Its Rise and Function in Latin Christianity*, 2nd ed. (Chicago, University of Chicago Press, 2015).

Treasure in Heaven: The Holy Poor in Early Christianity (Charlottesville, VA: University of Virginia Press, 2016).

Brown, Ras Michael, "The Immersion of Catholic Christianity in Kalunga," *Journal of Africana Religions*, 2:2 (2014), 246–55.

Burns, Kathryn, "Unfixing Race," in *Rereading the Black Legend: The Discourses of Religious and Racial Difference in the Renaissance Empires*, ed. Margaret R. Greer, Walter D. Mignolo, and Maureen Quilligan (Chicago: University of Chicago Press, 2007), 188–204.

Byron, Gay L., *Symbolic Blackness and Ethnic Difference in Early Christian Literature* (London: Routledge, 2008).

Cadden, Joan, *Meanings of Sex Difference in the Middle Ages: Medicine, Science, and Culture* (Cambridge: Cambridge University Press, 1993).

Cahill, David, "Colour by Numbers: Racial and Ethnic Categories in the Viceroyalty of Peru, 1532–1824," *Journal of Latin American Studies* 26:2 (1994), 325–46.

Camacho Martínez, Ignacio, and Antonio Domínguez Ortiz, *La hermandad de los mulatos de Sevilla: antecedentes históricos de la Hermandad del Calvario* (Seville: Area de Cultura del Ayuntamiento de Sevilla, 1998).

Camilli, E. Michael, "Six Dialogues, 1566: Initial Response to the 'Madgeburg Centurie,'" *Archiv für Reformationsgeschichte* 87 (1996), 141–52.

Cañizares-Esguerra, Jorge, "Demons, Stars, and the Imagination: The Early Modern Body in the Tropics," in *The Origins of Racism in the West*, ed. Miriam Eliav-Feldon, Benjamin H. Isaac, and Joseph Ziegler (New York: Cambridge University Press, 2009), 313–25.

"New World, New Stars: Patriotic Astrology and the Invention of Indian and Creole Bodies in Colonial Spanish America, 1600–1650," *The American Historical Review* 104:1 (1999), 33–68.

Puritan Conquistadors: Iberianizing the Atlantic, 1550–1700 (Stanford: Stanford University Press, 2006).

Cañizares-Esguerra, Jorge, and Erik R. Seeman, eds., *The Atlantic in Global History, 1500–2000* (Upper Saddle River, NJ: Pearson Prentice Hall, 2007).

Capone, Stefania, *La quête de l'Afrique dans le candomblé: pouvoir et tradition au Brésil* (Paris: Karthala, 1999).

Cardozo, Manoel S., "The Lay Brotherhoods of Colonial Bahia," *The Catholic Historical Review* 33:1 (1947), 12–30.

Carey, Brycchan, *From Peace to Freedom: Quaker Rhetoric and the Birth of American Antislavery, 1657–1761* (New Haven: Yale, 2012).

Carrera, Magali, "'El Nuevo [Mundo]: No se parece á el viejo': Racial Categories and the Practice of Seeing," *Journal of Spanish Cultural Studies* 10:1 (2009), 59–73.

Carrera, Magali Marie, *Imagining Identity in New Spain: Race, Lineage, and the Colonial Body in Portraiture and Casta Paintings* (Austin: University of Texas Press, 2003).

Carrocera, Buenaventura de, "Misión capuchina al reino de Arda," *Missionalla Hispanica* 6 (1949), 523–33.

Cartaya Baños, Juan, *La pasión de don Fernando de Añesco: limpieza de sangre y conflicto social en la Sevilla de los Siglos de Oro* (Seville: Universidad de Sevilla, 2014).

Carucci, Arturo, *La vergine Ifigenia negli "Acta" di San Matteo* (Salerno: Lino-typografia M. Spadafora, 1945).

Caso, Nicole, "Pragmatismo y el discurso ingenioso en el *Sermón de la Epifanía* del Padre Antonio Vieira," *Revista Iberoamericana*, LXXII:218 (2007), 79–92.

Caso Amador, Rafael, "El origen judeoconverso del humanista Benito Arias Montano," *Revista de Estudios Extremeños*, LXXI:3 (2015), 1665–712.

Castañeda, Felipe, "La esclavitud natural en Sepúlveda: De los escolios al de la política al Demócrates Segundo," in *Sobre la república-Libro I, de Aristóteles*, ed. F. Castañeda and A. Lozano-Vásquez (Bogotá: Universidad de los Andes, 2015), 135–232.

Castañeda García, Rafael, "Devociones y construcción de identidades entre los negros y mulatos en la Nueva España S. XVIII)," in *Fundación Visión Cultural, Memoria del VI Encuentro internacional sobre el Barroco* (La Paz: Visión Cultural, 2012), 241–7.

"La devoción a Santa Ifigenia entre los negros y mulatos de Nueva España. Siglos XVII y XVIII," *Esclavitud, mestizaje, y abolicionismo en los mundos Hispánicos*, ed. Aurelia Martín Casares (Granada: Universidad de Granada, 2015), 151–74.

"Modelos de santidad: Devocionarios y hagiografías a San Benito de Palermo en Nueva España," *Studia historica, Historia moderna* 38:1 (2016), 39–64.

"Santos negros, devotos de color. Las cofradías de San Benito de Palermo en Nueva España. Identidades étnicas y religiosas, siglos XVII-XVIII," in *Devoción, paisanaje e identidad: Las cofradías y congregaciones de naturales en España y en América*, ed. Óscar Álvarez Gila, Alberto Angulo Morales, and Jon Ander Ramos Martínez (Navarre: Servicios de Publicaciones Universidad de Pais Vasco, 2014), 145–64.

Castelnau-L'Estoile, Charlotte de, "The Uses of Shamanism: Evangelizing Strategies and Missionary Models in Seventeenth-Century Brazil," in *The Jesuits: Culture, Science and the Arts, 1540–1773*, ed. John O'Malley, Gauvin Alexander Bailey, et al. (Toronto: University of Toronto Press, 2006), 616–37.

Charney, Paul, "A Sense of Belonging: Colonial Indian Cofradías and Ethnicity in the Valley of Lima, Peru," *The Americas* 54:3 (1998), 379–407.

Childs, Matt D., "Gendering the African Diaspora in the Iberian Atlantic. Religious Brotherhoods and the Cabildos de Nación," in *Women of the Iberian Atlantic*, ed. Sarah E. Owens and Jane E. Mangan (Baton Rouge, LA: University of Louisiana Press, 2012), 230–61.

"Re-Creating African Ethnic Identities in Cuba," in *The Black Urban Atlantic in the Age of the Slave Trade*, ed. Jorge Cañizares-Esguerra, Matt D. Childs, and James Sidbury (Philadelphia: University of Pennsylvania Press, 2013), 85–100.

Christian Jr., William A., *Apparitions in Late Medieval and Renaissance Spain* (Princeton: Princeton University Press, 1981).

Local Religion in Sixteenth-Century Spain (Princeton: Princeton University Press, 1981).

Ciccarelli, Diego, and Simona Sarzana, eds., *Francescanesimo e cultura a Noto* (Palermo: Biblioteca francescana, 2005).

Clossey, Luke, *Salvation and Globalization in the Early Jesuit Missions* (New York: Cambridge University Press, 2008).

Coakley, John Wayland, *Women, Men, and Spiritual Power: Female Saints and Their Male Collaborators* (New York: Columbia University Press, 2006).

Codignola, Luca, "Les Amerindiens dans les archives de la Sacrée Congrégation 'De Propaganda Fide' a Rome," *Canadian Folklore* 17:1 (1995), 139–48.

Coello de la Rosa, Alexandre, *Espacios de exclusion, espacios de poder: el Cercado de Lima colonial (1568–1606)* (Lima: Instituto de Estudios Peruanos, 2006).

Colomer, José Luis, "Black and the Royal Image," in *Spanish Fashion at the Courts of Early Modern Europe*, vol. 1 (Madrid: Centro de Estudios Europa Hispánica, 2014), 77–112.

Cólon Mendoza, Iliona, *The Cristos yacentes de Gregório Fernández: Polychrome Sculptures of the Supine Christ in Seventeenth-Century Spain* (Aldershot: Ashgate, 2015).

Connors, Joseph, *Borromini and the Roman Oratory: Style and Society* (Cambridge, MA: MIT Press, 1980).

Conover, Cornelius, "Catholic Saints in Spain's Atlantic Empire," in *Empires of God: Religious Encounters in the Early Modern Atlantic*, ed. Linda Gregerson and Susan Juster (Philadelphia: University of Pennsylvania Press, 2011), 87–105.

"Saintly Biography and the Cult of San Felipe de Jesús in Mexico City, 1597–1697," *The Americas*, 67:4 (2011), 441–66.

Conrod, Frédéric, "The Greatest Collector: Ribadeneira's Hagiography of Loyola as Struggle against Dispersion," *Hispanic Review* (2013), 1–16.

Constable, Olivia Remie, *Housing the Stranger in the Mediterranean World: Lodging, Trade, and Travel in Late Antiquity and the Middle Ages* (Cambridge: Cambridge University Press, 2014).

Cope, R. Douglas, *The Limits of Racial Domination: Plebeian Society in Colonial Mexico City, 1660–1720* (Madison: University of Wisconsin Press, 1994).

Copeland, Clare, *Maria Maddalena de' Pazzi: The Making of a Counter-Reformation Saint* (Oxford: Oxford University Press, 2016).

Coria, Juan Carlos, *Pasado y presente de los negros en Buenos Aires* (Buenos Aires: Editorial J.A. Roca, 1997).

Cortés Alonso, Vicenta, *La esclavitud en Valencia durante el reinado de los Reyes Católicos (1479–1516)* (Valencia: Excmo. Ayuntamiento, 1964).

Cortés López, José Luis, *Esclavo y colono: introducción y sociología de los negroafricanos en la América española del siglo XVI* (Salamanca: Ediciones Universidad de Salamanca, 2004).

La esclavitud negra en la España peninsular del siglo XVI (Salamanca: Ediciones Universidad de Salamanca, 1989).

Los orígenes de la esclavitud negra en España (Salamanca: Ediciones Universidad de Salamanca, 1986).

Costa e Silva, Alberto da, "Africa-Brazil-Africa during the Era of the Slave Trade," in *Enslaving Connections: Changing Cultures of Africa and Brazil during the Era of Slavery*, ed. José C. Curto and Paul E. Lovejoy (Amherst, NY: Humanity Books, 2004), 21–8.

Cottias, Myriam, Alessandro Stella, and Bernard Vincent, eds., *Esclavage et dépendances serviles: histoire comparée* (Paris, France: L'Harmattan, 2006).

Cruz de Carlos Varona, María, Pierre Civil, Felipe Pereda, and Cécile Vincent-Cassy, eds., *La imagen religiosa en la monarquía hispánica: usos y espacios* (Madrid: Casa de Velázquez, 2008).

Cruz de Carlos Varona, María, "Una propuesta devocional femenina," in *La imagen religiosa en la monarquía hispánica: usos y espacios*, ed. María Cruz de Carlos Varona, Pierre Civil, Felipe Pereda, and Cécile Vincent-Cassy (Madrid: Casa de Velázquez, 2008), 83–99.

Cuadriello, Jaime, *Las glorias de la república de Tlaxcala o la conciencia como imagen sublime* (Mexico: Instituto de Investigaciones Estéticas Museo Nacional de Arte, INBA, 2004). English edition: *The Glories of the Republic of Tlaxcala: Art and Life in Viceregal Mexico*, trans. Christopher J. Follett (Austin: University of Texas Press, 2011).

Curcio-Nagy, Linda A., "Giants and Gypsies: Corpus Christi in Colonial Mexico City," in *Rituals of Rule, Rituals of Resistance: Public Celebrations and Popular Culture in Mexico*, ed. William H. Beezley, Cheryl English Martin, and William E. French (Wilmington, DE: Scholarly Resources, Inc, 1994), 1–26.

Curran, Andrew S., *The Anatomy of Blackness: Science and Slavery in an Age of Enlightenment* (Baltimore: Johns Hopkins University Press, 2011).

Cussen, Celia L., *Black Saint of the Americas: The Life and Afterlife of Martín de Porres* (New York: Cambridge University Press, 2014).

"The Search for Idols and Saints in Colonial Peru: Linking Extirpation and Beatification," *Hispanic American Historical Review* 85:3 (2005), 417–48.

Cymbalista, Renato, "The Presence of the Martyrs: Jesuit Martyrdom and the Christianisation of Portuguese America," *International Journal for the Study of the Christian Church* 10 (2010), 287–305.

D'Avenia, Fabrizio, *La Chiesa del re: monarchia e papato nella Sicilia spagnola (secc. XVI-XVII)* (Rome: Carocci Editore, 2015).

Dahan, Gilbert, *The Christian Polemic against the Jews in the Middle Ages*, trans. Jody Gladding (Notre Dame, IN: University of Notre Dame Press, 1998).

Dantas, Mariana L. R., "Humble Slaves and Loyal Vassals: Free Africans and Their Descendants in Eighteenth-Century Minas Gerais, Brazil," in *Imperial Subjects: Race and Identity in Colonial Latin America*, ed. Andrew B. Fisher and Matthew D. O'Hara (Durham, NC: Duke University Press, 2009), 115–40.

Black Townsmen: Urban Slavery and Freedom in the Eighteenth-Century Americas (New York: Palgrave Macmillan, 2008).

Daston, Lorraine, and Katharine Park, *Wonders and the Order of Nature, 1150–1750* (New York: Zone Books, 1998).

Dauverd, Céline, "Cultivating Differences: Genoese Trade Identity in the Constantinople of Sultan Mehmed II, 1453–81," *Mediterranean Studies* 23:2 (2015), 94–124.

Debrunner, Hans, *Presence and Prestige, Africans in Europe: A History of Africans in Europe before 1918* (Basel: Basler Afrika Bibliographien, 1979).

Dell'Aira, Alessandro. *Da San Fratello a Bahia: La rotta di San Benedetto il Moro* (Trent: Magazzini di Arsenale, 1999).

"La fortuna iberica di San Benedetto da Palermo," *Atti dell'Accademia di Scienze Lettere e Arti di Palermo* 12 (1993), 51–91.

"Le navire de la reine et du saint esclave de la Méditeranée au Brésil," *Cahiers de la Mediterranée* 65 (2002), 329–39.

"San Benedetto il Moro tra Sicilia e Galizia," *Kalós* (2003), 15–20, 30–5.

"St. Benedict of San Fratello (Messina, Sicily): An Afro-Sicilian Hagionym on Three Continents," in *Proceedings of the 23rd International Congress of Onomastic Sciences*, ed. Wolfgang Ahrens, Sheila Embleton, and André Lapierre (Toronto: York University Press, 2009), 284–97.

Delmas, Adrien, and Nigel Penn, eds., *Written Culture in a Colonial Context: Africa and the Americas, 1500–1900*, vol. 2 (Boston: Brill, 2012).

Denzler, Georg, *Kardinal Guglielmo Sirleto (1514–1585): Leben und Werk: Ein Beitrag zur Nachtridentinischen Reform* (Munich: M. Hueber, 1964).

Deslandres, Dominique, "In the Shadow of the Cloister: Representations of Female Holiness in New France," in *Colonial Saints: Discovering the Holy in the Americas, 1500–1800*, ed. Allan Greer and Jodi Bilinkoff (New York: Routledge, 2003), 129–52.

Devisse, Jean, "A Sanctified Black: Maurice," in *The Image of the Black in Western Art. Volume II, Part 1: From the Demonic Threat to the Incarnation of Sainthood*, ed. David Bindman and Henry Louis Gates, Jr. (Cambridge, MA: Belknap Press of Harvard University Press, 2010), 139–205.

Devisse, Jean, and Michel Mollat, "The Appeal to the Ethiopian," in *The Image of the Black in Western Art, Volume II: From the Early Christian Era to the "Age of Discovery," Part 2: Africans in the Christian Ordinance of the World*, ed. David Bindman and Henry Louis Gates, Jr., trans. William Granger Ryan (Cambridge, MA: Belknap Press of Harvard University Press, 2010), 83–152.

"The Frontiers in 1460," in *The Image of the Black in Western Art, Volume II: From the Early Christian Era to the "Age of Discovery," Part 2: Africans in the Christian Ordinance of the World*, ed. David Bindman and Henry Louis Gates, Jr., trans. William Granger Ryan (Cambridge, MA: Belknap Press of Harvard University Press, 2010), 153–84.

"The African Transposed," in *The Image of the Black in Western Art, Volume II: From the Early Christian Era to the "Age of Discovery," Part 2: Africans in the Christian Ordinance of the World*, ed. David Bindman and Henry Louis Gates, Jr., trans. William Granger Ryan (Cambridge, MA: Belknap Press of Harvard University Press, 2010), 185–279.

Dewulf, Jeroen, "Black Brotherhoods in North America: Afro-Iberian and West-Central African Influences," *African Studies Quarterly* 15:3 (June 2015), 19–38.

Díaz, Mónica, *Indigenous Writings from the Convent: Negotiating Ethnic Autonomy in Colonial Mexico* (Tucson: University of Arizona Press, 2010).

Díaz Rodriguez, Vicente, "La cofradía de los morenos de los primeros años de los dominicos en Cádiz," *Communio* 39:2 (2006), 359–484.

Díaz y Pérez, Nicolás, *Diccionario histórico, biográfico, crítico y bibliográfico de autores, artistas y extremeños ilustres*, vol. 1 (Madrid: Pérez y Boix, 1884).

Diène, Doudou, ed., *From Chains to Bonds: The Slave Trade Revisited* (New York and Paris: Berghahn Books and UNESCO, 2001).

Ditchfield, Simon, "Baronio storico nel suo tempo," in *Cesare Baronio tra santità e scrittura storica*, ed. Giuseppe Guazzeli, Raimondo Michetti, and Francesco Scorza Barcellona (Rome: Viella, 2012), 3–21.

Liturgy, Sanctity, and History in Tridentine Italy: Pietro Maria Campi and the Preseveration of the Particular (Cambridge: Cambridge University Press, 1995).

"Of Dancing Cardinals and Mestizo Madonnas: Reconfiguring the History of Roman Catholicism in the Early Moden Period," *Journal of Early Modern History* 8:3 (2004), 386–408.

"Tridentine Worship and the Cult of Saints," in *The Cambridge History of Christianity, vol. 6: Reform and Expansion, 1500–1660*, ed. R. Po-chia Hsia (New York: Cambridge University Press, 2007), 201–24.

"What's in a Title? Writing a History of the Counter-Reformation for a Postcolonial Age," *Archiv für Reformationsgeschichte*, 108:1 (2017), 255–63.

Domínguez Ortiz, Antonio, "La esclavitud en Castilla durante la edad moderna," *Estudios de historia social de España* 2 (1952), 376–8.

La esclavitud en Castilla en la edad moderna y otros estudios de marginados, 2nd ed. (Granada: Editorial Comares, 2003).

Dompnier, Bernard, and Paola Vismara, eds., *Confréries et dévotions dans la catholicité moderne (mi-XVe-début XIXe siècle)* (Rome: École française de Rome, 2008).

Donnelly, John Patrick, and Michael W. Maher, eds., *Confraternities & Catholic Reform in Italy, France, & Spain, Sixteenth Century Essays & Studie*s, vol. 44 (Kirksville, MO: Thomas Jefferson University Press, 1999).

Dos Santos Bezerra, Janaina, and Suely Creusa Cordeiro de Almeida, "'*Pompa e circunstância*' a um santo pardo: São Gonçalo Garcia e la luta dos pardos por inserção social no XVIII," *História Unisinos* 16:1 (2012), 118–29.

Dronke, Peter, "The Song of Songs and Medieval Love-Lyric," in *The Medieval Poet and His World* (Rome: Edizioni di Storia e Letteratura, 1984), 209–36.

Dursteler, Eric R., *Venetians in Constantinople: Nation, Identity, and Coexistence in the Early Modern Mediterranean* (Baltimore: Johns Hopkins University Press, 2006).

Earle, Rebecca, *The Body of the Conquistador: Food, Race, and the Colonial Experience in Spanish America, 1492–1700* (New York: Cambridge University Press, 2012).

Egoavil, Teresa, *Las cofradías en Lima, ss. XVII y XVIII* (Lima: Universidad Nacional Mayor de San Marcos, 1986).

Eire, Carlos, *From Madrid to Purgatory: The Art and Craft of Dying in Sixteenth-Century Spain* (Cambridge: Cambridge Univiersity Press, 1995).

Eisenbichler, Konrad, "Italian Scholarship on Pre-Modern Confraternities in Italy," *Renaissance Quarterly*, 50:2 (1997), 567–80.

El Alaoui, Youssef, *Jesuites, morisques et indiens. Étude comparative des methods d'évangélisation de la Compagnie de Jésus d'après les traités de José de Acosta (1588) et d'Ignacio de las Casas (1605–1607)* (Paris: Honoré Champion, 2006).

El-Leithy, Tamer, "Coptic Culture and Conversion in Medieval Cairo, 1293–1524 A. D.," unpublished Ph.D. dissertation, Princeton University (2005).

Eliav-Feldon, Miriam, Benjamin H. Isaac, and Joseph Ziegler, eds., *The Origins of Racism in the West* (New York: Cambridge University Press, 2009).

Elits, David, "The Volume and Structure of the Transatlantic Slave Trade: A Reassessment," *William and Mary Quarterly* 58:1 (2001), 17–46.

Elliott, John H., "A Europe of Composite Monarchies," *Past & Present* 137 (1992), 48–71.

Epstein, Steven, *Speaking of Slavery: Color, Ethnicity, and Human Bondage in Italy* (Ithaca, NY: Cornell University Press, 2001).

  Purity Lost: Transgressing Boundaries in the Eastern Mediterranean, 1000–1400 (Baltimore: Johns Hopkins University Press, 2007).

Esche-Ramschorn, Christiane, "The Multi-Ethnic Pilgrim Centre: Sharing Sacred Space in Renaissance Rome – The Diversity of Religions and Arts," in *Fremde in der Stadt: Ordnungen, Repräsentationen und soziale Praktiken (13.-15. Jahrhundert)*, ed. Peter Bell, Dirk Suckow, and Gerhard Wolf (New York: Peter Lang, 2010), 171–94.

Espinoza Rúa, Celes Alonso, "Un indio camino a los altares: santidad e influencia inquisitorial en el caso del 'siervo de Dios' Nicolás de Ayllón," *Histórica* 36:1 (2012), 135–80.

Estenssoro Fuchs, Juan Carlos, *Del paganismo a la santidad: la incorporación de los indios del Perú al catolicismo, 1532–1750*, trans. Gabriela Ramos (Lima: Pontifical Universidad Católica de Lima, 2003).

Falola, Toyin, and Matt D. Childs, eds., *The Yoruba Diaspora in the Atlantic World* (Bloomington: Indiana University Press, 2004).

Faü, Jean-François, "De la sainteté de Kaleb Ella Asheha dans l'iconographie baroque portugaise," *Aethiopica* 18 (2015), 7–21.

Fazio, Giuseppe, *La Madonna di Tindari e le vergini nere medievali* (Roma: L'Erma di Bretschneider, 2012).

Feitler, Bruno, and Evergton Sales Souza, eds., *A igreja no Brasil: Normas e Práticas durante a Vigência das Constituições Primeiras do Arcebispado da Bahia* (São Paulo: Editoria UNIFESP, 2011).

Felsi, Teobaldo, "Enrico, figlio del re del Congo, primo vescovo dell'Africa," *Euntes Docete* 19 (1966), 365–85.

Fernández Rojas, Matilde, *Patrimonio artístico de los conventos masculinos desamortizados en Sevilla durante el siglo XIX* (Seville: Press of the Diputación de Sevilla, 2009).

Ferreira Furtado, Júnia, *Chica da Silva: A Brazilian Slave of the Eighteenth Century* (Cambridge: Cambridge University Press, 2009).

Ferreira, Roquinaldo Amaral, *Cross-Cultural Exchange in the Atlantic World: Angola and Brazil during the Era of the Slave Trade* (New York: Cambridge University Press, 2012).

  "Slavery and the Social and Cultural Landscapes of Luanda," in *The Black Urban Atlantic in the Age of the Slave Trade*, ed. Jorge Cañizares-Esguerra, Matt D. Childs, and James Sidbury (Philadelphia: University of Pennsylvania Press, 2013), 185–206.

Ferrús Antón, Beatriz, "Sor Teresa Juliana de Santo Domingo, Chicaba o escribir en la piel del otro," *Cuadernos Dieciochistas* 9 (2010), 181–92.

Few, Martha, *Women Who Live Evil Lives: Gender, Religion, and the Politics of Power in Colonial Guatemala* (Austin: University of Texas Press, 2002).

Fikes, R., "Black Scholars in Europe during the Renaissance and the Enlightenment," *Crisis* 87 (1980), 212–16.

Finocchiaro, Giuseppe, *Cesare Baronio e la tipografia dell'Oratorio: Impresa e ideologia* (Florence: Leo S. Olschki, 2005).

Fisher, Andrew B., and Matthew D. O'Hara, eds., *Imperial Subjects: Race and Identity in Colonial Latin America* (Durham, NC: Duke University Press, 2009).

Fiume, Giovanna, "Antonio Etiope e Benedetto il Moro: il Santo scavuzzo e il Nigro eremite," in *Francescanesimo e cultura a Noto*, ed. Diego Ciccarelli and Simona Sarzana (Palermo: Biblioteca Francescana, 2005), 67–100.

"Il pantheon africano: Il caso di Antonio Etiope," in *Esclavitudes hispánicas (siglos XV al XXI): Horizontes socioculturales*, ed. Aurelia Martín Casares (Granada: Universidad de Granada, 2014), 59–88.

"Il processo 'de cultu' a Fra' Benedetto da San Fratello (1734)," in *Il santo patrono e la città. San Benedetto il Moro: culti, devozioni, strategie di età moderna*, ed. Giovanna Fiume (Venice: Marsilio, 2000), 231–52.

Il santo e patrono e la città: San Benedetto il Moro: culti, devozioni, strategie di età moderna (Venice: Marsilio, 2000).

Il santo moro: i processi di canonizzazione di Benedetto da Palermo (1594–1807). (Milano: F. Angeli, 2002).

"Lo schiavo, il re e il cardinale. L'iconografia secentesca di Benedetto il Moro (1524–1589)," *Quaderni Storici* 41: 1 (2006), 165–208.

"Saint Benedict the Moor: From Sicily to the New World," in *Saints and Their Cults in the Atlantic World*, ed. Margaret Cormack (Columbia: University of South Carolina Press, 2007), 16–51.

Schiavitù mediterranee: corsari, rinnegati e santi di età moderna (Sintesi. Milan: B. Mondadori, 2009).

Fiume, Giovanna, ed. *Schiavitù, religione e libertà nel Mediterraneo tra Medioevo ed età moderna* (Cosenza: L. Pellegrini, 2008).

Folda, Jaroslav, *The Nazareth Capitals and the Crusader Shrine of the Annunciation* (University Park: Pennsylvania State University Press, 1986).

Fonseca, Jorge, *Escravos no sul de Portugal. Séculos XVI-XVII* (Lisbon: Editora Vulgata, 2002).

"A historiografia sobre os escravos em Portugal," *Cultura* 33 (2014), 2–22.

Os escravos em Évora no século XVI (Evora: Câmara Municipal de Évora, 1997).

Religião e liberdade: Os negros nas irmandades e confrarias Portuguesas (séculos XV a XIX) (Ribeirão: Edições Húmus, 2016).

Fonseca, Jorge and João Sabóia, "Os Negros de Faro e a Confraria de Nossa Senhora do Rosário," *Anais do Município de Faro* 31–32 (2001–2002), 112–31.

Forsyth, Ilene H., *The Throne of Wisdom: Wood Sculptures of the Madonna in Romanesque France* (Princeton: Princeton University Press, 1972).

Fowler, Jessica, "Illuminated Islands: Luisa de los Reyes and the Inquisition in Manila," in *Devout Laywomen in the Early Modern World*, ed. Alison Weber (New York: Routledge, 2016), 152–70.

Fra Molinero, Baltasar, "Juan Latino and His Racial Difference," in *Black Africans in Renaissance Europe*, ed. T. F. Earle and K. J. P. Lowe (New York: Cambridge University Press, 2005), 326–44.

La imagen de los negros en el teatro del Siglo de Oro. Lingüística y teoría literaria (Mexico City; Madrid: Siglo Veintiuno Editores, 1995).

Fraccia, Carmen, "Constructing the Black Slave in Spanish Golden Age Painting," in *Others and Outcasts in Early Modern Europe: Picturing the Social Margins*, ed. Tom Nichols (Burlington, VT: Ashgate, 2007), 179–95.

Franco Silva, Alfonso, *La esclavitud en Sevilla y su tierra a fines de la Edad Media* (Seville: Diputación Provincial de Sevilla, 1979).

La esclavitud en Andalucia, 1450–1550 (Granada: Universidad de Granada, 1992).

Frazier, Alison Knowles, *Possible Lives: Authors and Saints in Renaissance Italy* (New York: Columbia University Press, 2005).

Frey, Sylvia R., "The Visible Church: Historiography of African American Religion since Raboteau," *Slavery & Abolition* 29:1 (2008), 83–110.

Fromont, Cécile, *The Art of Conversion: Christian Visual Culture in the Kingdom of Kongo* (Chapel Hill: University of North Carolina Press, 2014).

"Dancing for the Kings of Congo from Early Modern Central Africa to Slavery-Era Brazil," *Colonial Latin American Review* 22:2 (2013), 184–208.

Fuchs, Barbara, "A Mirror across the Water: Mimetic Racism, Hybridity, and Cultural Survival," in *Writing Race Across the Atlantic World*, ed. Philip Beidler and Gary Taylor (London: Palgrave MacMillan, 2005), 9–26.

Exotic Nation: Maurophilia and the Construction of Early Modern Spain (Philadelphia: University of Pennsylvania Press, 2009).

Fuente, Alejandro de la, and George Reid Andrews, "The Making of a Field," in *Afro-Latin American Studies: An Introduction*, ed. Fuente and Andrews (Cambridge: Cambridge University Press, 2018), 1–25.

Fuente, Alejandro de la, César García del Pino, and Bernardo Iglesias Delgado, *Havana and the Atlantic in the Sixteenth Century* (Chapel Hill: University of North Carolina Press, 2008).

Gage, John, *Color and Culture: Practice and Meaning from Antiquity to Abstraction* (Boston: Little, Brown and Company, 1993).

Gänger, Stefanie, "Circulation: Reflections on Circularity, Entity, and Liquidity in the Language of Global History," *Journal of Global History* 12:3 (2017), 303–18.

García Ayulardo, Clara, "A World of Images: Cult, Ritual, and Society in Colonial Mexico City," in *Rituals of Rule, Rituals of Resistance: Public Celebrations and Popular Culture in Mexico*, ed. William H. Beezley, Cheryl English Martin, and William E. French (Wilmington, DE: Scholarly Resources, Inc, 1994), 77–93.

García Ayluardo, Clara, and Manuel Ramos Medina, eds., *Manifestaciones religiosas en el mundo colonial americano* (Mexico: INAH Universidad Iberoamericana, 1993).

Garfield, Robert, *A History of São Tomé Island, 1470–1655: The Key to Guinea* (San Francisco: Mellen Research University Press, 1992).

Garofalo, Leo J., "The Shape of a Diaspora: The Movement of Afro-Iberians to Colonial Spanish America," in *Africans to Spanish America: Expanding the Diaspora*, ed. Sherwin K. Bryant, Rachel Sarah O'Toole, and Ben Vinson (Urbana: University of Illinois Press, 2012), 73–93.

Gaullera Sanza, Vicente, *La esclavitud en Valencia en los siglos XVI y XVII* (Valencia: Instituto Valenciano de Estudios Históricos, 1978).

Geary, Patrick J., *Living with the Dead in the Middle Ages* (Ithaca, NY: Cornell University Press, 1994).

Gerbner, Katharine, and Karin Vélez, "Missionary Encounters in the Atlantic World," Special Issue on Missionaries, *Journal of Early Modern History* 21:1–2 (2017), 1–7.

Germeten, Nicole von, *Black Blood Brothers: Confraternities and Social Mobility for Afro-Mexicans* (Gainesville: University Press of Florida, 2006).

"Black Brotherhoods in Mexico City," in *The Black Urban Atlantic in the Age of the Slave Trade*, ed. Jorge Cañizares-Esgerra, Matt Childs, and James Sidbury (Philadelphia: University of Pennsylvania Press, 2013), 248–67.

Violent Delights, Violent Ends: Sex, Race, and Honor in Colonial Cartagena de Indias (Albuquerque: University of New Mexico Press, 2013).

Gerritsen, Anne, and Giorgia Riello, eds., *The Global Lives of Things: The Material Culture of Connections in the Early Modern World* (London: Routledge, 2016).

Gestoso y Pérez, José, *Sevilla monumental y artística*, 3 vols. (Seville: El Conservador, 1889).

Gillespie, Jeanne, "Catarina de San Juan and the Politics of Conversion and Empire," in *Women's Voices and the Politics of the Spanish Empire: From Convent Cell to Imperial Court*, ed. Jennifer L. Eich, Jeanne Gillespie, and Lucia G. Harrison (New Orleans, LA: University Press of the South, 2008), 303–17.

Ginzburg, Carlo, *The Night Battles: Witchcraft and Agrarian Cults in the Sixteenth and Seventeenth Centuries* (Baltimore: Johns Hopkins University Press, 2013).

Goetz, Rebecca Anne, "Indian Slavery: An Atlantic and Hemispheric Problem," *History Compass* 14:2 (2016), 59–70.

Gold, Penny Schine, *The Lady and the Virgin: Image, Attitude, and Experience in Twelfth-Century France* (Chicago: University of Chicago Press, 1987).

Goldberg, K. Meira, *Sonidos Negros: On the Blackness of Flamenco* (Oxford: Oxford University Press, 2018).

Goldenberg, David M., *Black and Slave: The Origins and History of the Curse of Ham* (Berlin: Walter de Gruyter GmbH, 2017).

Gómez García, María del Carmen, and Juan María Martín Vergara, *La esclavitud en Málaga entre los siglos XVII y XVIII* (Malaga: Servicio de Publicaciones, Diputación Provincial de Málaga, 1993).

González Arévalo, Raúl, *La esclavitud en Málaga a fines de la Edad Media* (Jaén: Universidad de Jaén, 2006).

González Cruz, David, ed., *Religiosidad y costumbres populares en Iberoamérica* (Huelva: Universidad de Huelva, 2000).

González de León, Félix, *Historia crítica y descriptiva de las cofradías de penitencia, sangre y luz, fundadas en la ciudad de Sevilla: con noticias del origen, progresos y estado actual de cada una, y otros sucesos y curiosidades notables* (Valencina de la Concepción: Ediciones Espuela de Plata, 2005).

González García, Juan Luis, "Spanish Religious Imagery and Post-Tridentine Theory," *Hispanic Research Journal* 16:5 (2016), 441–55.

González Martínez, Javier J., "La transmisión impresa de un manuscrito dramático censurado: el caso de 'El santo negro,' 'El negro del Serafín' o 'El negro del mejor amo,'" *Castilla: Estudios de Literatura* 3 (2012), 403–17.

Gotor, Miguel, *I beati del papa: santità, inquisizione e obbedienza in età moderna* (Florence: Olschki, 2001).

Graubart, Karen B., "'So color de una cofradía': Catholic Confraternities and the Development of Afro-Peruvian Ethnicities in Early Colonial Peru," *Slavery & Abolition* 33:1 (2012), 43–64.

"Lazos que unen. Dueñas negras de esclavos negros en Lima, siglos XVI-XVII," *Nueva corónica* 2 (2013), 625–40.

Graullera Sanz, Vicente, *La esclavitud en Valencia en los siglos XVI y XVII* (Valencia: Instituto Valenciano de Estudios Históricos, Consejo Superior de Investigaciones Científicas, 1978).

Gray, Richard, "A Kongo Princess, the Kongo Ambassadors and the Papacy," *Journal of Religion in Africa* 29:2 (1999), 140–54.

"The Papacy and the Atlantic Slave Trade: Lourenço da Silva, the Capuchins and the Decisions of the Holy Office," *Past & Present* 115:1 (1987), 52–68.

Gray, Richard, and Lamin O. Sanneh, *Christianity, the Papacy, and Mission in Africa* (Maryknoll, NY: Orbis Books, 2012).

Green, R. L., "Africans in Spanish Catholic Thought, 1568–1647: Beyond Jesuit Hagiography," *Black Theology* 11:1 (2013), 96–116.

Green, Toby, "Building Creole Identity in the African Atlantic: Boundaries of Race and Religion in Seventeenth-Century Cabo Verde," *History in Africa* 36 (2009), 103–25.

"Building Slavery in the Atlantic World: Atlantic Connections and the Changing Institution of Slavery in Cabo Verde, Fifteenth–Sixteenth Centuries," *Slavery & Abolition* 32:2 (2011), 227–45.

Greenspan, Kate, "Autohagiography and Medieval Women's Spiritual Autobiography," in *Gender and the Text in the Later Middle Ages*, ed. Jane Chance (Gainesville: University of Florida Press, 1996), 216–36.

Greer, Allan, *Mohawk Saint: Catherine Tekakwitha and the Jesuits* (New York: Oxford University Press, 2005).

"Iroquois Virgin: The Story of Catherine Tekakwitha in New France and New Spain," in *Colonial Saints: Discovering the Holy in the Americas, 1500–1800*, ed. Allan Greer and Jodi Bilinkoff (New York: Routledge, 2003), 235–50.

Gregerson, Linda, and Susan Juster, eds., *Empires of God: Religious Encounters in the Early Modern Atlantic* (Philadelphia: University of Pennsylvania Press, 2011).

Groebner, Valetin, "Complexio/Complexion: Categorizing Individual Natures," in *The Moral Authority of Nature*, ed. Lorraine Daston and Fernando Vidal (Chicago: University of Chicago Press, 2004), 357–83.

"The Carnal Knowing of a Coloured Body: Sleeping with Arabs and Blacks in the European Imagination, 1300–1550," in *The Origins of Racism in the West*, ed. Isaac Eliav-Feldon and Joseph Ziegler (New York: Cambridge University Press, 2009), 217–31.

Gual Camarena, Miguel, "Una cofradía de negros libertos en el siglo XV," *Estudios de Edad Media de la Corona de Aragóna* 5 (1952), 457–66.

Guastella, Salvatori, *Fratello Negro. Antonio di Noto, detto l'Etiope* (Noto: Edizione Las Caritas diocesano, 1991).

Guazzelli, Giuseppe Antonio, "Cesare Baronio and the Roman Catholic Vision of the Early Church," in *Sacred History: Uses of the Christian Past in the Renaissance World*, ed. Katherine Van Liere (Oxford: Oxford University Press, 2012), 52–71.

Gudmundson, Lowell, and Justin Wolfe, eds., *Blacks and Blackness in Central America: Between Race and Place* (Durham NC: Duke University Press, 2010).

Guerrera Mosquera, Andrea, "Misiones, misioneros y bautizos a través del Atlántico: evangelización en Cartagena de Indias y en los reinos del Kongo y Angola. Siglo XVII," *Mem. Soc.* 18:37 (2014), 14–32.

Gutiérrez Azopardo, Ildefonso, "Los franciscanos y los negros en el siglo XVII," *Archivo Ibero-Americano* 197–200 (1991), 593–620.

Hahn, Cynthia J., *Portrayed on the Heart: Narrative Effect in Pictorial Lives of Saints from the Tenth through the Thirteenth Century* (Berkeley: University of California Press, 2001).

Hall, Gwendolyn Midlo, *Slavery and African Ethnicities in the Americas: Restoring the Links* (Chapel Hill: University of North Carolina Press, 2007).

Hall, Kim F., *Things of Darkness: Economies of Race and Gender in Early Modern England* (Ithaca, NY: Cornell University Press, 1995).

Hall, Marcia B., *Color and Meaning: Practice and Theory in Renaissance Painting* (Cambridge: Cambridge University Press, 1992).

Harms, Robert W., *The Diligent: A Voyage through the Worlds of the Slave Trade* (New York: Basic Books, 2002).

Harris, A. Katie, *From Muslim to Christian Granada* (Baltimore: Johns Hopkins University Press, 2000).

Harris, Max, *Aztecs, Moors, and Christians: Festivals of Reconquest in Mexico and Spain* (Austin: University of Texas Press, 2000).

Hastings, Adrian, *The Church in Africa: 1450–1950* (New York: Oxford University Press, 1994).

Heintze, Beatrix, ed., *European Sources for Sub-Saharan Africa Before 1900: Use and Abuse* (Stuttgart: Steiner, 1987).

Heldman, Marilyn E., *The Marian Icons of the Painter Fre Seyon: A Study in 15th-Century Ethiopian Art, Patronage and Spirituality* (Wiesbaden: Harrassowitz, 1994).

   "St. Luke as Painter: Post-Byzantine Icons in Early-Sixteenth-Century Ethiopia," *Gesta* 44:2 (2005), 125–48.

Hellwig, Karin, *La literature artística española del siglo XVII*, trans. Jesús Espino Nuño (Madrid: Visordis, 1999).

Hendrix, John Shannon, and Charles G. Carmon, eds., *Renaissance Theories of Vision* (Aldershot: Ashgate, 2010).

Heng, Geraldine, *The Invention of Race in the European Middle Ages* (Cambridge: Cambridge University Press, 2018).

   "Reinventing Race, Colonization, and Globalisms across Deep Time: Lessons for the Longue Durée," *PMLA* 103:2 (2015), 358–66.

Henriques, Isabel de Castro, *A herança Africana em Portugal, História e Memória, Séculos XV-XX* (Lisbon: CTT Correios de Portugal, 2007).

Hernández, Ángel Santos, "Orígenes históricos de la Sagrada Congregación 'De Propaganda Fide.'" *Revista española de derecho canónico* 28/81 (1972), 509–43.

Hernández Franco, Juan, *Sangre limpia, sangre española: el debate sobre los estatuos de limpieza (siglos XV-XVII)* (Madrid: Cátedra, 2011).

Herrera, Claudia, ed., *The African Presence in Mexico: From Yanga to the Present* (Chicago: Mexican Fine Arts Center Museum, 2006).

Herzog, Tamar, "How Did Early-Modern Slaves in Spain Disappear? The Antecedents," *Republic of Letters* 3:1. http://arcade.stanford.edu/rofl/how-did-early-modern-slaves-spain-disappear-antecedents.

Heywood, Linda M., "The Angolan-Afro-Brazilian Cultural Connections," in *From Slavery to Emancipation in the Atlantic World*, ed. Sylvia Frey and Betty Wood (Hoboken: Taylor and Francis, 2013), 9–23.

   Njinga of Angola: Africa's Warrior Queen (Cambridge, MA: Harvard University Press, 2017).

   ed., *Central Africans and Cultural Transformations in the American Diaspora* (New York: Cambridge University Press, 2002).

Heywood, Linda M., and John K. Thornton, *Central Africans, Atlantic Creoles, and the Foundation of the Americas, 1585–1660* (New York: Cambridge University Press, 2007).

Hill, Ruth, "Categories and Crossings: Critical Race Studies and the Spanish World," *Journal of Spanish Cultural Studies* 10:1 (2009), 1–6.

"Entering and Exiting Blackness: A Color Controversy in Eighteenth-Century Spain," *Journal of Spanish Cultural Studies* 10:1 (2009), 43–58.

Hilton, Anne, *The Kingdom of Kongo* (Oxford: Clarendon Press; Oxford University Press, 1985).

Hine, Darlene Clark, and Jacqueline McLeod, eds., *Crossing Boundaries: Comparative History of Black People in Diaspora* (Bloomington: Indiana University Press, 1999).

Hopkins, A. G., ed. *Global History: Interactions between the Universal and the Local* (London: Palgrave Macmillan, 2006).

Houchins, Sue E. and Baltasar Fra Molinero, "The Saint's Life of Sister Chicaba, c. 1676–1748: An As-Told-To Slave Narrative," in *Afro-Latino Voices: Narratives from the Early Modern Ibero-Atlantic World, 1550–1812*, ed. Kathryn Joy McKnight and Leo Garofalo (Indianapolis, IN: Hackett, 2009), 214–39.

Howard, Philip A., *Changing History: Afro-Cuban Cabildos and Societies of Color in the Nineteenth Century* (Baton Rouge: Louisiana State University Press, 1988).

Howe, Nicholas, *Visions of Community in the Pre-Modern World* (Notre Dame, IN: University of Notre Dame Press, 2002).

Hsia, R. Po-chia, *A Jesuit in the Forbidden City: Matteo Ricci, 1552–1610* (New York: Oxford University Press, 2010).

The World of Catholic Renewal, 1540–1770, 2nd ed. (New York: Cambridge University Press, 2005).

ed., *A Companion to Early Modern Catholic Global Missions* (Leiden: Brill, 2018).

ed., *The Cambridge History of Christianity, vol. 6: Reform and Expansion, 1500–1660* (New York: Cambridge University Press, 2007).

Ireton, Chloe, "'They Are Blacks of the Caste of Black Christians': Old Christian Black Blood in the Sixteenth- and Early Seventeenth-Century Iberian Atlantic," *Hispanic American Historical Review*, 97:4 (2017), 579–612.

Iyanaga, Michael, "Why Saints Love Samba: A Historical Perspective on Black Agency and the Rearticulation of Catholicism in Bahia, Brazil," *Black Music Research Journal* 35:1 (2015), 119–47.

Izco Reina, Manuel Jesús, *Amos, esclavos y libertos: estudios sobre la esclavitud en Puerto Real durante la Edad Moderna* (Cadiz: Universidad de Cádiz, 2002).

Izequiel, Batista de Sousa, *São Tomé et Principe de 1485 à 1755, une société coloniale: du blanc au noir* (Paris: L'Harmattan, 2008).

Iwasaki Cauti, Fernando, "Mujeres al borde de la perfección: Rosa de Santa María y las alumbradas de Lima," *Hispanic American Historical Review* 73:4 (1993), 581–613.

"Luisa Melgarejo de Soto y la alegría de ser tu testigo, Señor," *Histórico* 19:2 (1995), 219–50.

Jaffary, Nora E., *False Mystics: Deviant Orthodoxy in Colonial Mexico* (Lincoln: University of Nebraska Press, 2004).

"Virtue and Transgression: The Certification of Authentic Mysticism in the Mexican Inquisition," *Catholic Southwest: A Journal of History and Culture* 10 (1999), 9–28.

Jiménez de Baéz, Yvette, "Sor Teresa Juliana de Santo Domingo, Chikaba: una vida en frontera," in *La Orden de Predicadores en Iberoamérica en el siglo XVII: Actas del IX Congreso Internacional de Historiadores*, ed. J.B. Barquilla and Ó. Mayorga (Oaxaca: Editorial San Esteban, 2010), 265–310.

Jiménez Sureda, Montserrat, *Crist i la història: Els inicis de la historiografia ecclesiastica catalane* (Barcelona: Autonomous University of Barcelona Press, 2014).

Jones, Nicholas R. "Cosmetic Ontologies, Cosmetic Subversions: Articulating Black Beauty and Humanity in Luis de Góngora's 'En la fiesta del Santísimo Sacramento,'" *Journal for Early Modern Cultural Studies* 15:1 (2015), 26–54.

"Nuptials Gone Awry, Empire in Decay: Crisis, Lo Cursi, and the Rhetorical Inventory of Blackness in Quevedo's 'Boda de negros,'" *Arizona Journal of Hispanic Cultural Studies* 20 (2016), 29–47.

Staging Habla de Negros: Radical Performances of the African Diaspora in Early Modern Spain (University Park: Pennsylvania State University Press, 2019).

Jordan Gschwend, Annemarie, and K. J. P. Lowe eds., *The Global City: On the Streets of Renaissance Lisbon* (London: Paul Holberton Publishers, 2015).

Jotischky, Andrew, *The Carmelites and Antiquity: Mendicants and Their Pasts in the Middle Ages* (New York: Oxford University Press, 2002).

Jouve Martín, José Ramón, *Esclavos de la ciudad letrada: esclavitud, escritura y colonialismo en Lima (1650–1700)* (Lima: IEP, 2005).

"En olor de santidad: hagiografía, cultos locales y escritura religiosa en Lima, siglo XVII," *Colonial Latin American Review* 13:2 (2004), 181–98.

"Public Ceremonies and Mulatto Identity in Viceregal Lima: A Colonial Reenactment of the Fall of Troy (1631)," *Colonial Latin American History* 16:2 (2007), 179–201.

Kananoja, Kalle, "Central African Identities and Religiosity in Colonial Minais Gerais," unpublished Ph.D. Dissertation, Abo Akademi University (2012).

Kaplan, Paul, "Italy, 1490–1700," in *The Image of the Black in Western Art, Volume III: From the "Age of Discovery" to the Age of Abolition, Part 1: Artists of the Renaissance and Baroque*, ed. David Bindman and Henry Louis Gates, Jr. (Cambridge, MA: Belknap Press of Harvard University Press, 2010), 93–190.

The Rise of the Black Magus in Western Art (Ann Arbor, MI: UMI Research Press), 1985.

Karasch, Mary C., *Slave Life in Rio de Janeiro, 1808–1850* (Princeton: Princeton University Press, 1987).

Karras, Ruth Mazo, "Thomas Aquinas's Chastity Belt: Clerical Masculinity in Medieval Europe," in *Gender and Christianity in Medieval Europe: New Perspectives*, ed. Lisa M. Bitel and Felice Lifschitz (Philadelphia: University of Pennsylvania Press, 2008), 52–67.

Kasl, Ronda, et al. eds., *Sacred Spain: Art and Belief in the Spanish World* (New Haven, CT: Yale University Press/Indianapolis Museum of Art, 2009).

Katzew, Ilona, "Casta Painting: Identity and Social Stratification in Colonial Mexico," in *New World Orders: Casta Painting and Colonial Latin America*, ed. Ilona Katzew and John A. Farmer (New York: Americas Society, 1996), 8–29.

Casta Painting: Images of Race in Eighteenth-Century Mexico (New Haven, CT: Yale University Press, 2004).

Katzew, Ilona, and Susan Deans-Smith, eds., *Race and Classification: The Case of Mexican America* (Stanford: Stanford University Press, 2009).

Kea, Ray A., "From Catholicism to Moravian Pietism: The World of Marotta/ Magdalena, A Woman of Popo and St. Thomas," in *The Creation of the British Atlantic World*, ed. Elizabeth Mancke and Carole Shammas (Baltimore: Johns Hopkins University Press, 2005), 115–36.

Keenan, Charles, "Paolo Sarpi, Caesar Baronius, and the Political Possibilities of Ecclesiastical History," *Church History* 84: 4 (2015), 746–67.

Kelly, Samantha, "The Curious Case of Ethiopic Chaldean: Fraud, Philology, and Cultural (Mis)Understanding in European Conceptions of Ethiopia," *Renaissance Quarterly* 68/4 (2015), 1227–64.

Kenny, Joseph, *The Catholic Church in Tropical Africa, 1445–1850* (Ibadan, Nigeria: Ibadan University Press, 1983).

Kidd, Colin, *The Forging of Races: Race and Scripture in the Protestant Atlantic World, 1600–2000* (New York: Cambridge University Press, 2006).

Kiddy, Elizabeth W., *Blacks of the Rosary: Memory and History in Minas Gerais, Brazil* (University Park: Pennsylvania State University Press, 2005).

"The Regent, the Secretary and the Widow: Power, Ethnicity, and Gender in the Confraternity of Saints Elesbao and Iphigenia, Rio de Janeiro, 1784–1786," in *Afro-Latino Voices: Narratives from the Early Modern Ibero-Atlantic World, 1550–1812*, ed. Kathryn Joy McKnight and Leo Garofalo (Indianapolis, IN: Hackett, 2009), 153–69.

Kilroy-Ewbank, Lauren G., "Holy Organ or Unholy Idol? Forming a History of the Sacred Heart in New Spain," *Colonial Latin American Review* 23:3 (2014), 320–58.

Kirk, Stephanie, and Sarah Rivett, eds., *Religious Transformations in the Early Modern Americas* (Philadelphia: University of Pennsylvania Press, 2014).

Kitchen, John, *Saints' Lives and the Rhetoric of Gender: Male and Female in Merovingian Hagiography* (New York: Oxford University Press, 1998).

Klein, Herbert, and Francisco Vidal Luna, *Slavery in Brazil* (Cambridge: Cambridge University Press, 2010).

Koerner, Joseph Leo, "The Epiphany of the Black Magus Circa 1500," in *The Image of the Black in Western Art, Volume III: From the "Age of Discovery" to the Age of Abolition, Part 1: Artists of the Renaissance and Baroque* ed. David Bindman and Henry Louis Gates, Jr., trans. William Granger Ryan (Cambridge, MA: Belknap Press of Harvard University Press, 2010), 7–92.

Kraay, Hendrik, ed., *Afro-Brazilian Culture and Politics: Bahia, 1790s-1990s* (London: Routledge, 1998).

Kurt, Andrew, "The Search for Prester John, a Projected Crusade, and the Eroding Prestige of the Ethiopian Kings, c. 1200-c.1520," *Journal of Medieval History* 39:3 (2013), 297–320.

Lagerlund, Henrik, and Benjamin Hill, eds., *Routledge Companion to Sixteenth-Century Philosophy* (New York: Routledge, 2017).

Lahon, Didier, "Black African Slaves and Freedmen in Portugal," in *Black Africans in Renaissance Europe*, ed. T. F. Earle and K. J. P. Lowe (New York: Cambridge University Press, 2005), 261–79.

"Da redução da alteridade a consagração da diferença: As irmandades negras em Portugal (séculos XVI-XVIII)," *Projeto História São Paulo* 44 (2012), 53–83.

"Esclavage, confréries noire, sainteté noire et pureté de sang au Portugal (XVIᵉ et XVIIIᵉ siècles)," *Lusitana Sacra* 2nd series 15 (2003), 119–62.

"Exclusión, integration et métissages dans les confréries noires au Portugal (XVIe-XIXe siècles)," in *Negros, mulatos, zambaigos: derroteros africanos en los mundos ibéricos*, ed. Berta Ares Queija and Alessandro Stella (Seville: Consejo Superior de Investigaciones Científicas, 2000), 275–311.

"Le berger, le cuisinier, la princesse et l'empereur: Noirs et africains sur les autels du Portugal et du Brésil esclavagistes," in *Schiavitù, religione e libertà nel Mediterraneo tra Medioevo ed età moderna*, ed. Giovanna Fiume (Cosenza: L. Pellegrini, 2008), 215–39.

"Les confréries de noirs à Lisbonne et leurs privileges royaux d'affrachissemente. Relations avec le pouvoir (XVIe-XIX e siècles)," in *Esclavage et dépendances serviles: histoire comparée*, ed. Myriam Cottias, Alessandro Stella, and Bernard Vincent (Paris: L'Harmattan, 2006), 195–215.

O negro no coração do Império: uma memória a resgatar – séculos XV-XIX (Lisbon: Secretario Coordenador dos Programas de Educação Multicultural, Ministério da Educação: Casa do Brasil, 1999).

"Saints noirs et iconographie durant l'époque de l'esclavage dans la Péninsule Ibérique et au Brésil, 17e-19e siècles," *Cahier des Anneaux de la Mémoire* 12 (2009), 1–23.

Lameira, Francisco I. C., *Inventário artístico do Algarve: a talha e a imaginária* (Faro: Secretaria de Estado da Cultura, Delegação Regional do Sul, 1989).

Landers, Jane, *Black Society in Spanish Florida* (Urbana: University of Illinois Press, 1999).

Landers, Jane G., and Barry M. Robinson, eds., *Slaves, Subjects, and Subversives: Blacks in Colonial Latin America* (Albuquerque: University of New Mexico Press, 2006).

Lavrín, Asunción, *Brides of Christ: Conventual Life in Colonial Mexico* (Stanford: Stanford University Press, 2008).

Law, Robin, "Ethnicity and the Slave Trade: 'Lucumí' and 'Nago' as Ethnonyms in West Africa," *History in Africa* 24 (1997), 205–19.

"Religion, Trade and Politics on the 'Slave Coast': Roman Catholic Missions in Allada and Whydah in the Seventeenth Century," *Journal of Religion in Africa* 21:2 (1991), 42–77.

The Slave Coast of West Africa, 1550–1750: The Impact of the Atlantic Slave Trade on an African Society (Oxford: Clarendon Press; Oxford University Press, 1991).

Lawrence, Jeremy, "Black Africans in Renaissance Spanish Literature," in *Black Africans in Renaissance Europe*, ed. T. F. Earle and K. J. P. Lowe (Cambridge: Cambridge University Press, 2010), 70–94.

Leavitt-Alcántara, Brianna, "Holy Women and Hagiography in Colonial Spanish America," *History Compass* 12:9 (2014), 717–28.

Lefèvre, Renato, "Presenze etiopiche in Italia prima del concilio di Firenze del 1439," *Rassegna di Studi Etiopici* 23 (1967–1968), 5–26.

"Documenti e notizie di Tasfa Seyon e la sua attività romana nel sec. XVI," *Rassegna di studi etiopici* 24 (1969), 74–133.

Lewis, Charles, *An Elementary Latin Dictionary* (Oxford: Oxford University Press, 1998).

Lewis, Laura A., *Hall of Mirrors: Power, Witchcraft, and Caste in Colonial Mexico* (Durham: Duke University Press, 2003).

Chocolate and Corn Flour: History, Race, and Place in the Making of "Black" Mexico (Durham, NC: Duke University Press, 2012).

Lifshitz, Felice, "Beyond Positivism and Genre: 'Hagiographical' Texts as Historical Narrative," *Viator* 25 (1994), 95–114.

The Name of the Saint: The Martyrology of Jerome and Access to the Sacred in Francia, 627–827 (Notre Dame, IN: University of Notre Dame Press, 2006).

Lipski, John M., *A History of Afro-Hispanic Languages: Five Centuries, Five Continents* (Cambridge: Cambridge University Press, 2005).

Lockhart, James, *Spanish Peru, 1532–1560: A Social History*, 2nd ed. (Madison: University of Wisconsin Press, 1994).

Lombardi, Riccardo, *The Salvation of the Unbeliever* (Westminster, MD: Newman Press, 1956).

Lomas Salmonte, Francisco Javier, "Cádiz en la Antigüedad," in *Historia de Cádiz* (Madrid: Silex, 2005), 15–146.

Lopes, Inês Afonso, "Imagem-objeto: sinestesias da matéria com a mente. As imagens dos santos negros da igreja de Santa Clara do Porto," *Artis* 9–10 (2010–2011), 359–72.

López García, José Tomás, *Dos defensores de los esclavos negros en el siglo XVII, Francisco José de Jaca y Epifanio de Moirans* (Maracaibo: Biblioteca Corpozulia, 1982).

López García, José Miguel, Alberto Castroviejo Salas, and Luis Miguel Pozo Rincón, "Entre la marginación y integración. Los esclavizados en Madrid durante el antiguo regimen," in *Veinticinco años después: Avances en la historia social y económica de Madrid*, ed. Jesús Agua de la Roza, José Antolín Nieto Sánchez, et al. (Madrid: Ediciones Universidad Autónoma de Madrid, 2014), 251–78.

Lovejoy, Paul E., *The African Diaspora: Revisionist Interpretations of Ethnicity, Culture and Religion under Slavery* (Boston: Northeastern University Press, 1997).

Lovejoy, Paul, and David Richardson, "Trust, Pawnship, and Atlantic History: The Institutional Foundations of the Old Calabar Slave Trade," *American Historical Review* 104:2 (1999), 332–55.

Lowe, Kate, "Black Africans' Religious and Cultural Assimilation to, or Appropriation of, Catholicism in Italy, 1470–1520," *Renaissance & Reformation/Renaissance et Reforme [Special issue on Sub-Saharan Africa and Renaissance and Reformation Europe: New findings and New Perspectives]* 31:2 (2008), 67–86.

"The Global Population of Renaissance Lisbon," in *The Global City: On the Streets of Renaissance Lisbon*, ed. Annemarie Jordan Gschwend and K. J. P. Lowe (London: Paul Holberton Publishers, 2015).

"Introduction," *Renaissance & Reformation/Renaissance et Reforme [Special issue on Sub-Saharan Africa and Renaissance and Reformation Europe: New Findings and New Perspectives]* 31:2 (2008), 3–6.

"'Representing' Africa: Ambassadors and Princes from Christian Africa to Renaissance Italy and Portugal, 1402–1608," *Transactions of the Royal Historical Society* 17 (2007), 101–28.

"Visible Lives: Black Gondoliers and Other Black Africans in Renaissance Venice," *Renaissance Quarterly* 66:2 (2013), 412–52.

"Visual Representations of an Elite: African Ambassadors and Rulers in Renaissance Europe," in *Revealing the African Presence in Renaissance Europe*, ed. Joaneath Spicer (Baltimore: Walters Art Museum, 2012), 98–115.

Luebke, David M., *Hometown Religion: Regimes of Coexistence in Early Modern Westphalia* (Charlottesville: University of Virginia Press, 2016).

Lynch, John, *New Worlds: A Religious History of Latin America* (New Haven: Yale University Press, 2012).

Lyon, Gregory B., "Baudin, Flacius, and the Plan for the Madgeburg Centuries," *Journal of the History of Ideas* 64:2 (2003), 253–72.

Machielsen, Jan, "Heretical Saints and Textual Discernment: The Polemical Origins of the Acta Sanctorum (1643–1940)," in *Angels of Light? Sanctity and the Discernment of Spirits in the Early Modern Period*, ed. Clare Copeland and Jan Machielsen (Leiden: Brill, 2012), 103–41.

Maeso, María Eugenia, *Sor Teresa Chikaba: princesa, esclava y monja* (Salamanca: Editorial San Esteban, 2004).

Mancke, Elizabeth, and Carole Shammas, eds., *The Creation of the British Atlantic World* (Baltimore: Johns Hopkins University Press, 2005).

Manduca, Raffaele, "Uno spazio in movimento, ordini e conventi in Sicilia fra cinque e seicento," in *Il santo e patrono e la città: San Benedetto il Moro: culti, devozioni, strategie di età moderna*, ed. Giovanna Fiume (Venice: Marsilio, 2000), 281–311.

Mangan, Jane E., "A Market of Identities: Women, Trade, and Ethnic Labels in Colonial Potosí," in *Imperial Subjects: Race and Identity in Colonial Latin America*, ed. Andrew B. Fisher and Matthew D. O'Hara (Durham, NC: Duke University Press, 2009), 61–80.

Mansour, Opher, "Picturing Global Conversion: Art and Diplomacy at the Court of Paul V (1605–1621)," *Journal of Early Modern History* 17 (2013), 525–59.

Marcocci, Giuseppe, "Conscience and Empire: Politics and Moral Theology in the Early Modern Portuguese World," *Journal of Early Modern History* 18:5 (2014), 473–94.

   "Blackness and Heathenism: Color, Theology, and Race in the Portuguese World, c. 1450–1600," *Anuario Colombiano de Historia Social y de la Cultura* 43:2 (2016), 33–58.

Marcocci, Giuseppe, Aliocha Maldavsky, Wietse de Boer et al., eds., *Space and Conversion in Global Perspective* (Leiden: Brill, 2014).

Mark, Peter, *Africans in European Eyes: The Portrayal of Black Africans in Fourteenth and Fifteenth Century Europe* (Syracuse, NY: Syracuse University, 1974).

Marino, John A., *Becoming Neapolitan: Citizen Culture in Baroque Naples* (Baltimore: Johns Hopkins University Press, 2011).

Mariz, Carlos Domingues da Venda, *A Santa Casa da Misericórdia de Fão* (Fão: Santa Casa da Misericódia, 2000).

Marrone, Giovanni, *La schiavitù nella società siciliana dell'età moderna* (Caltanissetta-Rome: S. Sciascia 1972).

Martín Casares, Aurelia, "Free and Freed Black African in Granada in the Time of the Spanish Renaissance," in *Black Africans in Renaissance Europe*, ed. T. F. Earle and K. J. P. Lowe (New York: Cambridge University Press, 2005), 247–60.

   Esclavitudes hispánicas (siglos XV al XXI): Horizontes socioculturales (Granada: Universidad de Granada, 2014).

   La esclavitud en la Granada del siglo XVI: género, raza y religión (Granada: Editorial Universidad de Granada, 2000).

Martín Casares, Aurelia, and Margarita G. Barranco, "Popular Literary Depictions of Black African Weddings in Early Modern Spain," *Renaissance & Reformation/Renaissance et Réforme* 31:2 (2008), 107–21.

   "The Musical Legacy of Black Africans in Spain: A Review of Our Sources," *Anthropological Notebooks* XV:2 (2009), 51–60.

Martín Casares, Aurelia, and Christine Delaigue, "The Evangelization of Freed and Slave Black Africans in Renaissance Spain: Baptism, Marriage, and Ethnic Brotherhoods," *History of Religions* 52:3 (2013), 214–35.

Martínez, María Elena, "The Black Blood of New Spain: Limpieza de Sangre, Racial Violence, and Gendered Power in Early Colonial Mexico," *The William and Mary Quarterly* 61:3 (2004), 479–520.

Genealogical Fictions: Limpieza de Sangre, Religion, and Gender in Colonial Mexico (Stanford: Stanford University Press, 2008).

Martínez d'Alòs Moner, Andreu, *Envoys of a Human God: The Jesuit Mission to Christian Ethiopia, 1557–1632* (Boston: Brill, 2015).

Martínez Ferrer, Luis, "La preocupación médica y religiosa del doctor Pedro López por las personas de raza negra de la ciudad de México (1582–1597)," *Anuario de Estudios Americanos* 65:2 (2008), 71–89.

Martínez Gutiérrez, María Elisa, and Ethel Correa Duró, eds., *Poblaciones y culturas de origen africano en México* (Mexico City: Instituto Nacional de Historia Anthropología, 2005).

Martínez Montiel, Luz María, ed., *Presencia africana en Sudamérica* (Mexico: Consejo Nacional para la Cultura y las Artes, 1995).

Presencia africana en México (Mexico: Consejo Nacional para la Cultura y las Artes, 1997).

Martínez Montiel, Luz M., Juan Carlos Reyes G, et al., eds., *Memoria del III Encuentro Nacional de Afromexicanistas* (Mexico: Gobierno del Estado de Colima, 1993).

Martínez Suárez, Juan de Dios, *El culto a San Benito de Palermo en Venezuela* (Maracaibo, Venezuela: Editorial La Llama Violeta, 1999).

Masferrer León, Cristina Verónica, "Por las ánimas de negros bozales. Las cofradías de personas de origen African en la ciudad de México (siglo XVII)," *Cuicuilco* 18:51 (2011). www.scielo.org.mx/scielo.php?script=sci_arttext&pid=S0185-16592011000200006.

Massing, Jean Michel, *The Image of the Black in Western Art, Volume III: From the "Age of Discovery" to the Age of Abolition, Part 2: Europe and the World Beyond*, ed. David Bindman and Henry Louis Gates, Jr. (Cambridge, MA: Belknap Press, 2010), 93–190.

Mazurek, Antoine, "Réforme tridentine et culte des saints en Espagne: liturgie romaine et saints ibérique," in *The Council of Trent: Reform and Controversy in Europe and Beyond (1545–1700)*, ed. Violet Soen Wim François, vol. 1 (Göttingen: Vandenboeck and Ruprecht, 2018), 221–6.

McGaffey, Wyatt, "Dialogues of the Deaf: Europeans on the Atlantic Coast of Africa," in *Implicit Understandings: Observing, Reporting, and Reflecting on the Encounters Between Europeans and Other Peoples in the Early Modern Era*, ed. Stuart B. Schwartz (New York: Cambridge University Press, 1994), 249–67.

McGuire, Meredith B., *Lived Religion: Faith and Practice in Everyday Life* (Oxford: Oxford University Press, 2008).

McKee, Sally, "Domestic Slavery in Renaissance Italy," *Slavery & Abolition* 29:3 (2008), 305–26.

Melián, Elvira M., "Chikaba, la primera monja negra en el sistema esclavista finisecular español del siglo XVII," *Hispania sacra* 64:130 (2012), 565–81.

Méndez Rodríguez, Luis, "Bailes y fiestas de negros en España. Un estudio de su representación artísticas," *Archivo Hispalense: Revista Histórica, Literaria y Artística* 289 (2007), 397–413.

Melish, Joanne, *Disowning Slavery: Gradual Emancipation and Race in New England, 1780–1860* (Ithaca, NY: Cornell University Press, 1998).

Melchor Toledo, Johann Estuardo, "El arte religioso de la Antigua Guatemala, 1773–1821: Crónica de la emigración de sus imágenes," unpublished Ph.D. thesis, Universidad Nacional Autónoma de México (2011).

Mello e Souza, Marina, "Kongo King Festivals in Brazil: From Kings of Nations to Kings of Kongo," trans. Silvia Escorel, *African Studies Quarterly* 15:3 (2015), 39–45.

Reis negros no Brasil escravista: histórica da festa de coroação de rei congo (Belo Horizonte: Editora UFMG, 2002).

Melvin, Karen, "A Potential Saint Thwarted: The Politics of Religion and Sanctity in Late Eighteenth-Century New Spain," *Studies in Eighteenth-Century Culture* 36:1 (2007), 169–85.

Building Colonial Cities of God: Mendicant Orders and Urban Culture in New Spain (Stanford: Stanford University Press, 2012).

Meznar, Joan, "Our Lady of the Rosary, African Slaves, and the Struggle against Hereticsin Brazil, 1550–1660," *Journal of Early Modern History* 9 (2005), 371–97.

Miller, Joseph C., "Central Africa during the Era of the Slave Trade, c. 1490s–1950s," in *Central Africans and Cultural Transformations in the American Diaspora*, ed. Linda M. Heywood (New York: Cambridge University Press, 2002), 21–69.

The Problem of Slavery as History: A Global Approach (New Haven: Yale University Press, 2012).

"Retention, Reinvention, and Remembering: Restoring Identities through Enslavement in Africa and under Slavery in Brazil," in *Enslaving Connections: Changing Cultures of Africa and Brazil during the Era of Slavery*, ed. José C. Curto and Paul E. Lovejoy (Amherst, NY: Humanity Books, 2004), 81–121.

Mills, Kenneth, *Idolatry and Its Enemies: Colonial Andean Religion and Extirpation, 1640–1750* (Princeton: Princeton University Press, 1997).

Minnich, Nelson H., "The Catholic Church and the Pastoral Care of Black Africans in Renaissance Italy," in *Black Africans in Renaissance Europe*, ed. T. F. Earle and K. J. P. Lowe (New York: Cambridge University Press, 2005), 280–301.

Mira Caballos, Esteban, "Cofradías étnicas en la España moderna: Una aproximación al estado de la cuestión," *Hispania Sacra* LXVI, Extra II (2014), 57–88.

Miramon, Charles de, "Noble Dogs, Noble Blood: The Invention of the Concept of Race in the Late Middle Ages," in *The Origins of Racism in the West*, ed. Miriam Eliav-Feldon, Benjamin H. Isaac, and Joseph Ziegler (New York: Cambridge University Press, 2009), 200–16.

Modica, Marilena, "I processi settecenteschi di San Benedetto il Moro," in *Il santo e patrono e la città: San Benedetto il Moro: culti, devozioni, strategie di età moderna*, ed. Giovanna Fiume (Venice: Marsilio, 2000), 334–53.

Molina, J. Michelle, "True Lies: Athanasius Kircher's *China Illustrata* and the Life Story of a Mexican Mystic," in *Athanasius Kircher: The Last Man Who Knew Everything*, ed. Paula Findlan (New York: Routledge, 2004), 365–82.

Molineux, Catherine, *Faces of Perfect Ebony: Encountering Atlantic Slavery in Imperial Britain* (Cambridge, MA: Harvard University Press, 2012).

Momigliano, Arnaldo, *The Classical Foundations of Modern Historiography* (Berkeley: University of California Press, 1990).

Monti, James, *The Week of Salvation: History and Traditions of Holy Week* (Huntington, IN: Our Sunday Visitor, 1993).

Morabito, Vittorio, "San Benedetto il Moro da Palermo," in *Negros, mulatos, zambaigos: derroteros africanos en los mundos ibéricos*, ed. Berta Ares Queija and Alessandro Stella (Seville: Consejo Superior de Investigaciones Científicas, 2000), 223–73.

Moreno Navarro, Isidoro, *La antigua hermandad de los negros de Sevilla: etnicidad, poder y sociedad en 600 años de historia* (Seville: University Sevilla and Junta de Andalucía, 1997).

Morgado García, Arturo, *El estamento eclesiástico y la vida espiritual en la Diócesis de Cádiz en el siglo XVII* (Cadiz: Servicio de Publicaciones de la Universidad de Cádiz, 1996).

"The Presence of Black African Women in the Slave System of Cadiz (1650–1750)," *Slavery & Abolition* 34:1 (2013), 1–16.

"Los libertos en el Cádiz de la Edad Moderna," *Studia Histórica* 32:32 (2010), 399–436.

"Vidas reinventadas: la condición esclava en el Cádiz de la modernidad," *Bulletin for Spanish and Portuguese Historical Studies* 36:1 (2011), 70–96.

Morgado García, Arturo and Antonio Domínguez Ortiz, *Iglesia y sociedad en el Cádiz del siglo XVIII* (Cadiz: Universidad de Cádiz, Servicio de Publicaciones, 1989).

Morgan, David, "The Visual Piety of the Sacred Heart," *Material Religion* 13:2 (2017), 233–36.

Morgan, Philip D., and Sean Hawkins, eds., *Black Experience and the Empire* (New York: Oxford University Press, 2004).

Morgan, Ronald J., "Jesuit Confessors, African Slaves and the Practice of Confession in Seventeenth-Century Cartagena," in *Penitence in the Age of Reformations*, ed. Katharine J. Lualdi and Anne T. Thayer (Burlington, VT: Ashgate, 2000), 240–59.

"Postscript to His Brothers: Reading Alonso de Sandoval's *De Instauranda Aethiopum Salute* (1627) as a Jesuit Spiritual Text," *Atlantic Studies: Global Currents* 5:1 (2008), 75–98.

Spanish American Saints and the Rhetoric of Identity, 1600–1810 (Tucson: University of Arizona Press, 2002).

Morgan, Teresa, *Roman Faith and Christian Faith: Pistis and Fides in the Early Roman Empire and Early Churches* (Oxford: Oxford University Press, 2015).

Moriel-Payne, Juana, "La cofradía de la Limpia Concepción de los Pardos in San Joseph del Parral, 1600–1800: Reconstructing the Historical Memory of African-Mexican Community in the North of New Spain," *The Journal of Pan African Studies* 6:1 (2013), 19–34.

Morrison, Robert R., *Lope de Vega and the comedia de santos* (New York: Peter Lang, 2000).

Moss, Leonard W., and Stephen C. Cappannari, "In Quest of the Black Virgin: She is Black Because She Is Black," in *Mother Worship: Themes and Variations*, ed. James Preston (Chapel Hill: University of North Carolina Press, 1982), 53–74.

Mott, Luiz R. B., *Rosa Egipcíaca: uma santa africana no Brasil* (Rio de Janeiro: Bertrand Brasil, 1993).

Moura Ribeiro Zeron, Carlos Alberto de, ed., *Ligne de foi: la Compagnie de Jésus et l'esclavage dans le processus de formation de la société coloniale en Amérique portugaise, XVIe-XVIIe siècles* (Paris: H. Champion, 2009).

Muir, Edward, "The Eye of the Procession: Ritual Ways of Seeing in the Renaissance," in *Ceremonial Culture in Pre-Modern Europe*, ed. Nicholas Howe (Notre Dame, IN: University of Notre Dame Press, 2007), 129–53.

Mujica Pinilla, Ramón, Pierre Duviols, and Teresa Gisbert, eds., *El barroco peruano*, 2 vols. (Lima: Banco del Crédito, 2002).

Mulvey, Patricia A., "Black Brothers and Sisters: Membership in the Black Lay Brotherhoods of Colonial Brazil," *Luso-Brazilian Review* 17:2 (1980), 253–79.
  "Slave Confraternities in Brazil: Their Role in Colonial Society," *The Americas* 39:1 (1982), 39–68.

Mulvey, Patricia A., and Barry A. Crouch, "Black Solidarity: A Comparative Perspective on Slave Sodalities in Latin America," in *Manipulating the Saints: Religious Brotherhoods and Social Integration in Postconquest Latin America*, ed.
  Albert Meyers and Diane Elizabeth Hopkins (Hamburg: Wayasbah, 1988), 51–65.

Muñoz Martín, Arsenio, *Museos: Museo de Arte Sacro y de Ciencias Naturales* (Madrid: Franciscanos de la Provincia de Castilla, 2005).

Munro-Hay, S. C., *Ethiopia, the Unknown Land: A Cultural and Historical Guide* (London: I. B. Tauris, 2002).

Murray, Jacqueline, "One Flesh, Two Sexes, Three Genders?" in *Gender and Christianity in Medieval Europe: New Perspectives*, ed. Lisa M. Bitel and Felice Lifshitz (Philadelphia: University of Pennsylvania Press, 2008), 34–51.

Myers, Kathleen Ann, *Neither Saints nor Sinners: Writing the Lives of Women in Spanish America* (New York: Oxford University Press, 2003).

Navarro, Isidoro Moreno, *Cofradías y hermandades andaluzas: estructura, simbolismo e identidad* (Seville: Editoriales Andaluzas Unidas, 1985).

Neves, Maria João, Miguel Almeida, and Maria Teresa Ferreira Separados, "Separados na vida e na morte: retracto do tratamento mortuário dado aos escravos africanos na cidade moderna de Lagos," *XELB Rev.* 10 (2010), 547–60.

Newman, Barbara, "Preface," in *Send Me God: The Lives of the Ida the Compassionate of Nivelles, Nun of La Ramé, Arnulf, Lay Brother of Villers, and Abundus, Monk of Villers by Goswin of Bossut*, ed. and intro. Martinus Cawley (University Park: Penn State University Press, 2003), xxix–xlvii.

Newman, Jane, "'Race,' Religion, and the Law: Rhetorics of Sameness and Difference in the Work of Hugo Grotius," in *Rhetoric and Law in Early Modern Europe*, ed. Victoria Ann Kahn and Lorna Hutson (New Haven: Yale University Press, 2001), 285–317.

Nirenberg, David, "Was There Race Before Modernity? The Example of 'Jewish' Blood in Late Medieval Spain," in *The Origins of Racism in the West*, ed. Miriam Eliav-Feldon, Benjamin H. Isaac, and Joseph Ziegler (New York: Cambridge University Press, 2009), 232–64.

Nishida, Mieko, "From Ethnicity to Race and Gender: Transformations of Black Lay Sodalities in Salvador, Brazil," *Journal of Social History* 32:2 (1998), 329–48.

O'Malley, John, Gauvin Alexander Bailey, Steven Harris, and T. Frank Kennedy, eds., *The Jesuits: Culture, Science and the Arts, 1540–1773*, 2 vols. (Toronto: University of Toronto Press, 2006).

O'Neill, Charles E., and Joaquín María Domínguez, *Diccionario histórico de la Compañía de Jesús: biográfico-temático*, 4 vols. (Rome: Institutum Historicum; Universidad Pontificia Comillas, 2001).

O'Toole, Rachel S., *Bound Lives: Africans, Indians, and the Making of Race in Colonial Peru* (Pittsburg, PA: University of Pittsburgh Press, 2012).

"From the Rivers of Guinea to the Valleys of Peru: Becoming a Bran Diaspora within Spanish Slavery," *Social Text* 25:3 (2007), 19–36.

"'The Most Resplendent Flower in the Indies': Making Saints and Constructing Whiteness in Colonial Peru," in *Women, Religion, and the Atlantic World (1600–1800)*, ed. Lisa Vollendorf and Daniella J. Kostroun (Toronto: University of Toronto Press, 2009), 136–55.

"To Be Free and Lucumí: Ana de la Calle and Making African Diaspora Identities in Colonial Peru," in *Africans to Spanish America: Expanding the Diaspora*, ed. Sherwin K. Bryant, Rachel Sarah O'Toole, and Ben Vinson (Urbana: University of Illinois Press, 2012), 73–93.

Obregón, Julio Luna, *Efigenia, la negra santa: culto religioso de los descendientes africanos en el valle de Cañete* (Lima: Centro de Desarrollo de la muger Negra Peruana, 2005).

Olds, Katrina B., *Forging the Past: Invented Histories in Counter-Reformation Spain* (New Haven, CT: Yale Univesity Press, 2015).

Oleszkiewicz-Peralba, Małgorzata, *The Black Madonna in Latin America and Europe: Tradition and Transformation* (Albuquerque: University of New Mexico Press, 2007).

Oliveira, Anderson José Machado de, "Devoção e identidades: significados do culto de Santo Elesbão e Santa Efigênia no Rio de Janeiro e nas Minas Gerias no Setecentos," *Topoi* 7:12 (2006), 60–115.

Devoção negra: Santos pretos y catequese no Brasil colonial (Rio de Janeiro: Wartur; Faperj, 2008).

"Santos pardos e pretos na América portuguesa: Catolicismo, escravidão, mestiçagens e hierarquias de cor," *Studia histórica moderna* 38:1 (2016), 65–93.

Santos Oliveira, Vanessa dos, "Devoção distinção étnica na Irmandade do Homens Pretos do Rosário da Cidade de São Cristóvão-Sergipe," *Portuguese Studies Review* 20:1 (2012), 79–112.

Olsen, Margaret M., *Slavery and Salvation in Colonial Cartagena de Indias* (Gainesville: University Press of Florida, 2004).

Olson, Oliver K., *Matthias Flacius and the Survival of Luther's Reform* (Minneapolis: Lutheran Press, 2011).

Ortega, Rafael, "La cofradía de los negros en el Jaén del siglo XVII," *Boletín del Instituto de Estudios Giennenses* 12 (1957), 125–34.

Ostrow, Steven F., "Zurbarán's Cartellini: Presence and the Paragone," *Art Bulletin* 99:1 (2017), 67–96.

Osswald, Maria Cristina, "Goa and Jesuit Cult and Iconography before 1622," *Archivum Historicum Societatis Iesu* 74:147 (2005), 155–73.

Ota Mishima, María Elena, "Un mural novohispano en la cathedral de Cuernavaca: Los veintiseis mártires de Nagasaki," *Estudios de Asia y Africa* 16:4(50) (1981), 675–97.

Owens, Sarah E., and Jane E. Mangan, eds., *Women of the Iberian Atlantic* (Baton Rouge: Louisiana State University Press, 2012).

Owensby, Brian, *Empire of Law and Indian Justice in Colonial Mexico* (Stanford: Stanford University Press, 2011).

Pagden, Anthony, "The Peopling of the New World: Ethnos, Race and Empire in the Early-Modern World," in *The Origins of Racism in the West*, ed. Miriam Eliav-Feldon, Benjamin H. Isaac, and Joseph Ziegler (New York: Cambridge University Press, 2009), 292–312.

Palmer, Colin, "Afro-Latinos and the Bible: The Formative Years in Mexico, Brazil, and Peru," in *African Americans and the Bible: Sacred Texts and Social Textures*, ed. Vincent L. Wimbush and Rosamond C. Rodman (New York: Continuum, 2000), 179–92.

Slaves of the White God: Blacks in Mexico, 1570–1650 (Cambridge, MA: Harvard University Press, 1976).

Palomo, Federico, "Conexiones atlánticas: Fr. Apolinário da Conceição, la erudición religiosa y el mundo del impreso en Portugal y la América portuguesa durante el siglo XVIII," *Cuadernos de Historia Moderna Anejo* XIII (2014), 111–37.

"Un catolicismo en plural: identidades, disciplinamiento y cultura religiosa en los mundos Ibéricos de la edad moderna," in *Poder, sociedad, religión y tolerancia en el mundo hispánico, de Fernando el Católico al siglo XVIII*, ed. Eliseo Serrano Martín and Jesús Gascón Pérez (Zaragoza: Institución Fernando el Católico, 2018), 193–218.

Panford, Moses Etuah, "La figura del negro en cuatro comedias barrocas: 'Juan Latino' (Jimenez de Enciso), 'El Valiente Negro en Flandes' (Claramonte), 'El Santo Negro Rosambuco' (Lope de Vega) y 'El Negro del Mejor Amo' (Mira de Amescua)," unpublished Ph.D. thesis, Temple University (1993).

Pardo, Osvaldo, *The Origins of Mexican Catholicism: Nahua Rituals and Christian Sacraments in Sixteenth-Century Mexico* (Ann Arbor: University of Michigan Press, 2004).

Parés, Luis Nicolau, *The Formation of Candomblé: Vodun History and Ritual in Brazil*, trans. Richard Vernon (Chapel Hill: University of North Carolina Press, 2013).

Parker, Charles H., "The Reformation in Global Perspective," *History Compass* 12:12 (2014), 924–34.

Parrilla Ortíz, Pedro, *La esclavitud en Cádiz durante el siglo XVIII* (Cadiz: Diputación de Cádiz, 2001).

Passos, Maria José Spiteri Tavolaro, "Imaginária retabular colonial em São Paulo: Estudios Iconográficos," unpublished Ph.D. thesis, Universidade Estadual Paulista (2015).

Pastoureau, Michel, *Blackness: The History of a Color*, trans. Jody Gladding (Princeton: Princeton University Press, 2009).

Patton, Pamela Anne, ed., *Envisioning Others: Race, Color, and the Visual in Iberia and Latin America* (Leiden: Brill, 2016).

Paz, Octavio, *Sor Juana, or, The Traps of Faith*, trans. Margaret Sayers Peden (Cambridge, MA: Belknap Press, 1998).

Peabody, Sue, "'A Dangerous Zeal': Catholic Missions to Slaves in the Great Antilles, 1635–1800," *French Historical Studies* 25:1 (2002), 53–90.

Pearson, Timothy G., "'I Willingly Speak to You about Her Virtues': Catherine de Saint-Augustin and the Public Role of Female Holiness in Early New France," *Church History* 79:2 (2010), 305–33.

Pereda, Felipe, *Crimen e illusion: el arte de la verdad en el Siglo de Oro* (Madrid: Marcial Pons, 2017).

Pérez Guedejo, J. J., *Cofradías y Hermandades de Almendral, Historia y presente* (Badajoz: Diputación de Badajoz, 1999).

Periáñez Gómez, Rocío, "La investigación sobre la esclavitud en España en la edad moderna," *Norba. Revista de Historia* 21 (2008), 275–82.

Negros, mulatos y blancos: los esclavos en Extremadura durante la edad moderna (Badajoz: Diputación de Badajoz, 2010).

Perry, Mary Elizabeth, "The Manly Woman: A Historical Case Study," *American Behavioral Scientist* 31:1 (1987), 86–100.

Peterson, Jeanette Favrot, *Visualizing Guadalupe: From Black Madonna to Queen of the Americas* (Austin: University of Texas Press, 2014).

Phillips, William D., *Slavery in Medieval and Early Modern Iberia* (Philadelphia: University of Pennsylvania Press, 2013).

Pike, Ruth, "Sevillian Society in the Sixteenth Century: Slaves and Freedmen," *The Hispanic American Historical Review* 47:3 (1967), 344–59.

Portús, Javier, "Pintura y sociedad en la España del Siglo de Oro: Una aproximación desde la literature," *Studi Ispanici* 25 (2000), 25–40.

Poska, Allyson M., *Gendered Crossings: Women and Migration in the Spanish Empire* (Albuqueque: University of New Mexico Press, 2016).

Poutrin, Isabelle, *Le voile et la plume: autobiographie et sainteté féminine dans l'Espagne moderne* (Madrid: Casa de Velázquez, 1995).

Proctor III, Frank "Trey," "African Diasporic Ethnicity in Mexico City to 1650," in *Africans to Spanish America: Expanding the Diaspora*, ed. Sherwin K. Bryant, Rachel Sarah O'Toole, and Ben Vinson (Urbana: University of Illinois Press, 2012), 50–72.

"Slavery Rebellion and Liberty in Colonial Mexico," in *Black Mexico: Race and Society from Colonial to Modern Times*, ed. Ben Vinson and Matthew Restall (Albuquerque: University of New Mexico Press, 2009).

Prosperi, A., "L'Immaculée Conception à Séville et la fondation sacrée de la monarchie espagnole," *Revue d'Histoire de Philosophie Religieuses* 87 (2007), 435–67.

Putnam, Lara, "To Study the Fragments/Whole: Microhistory and the Atlantic World," *Journal of Social History* 39:3 (2006), 615–30.

Quiles, Fernando, "En los cimientos de la iglesia sevillana: Fernando III, rey y santo" *Boletín del Museo e Instituto Camón Aznar*, LXXV–LXXI (1999), 203–50.

Ramos, Frances L., *Identity, Ritual, and Power in Colonial Puebla* (Tucson: University of Arizona Press, 2012).

Ramos, Gabriela, *Death and Conversion in the Andes: Lima and Cuzco, 1532–1670* (Notre Dame: University of Notre Dame Press, 2010).

Redworth, Glyn, "Mythology with Attitude? A Black Christian's Defence of Negritude in Early Modern Europe," *Social History* 28:1 (2003), 49–66.

Reginaldo, Lucilene, "'África em Portugal': devoções, irmandades e escravidão no Reino de Portugal, século XVIII," *História* 28:1 (2009), 239–320.

"Irmandades e devoções de africanos e crioulos na Bahia setecentista: histórias e experiências atlânticas," *Stockholm Review of Latin American Studies* 4 (2009), 24–36.

"Rosários dos pretos, 'São Benedito de Quissama': Irmandades e devoções negras no mundo Atlântico (Portugal e Angola, século XVIII)," *Studia histórica. Historia Moderna* 38 (2016), 123–51.

Reis, João José, *Divining Slavery and Freedom: The Story of Domingos Sodré, an African Priest in Nineteenth-Century Brazil*, trans. H. Sabrina Gledhill (New York: Cambridge University Press, 2015).

Renoux, Christian, "Canonizzazione e santità femmenile in età moderna," *Storia d'Italia* 16 (2000), 735–6.

Restall, Matthew, *The Black Middle: Africans, Mayas, and Spaniards in Colonial Yucatan* (Stanford: Stanford University Press, 2009).

Ribeiro, René, "Relations of the Negro with Christianity in Portuguese America," *The Americas* 14:4 (1958), 454–84.

Rice, Robin Ann, "La 'Teresa Indiana': doctrina, herejía y creación del sujeto de la vida de la venerable Isabel de la Encarnación escrita por licenciado Pedro Salmerón (1675)," in *Vida conventual femenina (siglos XVI-XIX)*, ed. Miguel Ramos Medina (Mexico: Centro de Estudios de Historia de México Carso, 2013), 139–54.

Ritchey, Sara, *Holy Matter: Changing Perceptions of the Material World in Late Medieval Christianity* (Ithaca, NY: Cornell University Press, 2014).

Roach, Joseph R., *Cities of the Dead: Circum-Atlantic Performance* (New York: Columbia University Press, 1996).

Rodrigues Brandão, Carlos, *A festa do santo preto* (Rio de Janeiro: Funarte/INFl Goiânia: Universidade de Goiás, 1985).

Rodríguez, Luis R. Méndez, "Bailes y fiestas de negros: un estudio de su representación artística," *Archivo hispalense: Revista histórica, literaria y artística* 90:273 (2007), 397–412.
Esclavos en la pintura sevillana de los Siglos de Oro (Seville: Universidad de Sevilla, 2011).

Rodríguez, Vicente Díaz, "La cofradía de los morenos y primeros años de los dominicos en Cádiz," *Communio: revista semestral publicada por los Dominicos de la provincia de Andalucía* 39:2 (2006), 359–484.

Rodríguez Mateos, Joaquín, "De los esclavos y marginados: Dios de blancos y piedad de negros. La cofradía de los morenos de Sevilla," in *Andalucía Moderna: Actas del II Congreso de Historia de Andalucía* (Cordoba: Junta de Andalucía, 1995).

Rosal, Miguel Á, "La religiosidad católica de los afrodescendientes de Buenos Aires (siglos XVIII-XIX)," *Hispania Sacra* LX:122 (2008), 597–633.

Roselló Soberón, Estela, "La Cofradía de San Benito de Palermo y la integración de los negros y los mulatos en la ciudad de la Nueva Veracruz en el siglo XVII," in *Formaciones religiosas en la América colonial*, ed. María Alba Pastor and Alicia Mayer (Mexico: Universidad Nacional Autónoma de México, 2000), 229–42.

Rosolino, Riccardo, "Le reti sociali della santità: notai, giudici e testimoni al processo di canonizzazione di Benedetto il Moro (1625–1626)," in *Il santo e patrono e la città: San Benedetto il Moro: culti, devozioni, strategie di età moderna*, ed. Giovanna Fiume (Venice: Marsilio, 2000), 253–77.

Rothman, E. Natalie, "Becoming Venetian: Conversion and Transformation in the Seventeenth-Century Mediterranean," *Mediterranean Historical Review* 21:1 (2006), 39–75.
Brokering Empire: Trans-Imperial Subjects Between Venice and Istanbul (Ithaca, NY: Cornell University Press, 2012).

Rowe, Erin Kathleen, "After Death, Her Face Turned White: Blackness, Whiteness, and Sanctity in the Early Modern Hispanic World," *The American Historical Review* 121:3 (2016), 727–54.

Saint and Nation: Santiago, Teresa of Avila, and Plural Identities in Early Modern Spain (University Park: Pennsylvania State University Press, 2011).

"Visualizing Black Sanctity in Early Modern Spanish Polychrome Sculpture," in *Envisioning Others: Race, Color, and the Visual in Iberia and Latin America*, ed. Pamela Anne Patton (Leiden: Brill, 2016), 51–82.

Rubial García, Antonio, *La santidad controvertida: hagiografía y conciencia criolla alrededor de los Venerables no canonizados de Nueva España* (Mexico: Fondo de Cultura Económica, 1999).

El paraíso de los elegidos: una lectura de la historia cultural de Nueva España (1521–1804) (Mexico: Universidad Nacional Autónoma de México, 2010).

Rubiés, Joan-Paul, "The Concept of Cultural Dialogue and the Jesuit Method of Accommodation: Between Idolatry and Civilization," *Archivium Historicum Societatis Iesu*, 74:147 (2005), 237–80.

Rumeu de Armas, Antonio, *Historia de la previsión social en España; cofradías–gremios–hermandades–montepíos* (Madrid: Editorial Revista de derecho privado, 1942).

Russell-Wood, A. J. R., "Before Columbus: Portugal's African Prelude to the Middle Passage and Contributions to Discourse in Race and Slavery," in *Race, Discourse, and the Origin of the Americas: A New World View*, ed. Vera Hyatt and Rex Nettleford (Washington, DC: Smithsonian, 1995), 134–68.

"Black and Mulatto Brotherhoods in Colonial Brazil: A Study in Collective Behavior," *The Hispanic American Historical Review* 54:4 (1974), 567–602.

The Black Man in Slavery and Freedom in Colonial Brazil (New York: St. Martin's Press, 1982).

"Examination of Selected Statutes of Three African Brotherhoods," in *Manipulating the Saints: Religious Brotherhoods and Social Integration in Postconquest Latin America*, ed. Albert Meyers and Diane Elizabeth Hopkins (Hamburg: Wayasbah, 1988), 243–9.

"Iberian Expansion and the Issue of Black Slavery: Changing Portuguese Attitudes, 1440–1770," *American Historical Review* 83 (1978), 16–42.

Sá, Isabel dos Guimarães, "Ecclesiastical Structures and Religious Action," in *Portuguese Oceanic Expansion, 1400–1800*, ed. Francisco Bethencourt and Diogo Ramada Curto (New York: Cambridge University Press, 2007), 255–82.

Salvadore, Matteo, "The Ethiopian Age of Exploration: Prester John's Discovery of Europe, 1306–1458," *Journal of World History* 21:4 (2010), 593–627.

"Gaining the Heart of Prester John: Loyola's Blueprint for Ethiopia in Three Key Documents," *World History Connected* 10:3 (2013). http://worldhistoryconnected .press.uillinois.edu/10.3/forum_salvadore.html.

"The Jesuit Mission to Ethiopia (1555–1634) and the Death of Prester John," in *World-Building and the Early Modern Imagination*, ed. Allison B. Kavey (New York: Palgrave Macmillan, 2010), 141–72.

Sancho de Sopranis, Hipólito, *Las cofradías de morenos en Cádiz. Ensayo histórico* (Tangier: Instituto General Franco, 1940).

Las cofradías de morenos en Cádiz (Madrid: Instituto de Estudios Africanos, Consejo Superior de Investigaciones Científicas, 1958).

Sanok, Catherine, *Her Life Historical: Exemplarity and Female Saints' Lives in Late Medieval England* (Philadelphia: University of Pennsylvania Press, 2007).

Santana, Tânia Maria Pinto de, "Nossa Senhora do Rosário no santuário mariano: Irmandades e devoções negras em Salvador e no recôncavo baiano (século XVIII)," *Studia histórica moderna*, 38:1 (2016), 95–122.

Santos Hernández, Angel, "Orígenes históricos de la Sagrada Congregación 'De Propaganda Fide': En el 350 aniversario de su fundación," *Revista Española de Derecho Canónico* 28:81 (1972), 509–43.

Santos, Vanicléia Silva, "Uma política de ossos: As relíquias católicas na África e o culto aos mortos (1564–1665)," *Revista Latino-Americana de Estudos Avançados* 1:1 (2016), 138–57.

Saunders, A. C., *A Social History of Black Slaves and Freedmen in Portugal, 1441–1555* (New York: Cambridge University Press, 1982).

"The Legacy of Black Slavery in Renaissance Portugal," *Camões Center Quarterly* 4:1&2 (1992), 14–19.

Scarano, Julita, *Devoção e escravidão: a Irmandade de Nossa Senhora do Rosário dos Pretos no Distrito Diamantino no século XVIII* (São Paulo: Companhia Editora Nacional, 1976).

Scorza Barcellona, Francesco, "I santi neri di Sicilia," in *Schiavitù, religione e libertà nel Mediterraneo tra medioevo ed età moderna*, ed. Giovanna Fiume (Cosenza: Pellegrini, 2008), 163–77.

Scheer, Monique, "From Majesty to Mystery: Change in the Meanings of Black Madonnas from the Sixteenth to Nineteenth Centuries," *The American Historical Review* 107:5 (2002), 1412–40.

Schenone, Héctor H., *Iconografía del arte colonial* (Buenos Aires: Fundación Tarea, 1992).

Schlau, Stacey, "Flying in Formation: Subjectivity and Collectivity in Luisa Melgarejo de Soto's Mystical Practices," in *Devout Laywomen in the Early Modern World*, ed. Alison Weber (New York: Routledge, 2016), 133–51.

"Following Saint Teresa: Early Modern Women and Religious Authority," *MLN* 117:2 (2002), 286–309.

Schmidt-Nowara, Christopher, *Slavery, Freedom, and Abolition in Latin America and the Atlantic World* (Albuquerque: University of New Mexico Press, 2011).

Schmitt, Jean-Claude, *The Holy Greyhound: Guinefort, Healer of Children since the Thirteenth Century* (Cambridge: Cambridge University Press, 1983).

Schneider, Robert A., "Mortification on Parade: Penitential Processions in Sixteenth- and Seventeenth-Century France," *Renaissance and Reformation/Renaissance et Réforme* 10:1 (1986), 123–146.

Schorsch, Jonathan, *Swimming the Christian Atlantic: Judeoconversos, Afroiberians and Amerindians in the Seventeenth Century*, 2 vols. (Boston: Brill, 2009).

Schroeder, Susan, "Jesuits, Nahuas, and the Good Death in Mexico City, 1710–1767," *Hispanic American Historical Review* 80:1 (Feb. 2000), 1–43.

Schroeder, Susan, and Stafford Poole, eds., *Religion in New Spain* (Albuquerque: University of New Mexico Press, 2007).

Schuessler, Michael K., *Foundation Arts: Mural Painting and Missionary Theater in New Spain* (Tucson: University of Arizona Press, 2013).

Schutte, Anne Jacobson, *Aspiring Saints: Pretense of Holiness, Inquisition, and Gender in the Republic of Venice, 1618–1750* (Baltimore: Johns Hopkins University Press, 2001).

Schwartz, Stuart B., *All Can Be Saved: Religious Tolerance and Salvation in the Iberian Atlantic World* (New Haven, CT: Yale University Press, 2008).

"Black Latin America: Legacies of Slavery, Race, and African Culture," *Hispanic American Historical Review* 82:3 (2002), 429–33.

Scott, David, *Refashioning Futures: Criticism after Postcoloniality* (Princeton, NJ: Princeton University Press, 1999).

Seeman, Erik R., *Death in the New World: Cross-Cultural Encounters, 1492–1800* (Philadelphia: University of Pennsylvania Press, 2010).

Seijas, Tatiana, *Asian Slaves in Colonial Mexico: From Chinos to Indians* (New York: Cambridge University Press, 2014).

Selka, Stephen, "Black Catholicism in Brazil," *Journal of Africana Religions* 2:2 (2014), 287–95.

Selwyn, Jennifer D., "'Procur[ing] in the Common People These Better Behaviors': The Jesuits' Civilizing Mission in Early Modern Naples 1550–1620," *Radical History Review* 67 (1997), 4–34.

A Paradise Inhabited by Devils: The Jesuits' Civilizing Mission in Early Modern Naples (Burlinton, VT: Ashgate, 2004).

Sensbach, Jon, "Prophets and Helpers: African American Women and the Rise of Black Christianity in the Age of the Slave Trade," in *Women, Religion, and the Atlantic World (1600–1800)*, ed. Lisa Vollendorf and Daniella J. Kostroun (Toronto: University of Toronto Press, 2009), 115–35.

Serna, Juan Manuel de la, *Vicisitudes negro africanas en Iberoamérica: experiencias de investigación* (Mexico: Universidad Nacional Autónoma de México, 2011).

Serrera, Juan Miguel, "La Adoración de los Reyes Magos, un retrato casi de familia," in *Velázquez* (Madrid: Fundación Amigos del Museo del Prado, 1999), 351–65.

Sesma Muñoz, José Ángel and Carlos Laliena Corberta, *Crecimiento económico y formación de los mercados en Aragón en la Edad Media (1200–1350)* (Zaragoza: Universidad de Zaragoza, 2009).

Seth, Vanita, *Europe's Indians: Producing Racial Difference, 1500–1900* (Durham, NC: Duke University Press, 2010).

Shahîd, Irfan, *The Martyrs of Najrân. New Documents* (Brussels: Soc. des Bollandistes, 1971).

Sheehan, Jonathan, "Sacred and Profane: Idolatry, Antiquarianism and the Polemics of Distinction in the Seventeenth Century," *Past & Present* 192:1 (2006), 35–66.

Shelford, April G., "Race and Scripture in the Eighteenth-Century French Caribbean," *Atlantic Studies: Global Currents* 10:1 (2013), 69–87.

Sherman, William L., *Forced Native Labor in Sixteenth-Century Central America* (Lincoln: Unviersity of Nebraska Press, 1979).

Sidbury, James, and Jorge Cañizares-Esguerra, "Mapping Ethnogenesis in the Early Modern Atlantic," *The William and Mary Quarterly* 68:2 (2011), 181–208.

Sierra Silva, Pablo Miguel, "From Chains to Chiles: An Elite Afro-Indigenous Couple in Colonial Mexico, 1641–1688," *Ethnohistory* 62:2 (2015), 361–84.

Urban Slavery in Colonial Mexico: Puebla de los Ángeles, 1531–1706 (New York: Cambridge University Press, 2018).

Simms, Rupe, "Catholicism as an Instrument of Counterhegemony: The Religiopolitical Ingenuity of Afro-Mexican People," *Western Journal of Black Studies* 35:3 (2011), 163–75.

Silleras-Fernández, Núria, "Nigra Sum Sed Formosa: Black Slaves and Exotica in the Court of a Fourteenth-Century Aragonese Queen," *Medieval Encounters* 13 (2007), 546–65.

Smith, Denis Mack, *A History of Sicily, 800–1713: Medieval Sicily* (London: Chatto and Windus, 1968).

Soares, Mariza de Carvalho, *People of Faith: Slavery and African Catholics in Eighteenth-Century Rio de Janeiro*, trans. Jerry D. Metz (Durham, NC: Duke University Press, 2011).

Soria Mesa, Enrique, *La realidad tras el espejo: ascenso social y limpieza de sangre en la España de Felipe II* (Valladolid: Universidad de Valladolid, 2016).

Souza, Laura de Mello e, *The Devil and the Land of the Holy Cross: Witchcraft, Slavery, and Popular Religion in Colonial Brazil*, trans. Diana Grosklaus Whitty (Austin: University of Texas Press, 2003).

Spaulding, Rachel, "Covert Afro-Catholic Agency in the Mystical Visions of Early Modern Brazil's Rosa Maria Egipçíaca," in *Women's Negotiations and Textual Agency in Latin America, 1500–1799*, ed. Mónica Díaz and Rocío Quispe-Agnoli (New York: Routledge, 2017), 38–61.

Soyer, François, *The Persecution of the Jews and Muslims of Portugal: King Manuel I and the End of Religious Tolerance (1496-7)* (Leiden: Brill, 2007).

Spicer, Joaneath A., "European Perceptions of Blackness as Reflected in the Visual Arts," in *Revealing the African Presence in Renaissance Europe*, ed. Joaneath A. Spicer (Baltimore: Walters Art Museum, 2012), 35–59.

Stella, Alessandro, *Histoires d'esclaves dans la Péninsule Ibérique* (Paris: Ed. de L'ecole des Hautes Etudes en Sciences Sociales, 2000).

Stoichita, Victor, "The Image of the Black in Spanish Art: Sixteenth and Seventeenth Centuries," in *The Image of the Black in Western Art, Volume III: From the "Age of Discovery" to the Age of Abolition, Part 1: Artists of the Renaissance and Baroque*, ed. David Bindman and Henry Louis Gates, Jr. (Cambridge, MA: Belknap Press of Harvard University Press, 2010), 191–234.

Strasser, Ulrike, "A Case of Empire Envy? German Jesuits Meets an Asian Mystic in Spanish America," *Journal of Global History* 2:1 (2007), 23–40.

Sullivan-González, Douglass, *The Black Christ of Esquipulas: Religion and Identity in Guatemala* (Lincoln: University of Nebraska Press, 2016).

Sweet, James H., *Domingo Alvares, African Healing, and the Intellectual History of the Atlantic World* (Chapel Hill: University of North Carolina Press, 2011).

"The Hidden Histories of African Lisbon," in *The Black Urban Atlantic in the Age of the Slave Trade*, ed. Jorge Cañizares-Esguerra, Matt D. Childs, and James Sidbury (Philadelphia: University of Pennsylvania Press, 2013), 233–47.

"'Not a Thing for White Men to See': Central African Divination in Seventeenth-Century Brazil," in *Enslaving Connections: Changing Cultures of Africa and Brazil during the Era of Slavery*, ed. José C. Curto and Paul E. Lovejoy (Amherst, NY: Humanity Books, 2004), 139–48.

Recreating Africa: Culture, Kinship, and Religion in the African-Portuguese World, 1441–1770 (Chapel Hill: University of North Carolina Press, 2003).

"Reimagining the African-Atlantic Archive: Method, Concept, Epistemology, Ontology," *Journal of African History* 55:2 (2014), 147–59.

Tardieu, Jean-Pierre, *L'Eglise et les noirs au Pérou: XVIe et XVIIe siècles*, 2 vols. (Paris: L'Harmattan; Université de la Réunion, 1993).

"Origins of the Slaves in the Lima Region in Peru (Sixteenth and Seventeenth Centuries," in *From Chains to Bonds: The Slave Trade Revisited*, ed. Doudou Diène (New York: Berghahn, 2001), 43–54.

"La esclavitud de los negros y el plan de Dios: la dialéctica de los jesuitas del virreinato del Perú," in *Esclavitud, economía y evangelización: las haciendas jesuitas en la América virreinal*, ed. Sandra Negro Tua and Manuel M. Marzal (Lima: Pontificia Universidad Católica del Perú, Fondo Editorial, 2005), 67–81.

Tavárez, David, *The Invisible War: Indigenous Devotions, Discipline, and Dissent in Colonial Mexico* (Stanford: Stanford University Press, 2011).

"Legally Indian: Inquisitorial Readings of the Indigenous Identity in New Spain," in *Imperial Subjects: Race and Identity in Colonial Latin America*, ed. Andrew B. Fisher and Matthew D. O'Hara (Durham, NC: Duke University Press, 2009), 81–100.

Taylor, Scott K., *Honor and Violence in Golden Age Spain* (New Haven: Yale University Press, 2008).

Taylor, William B., *Theater of a Thousand Wonders: A History of Miraculous Images and Shrines in New Spain* (New York: Cambridge University Press, 2016).

Tedeschi, Salvatore, "Etiopi e Copti al Concilio di Firenze," *Annuarium Historiae Conciliorum* 21 (1989), 380–407.

"Paolo Giovio e la conoscenza dell'Etiopia nel Rinascimento," in *Paolo Giovio: il Rinascimento e la memoria: atti del convengo, Como 3–5 giungo 1983*, ed. T. C. Price Zimmerman (Como: Presso la Società a Villa Gallia, 1985), 93–116.

Terpstra, Nicholas, ed., *The Politics of Ritual Kinship Confraternities and Social Order in Early Modern Italy* (Cambridge: Cambridge University Press, 2000).

Thornton, John, *Africa and Africans in the Making of the Atlantic World, 1400–1800*, 2nd ed. (New York: Cambridge University Press, 1998).

"Afro-Christian Syncretism in the Kingdom of Kongo," *The Journal of African History* 54:1 (2013), 53–77.

"The Development of an African Catholic Church in the Kingdom of Kongo, 1491–1750," *The Journal of African History* 25:2 (1984), 147–67.

The Kongolese Saint Anthony: Dona Beatriz Kimpa Vita and the Antonian Movement, 1684–1706 (New York: Cambridge University Press, 1998).

Tiffany, Tanya J., *Diego Velázquez's Early Paintings and the Culture of Seventeenth-Century Seville* (University Park: Pennsylvania State University Press, 2012).

Tognetti, Sergio, "The Trade in Black African Slaves in Fifteenth-Century Florence," in *Black Africans in Renaissance Europe*, ed. T. F. Earle and K. J. P. Lowe (Cambridge: Cambridge University Press, 2010), 213–24.

Touber, Jetze, *Law, Medicine and Engineering in the Cult of the Saints in Counter-Reformation Rome* (Leiden: Brill, 2013).

Townsend, Camilla, "Burying the White Gods: New Perspectives on the Conquest of Mexico," *American Historical Review* 108:3 (2003), 659–87.

Traub, Valerie, "Mapping the Global Body," in *Early Modern Visual Culture: Representation, Race, Empire in Renaissance England*, ed. Peter Erickson and Clark Hulse (Philadelphia: University of Pennsylvania Press, 2000), 44–97.

Trexler, Richard C., *The Journey of the Magi: Meanings in History of a Christian Story* (Princeton: Princeton University Press, 1997).

Tudela, Elisa Sampson Vera, "Illustrating Sainthood: The Construction of Eighteenth-Century Spanish American Hagiography," in *Eve's Enlightenment: Women's Experience in Spain and Spanish America, 1726–1839*, ed. Catherine Marie Jaffe and Elizabeth Franklin Lewis (Baton Rouge: Louisiana State University Press, 2009), 84–100.

Turley, Steven E., *Franciscan Spirituality and Mission in New Spain, 1524–1599: Conflict Beneath the Sycamore Tree* (Farnham, UK: Ashgate Publishing, 2014).

Tutino, Stefania, "'For the Sake of the Truth of History and of the Catholic Doctrines': History, Documents, and Dogma in Cesare Baronio's *Annales Ecclesiastici*," *Journal of Early Modern History* 17:2 (2013), 125–59.

 Shadows of Doubt: Language and Truth in Post-Reformation Catholic Culture (Oxford: Oxford University Press, 2014).

Twinam, Ann, "Purchasing Whiteness: Conversations on the Essence of Pardo-ness and Mulatto-ness at the End of Empire," in *Imperial Subjects: Race and Identity in Colonial Latin America*, ed. Andrew B. Fisher and Matthew D. O'Hara (Durham, NC: Duke University Press, 2009), 141–65.

 Purchasing Whiteness: Pardos, Mulattos, and the Quest for Social Mobility in the Spanish Indies (Stanford: Stanford University Press, 2015).

Van Deusen, Nancy E., "Circuits of Knowledge among Women in Early Seventeenth-Century Lima," in *Gender, Race and Religion in the Colonization of the Americas*, ed. Nora E. Jaffary (Burlington, VT: Ashgate, 2007), 137–50.

 Embodying the Sacred: Women Mystics in Seventeenth-Century Lima (Durham, NC: Duke University Press, 2018).

 "Reading the Body: Mystical Theology and Spiritual Actualisation in Early Seventeenth-Century Lima," *Journal of Religious History* 33:1 (2009), 1–27.

 "'The Lord Walks among the Pots and Pans': Religious Servants of Colonial Peru," in *Africans to Spanish America: Expanding the Diaspora*, ed. Sherwin K. Bryant, Rachel Sarah O'Toole, and Ben Vinson (Urbana: University of Illinois Press, 2012), 136–61.

Van den Broek, R., *The Myth of the Phoenix: According to Classical and Early Christian Traditions*, trans. I. Seeger (Leiden: Brill, 1972).

Van Liere, Katherine Elliot, Simon Ditchfield, and Howard Louthan, eds., *Sacred History: Uses of the Christian Past in the Renaissance World* (Oxford: Oxford University Press, 2012).

Vaquero Rojo, Antonio E., *San Benito de Palermo: el primer negro canonizado* (Madrid: Atenas, 1985).

Veer, Peter van der, *Conversion to Modernities: The Globalization of Christianity* (New York: Routledge, 1996).

Velázquez Gutiérrez, María Elisa, and Ethel Correa Duró, *Poblaciones y culturas de origen africano en México* (Mexico: Instituto Nacional de Antropología e Historia, 2005.)

Vélez, Karin, "'A Sign that We Are Related to You': The Transatlantic Gifts of the Hurons of the Jesuit Mission of Lorette, 1650–1750," *French Colonial History* 12 (2011), 31–44.

Viana, Larisa, "Gonçalo Garcia: identidades e relações raciais na história de um santo pardo a América portuguesa," in *Escravidão e subjetividades no Atlântico luso-brasileiro e francês* (Séculos XVII-XX), ed. Myriam Cottas and Hebe Mattos (Marseille: OpenEdition Press, 2016). http://books.openedition.org/oep/786.

 O idoma da mestiçagem: as irmandades de pardos na América Portuguesa (Campinas: Editora da Unicamp, 2007).

Vila Vilar, Enriqueta, "Posibilidades y perspectivas para el estudio de la esclavitud en los Fondos del Archivo General de Indias," *Archivo hispalense: Revista histórica, literaria y artística* 68:207 (1985), 255–72.

Vilatte, Sylvie, "La 'dévote image noire de Nostre-Dame' du Puy-en-Velay: histoire du reliquaire roman et de son noircissment," *Revue belge de philologie et d'histoire* 74:3 (1996), 727–60.

Villa-Flores, Javier, *Dangerous Speech: A Social History of Blasphemy in Colonial Mexico* (Tucson: University of Arizona Press, 2006).

Vincent, Bernard, "Esclavage au Portugal: entre mer Méditerranée et océan Atlantique," *Arquivos do centro cultural Calouste Gulbenkian* 43 (2002), 61–70.

"Les confréries de noirs dans la péninsule Ibérique," in *Religiosidad y costumbres populares en Iberoamérica*, ed. David González Cruz (Huelva: Universidad de Huelva, 2000), 17–28.

"Pour une histoire des confrèries des noirs," in *Confréries et dévotions dans la catholicité moderne (mi-XVe-début XIXe siècle)*, ed. Bernard Dompnier and Paola Vismara (Rome: École française de Rome, 2008), 243–60.

"Saint Benoît de Palerme et l'Espagne," in *Schiavitù, religione e libertà nel Mediterraneo tra Medioevo ed età moderna*, ed. Giovanna Fiume (Cosenza: L. Pellegrini, 2008), 201–14.

"San Benito de Palermo en España," *Studia Historica: Historia Moderna* 38:1 (May 2016), 23–38.

Vincent-Cassy, Cécile, *Les saintes vierges et martyres dans l'Espagne du XVIIe siècle: culte e image* (Madrid: Casa de Velázquez, 2011).

Vinson III, Ben, *Bearing Arms for His Majesty: The Free-Colored Militia in Colonial Mexico* (Stanford: Stanford University Press, 2001).

Vinson III, Ben, and Matthew Restall, eds., *Black Mexico: Race and Society from Colonial to Modern Times* (Albuquerque: University of New Mexico Press, 2009).

Voigt, Lisa, *Spectacular Wealth: The Festivals of South American Mining Towns* (Austin: University of Texas Press, 2016).

Waldron, Jennifer, *Reformations of the Body: Idolatry, Sacrifice, and Early Modern Theater* (New York: Palgrave Macmillan, 2013).

Walker, Tamara J., "The Queen of *los Congos*: Slavery, Gender, and Confraternity Life in Late-Colonial Lima, Peru," *Journal of Family History* 40:3 (2015), 305–22.

Walsham, Alexandra, *The Reformation of the Landscape: Religion, Identity, and Memory in Early Modern Britain and Ireland* (Oxford: University of Oxford Press, 2011).

Ward, Haruko Nawata, "Women Apostles in Early Modern Japan, 1549–1650," in *Devout Laywomen in the Early Modern World*, ed. Alison Weber (New York: Routledge, 2016), 312–30.

Weber, Alison, *Teresa of Avila and the Rhetoric of Femininity* (Princeton: Princeton University Press, 1990).

Webster, Susan Verdi, *Art and Ritual in Golden-Age Spain: Sevillian Confraternities and the Processional Sculpture of Holy Week* (Princeton, NJ: Princeton University Press, 1998).

"Deus ex Sculptura: The Art and Ritual of Penitential Confraternities in Early Modern Seville," in *Confraternite, Chiesa e società: Aspetti e problemi dell'associazionismo europeo modern e contemporaneo*, ed. Liana Bertoldi Lenoci (Pugli: Schena Editore, 1994), 837–51.

"Sacred Altars, Sacred Streets: The Sculpture of Penitential Confraternities in Early Modern Seville," *Journal of Ritual Studies* 6:1 (1992), 159–77.

Wheat, David, *Atlantic Africa and the Spanish Caribbean, 1570–1640* (Chapel Hill: Omohundro Institute of Early American History and Culture by the University of North Carolina Press, 2016).

Wheeler, Roxann, *The Complexion of Race: Categories of Difference in Eighteenth-Century British Culture* (Philadelphia: University of Pennsylvania Press, 2000).

Whistler, Catherine, ed., *Opulence and Devotion: Brazilian Baroque Art* (Oxford: Ashmolean Museum, 2001).

Whitford, David M., *The Curse of Ham in the Early Modern Era: The Bible and the Justifications for Slavery* (Burlington, VT: Ashgate, 2009).

Wirtz, Kristina, *Performing Afro-Cuba: Image, Voice, Spectacle in the Making of Race and History* (Chicago: University of Chicago Press, 2014).

Wisch, Barbara, "Incorporating Images: Some Themes and Tasks for Confraternity Studies and Early Modern Visual Culture," in *Early Modern Confraternities in Europe and the Americas: International and Interdisciplinary Perspectives*, ed. Christopher F. Black and Pamela Gravestock (Burlington, VT: Ashgate, 2006), 243–63.

Wood, Alice L., "Religious Women of Color in Seventeenth-Century Lima: Estefania de San Ioseph and Ursula de Jesu Cristo," in *Beyond Bondage: Free Women of Color in the Americas*, ed. David Barry Gaspar and Darlene Clark Hine (Urbana: University of Illinois Press, 2004), 286–316.

Wright, Elizabeth R., *The Epic of Juan Latino: Dilemmas of Race and Religion in Renaissance Spain* (Toronto: University of Toronto Press, 2016).

Wunder, Amanda, *Baroque Seville: Sacred Art in a Century of Crisis* (University Park: Penn State University Press, 2017).

Yannakakis, Yanna, *The Art of Being In-Between: Native Intermediaries, Indian Identity, and Local Rule in Colonial Oaxaca* (Durham: Duke University Press, 2008).

Young, Jason, *Rituals of Resistance: African Atlantic Religion in Kongo and the Lowcountry South in the Era of Slavery* (Baton Rouge: Louisiana State University Press, 2007).

Young, Kydalla Etheyo, "Colonial Music, Confraternities, and Power in the Archdiocese of Lima," unpublished Ph.D. thesis, University of Illinois at Urbana Champaign (2010).

Zarri, Gabriella, "Living Saints: A Typology of Female Sanctity in the Early Sixteenth Century," in *Women and Religion in Medieval and Renaissance Italy*, ed. Daniel Ethan Bornstein and Roberto Rusconi (Chicago: University of Chicago Press, 1996), 219–303.

Zarza Rondón, Gloria de los Ángeles, "El rostro de los invisibles: esclavos hispanoamericanos en Cádiz al final de la época colonial," *Navegamérica* 8 (2012), 1–17.

Ziegler, Joseph, "Physiognomy, Science, and Proto-Racism, 1200–1500," in *The Origins of Racism in the West*, ed. Miriam Eliav-Feldon, Benjamin H. Isaac, and Joseph Ziegler (New York: Cambridge University Press, 2009), 181–99.

Županov, Ines G., *Missionary Tropics: The Catholic Frontier in India, 16th-17th Centuries* (Ann Arbor: University of Michigan Press, 2005).

"'One Civilly, But Multiple Religions': Jesuit Mission among St. Thomas Christians in India (16th-17th Centuries)," *Journal of Early Modern History* 9:3-4 (2005), 284–325.

"Twisting a Pagan Tongue: Portuguese and Tamil in Sixteenth-Century Jesuit Translations," in *Conversion: Old Worlds and New*, ed. Kenneth Mill and Anthony Grafton (Rochester, NY: University of Rochester Press, 2003), 109–39.

INDEX